Matthew Arnold and His Critics

MATTHEW ARNOLD

AND HIS CRITICS

A Study of Arnold's

Controversies

by Sidney Coulling

OHIO UNIVERSITY PRESS: ATHENS

In Memory of

My Parents

CONTENTS

PREFACE

I am concerned in this book with Matthew Arnold's polemical encounters with his contemporary critics—with those exchanges between him and his reviewers that comprised a kind of dialogue which shaped a significant portion of his prose work. Although much of what he wrote provoked controversy, my study treats only that part of his writing which elicited criticism he attempted to answer. The most controversial of the lectures he delivered in America, for example, was the one on Emerson, but because his sole answer to the criticism it received was a few minor revisions in the text, I have given less attention to the reception of the lecture than to the attacks on Arnold by American newspapers, which prompted an entire essay in response.

In examining Arnold's controversies I have tried to find every review of his work that was published during his lifetime and that he was likely to have read and answered. Sometimes, as in the Colenso matter, he apparently intended to reply not only to criticism in the press but also to objections that were expressed orally or in personal correspondence and thus have not always survived. In such instances I have sought to define the body of critical opinion to which Arnold responded by including comments that may not have reached him but are nevertheless representative.

My study began as a doctoral dissertation at the University of North Carolina under the direction of Professor Lyman A. Cotten, to whom I am indebted for the original suggestion. Since that time parts of it have appeared in somewhat different form in several journals: much of chapters two, four, and six as "Matthew Arnold's 1853 Preface: Its Origin and Aftermath" in the March 1964 issue of *Victorian Studies*, "The Background of 'The Function of Criticism at the Present Time' " in the January 1963 issue of *Philological Quarterly*, and "The Evolution of *Culture and Anarchy*" in the October 1963 issue of *Studies in Philology*, respectively; and segments of chapters five and eight as "Matthew Arnold and the *Daily Telegraph*" in the May 1961 issue of *The Review of English Studies* and "Swinburne and Arnold" in the April 1970 issue of *Philological Quarterly*, respectively. I am grateful to the editors of these journals for permission to use the articles here.

As my notes will indicate, in dealing with the more than thirty-five years of Arnold's literary career I have necessarily depended on the work of many scholars. From five in particular I have received help that I wish to acknowledge individually: the late Arthur Kyle Davis, Jr., who made available to me his entire collection of microfilmed letters; Professor David J. DeLaura, who has carefully read the entire manuscript and made many helpful suggestions; Professor Walter E. Houghton, who has patiently answered inquiries about the authorship of anonymous articles in nineteenth-century periodicals and informed me about yet unpublished items in the *Wellesley Index*; Professor R. H. Super, whose generous and unselfish help during the past decade has been as exemplary as his scholarship, and whose superb edition of Arnold's prose has made possible the completion of my study; and the late Arnold Whitridge,who gave both kind encouragement and the permission to quote from manuscript letters in his possession.

Throughout my research I have been assisted by librarians at a number of libraries in this country and at the British Museum. I express my appreciation to all of them, especially those at Washington and Lee University and the Virginia Military Institute, and to two in particular my gratitude for help extending over a period of time and going beyond the routine fulfillment of duty: the late Martha R. Cullipher, of the Washington and Lee Library, and Miss Marjorie G. Wynne, Edwin J. Beinecke Research Librarian at Yale.

I am indebted also to Washington and Lee University for a number of grants under the John M. Glenn and Robert E. Lee research programs and for a contribution toward the cost of publishing this book, and to Dr. William W. Pusey III and Dean William J. Watt, at different times chairman of the committee that recommended the grants. I am further indebted to the trustees of Washington and Lee for approving a semester's leave of absence during which I completed a portion of the writing, and to the Ford Foundation for its grant to the University that made possible a leave of absence.

My debt of longest standing is acknowledged in the dedication, which speaks for itself. To it I should like to add my thanks to Mary, Margaret, Anne, and Philip, who helped more than they knew.

Lexington, Virginia
December 26, 1973

The *dust* of controversy, what is it but the *false-hood* flying off from all manner of conflicting true forces, and making such a loud dust-whirl-wind,—that so the truths alone may remain, and embrace brother-like in some true resulting-force!

—Carlyle, *Past and Present*

ACKNOWLEDGMENTS

I gratefully acknowledge permission from the Clarendon Press, Oxford, to quote passages from *The Letters of Matthew Arnold to Arthur Hugh Clough*, edited by Howard Foster Lowry; from the University of Michigan Press, to quote passages from *The Complete Prose Works of Matthew Arnold*, edited by R. H. Super; and from Yale University Press, to quote passages from *Unpublished Letters of Matthew Arnold*, edited by Arnold Whitridge, and *The Swinburne Letters*, edited by Cecil Y. Lang.

Matthew Arnold and His Critics

CHAPTER ONE

The Writer and His Mission

So full of power, yet blithe and debonair,
    Rallying his friends with pleasant banter gay,
Or half a-dream chaunting with jaunty air
    Great words of Goethe, catch of Béranger.
We see the banter sparkle in his prose,
But knew not then the undertone that flows,
    So calmly sad, through all his stately lay.

                    —J. C. Shairp

In his absence the whole tone of discussion would have seemed more stupid, more literal. Without his irony to play over its surface, to clip it here and there of its occasional fustiness, the life of our Anglo-Saxon race would present a much greater appearance of insensibility.
—Henry James on Arnold

Opposition is true Friendship.—Blake

What we agree with leaves us inactive, but contradiction makes us productive.—Goethe

Wherever there is thought there is opposition.—Yeats

Like many of his contemporaries Benjamin Jowett was slow in learning to take Matthew Arnold seriously. But after going to his "dear friend M. Arnold's funeral" he wrote to Lady Taylor: "The world has been pleased to say many complimentary things of him since his death; but they have hardly done him justice because they did not understand his serious side—hard work, independence, and the most loving and careful fulfilment of all the duties of life."[1]

    John Duke Coleridge, who as a young man had more than once complained of Arnold's apparent levity, wrote in much the same manner to Ellis Yarnall:

. . . he was one of the noblest and most perfect characters I ever knew
. . . . from his very earliest years sorrow and trouble always calmed
and sobered him, his persiflage disappeared, and . . . you felt the warm,
generous heart, the just judgment, the tender sympathy which were
as natural to him as to breathe.[2]

When, several years later, Leslie Stephen expressed surprise at
"the immense seriousness"[3] revealed by Arnold's letters, which
had been deliberately edited to show his "serious" side because
his sister thought everyone knew his "lighter side,"[4] Charles
Eliot Norton pointed once again to the admirable person behind a deceptive facade:

One needed to see him under conditions of intimacy to know him as
he really was, and to know him thus, meant to love him. All the little
vanities, all the lack of humour in relation to himself, all the little
artificialities, disappeared or changed their aspect, and you found him
one of the simplest and sweetest of men, not taking himself too seriously, quite ready to smile at himself, absolutely unpretending, in-
variably pleasant, cheerful and sympathetic.[5]

Stephen's failure to see the serious side of Arnold, Noel
Annan has said, was the failure to penetrate "the disguise of
languor and preciosity which that great and refined critical
mind at times assumed."[6] It was not a unique failure, for Arnold, like Ernest Pontifex, discovered that "no matter how
serious he [was], he [was] always accused of being in jest."[7]
"I laugh too much," he wrote to John Duke Coleridge in 1844
about the lack of interest in his friends that they had attributed to him, "and they make one's laughter mean too much."[8]
The problem, Max Müller thought, was that Arnold seemed
to value a laugh from his hearers or readers more "than their
serious opposition, or their convinced assent. He trusted . . . to
persiflage, and the result was that when he tried to be serious,
people could not forget that he might at any time turn round
and smile, and decline to be taken *au grand sérieux*."[9]
    Arnold's persiflage, as Goldwin Smith astutely surmised,
was "in some measure a recoil from his father's sternness."[10]

Yet it was also in part the expression of a temperament that found natural release in wit, humor, banter, irony, "vivacities." The author of the preface to *Essays in Criticism*, of *Culture and Anarchy*, and of *Friendship's Garland*, was the same person whom his brother Tom, in an obituary written for the Manchester *Guardian*, recalled as having become at Oxford

one of the most popular men in the University. For though it is probable that he could have become a formidable satirist if he had chosen, he never did choose; he was too good-natured for that *rôle*; he did not go beyond banter, but in that no one ever surpassed him. Things which said by anyone else would have produced a deadly quarrel were said by him with such a bright playfulness, such a humorous masterfulness, that the victim laughed before he had time to feel hurt.[11]

He was the same person whom years earlier Clough's sister had described as "very merry and facetious,"[12] and the same whom Clough himself had depicted when his friend returned from the Continent ostentatiously displaying the results of a Parisian visit: hair innocent of English scissors, a chanson of Béranger on his lips, late breakfasts, and infrequent appearances at chapel.[13] He was also the same who later appeared in a memorable vignette painted by Max Müller:

. . . there was in all he said a kind of understood though seldom expressed sadness, as if to say, "It will soon be all over, don't let us get angry; we are all very good fellows," etc. He knew for years that though he was strong and looked very young for his age, the thread of his life might snap at any moment. . . . Not long before his death he met Browning on the steps of the Athenaeum. He felt ill, and in taking leave of Browning he hinted that they might never meet again. Browning was profuse in his protestations, and Arnold, on turning away, said in his airy way: "Now, one promise, Browning: please, not more than ten lines." Browning understood, and went away with a solemn smile.[14]

But persiflage was also part of a conscious strategy adopted by Arnold and not always understood or smiled at, even solemnly. To his family, who were gravely disapproving, he mentioned it time and again. "I felt sure that the preface would not exactly suit you or any member of my own family," he wrote to his mother about the preface to *Essays in Criticism*.[15] When she commented on the *Geist* letter he had published in the *Pall Mall Gazette*, he replied, "I understand what you feel about my graver and gayer manner, but there is a necessity in these things, and one cannot always work precisely as one would."[16] In describing to her the preface to *Culture and Anarchy*, which she may never have read, he said that it contained "much of that persiflage which I find necessary to use, but which I know you do not like."[17]

Persiflage, Arnold believed, was the necessary means by which he could gain a hearing. He once wrote to his sister "K" that "a certain amount of offence one may and must give, if one wants to introduce at all a new way of thinking. . . . sometimes one must lay aside Napoleon's excellent maxim il faut savoir *se borner*, in order to act on another good maxim of his —il faut quelquefois *se prodiguer*; for a people like ours, with a strong fund of imagination[,] genius and humour, are best reached by sometimes being audacious and giving oneself free play."[18] The principal form taken by his "audacity" was of course irony, which he said the middle class were "partly too good, partly too gross, to feel" but which was "the one arm" the aristocracy felt and respected.[19] Earlier, in a letter to his mother about the first installment of the "Anarchy and Authority" series, he had explained his point more fully:

It will amuse you though I am not sure you will altogether like it; but for my part I see more and more what an effective weapon, in a confused, loud-talking, clap-trappy country like this, where every writer and speaker to the public tends to say rather more than he means, is *irony*, or according to the strict meaning of the original Greek word, the saying rather less than one means. The main effect I have had on the mass of noisy claptrap and inert prejudice which chokes us has been, I can see, by the use of this weapon; and now, when people's minds are getting widely disturbed and they are beginning to ask themselves whether they have not a great deal that is new to learn, to increase this feeling in them irony is more useful than ever.[20]

The methods and aims here described raise a number of the central questions recurrently asked about Arnold as poet, essayist, and school inspector. Of these, three have particular relevance to a study of his work as controversialist. Why, in the first place, did he abandon poetry for polemics, or why, to employ the language of his landscape imagery, did he leave the serenity of the mountainside, with its lush vegetation and cool, clear springs, for the hot and dusty plain? Second, why did Arnold, while professing to be engaged in a disinterested pursuit of the truth, repeatedly engage in personalities as well? And, third, why was there in his strategy an apparent division of aims: between the professed desire on the one hand to avoid controversy and to "persuade" and "charm," and on the other an obvious delight in controversy that led to successive encounters with his opponents and frequent offense to his readers? All three of these questions, each involving ambivalences and seeming contradictions, deserve some consideration.

I

The wish that Tennyson wanted communicated to Arnold —that he not "write any more of those prose things like *Literature and Dogma,* but . . . give us something like his 'Thyrsis,' 'Scholar Gipsy,' or 'Forsaken Merman' "[21]—has been repeated on numerous occasions. "When I now think of Matthew Arnold," Logan Pearsall Smith sighed,

it makes me rather sad. . . . the advocate of Hellenism and sweet reasonableness who soon gave himself up to angry recrimination, and who, whether owing to exasperation with his contemporaries or to some arrogant streak in his own nature, more and more abandoned that serene aloofness from contemporary conflicts which had been his ideal, and adopted a pose of aggressive, self-satisfied contempt, and a harsh browbeating style full of derisive catchwords.[22]

"What we mourn," Paull F. Baum said in his concluding judgment of the Marguerite episode, ". . . is that in the test of character . . . Marguerite was not the woman to save him for poetry, and to save him from a life of school inspecting and journalistic controversies."[23] In a more theatrical expression of the wish that he might somehow have remained a poet, R. H. Ronson ended his account of Arnold's death by asking, "Who lay in Lucy's arms at the terrible moment of oblivion, the school inspector or the scholar gypsy?"[24]

Behind the lament that Arnold's life failed to follow a different course is the assumption that the artist may freely choose either to create or not to create and that retention of his poetic gift was thus within Arnold's power. But it is not at all certain that Arnold "abandoned" poetry. It would be more accurate, on the contrary, to say that poetry abandoned him. He wrote, to be sure, nothing that is quite the equivalent of a dejection or intimations ode, and he sometimes complained of the lack of leisure and of financial resources that would have made possible the life of a poet, such as that which Tennyson enjoyed. Even as late as 1861, when he was nearly twenty years older than the Keats who had expressed a similar wish in "Sleep and Poetry," he hoped to "finish off" his "critical writings . . . and give the next ten years earnestly to poetry."[25] Nevertheless, as we shall see in the next chapter, it is clear that Arnold was aware of how limited his poetical powers were and of how carefully they had to be protected and conserved. When in the latter years of his life he was asked why he wrote so little poetry, he replied, "Ah, if you knew how much harder it is than prose!"[26]

Nor is it certain that he would have wished to lead the life of a poet even had it been possible. The "worldly element," he once wrote to "K," entered "so much more largely" into his nature than into that of his family that there seemed to be a gulf between them.[27] For more than a decade, as Merle Bevington observed,[28] he entertained the worldly ambition of a political or diplomatic career. "How interesting"—how "absorbingly interesting"—"are public affairs!" he exclaimed. When the attraction they had for him manifested itself in *England and the Italian Question*, he was delighted to discover that he had inherited a "pamphleteering talent" from his father,[29] and in the years that followed he increasingly developed the sense not of a son in rebellion but of a son who, in his political and religious writings, was carrying on his father's work and deriving satisfaction from the realization. "I constantly feel, even while treading ground he did not tread," he wrote to his mother in 1863, "how much he influences me and how much I owe him."[30] In his "notions about the State" he was "quite papa's son, and his continuator," he told her, and after reading "in connexion with the New Testament a good deal of Aristotle and Plato," he reported that they had "brought papa very much to [his] mind again." When he several times failed to gain an appointment that would have relieved him of the drudgery of school inspecting, he resigned himself to doing his duty, "whatever that may be," determining to continue in "that variety of activity which is . . . necessary for producing a fruitful effect."[31] On the day after completing his forty-seventh year, the age at which his father had died and the kind of occasion that often moved him to self-analysis, he wrote to his mother about his failure to be appointed Lingen's successor as secretary to the Education Department:

> I soon settle myself, as David Hume did, into a cheerful acquiescence with whatever happens, and the Education Office vision always filled me with at least as much perturbation as hope. . . . There would have been much which I should have felt oppressive and depressive in the situation, and if it had not been for Fanny Lucy, who has a true woman's notions about *getting-on*, and who was very anxious for this promotion I should have been decidedly averse to it. I more and more wish to turn my thoughts from all notion of advancement in official and public life, and to go on quietly and soberly as I am. One begins almost to see one's way to the boys being out and settled in life; and when that point is once reached, a very simple *career* may satisfy one for the rest of one's days.[32]

The buried life of Arnold thus had more than one current, and Parnassus was not the only one of the hills "where his life rose."[33] We oversimplify, then, and indulge in preconceptions of our own if we see his polemical encounters as a betrayal of a call to the life of the poet. Things are what they are, as he was fond of quoting Bishop Wilson,[34] and it is part of the responsibility of criticism to see and describe them as such. This is precisely the point made years ago by Geoffrey Tillotson in a review pinpointing the weakness of E. K. Brown's curiously one-sided study of "conflict" in Arnold:

> Mr. Brown pictures the conflict he speaks of as taking place between the artist and the didactic writer. And this blinds him to something in the art of the prose—certainly to the art, as practiced in Arnold's prose, of being offensive. . . . Mr. Brown, it seems, tends to think that art is the means of producing a beautiful effect, rather than of producing an effect. But Arnold's writing *Culture and anarchy* rather than *Men and women* did not mean that he was any less the artist, but only that in the controversial prose art was engaged to other ends. There is as much art in, say, the attacks Arnold made on contemporary figures as in Browning's meditations on behalf of Cleon or Fra Lippo Lippi. . . . as art, these attacks are masterly, and the critic should rejoice in them as such—as he rejoices in Pope's attack on Sporus.[35]

II

Arnold's attacks on his contemporaries are an old source of complaint. "I often wished . . . that I too had a little sweetness and light," Leslie Stephen remarked, "that I might be able to say such nasty things of my enemies."[36] "More than once," John Morley added, "his literary tact did not save him from slips; the velvet glove in at least one case [presumably that of Frank Newman] wore cruelly thin, and devout people were more shocked by his artifices of polite letters than they were by the more plain-spoken negation."[37] John Duke Coleridge agreed: "Doubtless he was, like Horace, habitually urbane; but as Horace could drop his urbanity . . ., so there must be many living men (and still more some dead ones) towards whom contempt and indignation, rarely roused in him, are expressed in language moderate indeed, but plain and direct to the very verge of good manners."[38] His niece, Mrs. Ward, declared that he had "no malice—not a touch, not a trace of cruelty—so that men allowed him to jest about their most sacred idols and superstitions and bore him no grudge,"[39] but others believed with Crabb Robinson that he had "not much kindness in his nature."[40] And although his widow did not "think he *ever resented* adverse criticism,"[41] Walter Raleigh argued that he was insulated from resentment by arrogance:

> . . . he was adorably insolent, priding himself on his courtesy and humanity, walking delicately among the little people of the earth, like a kind of Olympian schoolmaster dandy. In controversy he wielded enormous powers of irritation, wielded them and enjoyed them, though it seems doubtful whether he ever quite understood why the poor victims of them were irritated. His courtesies are a graceful trellis-work which leave just space enough for his contempt to peep through. Politeness, which, in its genuine form, is a clothing for the modesty of good-will, with him is a suit of armour, worn to protect him from his adversaries. . . .[42]

About Arnold's attacks on his contemporaries several qualifying observations need to be made. First of all, they were less numerous and severe than a comment such as Leslie Stephen's would imply. In fact, after one has cited Frank Newman and Bishop Colenso, he has virtually exhausted the list of those who can properly be described as victims of personal attack by Arnold. What Stephen seems to have had in mind was the host of minor figures who appear incidentally in Arnold's writings as objects of criticism or satire—persons like Ichabod Wright, whose translation of Homer is said to have no reason for existing, or Joseph Hemington Harris ("Presbyter Anglicanus"), who was incapable of appreciating a joke—and representative groups of persons, such as Nonconformists or those with names Arnold thought hideous. That Arnold sometimes miscalculated the effect his language would have he himself recognized when, in expunging certain references to personalities, he expressed the desire "to die at peace with all men" as he drew "nearer to [his] bitter end."[43] But if it is true that he could at times show an insensitivity to the feelings of others, it is also true that some of his contemporaries could be humorless, obtuse, and hypersensitive, and thus a distinction must be drawn between a callousness or maliciousness that unnecessarily wounds and a satiric manner that, as Henry James suggested, raises debate above the banal and literal.

A distinction should also be drawn between attacks Arnold initiated and answers he made to attacks on himself. To do so is to make clear that he was more often the victim of attack than the aggressor. Even with the exclusion of unknown reviewers in the periodical press, the list of those who attacked him is a long one: John Duke Coleridge, Fitzjames Stephen, Goldwin Smith, James Macdonell, Robert Buchanan, and Oscar Browning, to name the most obvious. What is notable, too, is the number of times Arnold was sharply criticized in print by personal friends or acquaintances. To the first three of the names above, for example, may be added those of Clough, Harriet Martineau, and W. R. Greg. More than once Arnold had cause to complain that although he could defend himself from his enemies, he needed protection from his friends.

It should likewise be noted that in his polemical encounters Arnold wrote with an urbanity that lifted them well above the level on which much debate of the time was conducted. Even Leslie Stephen conceded that although "in controversy he took and gave many shrewd blows, he always received them with a courtesy, indicative not of mere policy or literary tact, but of dislike to inflicting pain and of incapacity for hating any tolerably decent antagonist in flesh and blood."[44] Having early learned the wisdom of turning away wrath by a soft answer, Arnold considered his procedure to be "sinuous, easy, unpolemical" and believed that even in "ridicule one must preserve a sweetness and good-humour."[45] He did "not read a purely personal article till it ha[d] been out at least a week," he once wrote to his sister. "Then one cannot be excited by it, for one says to oneself:['']It has already passed out of people's minds with the appearance of the new number; why trouble yourself about it?' "[46] He responded with imperturbable blandness to criticism from his peers, and attacks by younger men like Buchanan and Macdonell he answered with kindly restraint. He was "a delightful man to argue with," Max Müller said, never losing his temper,[47] and with critics who possessed a sense of humor, such as Frederic Harrison and Thomas Henry Huxley, he was able to engage in debates that enlivened with wit what was tempered by politeness.

One does well, therefore, to recall a judgment recorded nearly three-quarters of a century ago by Herbert Paul:

> It is a remarkable fact that, though an unsparing critic of English foibles, and also of the qualities upon which Englishmen particularly pride themselves, he never became unpopular. Such is the power of urbanity. . . . I can myself . . . testify to the fact that Mr. Sala, one of Mr. Arnold's favorite butts, regarded his facetious tormentor with friendly and respectful admiration. This was very creditable to Mr. Sala, but it was creditable to Mr. Arnold too. There was plenty of salt in his wit, but not much pepper.[48]

Arnold himself was aware of this paradoxical response to his work. "Lord Lytton," he wrote to his mother in 1868, "was right in saying that it is no inconsiderable advantage to me that all the writing world have a kind of weakness for me, even at the time they are attacking me," and a year later he again reflected on the point: "However much I may be attacked, my manner of writing is certainly one that takes hold of people and proves effective."[49]

This is why one is disinclined to agree altogether with Geoffrey Tillotson's conclusion that because Arnold's critics "could not take the urbanity of one who postured," he apparently "made a big strategical mistake. . . . if Arnold was bent on being urbane, he ought to have kept his urbanity more like

Newman's, which always seemed to exist by right of second nature."[50] More is contained in this statement than can be dealt with here, but at least one comment is called for. While it is manifestly impossible to ascertain the effect. Arnold might have achieved had he employed a different strategy, it is obvious that he succeeded in having a certain effect by the strategy he chose to employ. The frequency with which he was attacked testifies in itself to the effect he made, just as does the frequency with which reviewers of the periodical journals singled out his contributions as the most "striking" or "interesting" of those under consideration. Although he "less and less [went] out of [his] way to get hold of notices and read them," he wrote to his mother in 1867, he "constantly" came across "occasional notices . . . in the newspapers—sometimes violent attacks."[51] And later that same year he told her, with a pardonable vanity that should not obscure the truth he was conveying, "I constantly hear of the way my things are making, and people say to me that I am 'a power.' "[52]

III

Arnold's paradoxical relationship with his readers suggests that dichotomy of aim to which E. K. Brown devoted an entire book. "You will laugh," he wrote to his mother in 1868, "but fiery hatred and malice are what I detest, and would always allay or avoid, if I could." The last clause seems to imply a failure in knowledge of self as unmistakably as the first clause betrays maternal doubt. Again and again Arnold announced his intention of leaving the realm of controversy, only to return to it once more. "I had much rather avoid all the sphere of dispute," he wrote while preparing the published version of his answer to Frank Newman, and before the year was out, he had ridiculed Colenso in "The Bishop and the Philosopher." After the publication of an essay in its defense, he insisted that "no amount of noise or faultfinding [would] induce [him] to add another word," and yet for more than a decade he continued from time to time to criticize Colenso. In answer to Fitzjames Stephen's attack on the lecture that was an immediate product of the Colenso affair, "The Function of Criticism at the Present Time," he vowed that he would "religiously abstain" from anything like "direct controversy," but his response eventually led to one of his most controversial essays, "My Countrymen." Having defended it from his critics and expressed a desire "to leave irony and the Philistines," he was within months composing the first of the letters that comprise *Friendship's Garland*.[53] After the completion of the five articles on "Anarchy and Authority," written as sequels to the much-criticized "Culture and Its Enemies," he determined to leave his enemies "untouched for a year or two."[54] Within the year, however, he not only had returned to the pages of the *Pall Mall Gazette* but also had written the two papers on St. Paul that developed the criticism of Puritanism made in *Culture and Anarchy*. Declaring after a third paper that he would leave the subject, he resumed an essential part of it in *Literature and Dogma*. While working on a reply to its critics in *God and the Bible* he complained, "I really *hate* polemics."[55] And despite both the title of *Last Essays on Church and Religion* and the promise contained in its preface of a return to literature proper, Arnold repeatedly dealt with religious and ecclesiastical issues in the last years of his life. Nor did the promise preclude a series of debates with Goldwin Smith, Swinburne, Huxley, and the admirers of Emerson and Gladstone.

In addition to these instances of *volte-face*, there are other signs of an apparently divided purpose in Arnold's writing; for example, his surprising discovery that he had hurt Frank Newman and his admission that he had treated Colenso with excessive severity, the result being that he never republished the works that had given offense. There are the excisions of passages later regarded as too strong, such as the quotation from Revelation in "My Countrymen" and the reference in *Culture and Anarchy* to Dr. Arnold's cure for rioting.[56] And there are the softenings or total suppressions of passages that deal in personalities, such as the criticism of A. W. Kinglake and the use of Lord Shaftesbury's name, which created a *cause célèbre*. It was in these and similar passages that E. K. Brown detected that "uncertainty of touch" which indicated to him not only "some inner conflict, central and enduring," but also "a defective sense of art."[57]

Of this one may say, as Arnold said of an article by R. H. Hutton, that it has the "fault of seeing so very far into a millstone."[58] Inconsistencies and contradictions undeniably appear in Arnold's writing, just as do a certain superciliousness and airy dogmatism. The question, however, is not whether they exist, but how seriously they are to be regarded; and to believe that they "exhibit some gross and incredible flaw"[59] is to regard them too seriously. Moreover, it ignores the fact that Arnold was a busy man of affairs who of necessity subordinated literary to other responsibilities and often wrote under circumstances less than ideal: pressed by deadlines, harried by the duties of a school inspector, composing essays between the hours spent at marking stacks of examination papers or on railway carriages and in the midst of illness and domestic sorrow. To require of every utterance of such a writer that it meet some absolute standard of art, and then to find in whatever shortcomings are revealed a permanent and ineradicable defect of character, is to adopt the same mechanical view of human behavior that Arnold rejected in *God and the Bible*: that one "must be rigidly consistent, must show no conflicting aspects, must have no flux and reflux."[60]

It insufficiently takes into account, too, the different audiences and occasions for which Arnold wrote, and the different methods and styles he employed. Within the confines of Oxford he was cheered at the conclusion of his lectures on Homer and "Culture and Its Enemies," and bitterly assailed after their publication. The difference in response to the spoken and published versions suggests not so much a defective sense of art as the simple truth that what succeeds in one context does not necessarily succeed in another, just as the wide divergence of opinion about certain works intended only for publication (the preface to *Essays in Criticism,* "My Countrymen," and *Literature and Dogma* are notable examples) suggests that what is amusing or edifying to some readers is not so to all. We can speak intelligently of Arnold's effectiveness in achieving his aims only if we designate the audience or reader on whom the effect is to be determined, and even then there is the difficulty of distinguishing between the effect made by matter and that made by manner. Arnold unquestionably alienated Nonconformists as a group, but whether he could have made his ideas palatable to them by pursuing some other method is impossible to judge.

If there is a basic and persistent division of aim in Arnold, it is that between the writer who insists on "saying imperturbably what [he] thinks and making a good many people uncomfortable," and the writer who perceives that if he is to be successful he must check impulses likely to cause offense. The frank and iconoclastic Arnold, witty and ironic, chaffing his enemies and bent on destroying cherished illusions, is the author of an article such as "The Twice Revised Code." The Arnold who labored "hard to *persuade*" and, in an exercise of "moral discipline" to which he called the attention of his mother and favorite sister, suppressed all that "might wound, provoke, or frighten,"[61] is the author of *A French Eton.* In the one instance he risked his position in the Education Department by writing with a freedom that he later marvelled he was allowed.[62] In the other, addressing a middle class hostile to state action, he wrote with a tact that implied agreement with Diogenes Teufelsdröckh that "an ironic young man . . . may be viewed as a pest to society."[63] Yet in each case he wrote out of a concern and conviction that are the same.

Still, this does not answer the question of why Arnold engaged so frequently in controversy, being drawn again and again into polemical encounters despite his avowed intent to avoid them, and not always resisting the temptation to utter

the "sharp and telling things that [rose] to [his] lips."[64] It remains the central question to be asked about his career as prose
writer.

IV

In the obituary that he wrote for the Manchester *Guardian*
the young Thomas Arnold said of his brother:

> The natural bent of his mind was very different from that of his father.
> Matthew had the temper of an observer and an interpreter; his father
> that of a teacher and a reformer. Intellect was the chief weapon of
> the one; moral influence the chief weapon of the other. Matthew did
> not at first care about reforming the world or any part of it . . .; his
> ambition was to understand and estimate aright men and books.[65]

The Arnold described here is unrecognizable to those who
know him primarily as a moral teacher with a reformative
ideal, and yet it is the authentic Arnold of much of the poetry
and of such characteristic doctrines as that of disinterestedness. What occurred, clearly, was a gradual transformation
of the detached spectator into the *engagé* critic. Its beginnings
are early marked by a growing seriousness, such as that which
appears with rather startling inappropriateness in a letter to
"K" on her forty-second birthday:

> We have come a long way now, short as it seems to look back upon,
> but it is long as compared with the whole space which it is given to us
> to traverse; may we all remember the excellent advice of the astron-
> omer Ptolemy: 'As you draw nearer to your end, redouble your ef-
> forts to do good.'[66]

Accompanying this solemn view, almost indistinguishable
from the earnestness of his father that Lytton Strachey mer-
cilessly ridiculed, is a profound sense of a mission to perform
and of the possession of means to achieve it. "It is very ani-
mating to think that one at last has a chance of *getting at* the
English public," he wrote to his mother in the mid-sixties, and

he was "more and more . . . conscious of having something to do, and of a resolution to do it."[67]

The sense of having an influential role to play in fateful times—what Leslie Stephen described as the immensely serious, humorless, and oracular manner in which he viewed his vocation—is expressed repeatedly in Arnold's correspondence: "I more and more have the satisfaction of seeing that what I do produces its effect."[68] "I am sure there is great need of a power [such as that which he was said to possess] in our present troubled condition, if the power can but make or keep itself a good one."[69] "I do hope that what influence I have may be of use in the troubled times which I see are before us as a healing and reconciling influence, and it is this which makes me glad to find—what I find more and more—that I *have* influence." "The times are wonderful, and will be still more so; and one would not willingly lose by negligence, self-mismanagement, and want of patience what power one has of working in them and having influence on them." ". . . no one knows better than I do how little of a popular author I am; but the thing is, I gradually produce a real effect." ". . . it is a great and solid satisfaction . . . to find one's work, the fruit of so many years of isolated reflexion and labour, getting recognition amongst those whose judgment passes for the most valuable."[70]

While the solemnity of some of these passages may in part be discounted on the grounds that they were addressed to a family who disapproved of Arnold's vivacities and thus needed reassurance of the seriousness of his purpose, on the whole they accurately reflect the conception he held of himself as performing a mission. That mission, at least until after the completion of *Culture and Anarchy* in 1869, was an intellectual one: to assist in the "intellectual deliverance" that was the theme of his inaugural lecture at Oxford, and in the acquisition of ideas, which was the message of his epistles to Philistia; to exalt the "serious cheerfulness" of Sophocles and the nobility of Homer as examples of lucidity and grandeur for an age of confusion, vulgarity, and triviality of mind; to transform the middle class and thus equip it for its inescapable tasks as successor to the displaced aristocracy; to show in the Hellenic ideal the basis for a culture that could solve the political and social problems of modern life; and to find for Christianity an intellectual basis supported by rather than vulnerable to the advances of science.

"You must by this time begin to see what people mean by placing France *politically* in the van of Europe," Arnold wrote to "K" in one of the earliest of his letters that have survived; "it is the *intelligence* of their *idea-moved masses* which makes them, politically, as far superior to the *insensible masses* of England as to the Russian serfs." Nor was the idea here expressed a passing whim of the young secretary to Lord Lansdowne. He returned to it several weeks later in a letter that expressed grave concern about the future of England:

> How plain it is now . . . that England is in a certain sense *far be-hind* the Continent. In conversation, in the newspapers, one is so struck with the fact of the utter insensibility, one may say, of people to the number of ideas and schemes now ventilated on the Continent —not because they have judged them or seen beyond them, but from sheer habitual want of wide reading and thinking. . . . I am not sure but I agree in Lamartine's prophecy that 100 years hence the Continent will be a great united Federal Republic, and England, all her colonies gone, in a dull steady decay.[71]

To try to prevent the fulfillment of this prophecy became one of the chief burdens of Arnold's writing. After returning from the continental visit that produced *England and the Italian Question* (1859), the pamphlet in which he first spoke of aristocratic inaptitude for ideas, he defined the essence of his purpose as inculcating "*intelligence* . . . upon the English nation as what they most want." Six years later, after publishing *The Popular Education of France* and *A French Eton* and delivering the lectures, largely French in subject, that comprise *Essays in Criticism*, he wrote that he could not

admit that any countries are more worth studying, as regards secondary instruction, than those in which intellectual life has been carried farthest—Germany first, and, in the second degree, France. Indeed, I am convinced that as Science, in the widest sense of the word,
meaning a true knowledge of things as the basis of our operations,
becomes, as it does become, more of a power in the world, the weight
of the nations and men who have carried the intellectual life farthest
will be more and more felt; indeed, I see signs of this already. That
England may run well in this race is my deepest desire; and to stimu-
late her and to make her feel how many clogs she wears, and how
much she has to do in order to run in it as her genius gives her the
power to run, is the object of all I do.

But that she was not running well appeared obvious to him
after another educational mission two years later, causing him
to write with still greater anxiety:

I have a conviction that there is a real, an almost imminent danger of
England losing immeasurably in all ways, declining into a sort of
greater Holland, for want of what I must still call ideas, for want of
perceiving how the world is going and must go, and preparing herself accordingly. This conviction haunts me, and at times even over-
whelms me with depression; I would rather not live to see the change
come to pass, for we shall all deteriorate under it. While there is time
I will do all I can, and in every way, to prevent its coming to pass.[72]

It is this seriousness of purpose—this "almost painful anxiety about public matters"[73]—that accounts, more than any
other single factor, for the frequency of Arnold's polemical
engagements, for both the hostility of the critics who attacked
him and for his determination to defend and expand on what
had been attacked. Under a sense of urgency he was inclined
to represent issues as involving sharp dichotomies: the Greek
world was rational, the modern was capricious; Homer was
noble, Frank Newman was ignoble; Europe was educated,
England was uncritical. And the alternatives he presented
were equally sharp: get ideas *or* perish; choose culture *or* anarchy; have religion *or* dogma. Presented so, in a manner that
sometimes appeared conceited and dogmatic, developed with

a kind of fastidious disdain and superciliousness, and enlivened by banter and irony, Arnold's ideas understandably encountered an opposition that encouraged rather than deterred his persistence.

The controversies were not unrelated entities, however, but segments of what we now see as the continuity in his prose works and the steady evolution of his thought. The 1853 preface was shaped by criticism of his first two volumes of poetry, and then modified in the inaugural lecture by the attacks made on it. When *Merope* was almost universally condemned, the impulse to illustrate the Greek world that had produced it found expression in the lectures on Homer. The attempt made there to clarify the confusion about Homer that had been created by Newman foreshadowed the attempt to clarify the confusion about the Bible that had been created by Colenso, and the storm aroused in the two instances contributed to the most significant lectures and essays of the sixties, culminating in the final address at Oxford. From the replies to it emerged a book of social and political criticism, which in turn led to four volumes of biblical and religious commentary. Even while he engaged at the end of his life in a series of skirmishes with a variety of critics after ostensibly leaving the polemic arena, Arnold maintained a consistency of viewpoint by writing as the humanist he had always been.

But this is to anticipate the account that follows. We must return to 1848, when a young poet who has not yet published his first volume of verse is attempting to find his way in the confusion of the times, with a bewildering multitude of voices offering conflicting advice.

CHAPTER TWO

The Poet and His Readers

> Our young spirits,
> Who call themselves the masters of the age,
> Are either robed in philosophic mist,
> And, with an air of grand profundity,
> Talk metaphysics—which, sweet cousin, means
> Nothing but aimless jargon—or they come
> Before us in the broad bombastic vein,
> With spasms, and throes, and transcendental flights,
> And heap hyperbole on metaphor.—W. E. Aytoun

. . . what can be more important than the subject, and what is all the science of art without it? All talent is wasted if the subject is unsuitable. It is because modern artists have no worthy subjects, that people are so hampered in all the art of modern times.—Goethe

. . . Homer is the model of all models. He says, Nireus was fair; Achilles was fairer; Helen was of godlike beauty. But he is nowhere betrayed into a more detailed description of these beauties. Yet the whole poem is based upon the loveliness of Helen. How a modern poet would have revelled in descriptions of it!—Lessing

Poetry is not a turning loose of emotion, but an escape from emotion; it is not the expression of personality, but an escape from personality.—T. S. Eliot

. . . the period to which the work of Thucydides refers belongs properly to modern and not to ancient history; and it is this circumstance, over and above the great ability of the historian himself, which makes it so peculiarly deserving of our study.—Dr. Thomas Arnold

Early in 1848, at a time when Clough's poetry was still "predominantly subjective,"[1] Arnold wrote once again to express doubt that his friend was an artist. "A growing sense of the

23

deficiency of the *beautiful* in your poems, and of this alone being properly *poetical* as distinguished from rhetorical, devotional or metaphysical," he explained, made him speak as he did. He conceded that at the moment Clough had "most of the promising English verse-writers" with him. There was, for instance, Philip James Bailey. But despite the problem that still remained of producing the beautiful, Arnold declared, he would "die protesting against the world that the other is false and JARRING."[2]

The publication of Bailey's *Festus* (1839) nearly a decade earlier had announced the beginning in English verse of a vogue of introspection and extravagance that would become known as Spasmodic. The poetry it inspired could not survive the inevitable ridicule of its absurdities, and by 1855, the year after W. E. Aytoun had shattered its pretensions with a clever burlesque, *Firmilian*, a reviewer was welcoming Arnold's poems as "a relief, a balm, an anodyne, a delicious assuagement" following "all this hubbub of rhythmical rant, rhymed gibberish, vapouring mysticism, and conceited rhodomontade."[3] But before passing out of fashion, Spasmodic poetry exerted a considerable influence on literary taste during Arnold's most productive years as a poet. Bailey had written his poem, as Emerson remarked, by getting "his head brimful of *Faust*, and then pour[ing] away a gallon of ink." The result, the poet told his father with some uncertainty, was a dramatic poem, "if that may be termed dramatic which boasts no plot, no action." It consisted instead of "meditations, arguments, and reflections upon all sorts of subjects and sentiments," and in form it was so "elastic," admitting "almost every variety of classifiable thought," that Bailey spent a lifetime expanding it to forty thousand lines.[4] If there were flaws in *Festus*, they did not prevent it from being one of the most popular poems of the century. With unintentional irony its admirers praised it for demonstrating "great exuberance of thought" and "unrepressed vigour of imagination" and for containing "poetry enough to set up fifty poets."[5]

Among Bailey's most intoxicated readers was the Reverend

George Gilfillan, a Dundee Calvinist who hailed *Festus* as "the poem of the age's hope"[6] and soon became the foremost patron of the Spasmodics. It was his essays, comprising some of the most influential criticism of the time, that inspired a young muslin designer in Glasgow named Alexander Smith to write poetry of his own and introduce himself to Gilfillan as the "child" of the critic who had "first made him read and love poetry." Having in the meanwhile discovered in Sydney Dobell "another Shelley, of a manlier and Christian type," Gilfillan now believed he had found in Smith "another Keats." But though Smith was "a true poet," Gilfillan warned, he had thus far "only been plucking and weaving stray wild-flowers, and must bend himself to some enterprise of pith and moment." Accordingly he urged his protégé to write a long poem in order to show "the sustained concentration of his powers," an idea that appealed to Smith except for his lack of a subject. Rather than allow this to deter him, however, the "sincere and simple-minded" youth ignored the doubts of Gilfillan and brought together in a single work the poems he had composed. Written under the spell of *Festus* and entitled *A Life-Drama*, it reached a fourth edition in less than three years and was the "most successful poetical hit," Gilfillan noted with satisfaction, "since the days of Moore, Byron, and Scott."[7]

A Life-Drama (1853), as one of its most discerning critics has observed, is almost a parody of Spasmodic verse.[8] Its moody hero, sick with love, thirst for fame, and loss of faith, talks compulsively of his *Weltschmerz* and of the power of poetry to relieve it. To him poetry is variously the object of erotic desire:

> For Poesy my heart and pulses beat,
> For Poesy my blood runs red and fleet;

the expression of Shelleyan longing:

> I love thee, Poesy! Thou art a rock;
> I, a weak wave, would break on thee and die!

the medium for Byronic self-dramatization:

> This poor rhyme
> Is but an adumbration of my life,
> My misery tricked out in a quaint disguise;

and even the salvation of an uneasy time:

> To set this Age to music,—the great work
> Before the Poet now. I do believe
> When it is fully sung, —its great complaint,
> Its hope, its yearning, told to earth and heaven,—
> Our troubled age shall pass.

But in his sublimest moods he views poetry as prophetic and definitive utterance, as when he tells what his friend the bard had once said to him:

> a Poet must ere long arise,
> And with a regal song sun-crown this age,
> As a saint's head is with a halo crowned;—
> One, who shall hallow Poetry to God
> And to its own high use, for Poetry is
> The grandest chariot wherein king-thoughts ride;—
> One, who shall fervent grasp the sword of song
> As a stern swordsman grasps his keenest blade,
> To find the quickest passage to the heart.
> A mighty Poet whom this age shall choose
> To be its spokesman to all coming times.
> In the ripe full-blown season of his soul,
> He shall go forward in his spirit's strength,
> And grapple with the questions of all time,
> And wring from them their meanings.[9]

Smith's fame could not last, although at the time few said so. One was Dobell, who thought his "oriental luxury" was like "the exuberance of a strawberry-bed."[10] Tennyson saw that he had "fancy without imagination," and Elizabeth Barrett Browning that his imagery was excessive and his thought deficient.[11] Lowell, who declared that his book was "no more a poem than a brush-heap is a tree," compared his meteoric rise to a boy's launching a toy boat "with so strong a push as to run wholly under water."[12] But in the spring of 1853, according to Rossetti, "nothing [was] talked of . . . but Alexander Smith."[13]

At precisely the same time, Matthew Arnold was planning to publish his third volume of poetry and to introduce it with a preface[14] that, he later explained to his brother Tom in Tasmania, would be directed at "the sins and offences" of "numbers of young gentlemen with really wonderful powers of perception and expression, but to whom there is wholly wanting a 'bedeutendes Individuum,' so that their productions are most unedifying and unsatisfactory." Chief among these young gentlemen lacking a "noble or powerful nature" were, of course, Alexander Smith and the other Spasmodics.[15]

Arnold doubted that Tom would "care" for the 1853 preface, nor had he been altogether satisfied with it himself. Ten days after its completion he wrote to Clough, "The Preface is done—there is a certain *Geist* in it I think, but it is far less *precise* than I had intended."[16] His real difficulty, however, lay not so much in expression as in the attempt to make the preface serve a number of purposes. It was, first of all, a general attack on the critics who wrote for contemporary journals, and a specific attack on two of these critics. It was a general condemnation of romantic excesses in poetry, and a specific condemnation of Alexander Smith and his predecessors. It was a general reply to the reviewers of the 1849 and 1852 volumes of poetry, and a specific reply to the objections made to those volumes by Clough and other Oxford friends. And, finally and most important, it was a general defense of his own poetry, and a specific defense of his choice of classical subjects and of his refusal to be a spokesman for his age.

I

The immediate target of the preface was a writer for the *Spectator*, conjecturally identified by Arnold as its editor, Rob-

ert Stephen Rintoul,[17] who had asserted in an anonymous review of Edwin Arnold's poems earlier in 1853 that "the poet
who would really fix the public attention must leave the exhausted past, and draw his subjects from matters of present
import and therefore both of interest and novelty." Arnold
seized upon the passage, italicized the *therefore*, and then, as
if in astonishment, attributed the *non sequitur* to an "apparently intelligent critic."[18] Behind this scornful use of the quotation were both personal annoyance and profound disagreement. Rintoul is said to have been an editor of "chilly
temperament" who boasted that the *Spectator* was not "enthusiastic" and could not be.[19] Certainly it had not erred in that
direction when dealing with Arnold's first two volumes. Its
terse notice of *The Strayed Reveller* had complained of "un-
intelligibility" and "strangeness," and that of *Empedocles on
Etna* had denied Arnold "freshness of subject," "artistical
treatment," and "independence of mind."[20] Whether or not
the author of this latter notice was also the reviewer of Edwin Arnold, as has been supposed,[21] he at least shared with
him a tendency to be heavy-handed, solemn, and obsessed
by the notion that poetry must be both modern and moralistic.
Later, after the *Spectator* had "elaborately and rather mé-
chamment" attacked the Preface in a manner that seemed to
reveal Rintoul as the "apparently intelligent critic,"[22] Arnold
repented of his irony and deleted the damning adverb. Significantly, however, he retained the stricture that the quoted
comment was typical of the criticism of the age—a specious
criticism designed to confuse the reader and mislead the poet.

But to Arnold the criticism of the period not only prescribed
a false poetic practice with its insistence on contemporaneous
subject matter, it also prescribed false poetic aims with its insistence on romantic subjectivism. Just two months before the
completion of the preface, for example, David Masson had
declared in the *North British Review* that "a true allegory of
the state of one's own mind in a representative history,
whether narrative or dramatic in form, is perhaps the highest

thing that one can attempt in the way of fictitious art." Poetry, he argued, was simply "the embodiment of some notion or feeling, or some aggregate of notions and feelings, in appropriate objective circumstances." Ascribing this doctrine to Goethe and applying it to *A Life-Drama*, Masson found in Smith "certain real merits."[23] Arnold, however, was not to be intimidated by the appeal to Goethe's authority. Privately he denounced the doctrine as "a precious piece of cant,"[24] and in the preface he quoted it with the same incredulity with which he had quoted from the *Spectator*. Goethe had attempted something of the kind in *Faust*, he conceded, but despite its many beautiful passages *Faust*, judged as a whole, was defective; Goethe, the greatest of all critics, would have been the first to admit it.

II

In rejecting Masson's "precious piece of cant," Arnold was in effect rejecting not simply the poetry of Alexander Smith but that of his predecessors as well. The most obvious of these was certainly Keats, to whose poetry he had recently returned. On his reading list for June 1853 are the minor poems, followed by *Endymion* and *Lamia* in August, a month before the completion of the preface.[25] A rereading of the poetry seems only to have confirmed Arnold's response four or five years earlier to Monckton Milnes's *Life, Letters, and Literary Remains of John Keats*. "What a brute you were," he had exclaimed to Clough at that time, "to tell me to read Keats' Letters," and he had gone on to speak of the "harm [Keats] has done in English Poetry" and of the "perplexity Keats Tennyson et id genus omne must occasion to young writers of the ὁπλίτης ["heavy-armed foot soldier"] sort: yes and those d——d Elizabethan poets generally." In another letter to Clough, written several years afterwards, he resumed the subject with the assertion that "Keats and Shelley were on a false track when they set themselves to reproduce the exuberance of expression, the charm, the richness of images, and the felicity, of the Elizabethan poets." Modern poetry, he said, "can only subsist by . . . becoming a complete magister vitae as the poetry of the ancients did," and therefore its "language, style and general proceedings . . . must be very plain direct and severe: and it must not lose itself in parts and episodes and ornamental work, but must press forwards to the whole." Again, only a few months before writing the preface, Arnold told Clough that Alexander Smith's "kind does not go far: it dies like Keats."[26]

The response to Tennyson was no less emphatic. Perhaps as much as a year before he read Milnes's work Arnold had complained to Clough that "to *solve* the Universe as you try to do is as irritating as Tennyson's dawdling with its painted shell is fatiguing to me to witness." Two months after completing the preface he said of a line in *Sohrab and Rustum*, "[It] *is* rather Tennysonian—at any rate it is not good."[27] Later, though careful to veil his few public pronouncements on Tennyson in a formal politeness that partially obscures their unflattering intent,[28] he continued to speak privately with a merciless candor. He described *In Memoriam* as the archetype of "poems which have no beginning, middle or end, but are holdings forth in verse, which, for anything in the nature of the composition itself, may perfectly well go on for ever,"[29] and *Maud, and Other Poems* as "a lamentable production, and like so much of our literature thoroughly and intensely *provincial*, not European." By 1861 he had grown to like Tennyson's poetry "less and less" and to be "convinced both Alfred de Musset and Henri Heine are far more profitable studies, if we are to study contemporaries at all."[30] Despite "his temperament and artistic skill," Arnold concluded, Tennyson was "deficient in intellectual power" and not "a great and powerful spirit in any line."[31]

Arnold was understandably annoyed, therefore, when his readers detected the influence of Tennyson in his poetry. To John Duke Coleridge he admitted that "one has [Tennyson] so in one's head, one cannot help imitating him sometimes:

but except in the last two lines I thought I had kept him out of 'Sohrab and Rustum.' Mark any other places you notice, for I should wish to alter such."[32] Nor was Coleridge the only friend to hear the voice of Tennyson in his poetry. Goldwin Smith asserted in the *Times*, for instance, that Arnold was "a good deal influenced by Tennyson, and . . . in danger of inheriting some of that poet's faults."[33] Such criticism, in fact, had long since become commonplace in reviews of Arnold's poetry. W. M. Rossetti had included him among the "many writers of this generation" over whom Tennyson had exerted a "general influence."[34] Aytoun had noted a "Tennysonian tendency" in both his blank verse and his lyrics and had credited it with making "The Forsaken Merman" "by far the best poem in the [1849] volume."[35] Coventry Patmore also praised "The Forsaken Merman" but thought it recalled "certain poems of Tennyson rather too vividly."[36] A critic for the *English Review* considered "The New Sirens" to be "more Tennysonian than Tennyson himself,"[37] and Arnold scarcely derived much pleasure from Kingsley's intended compliment in *Fraser's*: " 'Mycerinus' is a fragment worthy of Tennyson."[38] Remarks like these could have acted only as re-enforcements of Arnold's decision to write a preface defending a poetical practice essentially opposed to Tennyson's aims.[39] It would not have done to attack Tennyson directly, to be sure, but in criticizing Keats he could attack obliquely.

III

Arnold was understandably annoyed, too, when the poems of Alexander Smith gained the popularity and in part the critical favor that his own poems failed to receive. "It can do me no good . . .," he wrote to "K" in the spring of 1853, "to be irritated with that young man, who has certainly an extraordinary faculty, although I think he is a phenomenon of a very dubious character; but—*it fait son métier—faisons le nôtre*."[40] Two weeks later he made the same criticism in writing to Clough, whose opinion of Smith's poetry he had previously inquired about: "As to Alexander Smith I have not read him—I shrink from what is so intensely immature—but I think the extracts I have seen most remarkable—and I think at the same time that he will not go far."[41] Arnold could hardly have been pleased, therefore, when Clough published in the July issue of the *North American Review* a thirty-page article devoted largely to praising the poetry of Smith for possessing virtues conspicuously absent from the poetry of Arnold.

This attack on "the whole structure of Arnold's mind," as Trilling calls it,[42] can be accounted for in part by the fact that its period of composition exactly coincided with a period in which Clough was experiencing unusual mental depression (the review was written in April, the same month in which he wrote to Arnold questioning their Oxford friendship) and temporary excitement about Smith's poetry. In May Clough was to write to his fiancée, Blanche Smith, "If you haven't read A. S. don't trouble yourself; 'tis hardly worth the while," and later he added, "I am rather sorry I recommended Master Alexander Smith to you." But in April he was "very much taken with Alexander Smith's life-drama," in which he found "really what I have had in my own mind."[43] And at the same time that he was seeing in the Scottish laborer a kindred spirit, he was harboring "a morbid suspicion" that Arnold was a doubtful friend who merely used him "as food for speculation."[44]

Thus it was that to Clough *A Life-Drama* was more appealing than *Tristram and Iseult* with its "obscurity" and *Empedocles on Etna* with its "pseudo-Greek inflation," for he preferred Smith's depiction of the "simple, strong, and certain" to Arnold's of the "subtle, shifting, and dubious." In this preference Clough was expressing both his discovery of qualities in Smith to which he himself aspired, and his view that Smith's poetry possessed two merits lacking in Arnold's: its subject matter was immediate rather than remote, and its tone was affirmative rather than negative. Hence the "grateful contrast," established at the outset of the article and sustained almost throughout, between Smith's poems with their "force of purpose and character" and "the ordinary languid collectanea published by young men of literary habits," a group presumably exemplified by Arnold. Clough concedes the literary value of "imitations and *quasi*-translations . . ., poems after classical models, poems from Oriental sources, and the like"—a summary clearly intended as a description of Arnold's 1852 volume—but he maintains that they do not "shake the hearts of men." To perform this function poetry must "deal more than at present it usually does, with general wants, ordinary feelings, the obvious rather than the rare facts of human nature . . .—the actual, palpable things with which our everyday life is concerned." The writer who tries "to build us a real house to be lived in . . . is more to our purpose than the student of ancient art who proposes to lodge us under an Ionic portico." Smith's great virtue is that he is a builder of houses and not, as is Arnold, a builder of porticoes. Smith's poems "were not written among books and busts. . . . They have something substantive and lifelike, immediate and first-hand, about them." And they make one "believe that, in these last days, no longer by 'clear spring or shady grove,' no more upon any Pindus or Parnassus, or by the side of any Castaly, are the true and lawful haunts of the poetic powers."[45]

Even more important for Clough are Smith's buoyant optimism and energy, which stand in sharp contrast to Arnold's enervating skepticism and introspection. The "charitable and patient" reader, he admits with perhaps unintentional irony, will find in Arnold's minor poems "some approximations to a kind of confidence, some incipiences of a degree of hope, some roots, retaining some vitality, of conviction and moral purpose." In general, however, the reader will choose to go "forth to battle in the armor of a righteous purpose" with Smith than to remain "reflecting, pondering, hesitating, musing, complaining" with Arnold. Clough recognizes that individuals combine in varying degrees "the two elements of thoughtful discriminating selection and rejection, and frank and bold acceptance of what lies around them," and between these two "extremes of ascetic and timid self-culture, and of unquestioning, unhesitating confidence" he will "tolerate every kind and gradation of intermixture." But "for the present age, the lessons of reflectiveness and the maxims of caution do not appear to be more needful or more appropriate than exhortations to steady courage and calls to action."[46]

Arnold's family was right: the review by Clough was indeed "peu favorable."[47] From it Arnold emerged as a poet with more "refined . . . and more highly educated sensibilities" than Alexander Smith possessed, with "a calmer judgment" and "a more poised and steady intellect," with "a finer and rarer aim perhaps, and certainly a keener sense of difficulty, in life." But it was precisely these characteristics, in Clough's view, that made Arnold's poetry less relevant than Smith's to the needs of the age. Even in poetic manner Arnold's superiority was not complete, for here, too, Clough qualified his praise. Although critical of Smith's lavish use of imagery, which he compared to a clerk's counting of "sovereigns at the Bank of England" and for which he blamed Keats and Shelley "with their extravagant love for Elizabethan phraseology,"[48] he seemed at times to prefer the robust vigor of Smith's style to the severe simplicity of Arnold's. Ultimately, of course, the question was not which of the two was the better poet, for in spite of the vagaries of his review, Clough was too sound a critic not to see Smith's basic deficiencies. Yet to him the central issue was which of the two more adequately met the demands made of poetry in mid-Victorian England (or, perhaps more accurately, the personal demands made by the irresolute Clough himself). It was because Smith attempted to meet these demands that Clough felt more strongly drawn to him than to Arnold.

IV

If Arnold rejected his family's opinion of the review, as he assured Clough he did, the reason is perhaps that he regarded it not so much as an expression of personal dissatisfaction with his poetry as a reflection of a general view of the age regarding the nature and function of poetry that manifested itself in two persistent demands imposed on the poet. The first was that he should choose subjects from contemporary life, subjects directly relevant to the people and their times. Mrs. Browning was to give this demand its most vigorous expression when she made her poetess Aurora declare:

> I do distrust the poet who discerns
> No character or glory in his times,
>
> .   .   .   .
>
> Nay, if there's room for poets in this world
> A little overgrown (I think there is),
> Their sole work is to represent the age,
> Their age, not Charlemagne's,—this live, throbbing age,
> That brawls, cheats, maddens, calculates, aspires,
> And spends more passion, more heroic heat,
> Betwixt the mirrors of its drawing-rooms,
> Than Roland with his knights at Roncesvalles.
> To flinch from modern varnish, coat or flounce,
> Cry out for togas and the picturesque,
> Is fatal,—foolish too. King Arthur's self
> Was commonplace to Lady Guenever;
> And Camelot to minstrels seemed as flat
> As Fleet Street to our poets.
>   Never flinch,
> But still, unscrupulously epic, catch
> Upon the burning lava of a song
> The full-veined, heaving, double-breasted Age:
> That, when the next shall come, the men of that
> May touch the impress with reverent hand, and say
> "Behold,—behold the paps we all have sucked!
> This bosom seems to beat still, or at least
> It sets ours beating: this is living art,
> Which thus presents and thus records true life."[49]

Browning supported her view while at the same time taking a sidelong glance at Arnold in *The Parleying With Gerard de Lairesse*:

> Earth's young significance is all to learn:
> The dead Greek lore lies buried in the urn
> Where who seeks fire finds ashes. Ghost, forsooth![50]

Tennyson confessed to the need to use something "modern" when dealing with the "antique" and in the introductory verse to "Morte d'Arthur" had the poet Everard Hall ask:

> Why take the style of those heroic times?
> For nature brings not back the mastodon,
> Nor we those times; and why should any man
> Remodel models?[51]

In the decade following Smith's *Life-Drama* the demand for "relevance" produced a series of long poems attempting to portray "modern life," including Tennyson's *Maud* (1855), Mrs. Browning's *Aurora Leigh* (1856), Clough's *Amours de Voyage* (1858), and Meredith's *Modern Love* (1862).

No less insistent was a second demand made of the poet, namely, that he should recognize and accept his responsibility to be not simply an interpreter and critic of his age, but a moral guide and spiritual comforter as well. Derived principally from Wordsworth and Shelley, this concept of the poet in a vatic role had been fittingly proclaimed at the outset of Bailey's *Festus*:

> Poetry is itself a thing of God;
> He made His prophets poets; and the more
> We feel of poesie do we become
> Like God in love and power,—under-makers.[52]

Tennyson had earlier depicted the poet as one who, born "in a golden clime" and with "the marvel of the everlasting will" lying open before him, "shook the world" through the power of his "winged shafts of truth,"[53] and in the same vein Browning's Sordello exclaimed, "A poet must be earth's essential king."[54] The reviewer who denounced Tennyson for not assuming the prophet's mantle, when he "might have been the herald of a new era; the prophet-preacher of a 'good time coming,' "[55] was simply writing out of a disappointed hope that would later inspire Alexander Smith's prophecy of the rise of a mighty poet.

The readers of Arnold's poetry had long since made him familiar with these demands imposed on the mid-Victorian poet. Both the reviewers and his friends, for example, repeatedly criticized his use of ancient subjects and his classical imitations. "What does the age want with fragments of an Antigone?" Kingsley asked in a "saucy" review written from the conviction that Arnold was "frittering away great talents."[56] "The man who cannot . . . sing the present age, and transfigure it into melody," he said, "or who cannot, in writing of past ages, draw from them some eternal lesson about this one, has no right to be versifying at all. Let him read, think, and keep to prose, till he has mastered the secret of the nineteenth century."[57] W. M. Rossetti said that Arnold's "predilection . . . for antiquity and classical association" lacked both "that strong love which made Shelley, as it were, the heir of Plato" and "that vital grasp of conception which enabled Keats . . . to return to and renew the old thoughts and beliefs of Greece."[58] The response of the *Gentleman's Magazine*, which confessed that the subjects of the 1849 volume had "not inspired us with much interest,"[59] was repeated at Oxford, where Arnold reported that "many complain[ed] that the subjects treated [did] not interest them."[60] J. C. Shairp wished that "Matt would give up that old Greek form."[61] Edward Quillinan deplored "all the heathen gods and goddesses that [held] him in enchantment."[62] And when his third volume appeared, Arnold received from Ralph Lingen, his former tutor, a letter of "four sheets on behalf of sticking to modern subjects."[63] Tom Arnold, by contrast, praised Clough's *Bothie of Tober-na-Vuolich* for portraying "with clearness and fidelity a portion of real human life passed on this actual world."[64]

Equally prevalent in the criticism of Arnold's poetry was the complaint that he was unsympathetic toward his age, expressing personal discontent rather than the desire to solve its problems. The most explicit and solemnly pious statement of this view was made, characteristically, by Kingsley:

> . . . here is a man to whom God has given rare faculties and advantages. Let him be assured that he was meant to use them for God. . . . Let him rejoice in his youth, as the great Arnold told his Rugby scholars to do, and walk in the sight of his own eyes; but let him remember that for all these things God will bring him into judgment. For every work done in the strength of that youthful genius he must give account, whether it be good or evil. And let him be sure, that if he chooses to fiddle while Rome is burning he will not escape unscorched. If he chooses to trifle with the public by versifying dreamy, transcendental excuses for laziness, for the want of an earnest purpose and a fixed creed, let him know that the day is at hand when he that will not work neither shall he eat.[65]

In much the same manner Patmore sternly reproached Arnold for his "indolent, selfish quietism," his "self-complacent reverie," and his lack of "severe manliness" and "sympathy with the wants of the present generation."[66] Aytoun was equally severe, declaring that Arnold could not expect a favorable response from the reader "so long as he appeal[ed] neither to the heart, the affections, nor the passions of mankind, but prefer[red] appearing before them in the ridiculous guise of a misanthrope. He would fain persuade us that he is a sort of Timon, who, despairing of the tendency of the age, wishes to wrap himself up in the mantle of necessity, and to take no part whatever in the vulgar concerns of existence."[67] The following year (1850) a writer for the *English Review*, in turning from the poetry of Clough, described Arnold as a "still more helpless, cheerless doubter." There was nothing, he thought, "more darkly melancholy, more painfully sombre, than . . . 'Resignation' "—nothing, that is, except "Mycerinus," a shocking "kind of apotheosis of despair" that seems "almost a profession of atheism!"[68] The reviewer for the *Guardian* was more restrained but voiced a similar reaction to the 1852 volume:

The despairing accents of Empedocles find an echo in the rest of the book. There is, indeed, a deep and tender sympathy for the sorrows, and perplexities, and inward struggles of mankind. But there is not much to heal these wounds. Hopeless apathy is not rest. . . . Passive contemplation alone is not meant for man. . . . Yet a poet, who can sympathise so feelingly as "A." with the things that vex the heart of man, its anxious questionings, fond regrets, fitful longings, might achieve the poet's noblest work—might leave morbid repinings, and sing the godlike repose of trustful energy—might soothe and elevate those that mourn.[69]

Arnold's friends likewise complained about the pervasive melancholy of his poetry. Froude even detected something spurious in it, for early in 1849, while the controversy over *The Nemesis of Faith* was still raging, he wrote to Clough, "I don't see what business he has to parade his calmness and lecture us on resignation when he has never known what a storm is and doesn't know what he has to resign himself to. I think he only knows the shady side of nature out of books."[70] But Shairp took Arnold more seriously. Writing to Clough at the very time that Clough was preparing his review of Arnold, he voiced his regret

to see so much power thrown away upon so false and uninteresting (too) a view of life. Since you have gone from England, it's well you've gone to a hearty fresh young people, rather than into the "blank dejection of European Capitols." Anything that so takes the life from out things must be false. It's this I like about your things that though in theory you maintain the contrary, yet in fact the "great human heart" will out and you can't hinder it: Stick to this. Mat, as I told him, disowns man's natural feelings, and they will disown his poetry. If there's nothing else in the world but blank dejection, it's not worth while setting them to music.

And the following month he said again, "The terrible want of fresh heart spoils Mat. to my taste. I can't read much of his last book without pain. That 'blank dejection of European Capitols' which you speak of weighs him down. There's not one skylark tone in them."[71]

V

Rightly viewed, the entire preface of 1853 is an answer to these two major criticisms of Arnold's poetry. As a defense of his use of classical subjects and of his refusal to regard poetry as a medium through which to address the age, moreover, it is all of a piece. The attack on the *Spectator*'s critic and on romantic excesses in language and imagery is an application of the central thesis that asserts the imperishable value of the ancients. The attack on Masson's "precious piece of cant" in the *North British Review* and on subjectivity in poetry in general is an application of the complementary thesis that denies the poet's mission to be a narrowly moralistic and utilitarian one. Significantly, the explanation for the withdrawal of *Empedocles* serves both purposes. Arnold carefully states that he withdraws the poem not because its subject is ancient and not because he failed to execute his intention, but rather because his delineation of one who lived after the calm cheerfulness of the Greeks had disappeared and into whose feelings there entered much that was "exclusively modern"—doubt, despair, "the dialogue of the mind with itself"—did not provide enjoyment.[72] The friends' and reviewers' insistence on modernity is thus paradoxically turned against them.

The preference of classical to modern subjects that is declared in the preface was basically a preference that reflected the characteristic tendency of Arnold's thought—a disposition toward order, authority, and centrality; the same disposition that would lead him to emphasize the value of the French Academy, the need for state action, the importance of the Established Church, the usefulness of touchstones in judging poetry. It was likewise a preference that, in opposing romantic subjectivism, reaffirmed the concept of the poet as "maker" and approved the "disinterested objectivity" of the Greeks. In writing to "K" about the lack of interest in the subjects of his poems Arnold had added, "But as I feel rather as a reformer in poetical matters, I am glad of this opposition.

If I have health & opportunity to go on, I will shake the present methods until they go down, see if I don't. More and more I feel bent against the modern English habit (too much encouraged by Wordsworth) of using poetry as a channel for thinking aloud, instead of making anything."[73] Finally, and most important, the preference expressed Arnold's sense of his limitations as a poet and his frustration in lacking a sympathetic audience and the adequate leisure to devote to his art. In 1858, after the cold reception of *Merope*, he wrote to "K" that "if the opinion of the general public about my poems were the same as that of the leading literary men . . . I should gain the stimulus necessary to enable me to produce my best—all that I have in me, whatever that may be,—to produce which is no light matter with an existence so hampered as mine is." Then, in one of his rare comments on the actual process of artistic creation, he continued:

People do not understand what a temptation there is, if you cannot bear anything not *very good*, to transfer your operations to a region where form is everything. Perfection of a certain kind may there be attained, or at least approached, without knocking yourself to pieces, but to attain or approach perfection in the region of thought and feeling, and to unite this with perfection of form, demands not merely an effort and a labour, but an actual tearing of oneself to pieces, which one does not readily consent to (although one is sometimes forced to it) unless one can devote one's whole life to poetry.

There was the further difficulty, Arnold went on to say, of submitting

voluntarily to the exhaustion of the best poetical production in a time like this. . . . It is only in the best poetical epochs (such as the Elizabethan) that you can descend into yourself and produce the best of your thought and feeling naturally, and without an overwhelming and in some degree morbid effort; for then all the people around you are more or less doing the same thing. It is natural, it is the bent of the time to do it; its being the bent of the time, indeed, is what makes the time a *poetical* one.[74]

This is why the significance of the preface eludes us if we stress its repudiation of the forces that created Arnold's best poetry without at the same time understanding the reasons for that repudiation. For the "classicism" of the preface, as Kenneth Allott accurately observes, is "at least in part an evasion of the anxieties of genuine poetic creation."[75] Arnold's meaning in 1853 is essentially the same as when he writes to Clough in the forties and to "K" in 1858 that lacking robust genius and abundant opportunity, he can attain excellence of a kind more readily in one type of poetry than in another and thereby avoid the "cracking" of his "sinews" in the effort to unite matter and form.[76] Although Froude could object that it was easy thus "to sit calm,"[77] Yeats would be more to the point in citing Coleridge and Rossetti as examples of poets who made what Arnold called a "morbid effort" and "suffered in their lives because of it."[78] The preface, then, is primarily concerned with helping the young poet who is not endowed with a poetic gift of the highest kind and who is confronted with false and conflicting advice. Arnold had earlier complained about the harm done in English poetry by Keats and the perplexity that Keats, Tennyson, and the Elizabethans in general cause young writers of the "heavy-armed foot soldier" sort. Now he declares in the preface that in the confusion of the present times, with a bewildering multitude of voices offering different counsel and an immense number of works that can become models, the young writer needs "a hand to guide him through the confusion, a voice to prescribe to him the aim which he should keep in view, and to explain to him that the value of the literary works which offer themselves to his attention is relative to their power of helping him forward on his road towards this aim."[79]

The voice Arnold invokes in this confusion is that of Goethe, speaking in a manner very much different from that in which he had been heard by David Masson. Goethe had also known the difficulty of achieving a major work of art: "What exertion and expenditure of mental force are required

to arrange and round off a great whole, and then what powers, and what a tranquil, undisturbed situation in life, to express it with the proper fluency." He had known, too, that for
the modern writer the difficulty was all the greater because of
"criticizing and hair-splitting journals," the lack of "worthy
subjects," and "the general sickness of the present day—subjectivity." He had said that much of Shakespeare's greatness
was due to "his great vigorous time" and that such a phenomenon was no longer possible. Having himself experienced
the perplexity of the modern writer, Goethe could speak to
the young poet with compelling force. He emphasized the advantage of "a *given* material" and advised "the choice of subjects which have been worked before." He insisted on the
primacy of the whole: "if you fail anywhere, the whole is a
failure, however good single parts may be." And he had held
up the ancients as models: "One should not study contemporaries and competitors, but the great men of antiquity,
whose works have, for centuries, received equal homage and
consideration. . . . Let us study Molière, let us study Shakespeare, but above all things, the old Greeks, and always the
Greeks."[80]

Like Goethe, Arnold in the preface speaks "not of the best
sources of intellectual stimulus for the general reader, but of
the best models of instruction for the individual writer"—and
the best models are the ancients. Admittedly they have their
limitations. Their expression is often bald; their range of experience is restricted; some of their subjects are no longer of
deep interest. But from them can be learned, better than anywhere else, three things that are essential for the young poet
to know: "the all-importance of the choice of a subject; the
necessity of accurate construction; and the subordinate character of expression." From the ancients the poet will learn to
select an excellent action, one that appeals, Arnold says in a
phrase recalling Wordsworth, "to the great primary human
affections: to those elementary feelings which subsist permanently in the race, and which are independent of time." The

date of the action is thus irrelevant; what is important is the greatness of the action and its representation. From the ancients also the poet will learn the importance of execution, of construction, of what Goethe calls *Architectonicè*. And from them, finally, he will learn that the impression left by treating an action as a whole is superior in effect to the impression left by the individual parts, however striking a single thought may be or however felicitous an image.[81]

If the poet penetrates into the spirit of the ancients, moreover, "he will deliver himself from the jargon of modern criticism, and escape the danger of producing poetical works conceived in the spirit of the passing time, and which partake of its transitoriness." Indeed, those who know the ancients "wish neither to applaud nor to revile their age: they wish to know what it is, what it can give them, and whether this is what they want." Nor do they inflate "themselves with a belief in the pre-eminent importance and greatness of their own times. They do not talk of their mission, nor of interpreting their age, nor of the coming poet; all this, they know, is the mere delirium of vanity; their business is not to praise their age, but to afford to the men who live in it the highest pleasure which they are capable of feeling." The passage is directly aimed, of course, at Alexander Smith, whose pompous prediction that "A mighty Poet" would arise to be the age's "spokesman to all coming times" had been quoted contemptuously in the *North British Review*.[82] Yet it is also aimed at the reviewers and friends who had objected that Arnold's poetry did not attempt to solve the problems of the age, and in reply he declares that such an objection merely encourages ephemeral poetry and pretentious poets.

But poetry conceived in the spirit of the times may be worse than ephemeral. It may also be inadequate, as in the nineteenth century, simply because the era in which it is produced lacks the qualities essential to the creation of great poetry. More than two years previously Arnold had written to "K" that he was retiring "more and more from the modern world and modern literature, which is all only what has been before and what will be again, and not bracing or edifying in the least";[83] and nearly two years before that he had said to Clough, "Reflect . . ., as I cannot but do . . . more and more, in spite of all the nonsense some people talk , how deeply *unpoetical* the age and all one's surroundings are. Not unprofound, not ungrand, not unmoving:—but *unpoetical*."[84] This fulfillment of his earlier prophecy of "a wave of more than American *vulgarity*, moral, intellectual, and social, preparing to break over us"[85] is asserted once again in the preface. The poet, Arnold says, would gladly discover great actions in the present, but "an age wanting in moral grandeur can with difficulty supply such, and an age of spiritual discomfort with difficulty be powerfully and delightfully affected by them." Great demands are thus made of a poet in such an age, although the rightful demands are not those made by the periodical critics. In a concluding paragraph that looks forward to the thesis of "The Function of Criticism at the Present Time," Arnold declares that the really compelling demand is to make the creation of great poetry once more possible. If the present age is unpoetic, if the poet is unable under the circumstances in which he lives "to think clearly, to feel nobly, and to delineate firmly," if he cannot "attain to the mastery of the great artists," he can at least not bewilder his successors but "transmit to them the practice of poetry, with its boundaries and wholesome regulative laws, under which excellent works may again, perhaps, at some future time, be produced."[86]

VI

Arnold's manner in the 1853 preface was calculated to invite rather than to avoid criticism. Its traits were precisely those that would continue to annoy and even infuriate many of his reviewers: the careful iteration of words and phrases, the delicate strokes of irony, the occasional tendency to overstate and dogmatize, the slight but unmistakable air of superiority. Understandably, therefore, the preface was not always kindly received. The *Examiner*, in fact, categorically denounced it as "pugnacious" and "impertinent."[87] The *Daily News* declared that its "somewhat superciliously announced" theory of poetry was illustrated by an "absurd servility to antique fashions."[88] John Duke Coleridge, in the *Christian Remembrancer*, described its thesis as "entirely fallacious and inadequate, based upon untenable assumptions, and conducting us to conclusions which we utterly repudiate."[89] In his brief notice of the 1853 volume John A. Heraud, of the *Athenaeum*, virtually ignored the poetry altogether and concentrated on attacking Arnold's "theoretical crotchets."[90]

But if the criticism of the preface was predominantly hostile, it was not entirely unfair. W. C. Roscoe, for example, pointed out in the *Prospective Review* an obvious weakness in Arnold's argument—the apparent exclusion of all but narrative and dramatic poetry.[91] What then "becomes of lyrical poetry?" Robert Lytton (Owen Meredith) asked John Forster; "and shall we have nothing but epics?"[92] Another weakness, as Froude observed, was Arnold's seeming implication that great actions were confined to the classical age:

It is indeed idle nonsense to speak . . . of the "present" as alone having claims upon the poet. Whatever is great, or good, or pathetic, or terrible, in any age, past or present, belongs to him, and is within his proper province; but most especially, if he is wise, he will select his subjects out of those which time has sealed as permanently significant. . . . But why dwell with such apparent exclusiveness on classic antiquity, as if there was no antiquity except the classic, and as if time were divided into the eras of Greece and Rome and the nineteenth century?[93]

Froude's point was developed at greater length—and in narrower terms—by the journal that had raised the issue in the first place, the *Spectator*. Although admitting that the dispute was not to be settled by a revival of the quarrel between the ancients and the moderns (for the real question was "whether

the poet of the nineteenth century should seek the subjects
of his art in the facts he gathers out of ancient Greek books,
rather than in the world of his own experience, action, and
emotion"), the reviewer nevertheless insisted that "the poet
must seek such subjects as both he and his audience [can]
realize vividly and distinctly, and which [deal] with ideas
and feelings sufficiently akin to those of our living world, to
be not only grasped by an act of intellectual apprehension, but
appropriated by an act of moral sympathy." Such subjects "are
to be found in modern times more easily and more abundant-
ly than in ancient times," of which "we have the extremest
difficulty in forming a full adequate conception, such as alone
can satisfy in a poetic representation." This is why Arnold is
mistaken in placing Macbeth with the legend of Oedipus as
a subject of the past. Greek life, the writer concluded in utilitarian fashion, "gives us nothing new that we can tell to
others," and any attempt to revive it ends inevitably "in the
composition of a mummy, not the creation of a life." The true
poet, on the other hand, will recognize that his special work
"consists in discerning the elements of beauty and of grandeur
that the spirit of man can develop today, under the conditions
of today, not in vain attempts to fly from those conditions
into the primaeval forests of old Greece, and recreate the life
of Dryad and of Faun."[94]

Implicit in this debate over subject matter was the question
of the distinction between *poesis* and *mimesis*, and at least
one reviewer believed that Arnold's emphasis on the ancients
as guides to the young writer could lead to an excessively mi-
metic view of poetry. The reviewer was the literary editor of
the *Leader*, George Henry Lewes,[95] who was known for his
encouragement of young and undiscovered talent and who
earlier in the year had praised Alexander Smith's "luxuriant
imagery and exquisite felicity of expression" as portents of
"the great poet he will be when age and ripe experience lend
their graver accent to his verse."[96] Valuing originality, Lewes
declared that "all conscious imitation is weakness, and that

'models' produce no real good, though little harm, because the servile mind is one which if emancipated would not be strong. To study models with a view to *emulate* them is not the same as to study them with a view to *imitate* them; the one is an envigorating—the other an enervating study." The following week Lewes resumed the argument by repeating that "instead of Imitation we counsel Emulation; instead of following the mere fashions of Greek Art, follow no fashions but those which bear the general verdict of your age, and while learning from the Greeks the lessons they and all great artists have to teach, beware, above all things, of imitating them."[97]

The objection of Lewes was reiterated by other reviewers. The *Daily News* condemned Arnold's "almost exclusive regard for ancient models" as well as Alexander Smith's "mosaic showiness."[98] A writer for the *New Quarterly Review* recognized Arnold's superiority to Smith (Arnold being solid and true, and Smith hollow and meretricious) but nevertheless found Arnold's volume "disfigured with mannerisms and blotted with absurdities" that were the "faults of a scholar." Arnold was therefore "wrong," the reviewer asserted, "in advising a modern writer to cultivate any style, or form himself upon any model whatsoever."[99] And Aytoun, developing in detail the thesis that imitation was Arnold's "curse," suggested that he "abandon all imitation, whether ancient or modern— identify himself with his situation—trust to natural impulse —and give art-theories to the winds."[100]

Of all the attacks on the preface, the longest and most thoroughgoing was the unaccountably vicious review by John Duke Coleridge, who echoed each of the earlier objections raised against it and added some of his own. Like the *Spectator* and Froude before him, he disputed Arnold's argument for classical models and subject matter, questioning the classification of Macbeth and Oedipus together (which "altogether baffles our best endeavours to comprehend the meaning of his rule") and declaring that recognition of the value of ancient writers does not lead "to the conclusion that an Englishman should write of Medea or of Empedocles in preference to Mary Queen of Scots or Cromwell; that an English poet's allusions should be to classical events, or to the heroes of the ancient world, his style be formed upon that of writers in a foreign language, and his thoughts moulded upon those of believers in a heathen creed." Arnold's comments on Shakespeare and Romantic poets he called "so little creditable to his taste, that we cannot help feeling they would hardly have been ventured upon except under the stimulus of thoroughly defending a thesis, which, from the time of Aristotle, has made men intellectually unscrupulous." And Arnold's narrow view of poetry, he said, would not only make it the enjoyment of a cultivated few but also strike a long list of familiar names from the role of the world's great poets.[101]

Even more offensive was Coleridge's stern rebuke of Arnold for not using poetry as a pulpit from which to spread the gospel of Christianity. Since *Empedocles* had already been withdrawn, he advised, Arnold would do well to "drop sundry other moral and quasi-religious musings, which are very painful if they represent the author's real opinions, and hardly ought to be published if they do not." Pointing ominously to "the incalculable mischief of a sceptical and irreligious train of thought when presented to the mind in melodious verse, and clothed with the graces of a refined and scholarlike diction," Coleridge spoke of the dangerous problem created by authors who "appear to think themselves justified in standing *ab extrà* to Christianity"; he reproached Arnold for failing to use the beauty of nature to inculcate Christian morals and for apparently believing that poetry should be "high, distant, and apart from the turmoil of sinful life, and the everlasting conflict of Our Lord with Satan," a belief "as bad in art as it is mischievous to religion and to truth"; and in the concluding pages of his review he implied that as a poet Arnold was an infidel undermining the fortress of religion while the garrison remained within, totally unaware of its peril.[102]

The most insulting of Coleridge's strictures, however, was

the charge that "Sohrab and Rustum" had been plagiarized from Sainte-Beuve's *Causeries du Lundi,* a volume containing a notice of Mohl's translation of Firdausi and several passages from it. The fact that Arnold makes no reference to his source, Coleridge remarked in a captious spirit, "leaves us in uncertainty whether the whole work of M. Mohl, which we have never seen, may not have been used throughout, and the study of antiquity carried so far as simply to reproduce an ancient poem as well as an ancient subject. For Mr. Arnold has not thought fit to offer a single syllable of acknowledgment to an author to whom he has been manifestly very largely indebted."[103] What made the accusation seem even more unfair was Arnold's belief that Coleridge knew of the source only through Arnold's own admissions. Although the editor of Coleridge's correspondence believed that he made the discovery himself, A. P. Stanley, with whom Coleridge corresponded about the matter, said that he understood the charge to be grounded solely on information derived from Arnold. It seemed to him, he told Coleridge reprovingly, "an eminent case of 'seething a kid in the mother's milk.' "[104]

VII

When Arnold published a second edition of the *Poems* in June 1854—some seven months after the appearance of the first edition—he introduced the volume with the 1853 preface, reprinted with only minor alterations, and another preface[105] in which he stated that he had allowed the original preface "to stand almost without change" because he still believed "it to be, in the main, true." He was not "insensible to the force of much that ha[d] been alleged against portions of it, or unaware that it contain[ed] many things incompletely stated, many things which need[ed] limitation." But he did not then have time "to supply these deficiencies," nor did he regard this as "the proper place for attempting it."

On a few points, however, Arnold wished to offer some explanation to the critics of the preface. After first conceding that he had not touched on the question of lyric poetry, he turned to the objection, "ably urged" by the *Spectator* and by Coleridge ("ably" would later be changed to "warmly"), to the classing together of Oedipus and Macbeth as subjects. Arnold admitted that to the Elizabethan the age of Macbeth was more familiar than that of Oedipus, but he was speaking of the manner in which the subjects appear to the modern reader. And to him the times of Macbeth are scarcely closer than the times of Oedipus. He is merely attracted toward a certain character and has a capacity for imagining him "irrespective of his times, solely according to a law of personal sympathy," and the poet hopes to treat successfully the subjects for which he feels "this personal attraction most strongly." Joan of Arc is not really nearer the modern than Alcestis (whose position is later taken, less appropriately, by Prometheus), nor Charlemagne than Agamemnon. "Each can be made present only by an act of poetic imagination; but this man's imagination has an affinity for one of them, and that man's for another."

To the criticism of Froude and Coleridge that he had seemed to restrict the period of great actions to the classical age, Arnold replies that he merely advised the poet "to choose for his subjects great actions, without regarding to what time they belong." Though he admits that poetry can be made of "the most trifling action, the most hopeless subject," he believes (as did Goethe) that the poet should not waste his power by being "compelled to impart interest and force to his subject, instead of receiving them from it, and thereby doubling his impressiveness." Since there is "an immortal strength in the stories of great actions," the poet "may well be glad to supplement with it that mortal weakness, which, in presence of the vast spectacle of life and the world, he must for ever feel to be his individual portion."

Finally, to Lewes's distinction between imitating classical writers and emulating them Arnold makes no objection. The important thing, he says, is to study them. They can help, he

declares in a passage that points forward to much of his literary, social, and biblical criticism, to cure the great vice of the
modern intellect—a want of sanity that is manifested in literature, art, religion, morality. Sanity is the great virtue of ancient literature; the want of it is the great defect of modern
literature. "I call the classic *healthy*," Goethe had said, "the
romantic *sickly*. . . . Most modern productions are romantic,
not because they are new, but because they are weak, morbid,
and sickly; and the antique is classic, not because it is old, but
because it is strong, fresh, joyous, and healthy."[106] The echo in
Arnold's conclusion could scarcely have been missed by Lewes,
whose *Life of Goethe* would be published the following year:
"It is impossible to read carefully the great ancients, without
losing something of our caprice and eccentricity; and to emulate them we must at least read them."

The brevity of this preface of 1854 is uncharacteristic of
Arnold's polemic writing and suggests a weakening, in the
face of overwhelmingly hostile criticism, of the position he
had adopted in the original preface. Nor does his apologetic
appeal to the pressure of time carry much conviction. It was,
as a matter of fact, later withdrawn, when Arnold had even
less free time than he had in 1854 but nevertheless managed
to engage in more extensive controversies. The second preface is further marked by an altered tone that also suggests a
weakening. In it Arnold's attitude is less supercilious, his
manner more conciliatory, his method more flexible and less
dogmatic than in the 1853 preface. He expresses, too, more
willingness to admit flaws in logic and the limitations of his
thesis, and a greater readiness to concede and not to employ
concession as an argumentative device.

Still another indication of Arnold's sensitivity to his critics
was the long note to "Sohrab and Rustum" which he wrote for
the 1854 volume and in which he answered Coleridge's charge
of plagiarism.[107] Here he summarized the story as told by Sir
John Malcolm in his *History of Persia*, quoted at length the
extracts from Mohl's translation of Firdausi's poem which he

had found in Sainte-Beuve's *Causeries,* declared that he had not been able to see Mohl's book, and indicated with gentle irony that the reviewer for the *Christian Remembrancer* would have been "more charitable" had he, before making the "good-natured suggestion" of plagiarism, "ascertained, by reference to M. Mohl's work, how far it was confirmed by the fact"—all this despite the patent injustice of Coleridge's charge and "the limited circulation" of the *Remembrancer,* which made his review "of little importance."[108]

VIII

After the note in answer to Coleridge's accusation, the polemic voice of Matthew Arnold remained silent for more than three years. Then, in the fall of 1857, Arnold delivered his inaugural lecture as professor of poetry at Oxford. Entitled "On the Modern Element in Literature," it was a continuation of the thesis he had presented in the preface—that the ancient Greek writers are invaluable guides for the modern poet. But the lecture is more than a mere sequel to the preface; it is also a significant modification of it. As Louis Bonnerot has observed, the position taken by Arnold in 1857 "est bien différente de l'attitude assez intransigeante et rigide que révélait la 'Preface' de 1853: Arnold reconnaît que le monde modern existe et que le classicisme doit nous donner le moyen non de le fuir, mais de le comprendre. Il ne s'agit plus de construire une retraite sereine hors du temps, mais de fournir la nourriture spirituelle la plus appropriée à des hommes, dit-il dans l'essai sur Marc Aurèle 'engaged in the current of contemporary life and action.' "[109]

This modification of Arnold's thesis resulted in part from correspondence with Sainte-Beuve, to whom, in January 1854, he sent a copy of the *Poems* with an accompanying letter acknowledging his debt for the story of Sohrab. Sainte-Beuve later replied, thanking Arnold for his gift and discussing the preface, on which he was considering doing an article.[110] The letter has apparently been lost, but we may infer its contents by the reply Arnold wrote to it in September. He declared that he had given much attention to what Sainte-Beuve had said regarding the superior interest of modern subjects, which, he admitted, Sainte-Beuve and Homer were right in preferring to subjects from the past. Yet he wondered whether there were not "des époques *trop claires* où les événements présents deviennent, pour le poète, presque intraitables." Have Virgil and Apollonius of Rhodes, he asked, "mal fait, à l'époque où ils vécurent[,] de laisser à côté les événements contemporains pour s'occuper des faits d'Enée et de Jason? Ces oeuvres de *cabinet et d'étude* ne sont-elles pas, quelquefois, les seules possibles?—et n'ont-elles pas bien, elles aussi, leur valeur? Mais, me direz-vous, il faut de la nouveauté dans la maniére de présenter les choses passées et de les approprier au temps. Oui, sans doute, cela est vrai, je le sens peut-être même que toute la *question* est là!"[111] Early in November[112] Sainte-Beuve replied that he thought he and Arnold were not far from agreement about the choice of the best subjects for poetry and that Arnold was right in contending that "les sujets modernes sont trop clairs et ne [se] prêtent guère qu'à l'histoire." He would make a distinction, however, between Arnold's two examples:

L'Enéide a vécu et vit par l'appropriation d'un sujet antique à un temps présent et par l'infusion d'un souffle et d'un esprit tout romain refluant jusqu'aux origines. L'âme des Scipions y respire par endroits, et on pleure au: 'tu marcellus eris.'—Apollonius, au contraire, malgré son admirable chant sur Médée dont Virgile s'est tout [tant?] servi n'a fait dans l'ensemble qu'un poème savant et mort, et pas un coeur Alexandrin n'a palpité au moment de sa naissance comme faisait le jeune Romain pour l'Enéide.[113]

The debate continued into the following months, for in January 1856, when Saint-Beuve published in the *Moniteur* the third of the lectures on Virgil that he had prepared for the Collège de France, he referred approvingly to the contention of the preface that the poet should choose from the past those subjects that appeal to the eternal feelings of human nature, and to the contention in Arnold's letter that the events of some epochs are almost impossible for the poet to treat and hence properly belong to the historian. All this, said Sainte-Beuve, is true. But then he added:

Pourtant . . . il est un point que je n'abandonnerai jamais, à savoir l'importance et la nécessité pour que le poème ait vie,—une vie réelle à sa date et parmi les contemporains, et non pas une vie froide pour quelques amateurs de cabinet,—la nécessité d'un élément moderne, d'un intérêt modern actuel et jeune, cet intérêt ne fût-il qu'adapté et comme infusé dans un sujet ancien.[114]

Behind the lecture was also a force that at the time seems to have been even stronger than Sainte-Beuve's—that of Dr. Thomas Arnold, whose influence Arnold had grown increasingly to appreciate. When a letter by Dr. Arnold concerning his children's education was discovered in 1855, Arnold wrote with obvious emotion to his mother that it illustrated "what makes him great—that he was not only a good man saving his own soul by righteousness, but that he carried so many others with him in his hand, and saved them, if they would let him, along with himself"; and two years later, in supporting Frederick Temple for the headmastership of Rugby, he spoke of him as "the *one* man who *may* do something of the same work papa did."[115] Arnold's lecture, significantly, was delivered in the same month in which he may have begun "Rugby Chapel," the elegiac poem about his father that expressed what the younger Thomas Arnold was later to describe as a "profound and yearning appreciation."[116] The "main idea" of the lecture, Arnold explained to his mother, was "Papa's. His admirable expression—'what is falsely called ancient history, the really modern history of Greece and Rome'—might have stood as the text of it."[117]

The key words in the lecture are "intellectual deliverance." At other times Arnold used different words—"disinterested objectivity," "criticism," "Hellenism"—to designate essentially the same thing: that attitude which results when, in the face of the complexity and multitudinousness of life, the mind gains a comprehension of the past and present, when it comes into possession of the general ideas that control the vast number of facts that confront it. The demand for intellectual deliverance, Arnold says, is characteristic of ages called "modern." In 1853 he had implied that modernity is characterized by intellectual sterility—doubt, discouragement, "the dialogue of the mind with itself." But in 1857 he declares that modernity is also characterized by intellectual vitality, for he goes on to say that this demand for intellectual deliverance that is characteristic of modern ages is the emphatic demand of the present time. This is why the literature of ancient Greece is "an object of indestructible interest": it is for the present age "a mighty agent of intellectual deliverance." It is so because it was a great, an "adequate" literature coexisting with a highly developed, distinctively "modern" epoch. The poetry of Sophocles, with its "consummate, . . . unrivalled *adequacy*," represents "the highly developed human nature of that age—human nature developed in a number of directions, politically, socially, religiously, morally developed—in its completest and most harmonious development in all these directions; while there is shed over this poetry the charm of that noble serenity which always accompanies true insight." Aristophanes, who saw life from the comic side as Sophocles saw it from the tragic side, is also adequate. But Menander is not, for he depicted the Athens that remained after the failure of the expedition to Syracuse and the unsuccessful conclusion of the Peloponnesian War, an Athens that had lost its vitality. The Athenian whom he portrayed was "refined and intelligent indeed, but sceptical, frivolous, and dissolute." Therefore Aristophanes has survived and Menander has perished, because, as Arnold rather curiously reasons, humanity "has the strongest, the most invincible tendency to *live*, to *develop* itself," clinging to "the literature which exhibits it in its vigour" and rejecting that "which exhibits it arrested and decayed."[118]

An even greater age than that of Pericles was the culminat-

ing age in Roman history—"perhaps, on the whole, the greatest, the fullest, the most significant period on record." But the
literature of this great epoch is not a great literature. Lucretius, with his predominantly thoughtful and reflective disposition, his feeling of depression and ennui, is eminently modern. Yet he is not adequate:

> Think of the varied, the abundant, the wide spectacle of the Roman
> life of his day; think of its fulness of occupation, its energy of ef-
> fort. From these Lucretius withdraws himself, and bids his disciples
> to withdraw themselves; he bids them to leave the business of the
> world, and to apply themselves *"naturam cognoscere rerum*—to learn
> the nature of things;" but there is no peace, no cheerfulness for him
> either in the world from which he comes, or in the solitude to which
> he goes. With stern effort, with gloomy despair, he seems to rivet
> his eyes on the elementary reality, the naked framework of the world,
> because the world in its fulness and movement is too exciting a spec-
> tacle for his discomposed brain. He seems to feel the spectacle of it
> at once terrifying and alluring; and to deliver himself from it he has
> to keep perpetually repeating his formula of disenchantment and an-
> nihilation.

Lucretius is thus "morbid; and he who is morbid is no adequate interpreter of his age." Nor is Virgil adequate. Had he
"been inspired to represent human life in its fullest significance, he would not have selected the epic form," which is
less vital than the dramatic form. The dramatic poet represents only what is universal and eternal—the thoughts and
feelings of man. The epic poet, on the other hand, must also
represent what is local and transient—customs, manners, the
appearance of nature. The *Aeneid*, accordingly, lacks the
depth, the completeness of the plays of Aeschylus and Sophocles, and, more significantly, it lacks the "serious cheerfulness of Sophocles, of a man who has mastered the problem
of human life, who knows its gravity, and is therefore serious,
but who knows that he comprehends it, and is therefore cheerful." Over the whole of the *Aeneid* "there rests an ineffable
melancholy . . . which is at once a source of charm in the poem,

and a testimony to its incompleteness." Horace, too, is inadequate; he lacks seriousness. He is without prejudice, illusion, or blunder; but he is also "without faith, without enthusiasm, without energy."[119]

"I am glad you like the Gipsy Scholar," Arnold had written Clough four years earlier, "but what does it *do* for you? Homer *animates*—Shakespeare *animates*—in its poor way I think Sohrab and Rustum *animates*—the Gipsy Scholar at best awakens a pleasing melancholy. But this is not what we want."[120] What is wanted, of course, is literature that animates and ennobles—the essential functions, presumably, of that literature Arnold will later pronounce to be "adequate." In 1857, however, an additional demand is made of literature if it is to be adequate: it must express sympathy with the age in which it is written. "Yes, Lucretius is modern; but is he adequate?" Arnold asks in his inaugural lecture, and then answers with a rhetorical question: "And how can a man adequately interpret the activity of his age when he is not in sympathy with it?"[121] Between this and the pointed assertion of the 1853 Preface that "the old artists . . . attained their grand results by penetrating themselves with some noble and significant action, not by inflating themselves with a belief in the pre-eminent importance of their own times" there have intervened a critical dispute and a father's influence that have noticeably altered Arnold's position.[122]

Sainte-Beuve and Dr. Arnold were not alone in helping to effect this change, however. There were also the critics of Arnold's poems who had persistently complained—often crudely enough, certainly, but still with a general understanding of what Sainte-Beuve meant when he spoke of the necessity for adapting subjects from the past to modern times— that Arnold's poetry did not have sufficient relevance to the age. To their complaints Arnold was in 1853 unwilling to make concessions. He withdrew *Empedocles*, to be sure, because it suffered from the same deficiency that fatally weakened the poetry of Lucretius. But his other pronouncements in the preface were almost wholly literary and aesthetic, not social and ethical as his statements about poetry would largely become. He spoke not of the adequacy of the ancient writers but of their value as guides to the young poet, and guides in a strictly artistic sense—they taught the importance of form and structure, of simplicity of style, of the subordination of the parts to the whole. He spoke of great actions that dealt with the primary human affections and whose representation gave delight to the reader, not of actions and themes that provided an adequate interpretation of life. He spoke of the poet's being fortunate if he could "delight himself with the contemplation of some noble action of a heroic time"[123] and ridiculed the notion that the poet should speak of his mission or of interpreting his age. It was impossible, he concluded, to create great poetry in the present time. All that could be done was to preserve the form and laws of poetry as handed down by the ancients.

Four years later Arnold was to declare that the fault lay not with the Victorian age but with its poetry. The "*time* is a first class one," he wrote to his brother Tom in December 1857, "—an infinitely fuller richer age than Pope's; but our poetry is not *adequate* to it: it interests therefore only a small body of sectaries: hundreds of cultivated and intelligent men find nothing that speaks to them in it." And why was this so? Because "it is a hard thing to make poetry adequate to a first-class epoch."[124] This, we may suppose, is the reason for *Merope*, which is thus linked with Arnold's earlier attempts to avoid the agony of creative effort. To his sister Frances he wrote that the poem was intended as "a specimen of the world created by the Greek imagination," an imagination "different from our own" but one with "a peculiar power, grandeur, and dignity . . . worth trying to get an apprehension of." To his friend Fanny Blackett du Quaire he added that the poem was "calculated rather to inaugurate [his] Professorship with dignity than to move deeply the present race of *humans*."[125] To the reader of the "Preface to *Merope*" he explained in more detail that, "the power of true beauty, of consummate form" being indestructible and therefore of perennial interest, he had sought "to come to closer quarters with the form which produces such grand effects in the hands of the Greek masters; to try to obtain, through the medium of a living, familiar language, a fuller and more intense feeling of that beauty." And at the conclusion of the preface he made the modest disclaimer (the first of those half-insincere confessions of inadequacy that he effectively used for polemic purposes) that he had been "emboldened to undertake" the poem only because "the many poets of the present day who possess[ed] that capacity" which he lacked had not attempted to enrich English literature by extending "its boundaries in the one direction, in which, with all its force and variety, it has not yet advanced!"[126]

Yet we should not be surprised that "On the Modern Element in Literature" and *Merope* celebrated the same occasion, for their coincident appearance reflects a characteristic dichotomy everywhere present in Arnold's work. If he insists on critical detachment, he also insists on the passionate commitment to make reason and the will of God prevail. If he admires the spontaneity of consciousness of Hellenism, he also admires the strictness of conscience of Hebraism. If he declares that the grand style requires a poetic gift, he also declares that it requires a noble nature; and if it requires simplicity of language, it also requires seriousness of subject.

The inaugural lecture nevertheless marks a turning point in Arnold's career. The difference between 1853 and 1857 becomes the difference between "Obermann" and "Obermann Once More": previously driven "to solitude," Arnold is now driven "to the world without."[127] The lecture establishes, moreover, a pattern for future turning points. Commitment later takes precedence over detachment, Hebraism over Hellenism, high seriousness over simplicity. Arnold would continue to insist, as he had insisted in the preface, on the weaknesses of romanticism—on its eccentricity and arbitrariness (in the lectures on Homer), on its deficiency of intellectual content (in "The Function of Criticism at the Present Time"). But he would never again be the critic who wrote the preface.

Nor would he be the poet for whom the preface was written. Of *Merope*, that dreary piece of antiquarianism, that lifeless product *"de cabinet et d'étude,"* Swinburne was to ask, "The clothes are well enough but where has the body gone?" Jowett, representative of the classical scholars to whom Arnold looked for approval, called it "too much a direct imitation of extant Greek examples to be a genuine poetic reproduction of the Greek type."[128] Arnold's old adversary, the *Spectator*, declared that it was "more deficient in what is popularly thought poetry, than even his previous attempts on classical subjects."[129] And if Arnold himself showed toward the poem "the fondness of a mother for a subnormal child," as Douglas Bush puts it,[130] he was still too perceptive a critic not to see its limitations. When he sent a copy to Fanny du Quaire, he included the warning that she would not find in it what she wished to find and excused her "beforehand for wishing to find something different, and being a little dissatisfied with" him. But he had such "a real love" for the "old Greek world," he added, that he promised to give her "a better satisfaction some day."[131] The fulfillment of his promise was to be what neither could have anticipated at the time, but it was to afford the same "better satisfaction" that Johnson gave when he wrote his *Lives of the Poets* rather than continue "producing more *Irenes*."[132]

CHAPTER THREE

Homer and His Translators

Jowett once described Professor F. Newman to me, in his most inci-
sive and thinnest voice, as 'a good man—who is always in the wrong.'
—Swinburne

. . . in the serious style, Homer is pre-eminent among poets . . . .
—Aristotle

. . . Great Art is like the writing of Homer . . . .—Ruskin, paraphrasing Sir Joshua Reynolds

. . . j'ai été bien charmé et satisfait de tout ce que vous dites du père
et de l'océan de toute Poësie . . . .—Sainte-Beuve to Arnold

. . . heap up in one scale all the literary criticism that the whole nation
of professed scholars ever wrote, and drop into the other the thin
green volume of Matthew Arnold's Lectures on Translating Homer,
. . . and the first scale, as Milton says, will straight fly up and kick
the beam.—Housman

In the autumn of 1860, three years after his inaugural address
at Oxford, Arnold began the series of lectures that he later
published as *On Translating Homer*. The subject was chosen,
he explained in a letter to his mother, "partly because I have
long had in my mind something to say about Homer, partly
because of the complaints that I did not enough lecture on
poetry." The first of the lectures offered advice to the translator of Homer and indicated how previous translators had
failed to render three of the four preeminent Homeric qualities: Cowper and Wright failed to render Homer's rapidity,
Pope and Sotheby failed to render his plainness and directness of style and diction, and Chapman failed to render his
plainness and directness of ideas. The second lecture was devoted to a discussion of the fourth and most important qual-

ity, nobility, which Francis Newman so conspicuously failed to render as to place his translation in a category all its own. In the third lecture Arnold examined the meters capable of conveying the general effect of Homer and gave specimens of his own hexameters, the meter he preferred to the heroic couplet and blank verse. This final lecture was delivered to a full audience, and at its conclusion Arnold was cheered, "which is very uncommon at Oxford."[1]

There was less cheering, however, when the lectures appeared in published form. The *Spectator*, to be sure, gave them a laudatory review, praising Arnold for his "delicacy of taste, keenness of insight, and evidence of true poetic culture";[2] and later in the year E. S. Dallas in the *Times*[3] spoke admiringly of "their eloquence, their acuteness, and their suggestiveness."[4] The *Daily News* even declared that Arnold was "as clear in his criticism of the principles of his craft as he [was] successful in the actual exercise of it."[5] Additional support came from letters of approval, one of which—from W. H. Thompson, Regius Professor of Greek at Cambridge and "one of the most able and at the same time most fastidious [of] men"—Arnold "particularly value[d]."[6] But this response from his admirers was not representative. In both manner and substance the lectures had been controversial, and even as late as four years afterwards Arnold could still hear rumblings from the storm he had aroused.

Yet the noise rather pleased him. It testified, for one thing, to his growing fame and influence; hence the mock-serious motto with which he introduced the answer he made to his critics: "Multi, qui persequuntur me, et tribulant me: a testimoniis non declinavi."[7] More important, it gave him an opportunity to solidify his position, as he told his mother after reading the *Saturday Review*'s long-awaited attack on the lectures:

When first I read a thing of this kind I am annoyed; . . . then I begin to think of the openings it gives for observations in answer, and from that moment, when a free activity of the spirit is restored, my gaiety and good spirits return, and the article is simply an object of interest to me. To be able to feel thus, one . . . must be on ground where one feels at home and secure—that is the great secret of good-humour.[8]

Arnold, in fact, was relishing a debate that enabled him to deliver a fourth lecture on Homer. "As I get into it," he wrote during its composition, "it interests me and amuses me. There will be very little controversy in it, but I shall bring out one or two points about the grand style and the ballad style, so as to leave what I have said in the former lectures as firm and as intelligible as possible, and then I shall leave the subject." Early the next year, however, in preparing the lecture for publication (it appeared separately as *On Translating Homer: Last Words*), Arnold admitted that he was "afraid" his reply would provoke further dispute:

I sincerely say "afraid," for I had much rather avoid all the sphere of dispute. One begins by saying something, and if one believes it to be true one cannot well resist the pleasure of expanding and establishing it when it is controverted; but I had rather live in a purer air than that of controversy, and . . . I mean to leave this region altogether and to devote myself wholly to what is positive and happy, not negative and contentious, in literature.[9]

The sincerity of this passage has been questioned by critics who regard Arnold as a controversialist insensitive to the feelings of his opponents, and indeed there is an apparent discrepancy here between his delight in controversy and his avowed intent to avoid it. Yet if there is an explanation for this, it is to be found in the central theme of Arnold's lectures. Once again, as in 1853, he was condemning "eccentricity" and "arbitrariness" in English life and letters, and as a prime exhibit of these faults he had paraded before his Oxford audience the work of one of her most distinguished graduates, the professor of Latin at the University of London and a former Balliol Fellow who "without any apparent effort" had earned one of the best double firsts ever known[10]—Francis William Newman.

About Frank Newman opinion has diverged as sharply as about his more famous brother. Respected by Basil Willey as an honest doubter and by William Robbins as a humanitarian, he is to J. M. Cameron simply a fool.[11] Mrs. Gaskell thought he was "high, and noble," and George Eliot considered him such "a very pure, noble being" that it was "good only to look at" him.[12] George Gilfillan, however, had only contempt for this "learned, pious, and sincere fribble."[13] Carlyle admired his "sharp-cutting, restlessly advancing intellect" and "pious enthusiasm," but Anthony Froude was "repelled" by his "unimaginative way of dealing with Jesus," and Archbishop Whately believed that his piety consisted "mainly of a sort of self-adoration."[14]

Dr. Arnold had once said of Frank and John Henry Newman "that in them you saw very plainly the difference between the great man and the little man."[15] But the father's view was not shared by the son, who had never engaged in angry debate with the elder Newman during the Hampden controversy or exchanged insulting innuendos throughout the Tractarian movement. Nor is it likely that Dr. Arnold's view would have remained unchanged had he lived to see the direction in which Frank eventually went. His prize student and biographer, A. P. Stanley, was later to describe Newman's *History of the Hebrew Monarchy* as "offensive," though adding "that poor Newman being insane should not be judged harshly."[16] And in 1850 the appearance of Newman's *Phases of Faith* elicited from Matthew Arnold a still more devastating response:

F. Newman's book I saw yestern at our ouse. He seems to have written himself down an hass. It is a display of the theological mind, which I am accustomed to regard as a suffetation, existing in a man from the beginnnig, colouring his whole being, and being him in short. One would think to read him that enquiries into articles, biblical inspiration, etc. etc. were as much the natural functions of a man as to eat and copulate. . . .

The world in general has always stood towards religions and their

doctors in the attitude of a half-astonished clown acquiescingly duck-
ing at their grand words and thinking it must be very fine, but for its
soul not being able to make out what it is all about. This beast talks
of such matters as if they were meat and drink. What a miserable
place Oxford and the society of the serious middle classes must have
been 20 years ago. He bepaws the religious sentiment so much that
he quite effaces it to me. . . .[17]

The book thus dismissed in the language of a cockney Dog-
berry is Newman's spiritual autobiography. A classic example of the negative and mechanical approach to the Bible that
Arnold later deplored in Bishop Colenso's work and sought
to counteract in *Literature and Dogma*, it has been called "the
most formidable direct attack ever made against Christianity
in England."[18] Starting from "an unhesitating unconditional
acceptance of whatever was found in the Bible,"[19] Newman
eventually renounced his early faith and concluded that Jesus
was an impostor who deliberately flouted authority in order
to bring about his execution and thereby conceal his fantastic
pretensions.

The passage between these antipodal positions is described
with none of the literary skill that distinguishes the *Apologia
Pro Vita Sua*, and with none of the dramatic force. Frank
Newman's painful search after truth may be, as Basil Willey
says, an "interesting and touching spectacle";[20] but his account
of it seems naive and gratuitous when compared with his
brother's reply to Kingsley's charge of intellectual dishonesty.
Frank's basic purpose is to relate a series of crises he had experienced, the first of which, over the question of infant baptism,[21] had turned his allegiance from dogmatic articles of
faith to the supposed simplicities of scripture. Here, however,
his difficulties increased. Having noticed that the first chapter
of Matthew omits four generations from the genealogy of
Jesus, he discovered that the corruption of the two names Aha-
ziah and Uzziah into the same sound had caused the merging
of four generations into one, and the similarity of Jehoiakim
to Jehoiachin had led to their blending. Not all of the first

gospel, consequently, could have been divinely inspired. Similarly, the author of Acts betrays his human fallibility when he confuses the land that Jacob bought from the children of Hamor with that which Abraham bought from Ephron the Hittite, and again when he incorrectly makes Gamaliel say that Theudas preceded Judas the Galilean. Already we are in the world of the bishop of Natal with his three priests and 264 pigeons.

As his perplexities grew, Newman turned to Dr. Arnold for help. He had become troubled by the difficulty of explaining how all of mankind could have proceeded in some six thousand years from a single Adam and Eve, and how the patriarchs could have lived to the old age attributed to them. "It was a novelty to me," he writes,

> that Arnold treated these questions as matters of indifference to religion; and did not hesitate to say, that the account of Noah's deluge was evidently mythical, and the history of Joseph "a beautiful poem." I was staggered at this. If all were not descended from Adam, what became of St. Paul's parallel between the first and second Adam, and the doctrine of Headship and Atonement founded on it? If the world was not made in six days, how could we defend the Fourth Commandment as true, though said to have been written in stone by the very finger of God?[22]

This, then, was the man who in 1856 published *The Iliad of Homer Faithfully Translated into Unrhymed English Metre*—a man who, notwithstanding his many admirable qualities, was humorless, literal minded, unimaginative, and totally devoid of poetic feeling; a man whose uncompromising honesty led him to place over his wife's grave an epitaph declaring that she had "no superiority of intellect,"[23] and whose "rigorously logical" mind, as James Martineau observed, prevented his attaining "largeness of view."[24] Arnold was later to insist that his criticism of the translation had not been personal. In a letter to his mother after Newman had replied to the lectures, Arnold wrote, in his customary manner of veiling the serious behind the playful: ". . . as you know, my

sweetness of disposition is my most distinguishing characteristic, and indeed the one feeling this answer of Newman's
gives me is sorrow that he should be so deeply annoyed by
what I intended far more as an illustration of the want of
justesse d'esprit to which the English are prone, than as an
attack upon him."[25] Years later Arnold's widow recalled his
"being troubled at finding how much Mr. Newman had taken
to heart all he had said about his Homer work: indeed it was
in consequence of this that Matt did not republish the book."[26]
Yet despite these protestations, there is no reason to believe
that Arnold had altered his opinion of Newman. After completing the second lecture he wrote to Clough, in a revealing
comment, that he had "done" Newman,[27] and the lecture itself he had concluded with a crushing judgment: ". . . I have
pointed out how widely, in translating Homer, a man even of
real ability and learning may go astray, unless he brings to the
study of this clearest of poets one quality . . .—simple lucidity of mind."[28]

I

To the task of translating Homer Newman had brought
not lucidity of mind but the same passion for literal fidelity
that he had brought to his reading of scripture. The translator's "first duty," he held, "is a historical one: to be *faithful*."[29]
In a popular translation such as his own, moreover, there was
absolute necessity for being truthful, since the general public
reads an English version of Homer only in order "to know all
his oddities, exactly as learned men do."[30] Newman's central
aim, accordingly, had been "to retain every peculiarity of the
original, so far as I am able, *with the greater care, the more
foreign it may happen to be*."[31] And to Newman the *Iliad*
seemed as foreign as scripture. Later he would argue that just
as a missionary translating the Bible into Fiji could not "remove the deep-seated eccentricity of its very essence" by avoid-
ing a few eccentric phrases like "kingdom of heaven" or
"Lamb of God," so a translator of Homer could not escape the
fact of his being odd "to the very core."[32]

The "oddities" and "peculiarities" of Homer, Newman thought, were the result of his writing in a primitive era before the distinctions between prose and poetry had been made. Thus he "is alternately Poet, Orator, Historian, Theologian, Geographer, Traveller, jocose as well as serious, dramatic as well as descriptive." This is why he is not "always at the same high pitch of poetry." On the contrary, he "rises and sinks with his subject, is prosaic when it is tame, is low when it is mean." The Homeric style, in short, "is direct, popular, forcible, quaint, flowing, garrulous, abounding with formulas, redundant in particles and affirmatory interjections, as also in grammatical connectives of time, place, and argument."[33]

In order to render such poetry into English, Newman believed, it was necessary to employ "a diction sufficiently antiquated to obtain pardon of the reader for its frequent homeliness." Yet because the dialect of Homer was itself "essentially archaic," the language used should derive from Anglo-Saxon and French, not Greek and Latin. Newman himself had sought to attain "a plausible aspect of moderate antiquity, while remaining easily intelligible," being "quaint" but not "grotesque." He had therefore given an antique flavor to his translation with archaisms like *bragly, bulkin, gramsome,* and *skirl,* appending for the reader unfamiliar with the words (as if there were another kind of reader) a two-page glossary explaining their meanings: "proudly fine," "calf," "direful," "to cry shrilly."[34]

The metrical counterpart to archaic diction was, for Newman, to be found in the old English ballad, which was "fundamentally musical and popular." It was not to be found in the polished pentameters of the eighteenth century, products of "a cultivated age"; Scott, and not Pope, was "the most Homeric of our poets." Experimenting with the three- and four-foot lines of the ballad, Newman satisfied himself that he could reproduce the effect of Homer's hexameter by combining a line of four beats with one of three. When "an unpleasant void" was created by the elimination of rhyme ("the exigencies of rhyme positively forbid faithfulness"), he filled it by giving each second line a feminine ending. Thereupon, he said, "I found with pleasure that I had exactly alighted on the metre which the modern Greeks adopt for the Homeric hexameter, ever since they have abandoned the musical principle of *quantity* . . . as determining metre, and have betaken themselves to *accent*."[35] With the additional novelty of a typographical arrangement by which two lines are printed together, Newman's modified ballad stanza appears thus in his translation of the opening lines of the *Iliad*:

> Of Peleus' son, Achilles, sing, oh goddess, the resentment
> Accursed, which with countless pangs Achaia's army wounded.

For Matthew Arnold the Homer of Frank Newman was as impossible as his brother's solution to the religious problem of the age. It was, in the first place, based on a fundamental misconception of the nature and purpose of a translation, which should reproduce the general effect of Homer and not the particular effect of single words and lines. Newman's version might "help schoolboys to construe Homer,"[36] but this is not the same as to translate him poetically into English. The *Iliad* is no more adequately rendered by philological accuracy than scripture is comprehended by literal interpretation. Faithfulness in translation involves reproducing the manner as well as the matter of the original; to believe that rendering the parts also renders the whole is to fall into the error of the Spasmodic poets or of the Pre-Raphaelite painters. To his initial error, moreover, Newman adds that of resting his translation on another fallacious principle: if Homer is "archaic," "quaint," and "foreign," it is manifestly impossible to reproduce in English the effect he had on a fifth-century Athenian, even if we could determine what that effect was, for equivalents in language are lacking. The only way in which Homeric translation can be judged, therefore, is to test its effect not upon the general reader for whom Newman had written, but upon the scholar who both knows Greek and has poetic taste and feeling. The implication is inescapable: though "a man of great ability and genuine learning,"[37] Newman was clearly not a poet.

Yet the basic point at issue between Arnold and Newman was not an eccentric translation resulting from a pedantic notion of what constitutes faithfulness. It was, rather, an eccentric translation resulting from what Arnold believed to be a grotesque misconception of Homer himself. The important question was not whether Newman should have preserved every peculiarity of the original, but how well he understood the original. And what, Arnold asks, is the general effect Homer produces on him? It is that of a poet, he says—answering his own question by isolating four adjectives Newman had used—who is quaint, garrulous, prosaic, and low. This is how Newman conceives of the poet who, "clearest-souled of men," had been one of Arnold's chief props "in these bad days"[38] and in whose poetry he had immersed himself for a decade, the poet whose grandeur is "a perfect, a lovely grandeur," and not "the mixed and turbid grandeur" of Shakespeare and Goethe. The "man who could apply those words to Homer," Arnold replies, "can never render Homer truly."[39]

Homer is neither quaint nor antiquated, he says, any more than *bragly* or *bulkin* is "easily intelligible." Sir Thomas Browne is quaint; Chaucer is antiquated; Shakespeare is sometimes both quaint and antiquated. How Homer affected Sophocles there is no way of determining, Arnold admits. But he denies that he ever seems archaic to the scholar, who is the only judge of the matter.[40]

Nor is Homer garrulous. Arnold quotes six lines of leisurely narration from a medieval metrical romance and asks rhetorically whether Homer's style in any way resembles it. Similar disposal is made of Newman's statement that Homer "rises and sinks with his subject." On the contrary, Arnold declares, Homer "invests his subject, whatever his subject be, with nobleness." An author to whom Newman's remark properly applies is Defoe, whose style in *Moll Flanders* is consistently pitched to a low subject matter. Does Homer's style, Arnold again asks rhetorically, at all resemble Defoe's?[41]

Homer thus has none of the characteristics Newman ascribes to him. And because he has failed so entirely to understand that Homer is noble, Newman has necessarily been false to his original. He is false in being grotesque, as in the incongruity of

> O brother thou of me, who am a mischief-working vixen,
> A numbing horror;

He is false in being odd, as in the quaintness of "dapper-greaved Achaians." He is false in being familiar, as in

> A thousand fires along the plain, I say, that night
>   were burning.[42]

He is false also in his "metrical exploits." Homer is in the grand style, and the ballad is not. "Homer's manner and movement are always both noble and powerful: the ballad-manner and movement are often either jaunty and smart, so not noble; or jog-trot and humdrum, so not powerful." In execution, too, Newman's meter is faulty. Arnold is unwilling to look "for passages likely to raise a laugh; that search, alas! would be far too easy." It is enough, he suggests, to point to the forced accentuation on *wert* in

> Infatuate! O that thou wert lord to some other army—

and to the hopelessly un-Homeric manner of

> Myself right surely know also, that 'tis my doom to perish.[43]

In almost every respect, therefore, Newman's translation is a failure—an "eminently ignoble" one, as Arnold puts it. Why dwell at such length, then, on what is so patently bad? Arnold's answer seems at least partially disingenuous. "Newman is a writer of considerable and deserved reputation," he says; "he is also a Professor of the University of London, an institution which by its position and by its merits acquires every year greater importance. It would be a very grave thing if the authority of so eminent a Professor led his students to misconceive entirely the chief work of the Greek world." There is the suggestion here of a sop thrown in Newman's direction, for one wonders how seriously an Oxford audience regarded the authority of a London professor, or how deeply had been taken to heart the view of Homer proclaimed in a translation published four years earlier and scarcely noticed at all. The primary reason for singling Newman out is found instead in the passage that follows: the "eccentricity" and "arbitrariness" of Newman were not his "peculiar failing," but "the great defect of English intellect, the great blemish of English literature."[44] Newman's name was sufficiently famous at Oxford to lend significance to his exemplifying a national shortcoming, and his views about Christianity, if not those about Homer, were well known. Neither Arnold nor his audience need have been aware of those idiosyncrasies of dress and manner that captivated Newman's biographer and later arrested the attention even of Lionel Trilling; nor need Arnold have been motivated by personal antipathy. What was important was that Newman's translation of Homer, like his *Phases of Faith*, represented in a striking way those qualities of his countrymen that Arnold had dedicated his professorship to combatting.

II

Homeric Translation in Theory and Practice, Newman's answer to Arnold, is the kind of reply one might have expected of the author. Learned, solemn, and almost as long as the three lectures combined, it is at times a careful, point-by-point refutation, at other times an angry, childish outburst of injured feelings. "I suppose I am often guilty of keeping low company," Newman gravely comments in response to Arnold's puzzlement over his strange diction; and about Arnold's professing to refrain from ridicule he says with naive presumption, "I could not be like Homer without being easy to ridicule." The poignant and ingenuous mingle as he recalls having "devoted every possible quarter of an hour for two years and a half to translate the Iliad, toiling unremittingly in my vacations and in my walks, and going to large expenses of money, in order to put the book before the unlearned; and this, though I am not a Professor of Poetry nor even of Greek." Having recently seen a translation of Homer that apparently had "perished uncriticised, unreproved, unwept, unknown," he is willing to have his own work "slain in battle" but not sentenced to death by the Oxford professor of poetry.[45]

Like many readers of *On Translating Homer*, Newman finds objectionable Arnold's tone of superiority, his dogmatic manner, his clever and exasperating use of insinuation.[46] It is effective, he admits, to call one's translation ignoble, to speak of the translator's "metrical exploits," to sigh "alas!" at the ease with which risible passages could be found. But Newman refuses to yield to a critic who, he says, often makes ex-cathedra pronouncements without either knowledge or proof in their support. He complains, too, that Arnold pretends to regard him with respect but in reality treats him with contempt; that he distorts the meaning of his words or represents it incompletely; that he fails to quote adequately and fairly from his translation; and that by misstatement and implication he gives a false impression of individual passages.

Newman's pamphlet as a whole, however, is directed toward the substance rather than the manner of Arnold's remarks. Essentially, it is concerned with three topics: the nature of Homeric poetry, the meter employed by Newman, and the hexameters of Arnold.

In a display of erudition unmatched by Arnold, but tinged with pedantry and a fondness for statistics, Newman reaffirms his view that Homer was an archaic poet. As if numbers were germane to the central question, he cites the 548 octavo pages of Buttman that discuss 106 poorly explained Homeric words, some of which Sophocles may have understood but all of which he would have found antiquated, and the 206 pages of the supplement to Thiersch that are devoted to the Homeric noun and verb alone. "Every sentence of Homer," he asserts, "was more or less antiquated to Sophocles." New case endings for nouns, unusual pronominal forms and verbal inflections, the orthographical changes effected by the loss of the digamma—all these differences cause a wide separation between Homeric and Attic Greek. To suggest this antiquity by the use of such words as *bragly* and *bulkin* is quite proper in an English version of Homer, Newman thinks, and he looks to the time when the translator may replace *lands* and *hounds* with *landis* and *houndis* and restore *ye* or *y* before the past participle.[47]

This method of suggesting the archaic requires the distinction Newman makes between "familiar" and "unfamiliar" language. Homer's words, he argues, may have been "familiar" (by which he means "often heard") to the Athenian even when they were not understood or, when understood, seemed foreign. When thus familiar they could not have "surprised" him. Similarly, the modern reader is "familiar" with the language of Pope and Cowper and accepts it as Newman believes his archaic diction should be accepted.[48]

But the fundamental question does not lie even here. Homer might have been completely unintelligible to Pericles, Newman says, and yet still be improperly translated into archaic English. The real question is whether Homer is absolutely or only relatively antiquated, whether he is the poet of a barbarian or of a refined age. Newman himself has no doubt at all as to the answer. "Homer sang to a wholly unfastidious audience, very susceptible to the marvellous, very unalive to the ridiculous, capable of swallowing with reverence the most grotesque conceptions." This is why the translator must make liberal use of archaisms: "a broad tinge of antiquity in the style is essential, to make Homer's barbaric puerilities and eccentricities less offensive."[49]

And if Homer is antiquated, he is even more noticeably quaint. Newman finds in him "inexhaustible quaintnesses." It is quaint, he says, "to call waves *wet*, milk *white*, blood *dusky*, horses *singlehoofed*, a hero's hand *broad*, words *winged*, Vulcan *Lobfoot*," and so on. It may be true, as Arnold maintains, that such epithets had become familiar to the Greeks and thus for them had lost their oddness. But Newman denies that this means they are oddities any the less. It is still "quaint to say that Menelaus was as brave as a bloodsucking fly, that Agamemnon's sobs came thick as flashes of lightning; and that the Trojan mares, while running, groaned like overflowing rivers. All such similes come from a mind quick to discern similarities, but *very dull to feel incongruities*." Nor does Newman regard Homer's quaintness as a fault; it is rather, he thinks, the picturesque expression of a barbarian and illogical mind.[50]

Homer is likewise garrulous. Despite the "tones of great superiority" assumed by Arnold, Newman says, "every schoolboy knows that diffuseness is a distinguishing characteristic" of the poet. His garrulity at times takes the form of "a mere love of chatting," telling of the toilet of Juno, or the history of Agamemnon's breastplate, or the arming of a hero. No detail—the opening of a door with a key or the precise place where one warrior wounds another—is too trivial for his attention. At other times garrulity appears in the form of expletives. Newman's use of these, as in the line Arnold had criticized and misquoted—"A thousand fires along the plain, I say, that night were gleaming"—is "moderate indeed compared to Homer's." Garrulity appears in Homer's circumlocutions, as well, as in "my heart in my bosom is divided" for "I doubt."[51]

Homer is also, Newman repeats, frequently prosaic and low. How can he convince Arnold of this fact, he wonders face-

tiously, when Arnold submits as a guide for the translator a
flat line like "In the plain there were kindled a thousand fires;
by each one there sate fifty men"? Homer's style is not the
sustained style of Virgil or of Milton, and at times it seems
intentionally unpoetic:

> Then visiting he urged each man with words,
> Mesthles and Glaucus and Medon and Thersilochus
> And Asteropeus and Deisenor and Hippothoüs
> And Phorkys and Chromius and Ennomus the augur.

Although the *Iliad* is generally noble, Newman believes, much
of it is ignoble to the modern reader and actually offensive in
some of its details: Hecuba's wish to eat Achilles' liver, Juno's
willingness to devour Priam's children raw, Jupiter's hanging
up Juno and fastening anvils to her feet.[52]

Homer's language, moreover, is often crude. The Greek
phrase Newman had rendered by *vixen*, a word Arnold ridiculed as grotesque, was in fact exceedingly coarse. Helen intended to describe herself as impure, Newman says, and by
making her say *vixen* instead of *bitch*, the only word that
faithfully translates the original, he performs a service for
which Arnold should be grateful. In descriptions of physical
action, too, Homer is much less elegant and refined than Arnold supposes. When the fastidious professor of poetry criti-
cizes Newman for making Achilles *yell*, he forgets that Homer
portrays him as grinding his teeth, rolling on the ground, and
covering his hair with dust. Cowper makes a similar error in
rendering as "The pow'rs of Ilium gave the first assault,/
Embattled close," a passage which should read, "The Trojans
knocked-forward (or, thumped, *butted*, forward) in close
pack." Newman suggests that "Forward in *pack* the Trojans
pitch'd" would not be "really unfaithful to the Homeric col-
our," and "Forward in mass the Trojans pitch'd" would be "an
irreprovable rendering."[53]

Homer, in short, is a popular poet, and thus he should be
translated into the ballad meter, which "is essentially a noble

metre, a popular metre, a metre of great capacity." Newman concedes that his own meter has the fault of monotony—whereas no pause is required between the two Doric lines comprising the Homeric hexameter, there tends to be a pause between the two ballad lines he himself has employed—but he refuses to admit that this makes the movement of his lines un-Homeric. Indeed, Arnold misrepresents his aim when he tells him to "reproduce . . . on our ear something of the effect produced by the movement of Homer." Because English meter is accentual and the English language highly consonantal, and Greek meter quantitative and the Greek language highly vocalized, Newman has sought to create not "audible sameness of metre, but a likeness of *moral genius*." The only similarity of sound he admits is that both Homeric and ballad meter are "primitively made *for music*."[54]

However imperfectly he may have succeeded with his modified ballad meter, Newman is pleased (rather maliciously so) to note that Arnold has totally failed in his hexameters. After quoting six of them Newman exclaims, "I sincerely thought, this was meant for prose; at length the two last lines opened my eyes. He *does* mean them for Hexameters!" Seven more lines are quoted, with incredulity once again giving way to astonishment. In answer to Arnold's reproach for the arbitrary accentuation on *wert* in one of his lines, moreover, Newman points to the identical error committed nine times by Arnold in thirteen lines. And these, he says, are lines ostensibly written as models for the translator of Homer! Arnold has not only destroyed quantity, but, after theoretically substituting accent for it, destroyed accent also. In so doing, Newman warns, Arnold has shown scholars "the pit of delusion into which they will fall, if they allow themselves to talk fine about the 'Homeric rhythm' *as now heard*, and the duty of a translator to reproduce something of it."[55]

Newman's objection to the hexameter rests essentially on his conviction that both Arnold's practice and his theory run counter to the nature of the English language. Although Arnold calls an accentual trochee such as *between* a spondee, in practice he advocates the trochee as a basis for the hexameter. Nothing could be worse, Newman thinks, because a trochaic beginning of the line in a long poem repeatedly violates the tendency of English sentences to begin with unaccented syllables. In fact, he says, the task Arnold proposes is, if not impossible, at least too difficult to accomplish well, the English language being full of consonants and of syllables that are neither distinctly long nor distinctly short. And for Newman there is the final objection that a popular poet should be translated into a popular measure. The argument has thus turned full circle: English hexameters are not popular, and so they are not the meter for translating Homer.[56]

III

When Newman's pamphlet was followed several weeks later in the summer of 1861 by the *Saturday Review*'s attack, Arnold wrote to his mother that he would "probably give a fourth lecture . . . to conclude the subject, and . . . try to set things straight, at the same time soothing Newman's feelings —which I am really sorry to have hurt—as much as I can without giving up any truth of criticism."[57] He delivered the lecture in November and published it in March. "The Homer lecture you will like," he told his mother after its completion, "and I think it will be liked generally." One reason was that it had enabled Arnold to make a suitable response to Newman "while retaining and still plainly expressing my judgment of his translation."[58] But, more important, it had reassured Arnold of the truth of his position. After the initially favorable reception of *On Translating Homer* he had said, "What takes people in my lectures is the stress laid on what is *tonic* and *fortifying* in Homer. This sort of thing always attracts attention from English people, however barbarous they may be."[59] When some of this conviction was shaken by an occasional eruption of barbarousness in reviews of the lectures, however, a fourth lecture was necessary to reestablish it. "The truth is," Arnold wrote confidently to his mother after delivering it, "they may talk till doomsday but they will never upset the main positions of those lectures, because they are founded upon the rocks."[60]

Although it has been called "a unique piece of sustained irony,"[61] the fourth lecture is in truth ironic only in the opening and closing passages. Arnold's strategy at the outset is to imply that he, not Newman, has been the victim of attack. He has always sought to emulate the example of Buffon in resolutely abstaining from controversy, Arnold says, and he now resumes the subject of translating Homer only because "a learned and estimable man" has misunderstood his language and intention. He has no desire to engage in a personal quarrel, but by making an explanation to Newman he may serve the more important purpose of clearing the dust of controversy that has temporarily obscured the view of Homer. Yet at the same time that he claims for himself a positive and useful role, Arnold employs the language of self-deprecation, describing himself as "humble" and "unworthy" and freely confessing his ignorance. This mock humility is in turn tempered by a banter made all the more effective by its contrast with the solemnity of Newman and the *Saturday Review*. And with its inane comment about the source of Newman's diction—that "he 'lived with' the other Fellows of Balliol"— the *Saturday* itself had given Arnold the opportunity to show an amused Oxford audience how faintly his adversaries perceived the real points at issue.[62]

The explanation to Newman himself, on the other hand, is without irony (unless, of course, the sincerity of Arnold's professed regard should be denied). The tone is, rather, apologetic, conciliatory, and respectful. Arnold regrets any "vivacities of expression" that may have caused pain, assuring Newman that they were used "without a thought of insult or rancour." He regards Newman "as one of the few learned men we have, one of the few who love learning for its own sake." His own love of literature, he hopes, is comparable, allowing him to deal with literary works quite apart from personalities. His criticism of Newman's translation was prompted, then, not by disrespect for the translator himself, but by the belief that he had wrongly applied his learning and ability. It is an error to which the English, with their want of an academy, are particularly susceptible. But the charge that Newman had undertaken a work for which he was unsuited does not "exclude a great respect for himself personally, or for his powers in the happier manifestation of them."[63]

All of this by way of soothing Newman's feelings. But on the question of how Homer is to be translated, Arnold refuses to yield ground. He solidifies his position, in fact, by an argument that cancels the apparent advantage Newman possesses in his greater learning. "To handle these matters properly," Arnold says, "there is needed a poise so perfect that the least overweight in any direction tends to destroy the balance. Temper destroys it, a crotchet destroys it, even erudition may destroy it." In Newman the destructive force has been erudition, and thus it turns out that his failure in translating Homer results not simply from his want of the poetical gift, but also from his having to excess the very thing for which Arnold has just expressed admiration for his having! He fails also because, like all learned men who seek final rules, "he draws his conclusions too absolutely; he wants to include too much under his rules; he does not quite perceive that in poetical criticism the shade, the fine distinction, is everything."[64]

Newman's entire position is false, Arnold demonstrates, because it is an attempt to apply a philological view where the poetical view alone is applicable. The question "is one not of scholarship, but of a poetical translation of Homer." If in its general effect the poetry of Homer is perfectly plain and intelligible, and if the aim of the translator is to reproduce this general effect, the scholar's doubt as to the meaning of individual words cannot change either that effect or that aim. When Newman insists, moreover, that every sentence of Homer was antiquated to Sophocles, he fails to distinguish between the language of ordinary life and the language of poetry. Homer's language was not the practical, everyday language used by the Athenian, but the poetical language that he was taught from childhood and in which he composed when he wrote verse. It was part of his poetical vocabulary as much as words like *perchance* and *spake* are part of the poetical vocabulary of the modern Englishman. Even when he was uncertain of the precise meaning of a word, he had what might be called a poetical sense of it, just as the reader of the Bible has a clear sense of *mote* and *beam* even though he may not have a strictly accurate one. But this parallel is not adequately suggested by Newman's use of words like *bragly*, *libbard*, *withouten*, and *muchel*. The first two are not familiar to the Englishman as Homer's words were familiar to the Athenian, and the latter two sound antiquated even as poetical expressions.[65]

Newman's philological interests again mislead him into conceiving of Homer as a primitive eccentric. Intent upon finding a literal equivalent for each word, he eventually finds oddities everywhere, and to share these discoveries with the reader becomes his central aim. "Terrible learning," Arnold exclaims, "terrible learning, which discovers so much!"[66]

The same error leads to the view of Homer as quaint. Arnold does not concede Newman's argument that it is quaint to call waves *wet* and milk *white*, and he is not sure that it is quaint to call blood *dusky*. It is quaint, he admits, to call Vulcan *Lobfoot*, but this does not mean that the epithet is quaint in the original. Newman "knows the literal value of the Greek so well," he says, "that he thinks his literal rendering identical with the Greek, and that the Greek must stand or fall along with his rendering."[67]

Nowhere is this confusion of pedantry with poetry more obvious than in Newman's assertion that Homer rises and sinks with his subject and that he is frequently prosaic and coarse. Homer never sinks with his subject, Arnold repeats. The subject may sink, but not Homer. In level as well as in elevated passages, he is always perfectly sound and poetical.[68] The lines Newman claims he found it impossible to believe were intended for poetry are, Arnold declares, "very good poetry indeed, poetry of the best class, *in that place*." Nor is Newman's poetic taste more evident when he tries to illustrate Homer's use of coarse descriptive phrases. In "The Trojans knocked forward in close pack," he offers what is a good literal translation, Arnold grants, but in the attempt to improve the line with "Forward in mass the Troians pitch'd," he loses both Homeric color and literal faithfulness.[69]

With this final proof of Newman's incapacity for poetic translation, Arnold concludes that portion of the lecture specifically aimed at him.[70] What Newman had said about ballads and hexameters he considers only indirectly in answering two critics who had entered the controversy with articles on the disputed matter of metrics. One of these, John Stuart Blackie, had supported Newman's belief that the proper medium for translating Homer was the ballad measure, and Arnold, partly in order to recognize every important critic of the lectures, directs his reply to Blackie rather than to Newman when he turns once again to the question of Homer and the balladists.

IV

John Stuart Blackie, translator of Homer, Aeschylus, and Goethe and tireless author of books on subjects ranging from atheism to German war songs, was "an animated, pleasant man," Arnold informed his sister, "with a liking for all sorts of things that are excellent." But as a critic and translator of Homer he was another Frank Newman. "*Au reste*," Arnold continued, "an *esprit* as confused and hoity toity as possible, and as capable of translating Homer as of making the Apollo Belvedere."[71]

In the August *Macmillan's* Blackie had paid tribute to Arnold's "ingenious and graceful lectures" but had rebuked him, in a thinly veiled comment, for his severity toward "a personal friend of my own, and a man whom I love and respect with no common reverence." Although he agreed that Newman's translation was a mistake and that Newman was not a poet, he thought him "a man altogether of such fine qualities . . . that no man of good feeling would like to fling a stone at him."[72]

The purpose of Blackie's article, however, was not to defend Newman personally but to defend part of his thesis: to demonstrate the characteristics of Homer—"his materials," "his tone," and "his method of handling"—that are shared with the balladists. The ballad medium itself, Blackie argues, is more elevated than Arnold admits in his "one-sided" view that there is something "vulgar in the mere form of the ballad. Locksley Hall is in ballad measure . . . and no person ever accused Mr. Tennyson's muse of vulgarity in any shape." This medium, moreover, Homer so invests with nobility that his work becomes grander than other ballad poetry. He "rises above all ballad-singers in the vividness of his genius, in the grandeur of his conceptions, and in the constructiveness of his intellect." Blackie thus concludes that "a new translation of Homer should be attempted in some of our well-known ballad measures."[73]

Blackie's argument is rather curtly dismissed by Arnold, who in paraphrasing reduces it to absurdity: "Professor Blackie proposes a compromise: he suggests that those who say Homer's poetry is pure ballad-poetry, and those who deny that it is ballad-poetry at all, should split the difference between them; that it should be agreed that Homer's poems are ballads *a little*, but not so much as some have said." But Arnold will not "allow that Homer's poetry is ballad-poetry at all." Homer not only belongs "to an incomparably more developed spiritual and intellectual order than the balladists"; his poetic medium has a "capacity for sustained nobleness" that the ballad form lacks. Arnold does not deny that the ballad may achieve a certain grandeur, as in the "lyrical cry" of "Sir Patrick Spens," but he is speaking of narrative poetry, where the

ballad style leads "away from the grand style rather than towards it."[74] Furthermore, Homer is not simply a better poet
than the balladists. He is "so essentially different" that he "is
not to be classed with them at all." Whereas in the balladists
the narrative is almost everything, the ideas being few and simple, in Homer there is not only the narrative; there is also
"the noble and profound application of ideas to life—. . . the
most essential part of poetic greatness."[75]

A much more substantial article than Blackie's was one that
had appeared two months earlier in *Fraser's*. It was by the able
editor and biographer of Francis Bacon, James Spedding,
whom FitzGerald once described as "the wisest man I have
known."[76] Before reading it, Arnold said that it was "sure to
be interesting, as it is by James Spedding,"[77] and later conceded that there was "much to be said" for it. But at the same
time he believed that Spedding, like Newman, was "not *ondoyant* and *divers* enough . . . to deal rightly with matters of
poetical criticism."[78]

Spedding's primary purpose is to dispel the notion that
Homer can be successfully rendered by the English hexameter,
which he regards as the meter the translator "should of all
others avoid." Arnold's error in proposing it, he implies, is
linked to the fallacious assumption that the scholarly tribunal
is alone competent to evaluate Homeric translation. The real
question, according to Spedding, is not whether the translation
produces upon the scholar the same general effect as the original, but whether it produces upon one who cannot read the
original the same general effect the original produces upon
one who can. To the scholar, "the original shows through the
translation, and gives it new colours and qualities. In reading the English he feels the Greek within it; and the illusion
thereby produced is seen in no more conspicuous example than
that of . . . reading a page of English hexameters, and fancy-
ing that the 'movement' of them is like that of the Greek or
Latin." Although Spedding admits that there is in Homer
"now and then a line which reads like an English hexameter,"

he insists that in general the resemblance is one "not of mimicry but of mockery; a mere exaggeration of the characteristic peculiarity, without any of the other features by which it is balanced, softened, varied, or harmonised; and the conditions being such, that the better you make your English hexameter, the more it will resemble the worst form of the measure which the Greek allows."[79]

Spedding seeks to demonstrate the unsuitability of the English hexameter by distinguishing between it and the Virgilian hexameter, which he chooses because it is "the most perfectly developed form of the metre under conditions which enable us to judge of it" and because the Homeric hexameter, when read in respect to accent exactly as Latin is read, "is in its fundamental conditions the same as the Virgilian." Whereas the English hexameter considers accent alone, entirely disregarding quantity, and requires that the first four accents be placed where the first four long syllables are placed in the Latin, the Virgilian hexameter permits much freedom with regard to accent but none at all with regard to quantity, and requires that the first four accents never coincide with the first four long syllables. These essential differences, Spedding argues, prevent the English hexameter as now constituted from ever rendering the effect of Homer.[80]

He thinks it possible, however, that "a new English metre may be invented, resting upon six regularly recurring accents as the ground, and made musical by some variation played upon it with quantity; just as the Latin takes quantity for its ground, and obtains its variations through the management of the accent." Spedding's belief in the possibility of such a meter stems from his conviction that quantity is "distinguishable in English through all its degrees, by any ear that will attend to it." The word *slumbers*, for example, has two long syllables; *supper*, two short syllables; *bittern*, a short and a long syllable. *Quantity* is a dactyl; *quiddity*, a tribrach; *rapidly*, a word for which there is no parallel in Latin. Illustrating these quantitative distinctions in the hexameter itself, Spedding submits

Sweetly cometh slumber, closing th' o'erwearïed eyelid

as a correct Virgilian hexameter, and

Sweetly falleth slumber, closing the wearïed eyelid

as a hexameter with two false quantities. Although he recognizes that this new meter is not an immediate possibility, he offers in the meanwhile a specimen of the Virgilian hexameter transposed into English:

> Verses so modulate, so tuned, so varied in accent,
> Rich with unexpected changes, smooth, stately, sonorous,
> Rolling ever forward, tidelike, with thunder, in endless
> Procession, complex melodies—pause, quantity, accent,
> After Virgilian precedent and practice, in order
> Distributed—could these gratify th' Etonian ear-drum?[81]

Such a measure being presently impossible, Spedding looks elsewhere for an established meter capable of rendering the Homeric movement. Among the alternatives he prefers blank verse, in which Tennyson has written hundreds of lines with "all the characteristic qualities which Mr. Arnold finds in Homer . . . as conspicuous as in Homer himself." Yet Spedding goes on to reject even blank verse, expressing doubt at the end whether it is wise, in view of Arnold's statement that no translation is very valuable compared with the original, to attempt to translate Homer at all. In a crashing anticlimax he suggests that those who wish to know what Homer is like should learn Greek.[82]

Before Arnold was able to reply to Spedding's article, it was answered by H. A. J. Munro, Fellow of Trinity College, Cambridge, and translator of Lucretius. During the previous year, Munro had read a paper on the loss of quantity in classical languages in the third century and was now induced to publish it in order to vindicate the accentual English hexameter that Spedding had condemned. Munro had argued in his paper that the Latin accent, like the Greek, "had no relation to quantity or the length of the syllable, but was a mere *raising or sharpening* of the tone of voice at the syllable on which it was placed." Yet in reading Latin today, we make accent "a mere stress, instead of a simple raising of the tone without any lengthening of the quantity." Greek also we read "with this debased Latin accent, and fancy that we preserve the quantity while sacrificing the accent."[83]

This misreading of classical versification, Munro contends in an appendix to the original paper, leads to errors that vitiate Spedding's thesis. He does not understand, for example, that "accent has nothing to do with the Virgilian hexameter. Its rhythm depends entirely on caesura, pause and a due arrangement of words." Thus when he says that there are few Homeric lines like the English hexameter (that is, lines in which all six long syllables are accented), he fails to perceive that our English reading of Homer and Virgil is in itself meaningless, and that these lines "are among the very commonest types of Homeric rhythm." Equally false are Spedding's remarks on quantity in English. "Neither my ear nor my reason," Munro declares, "recognises any real distinction of quantity except that which is produced by accentuated and unaccentuated syllables." To say with Spedding that *rapidly* is a word for which there is no parallel in Latin, or that "Sweetly cometh slumber, closing th' o'erwearïed eyelid" is a correct Virgilian hexameter, is to convey "no intelligible idea." *Rapidly* is an accentual dactyl, *cometh* an accentual trochee, and nothing more. "The argument of quantity is a mere paralogism arising from our misreading Virgil."[84]

Munro believes that the usual English meters are accentual adaptations of quantitative Latin measures. In the blank verse of Shakespeare and Milton, for example, accent has simply replaced the Latin metrical beat. The remarkable improvement by the Elizabethan poets of what had previously been an undistinguished meter suggests to Munro the possibility that "in the hands of genius the English hexameter might be rendered even more majestic and sonorous than the iambic." But be-

fore this can be accomplished, he says, "six accentuated syllables must take the place of . . . six rhythmical beats . . . .
Quantity must be utterly discarded."[85]

Although Munro's paper nowhere mentions Arnold, it is
pertinent because of its suggestions for answering Spedding.
Arnold. is not in complete agreement with Munro, differing
from him in thinking that the translator of Homer should distinguish between "th' o'erwearïed eyelid" and "the wearïed
eyelid" and that he should not utterly discard quantity. But,
more important, he agrees that Spedding is probably mistaken
in believing that the classical hexameter was pronounced as
the English pronounce it, that he may have too nice an ear in
describing *rapidly* as a word for which there is no parallel in
Latin, and that he misses a crucial point in failing to see that
the rhythm of the Virgilian hexameter depends on caesura
and pause.[86]

Arnold's reply to Spedding closely resembles in technique
the reply to Newman. He first praises Spedding as a critic
"whom it is impossible to read without pleasure" and describes
his remarks on accent and quantity as "most interesting and
instructive"—indeed, quite above Arnold's "humble function"
of merely giving practical advice to the translator of Homer.
But the effect of these compliments is instantly canceled by
the criticism that Spedding, like Newman, is too inflexible,
too absolute in imposing rules, too lacking in finesse and in
the capacity for being *ondoyant* and *divers* to deal adequately
with the subject at hand. When, for example, he rejects the
scholarly tribunal as an imperfect judge of Homeric translation, he rejects the only means we have of judging. The proposed test that a translation should produce upon the unlearned the same general effect the original produces upon the
scholar is an impossibility, Arnold says, because the impressions of the two can never be accurately compared.[87]

Spedding's rigidity is nowhere more apparent than in his
condemnation of the English hexameter. Arnold agrees that
it does not perfectly represent the classical meter, being "mere-

ly an attempt to imitate the effect of the ancient hexameter, as read by us moderns." Yet what must the translator of Homer do? Must he abandon the English hexameter completely and resort to lines like "Procession, complex melodies—pause, quantity, accent"? Clearly some more practical step must be taken. The English hexameter is one by which "the English ear, the genius of the English language, have, in their own way, adopted, have *translated* for themselves the Homeric hexameter." Spedding, on the other hand, proposes revolution in a meter that has so grown up as to admit change "only within narrow limits," to preclude change that is "sweeping and essential." His hexameter, moreover, is based on a false theory of quantity, for quantity in English, unlike quantity in Greek or Latin, is not felt when unsupported by accent. In "Sweetly cometh slumber, closing th' o'erwearïed eyelid" the English reader so feels the accent on the first syllable of *closing* that he has no sense of any length in the second syllable, and therefore the rhythm of the line is destroyed.[88]

Arnold concedes that the translator of Homer may find it necessary to turn to blank verse, but if so it must not be the blank verse of Spedding, whose specimens Arnold finds "slow," "ungainly," and "artificial." Nor must it be the blank verse of Tennyson, the "essential characteristic" of which is "an extreme subtlety and curious elaborateness" of thought and expression. His poetry, as in a line like "Now lies the Earth all Danaë to the stars," is "the least *plain*, the most *un-Homeric*, which can possibly be conceived." The Homeric simplicity that Spedding believes he sees in it is in reality the artificial simplicity the French call *simplesse*.[89]

Yet the English hexameter, Arnold repeats, and not blank verse, is the meter most capable of rendering the Homeric rhythm. It must be somewhat modified, however, and he hopes that continued efforts will be made to use and perfect it. He himself has tried to relieve its monotony by occasionally beginning a line with an iambic foot, as in "Be*twéen*" or "There sát," which both Newman and Spedding misread. But he does not believe that the English hexameter is likely to enjoy the immediate success some have supposed him to predict. It is a meter still unfamiliar, a meter disliked by many (though chiefly among critics, Arnold thinks, rather than the general public). Nevertheless, with the work of poets like Longfellow in original poetry and of lesser poets in translation, the hexameter may become familiar, and with gradual improvement it may become the established meter for which modern poetry has great need.[90]

Meanwhile Arnold makes only the most modest claims for his own hexameters. Soon after the publication of *On Translating Homer* he had written, in response to criticism by a clergyman named Herbert Hill, that the "doctrine" of the lectures was "the chief matter" and "the merit of the hexameters . . . a secondary matter." He had not composed them "as I should try to make the hexameter if I set to work to use it on a large scale."[91] Now, publicly, he calls his hexameters "perishable objects" that he regards with "Oriental detachment." They were not submitted to compete with translations of Homer but only to illustrate certain characteristics of Homer that the translator should endeavor to reproduce. In fact—he confesses in a conclusion that cedes in one clause what is reclaimed in the next—they may not have Homeric rapidity, plainness, simplicity, and nobility, but he hopes that a translator who reads them sympathetically will see what he means when he says that Homer has all of these qualities.[92]

V

Spedding's inflexibility—his "obduracy and over-vehemence"[93] in declaring that he would never read a translation of Homer into English hexameters—becomes for Arnold an effective means of answering another critic, Philip Stanhope Worsley, the consumptive young scholar and poet who earlier in 1861 had published the first volume of his translation of the *Odyssey* into Spenserian stanzas. Spedding should welcome a good translation in any meter, Arnold says, just as he himself welcomes a new translation in the very form against which he had advised on the grounds that its intricate rhyme scheme radically changed the Homeric rhythm. But there is no necessary connection between the two, Worsley replied in the preface to his translation. A reader who is conscious of tyranny in a simple rhyme scheme, he argued, may not be conscious of it in a complex one. In Pope's *Essay on Man*, for example, the ear is "kept unceasingly on the alert, and one is scarcely able to repress a kind of self-congratulation on every successive rhymic achievement." In *The Faerie Queene*, on the other hand,

> the feeling to the ear is that of placid satisfaction, wholly subordinate to the general interest of the poem. We are no longer offended by unnatural pauses; indeed it is scarcely possible for a pause to seem unnatural. The very intricacy of the metre saves us from this, and a full stop may occur almost anywhere without detriment to the general effect of the stanza. . . . On the whole . . . it appears that the more complicated the correspondences the less obtrusive and absolute are the rhymes. . . .[94]

Although relegated to a footnote in the published lecture, Arnold's answer to Worsley is the most gracious of his replies to the critics of the Homer lectures and is in keeping with his habitual courtesy toward younger writers. "This is true, and subtly remarked," he says of Worsley's statement that rhymes are less obtrusive in complicated than in simple schemes. To the work of translating Homer, moreover, he brings "a truly poetical sense and skill" that make his *Odyssey* "delightful to read" and "much the most pleasing of those hitherto produced." But Arnold stands firmly by his original position. He never denied, he says, that the rhymes in the couplet are more strongly felt than those in the stanza. He contended only that the more frequent recurrence of the same rhyme in the stanza creates a more intricate pattern and thus changes the Homeric movement even more radically than does the couplet. Consequently, he believes that the perfect translation of Homer is more nearly possible in the couplet than in the stanza, and while Worsley's translation may suffice for the general public, for whom it was intended, it is still not enough for the critic.[95]

The reply to Worsley was prompted in part by Arnold's liking "very much" the preface to the second volume of his translation,[96] published early in 1862. "It seems to me almost a truism," Worsley had written there, "that the absolutely fittest instrument for Homeric translation is, as Mr. Arnold has so ably maintained, the English hexameter." Worsley admitted that it had not been successfully employed on a large scale and that its use was "still in a great degree chaotic and unformed." But two lines from Arnold's specimens he thought "the very best and most Homeric hexameters" he had yet seen:

> But let me be dead, and the earth be mounded above me,
> Ere I hear thy cries, and thy captivity told of.[97]

Worsley was virtually alone, however, in his admiration for Arnold's hexameters. They had met with almost universal disapproval in the periodical press, and when Dallas in the *Times* called them "novel and strange," Arnold told his mother with a sense of resignation that "hexameters are in themselves something 'novel and strange' which it is always a question if a person likes—and mine owing to my desire to be plain and copied are perhaps more novel and strange than usual."[98] But he was probably unprepared for the intensity of feeling that inspired Tennyson's parody in the *Cornhill* for December 1863:

> These lame hexameters the strong-wing'd music of Homer!
>   No—but a most burlesque barbarous experiment.
> When was a harsher sound ever heard, ye Muses, in England?
>   When did a frog coarser croak upon our Helicon?
> Hexameters no worse than daring Germany gave us,
>   Barbarous experiment, barbarous hexameters.

In "the only compliment of the kind" he had ever paid Arnold (despite the fact that "there [was] no one whose judgment he value[d] so much"),[99] Tennyson said that among those who had attempted to translate Homer into the English hexameter was one "of our best and greatest." Their failure, he thought, had "gone far to prove the impossibility of the task."[100]

Arnold did not have occasion until several years later to refer in print to Tennyson's parody, which appeared after the final lecture had been delivered. In the meantime he was engaged in answering another critic, the *Saturday Review*, which was to become one of his most persistent opponents during the sixties. Established in 1855 "with a view to injure the *Guardian*,"[101] it was edited by John Douglas Cook, "a stout, square, bull-necked, red-faced, apoplectic-looking man"[102] who had gathered about him a group of writers with such a talent for attacking eminent men that they earned for the paper the title of *Saturday Reviler*. Among these masters of the slashing style was Goldwin Smith, whom J. A. Symonds described at the time as "a very strange, carking, bitter man— with a good deal of the Saturday Review's verjuice in him."[103] The authorship of the *Saturday*'s attack on the Homer lectures in July 1861 had apparently been ascribed to Smith—Arnold wrote that year that he was "a great element of bitterness and strife"[104] who "looked ill and miserable, . . . pass[ing] his life in the most acrimonious attacking and being attacked"[105]— for in October he approached Arnold in the Athenaeum and said, "I wish you to know that I had nothing to do with that article on you in the Saturday Review."[106] Yet whoever the author (Smith did not divulge his identity),[107] Arnold had just cause to complain of the *Saturday*'s "villainy."[108] "I do not much care for them," he had remarked even before the publication of the attack. "They praise or blame from some absurd pique or whim, not because the thing is praiseworthy or blameworthy."[109]

The puerility and heavy-handedness of the *Saturday*'s attack should have made Smith's denial unnecessary. "Here is a good stand-up fight," the writer began, enjoying the "amusement" provided by "scholars and professors [who] can pitch into one another with a good will when they take it into their heads" and wishing only for "a little more fighting." But his professed neutrality soon yielded to partisanship. Although admitting that the Homer lectures were "intensely amusing" and "very clever," he reproached Arnold for abusing the Oxford Chair of Poetry by his ridicule of a scholar who had, "as a scholar, a very much higher reputation." Arnold's "contemptuous and insulting language," "personal abuse," and "low buffoonery" were "utterly out of place." Nor was he "so free from glass windows as to be entitled to throw many stones." Newman's translation was "very bad," but Arnold's hexameters were "still worse."[110]

In language as unrefined as the thought it expressed, the reviewer declared that on questions of both reasoning and scholarship Newman "makes very short work" of Arnold. Although we are frequently told that Homer is in "the grand style," he complained, what the grand style is Arnold never says. "We only learn that Dante and Milton are the only modern poets who have reached it; that Shakespeare has it not, and yet that Shakespeare has the 'supremacy' over Milton; from which we infer that, after all, there is some other style grander, or at least, so to speak, supremer, than 'the grand style' itself." Likewise, on the matter of whether Homer seemed quaint and antiquated to Sophocles, Newman takes "a far broader historical and philological view." He pushes this view too far in his translation, to be sure, but "on the score of history and philology" he "pounds Mr. Arnold to pieces."[111]

In a final, sarcastic outburst, which Thackeray later told Arnold was "the most amusing piece of audacity he ever knew,"[112] the writer called Arnold "a clever man" who "sometimes shows signs not only of cleverness, but of good sense; but all is spoilt . . . by his outrageous self-conceit. The whole of the lectures are one constant I—I—I—*Das grosse ich* reigns from one end to the other." He "has yet to learn," moreover, "that it is possible . . . to point out errors of taste without such monstrous personal insolence as asking 'with whom' a man 'can have lived' "—a question the reviewer had earlier answered as gravely as had the person about whom it had been asked. Despite "all his defects and eccentricities," he concluded, Newman "still remains in most respects . . . much Mr. Arnold's superior."[113]

The "disadvantage" under which his anonymous critic labored, Arnold blandly observed, was "that the subject is not one for . . . violence."[114] Neither was the article one for the retort courteous. It called, rather, for irony. In his reply, therefore, Arnold never accords the *Saturday* the dignity of being referred to by name. It is instead one of Newman's "friends" or "his admirer." But there is never any doubt that the *Saturday Review* is being equated with the *Gazetier Janséniste*, the journal that attacked Montesquieu's great work, the *Esprit des Lois*, and that was "very pretentious, very aggressive, and, when the point to be seized was at all a delicate one, very apt to miss it." Nowhere does the *Saturday* miss it more completely than in its explanation of Newman's diction—"As if he could have got his glossary from the fellows of Balliol!"—or in its inference that there is a style grander than the grand style itself. To the complaint, made by more than one of his critics, that his remarks on the grand style were vague, Arnold at first impatiently responds by declaring that it is like faith ("One must feel it in order to know what it is"), and then in more detail explains, defines, and illustrates it. But for the *Saturday*'s ridicule there is a sharper answer. "How vain to rise up early, and to take rest late," Arnold half-seriously sighs with the Psalmist, "from any zeal for proving [to such a critic] . . . that one poet may be a greater poetical force than another, and yet have a more unequal style."[115]

With his reply to the *Saturday Review*, Arnold answered the last of the major critics of the Homer lectures. In 1864, however, there was another attack, this one by Ichabod Charles Wright, a banker and translator of Dante who had pub-

lished the first part of his translation of the *Iliad* in 1859 only
to have it dismissed by Arnold as repeating "in the main
Cowper's manner" and thus having no "proper reason for existing."[116] Outraged, Wright prepared a thirty-five page pamphlet, most of it in the form of a letter to the dean of Canterbury (who had dedicated his recent version of the *Odyssey*
to Wright), proclaiming the favorable verdict passed upon
his translation by the scholarly tribunal that Arnold himself
had designated as the sole judge: "a truer version of Homer
without the dulness of Cowper" and "Homer himself, speaking in our nervous Saxon English." While unanimously praising Wright's translation, moreover, this same tribunal unanimously rejected Arnold's hexameters. Thus refuted by the
very authorities he had chosen, the "crest-fallen" Arnold now
longed to be rid of these "perishable objects" which had once
been part of the "visions of glory" that "flitted across his soul,
and exalted him in his rapt imagination to a throne inferior
only to that of Homer himself!" The thought of a humiliated
Arnold inspired Wright to compose some wretched doggerel
which he quoted with the superfluous observation that although "not very complimentary" to Arnold it was "tame"
compared with Tennyson's recent attack. The poet laureate,
he exclaimed triumphantly, had "put an extinguisher on the
Poetry-Professor as a writer of Hexameters."[117]

Arnold regarded Wright's pamphlet as being "of no consequence,"[118] and until he reread the offending comment he
thought Wright had "no just cause for complaint."[119] Besides,
the occasion for the pamphlet had already receded several
years into the past, and at the moment Arnold was faced by a
more pressing attack from Fitzjames Stephen. But in the preface to *Essays in Criticism*, which he was preparing for publication early the next year, Arnold found his opportunity for
an appropriate and amusing reply. The phrase, he confessed,
"had, perhaps, too much vivacity." The work of every author
had a right to exist, and an unpopular writer was the last to
call it into question. Wright had enjoyed his revenge, how-

ever, in Tennyson's "remarkable pentameter" with its "exquisite stroke of pleasantry," aimed at one who now returned it
with irony.[120] Furthermore, Wright would view his critic's vivacity more indulgently, Arnold said, turning toward the opponents who had increasingly engaged his attention during
the early sixties, if he saw it as a final sparkle before the world
was plunged into the gloom of Philistinism, ruled by the gravity of the *Guardian* and ennobled by the roaring of the young
lions of the *Daily Telegraph*. In such a future there would be
no more room for Wright's *Iliad* than for Arnold's paradoxes
and hexameters.[121]

Yet there was more than facetiousness in Arnold's reply.
Underlying the humor was a seriousness found in nearly all
his work, and Wright's pamphlet became the means, in a way
illustrative of Arnold's practice in turning adverse criticism to
his own purposes, of commenting on contemporary life and
touching issues broader than personal ones. Thus the address
of Wright's letter to the dean of Canterbury—Mapperley
Hall, Nottingham—acted as a reminder of what Arnold had
said in "The Function of Criticism at the Present Time" about
John Roebuck, Elizabeth Wragg, and a child found dead on
the Mapperley Hills:

> Partly, no doubt, from being crest-fallen, but partly, too, from sin-
> cere contrition for that fault of over-vivacity which I have acknowl-
> edged, I will not raise a finger in self-defence against Mr. Wright's
> blows. I will not even ask him,—what it almost irresistibly rises to
> my lips to ask him when I see he writes from Mapperly,—if he can
> tell me what has become of that poor girl, Wragg? She has been tried,
> I suppose: I know how merciful a view judges and juries are apt to
> take of these cases, so I cannot but hope she has got off. But what I
> should so like to ask is, whether the impression the poor thing made
> was, in general, satisfactory: did she come up to the right standard as
> a member of "the best breed in the whole world?" were her life-
> experiences an edifying testimony to "our unrivalled happiness?"
> did she find Mr. Roebuck's speech a comfort to her in her prison?
> . . .[122]

The Arnold who wrote this passage had noticeably different concerns from the Arnold who three years earlier had delivered a fourth lecture on Homer that "every one thought . . . perfect in tone and convincingness."[123] Even as he prepared the fourth lecture for publication, he was busy correcting proofs of "The Twice Revised Code," which had grown out of his involvement in yet another issue. During the sixties his thoughts had been turning steadily from literary to social and political criticism, from the ancient Greece of Homer and Sophocles to the contemporary England of Wragg and her murdered child. Nevertheless, there is a continuity in his work of this period that derives from a singleness of purpose: to supplant the negative, the mechanical, and the pedantic with the fortifying, the imaginative, and the enlightening. Characteristically, then, in November 1862, two years after the first of the Homer lectures had been given, he described in the same letter both his nightly habit of reading "about a hundred lines of the *Odyssey* to keep [him]self from putrefaction" and his intention of writing an article on a "jejune and technical manner" of dealing with the Bible.[124] The article would be concerned with the bishop of Natal, who had recently done to the Pentateuch what Frank Newman had done to the *Iliad*.

CHAPTER FOUR

Bishop Colenso and the Pentateuch

. . . the more I know of Eastern minds and thought, its luxuriance and inexactness in the commonest statements, the less disposed I am to find difficulties and food for doubt in the things that seem to have thrown poor dear Colenso into a sea of mental trouble and difficulty. —Bishop T. F. McDougall

There are obviously . . . two ways of affecting the minds of men: the one by treating the matter so as to carry it immediately to the sympathies of the many, and the other by aiming at a few select and superior minds. . . .—Wordsworth

. . . there is a duty to speak the truth as well as a duty to withhold it. . . . truth is not truth to those who are unable to use it; no reasonable man would attempt to lay before the illiterate such a question as that concerning the origin of the Gospels. And yet . . . the healthy tone of religion among the poor depends upon freedom of thought and inquiry among the educated.—Benjamin Jowett

I dislike Articles because they represent truth untruly, that is, in an unedifying manner, and thus robbed of its living truth, whilst it retains its mere literal form. . . .—Dr. Thomas Arnold

If Galileo had said in verse that the world moved, the Inquisition might have let him alone.—Thomas Hardy

During his educational mission to the Continent in 1859, Arnold read John Stuart Mill's recently published *On Liberty* and praised it as "worth reading attentively, being one of the few books that inculcate tolerance in an unalarming and inoffensive way."[1] He appears to have read with particular attentiveness the second chapter, where Mill's comments on Christian morality provided him with the point of departure for the essay on Marcus Aurelius four years later. A passage in the chapter that prompted a more famous reply, however, was one in which Mill answered an imaginary opponent of free discussion who argued that the masses need not understand their opinions sufficiently well to defend them as long as there is someone capable of doing so. The Catholic Church, Mill conceded, does indeed so distinguish between clergy and laity: "the clergy . . . may admissibly and meritoriously make themselves acquainted with the arguments of opponents, in order to answer them, and may, therefore, read heretical books; the laity, not unless by special permission, hard to be obtained." But this solution to an "embarrassing problem" is denied to Protestants and is in fact unrealistic in the modern world, where "it is practically impossible that writings which are read by the instructed can be kept from the uninstructed." Furthermore, Mill argued, even the instructed few are adequately informed only when everything can "be written and published without restraint."[2]

The following year Mill's thesis was put to its first significant test by the seven authors of *Essays and Reviews*. In an introductory statement, they expressed hope that the volume would "be received as an attempt to illustrate the advantage derivable to the cause of religious and moral truth, from a free handling, in a becoming spirit, of subjects peculiarly liable to suffer by the repetition of conventional language, and from traditional methods of treatment," and throughout the volume they stressed the desirability of free inquiry. Thus in the first essay, "The Education of the World," Frederick Temple, headmaster of Rugby, wrote:

He is guilty of high treason against the faith who fears the result of any investigation, whether philosophical, or scientific, or historical. And therefore nothing should be more welcome than the extension of knowledge of any and every kind—for every increase in our accumulations of knowledge throws fresh light upon these the real problems of our day. If geology proves to us that we must not interpret the first chapters of Genesis literally; if historical investigations shall show us that inspiration, however it may protect the doctrine, yet was not empowered to protect the narrative of the inspired writers from occasional inaccuracy; if careful criticism shall prove that there have been occasionally interpolations and forgeries in that Book, as in many others; the results should still be welcome.[3]

Nor should this freedom of inquiry be restricted to the laity. Henry Bristow Wilson, who in his Bampton Lectures of 1851 had "scandalized many of the Heads of Houses" with his demand for theological freedom[4] and who later would be tried and acquitted as one of the "Septem Contra Christum," argued that "the freedom of opinion which belongs to the English citizen should be conceded to the English Churchman; and the freedom which is already practically enjoyed by the members of the congregation, cannot without injustice be denied to its ministers." Still, the Essayists were aware that anyone who advanced novel or unpopular religious views invited opposition and thus risked martyrdom in the cause of freedom. To one so martyred, Benjamin Jowett could offer only the imperfect solace with which the final essay concluded: "He may depart hence before the natural term, worn out with intellectual toil; regarded with suspicion by many of his contemporaries; yet not without a sure hope that the love of truth, which men of saintly lives often seem to slight, is, nevertheless, accepted before God."[5]

The prophetic force of these words was evident in the heated controversy that followed the publication of *Essays and Reviews*. But it was even more strikingly evident two years later, in October 1862, when John William Colenso, bishop of Natal, published the first volume of *The Pentateuch and Book of Joshua Critically Examined* and precipitated one of the bitterest theological disputes of the century. Ruskin had rightly predicted that the outcry over *Essays and Reviews* would be "nothing to it."[6]

Colenso, a conscientious, serious-minded, unimaginative man, had grown up in a predominantly Evangelical and Nonconformist environment where he appears at first to have wavered between the Anglican and the Independent ministries. At the age of sixteen, however, he made his decision on grounds that would later prove ironic. "I am now . . . fully convinced," he wrote to an aunt in 1830,

> that a Church minister may be a man of God; and his opportunities of being useful must far exceed those of a Dissenting one. The first, and a very striking, advantage (so, at least, it appears to me) of the Church minister over the Independent is his actual *Independence*. There are not so many bigots in the Church as there used to be, nor have the bishops the same tyrannical power which they used to have over the body of which they represent the head. . . . When once the Church minister is settled in his church, unless guilty of some heinous dereliction of duty, he cannot be expelled. . . . Not so, however, with the Independent. He must preach not what he likes, but what his congregation likes: he must obey the voice of his flock, and in too many instances the flock turns out a flock of wolves in sheep's clothing. . . .[7]

After taking his degree at Cambridge, he was for several years mathematics tutor at Harrow and at St. John's College, writing textbooks, J. A. Symonds complained, with "stupid long proofs & demonstrations which might have been made simple & clear in a moment if he would have been a little less scientific."[8] Later he served as rector of Forncett St. Mary in Norfolk until he was appointed in 1853 the first bishop of the newly created diocese of Natal. It was a difficult position and one not much sought after, a recent writer has observed, and despite the implicit warning contained in the dedication of his *Village Sermons* to the heterodox Maurice,[9] Colenso must have seemed to those responsible for the appointment a man of zeal and dedication who would be capable of having the desired effect upon the Zulus. They had no reason at the time to consider the effect the Zulus would have upon him.[10]

That effect was made known early in 1861 in a letter from Colenso to Dr. Harold Browne, then Norrisian Professor at Cambridge and later bishop of Winchester:

While translating the story of the Flood, I have had a simple-minded, but intelligent, native—one with the docility of a child, but the reasoning powers of mature age—look up, and ask, "Is all that true? Do you really believe that all this happened thus,—that all the beasts, and birds, and creeping things upon the earth, large and small, from hot countries and cold, came thus by pairs, and entered into the ark with Noah? And did Noah gather food for them *all*, for the beasts and birds of prey, as well as for the rest?" My heart answered in the words of the prophet, "Shall a man speak lies in the name of the Lord?" I dared not do so. . . . I felt that I dared not, as a servant of the God of Truth, urge my brother-man to believe that which I did not myself believe, which I knew to be untrue as a matter-of-fact historical narrative.

Colenso "was thus driven—against my will at first, I may truly say—to search more deeply into these questions," and now he would "tremble" at the results of his inquiries were it not for his belief in a God of Truth who rewarded those who sought Him: "Our duty, surely, is to follow the truth wherever it leads us, and to leave the consequences in the hands of God."[11]

A clear sign of the direction in which truth was leading Colenso was provided the following summer by the publication of *St. Paul's Epistle to the Romans Newly Translated and Explained from the Missionary Point of View*, in the course of which he challenged the doctrines of atonement and eternal punishment and so invited some of the opposition he later encountered.[12] Robert Gray, bishop of Cape Town, denounced it as "full of the most objectionable views, . . . entirely substituting a new scheme for the received system of Christianity,"[13] and the *Guardian* declared that it uttered "words to the English public which no Churchman, least of all a Bishop, should ever have put together."[14] By this time Colenso's friends were alarmed by the bent of his biblical inquiries, and when they learned that he planned next an attack upon the Pentateuch, they tried to persuade him not to publish it. His brother-in-law, Bishop McDougall, even pointed explicitly to the contradiction underlying the entire work: Colenso could believe in a miraculous occurrence but not in faulty arithmetic.[15] He was not to be dissuaded, however, and thus in 1862 provoked the controversy that eventually led to his deposition and excommunication by Bishop Gray (decisions later reversed by the Privy Council) and to a host of replies to his work. Most of these, such as *The Pentateuchal Narrative Vindicated from the Absurdities Charged Against It by the Bishop of Natal* and *The Increase of the Israelites in Egypt Shewn to be` Probable from the Statistics of Modern Populations, with an Examination of Bishop Colenso's Calculations on This Subject*,[16] are preserved today as little more than quaint titles. But one of the replies has survived—that of Arnold, whose position in the controversy was a puzzling anomaly to a public that knew him as the son of the liberal Thomas Arnold and the author of *Empedocles on Etna*.

I

Less than a month after the appearance of Colenso's volume, Arnold had already planned an answer, for on November 19 he told his mother of his intention

to write an article called "The Bishop and the Philosopher," contrasting Colenso and Co.'s jejune and technical manner of dealing with Biblical controversy with that of Spinoza in his famous treatise on the *Interpretation of Scripture*, with a view of showing how, the heresy on both sides being equal, Spinoza broaches his in that edifying and pious spirit by which alone the treatment of such matters can be made fruitful, while Colenso and the English Essayists, from their narrowness and want of power, more than from any other cause, do not.[17]

Published in the January issue of *Macmillan's Magazine*, the article begins on a familiar note as Arnold once again contrasts the critical spirit of the Continent with the uncritical spirit of England: while "educated Europe" watched with "a titter," the English performed "a great public act of self-humiliation" by sending forth the bishop of Natal as their "scapegoat into the wilderness." But here ends the reminiscence of the second lecture on Homer, for it soon becomes clear that Arnold is claiming for literary criticism a wider province and a greater authority than he had previously claimed. Literary criticism is now the "appointed guardian" of "the general culture of single nations" and "of the world at large," and its function is to "try books as to the influence which they are calculated to have" upon this culture. All books, to be sure, undergo a specialized criticism—theological works by theologians, historical works by historians, philosophical works by philosophers—but they must undergo literary criticism as well. Accordingly, Arnold judges the work of Colenso not from the theological point of view, but from the point of view of its influence on the "general culture."[18]

And how is this influence to be determined? There are but two criteria: the work in question must either edify the uninformed many or instruct the educated few. A third possibility —enlightenment of the many by removing their prejudices— is disallowed:

The highly-instructed few, and not the scantily-instructed many, will ever be the organ to the human race of knowledge and truth. Knowledge and truth, in the full sense of the words, are not attainable by the great mass of the human race at all. The great mass of the human race have to be softened and humanised through their heart and imagination, before any soil can be found in them where knowledge may strike living roots. Until the softening and humanising process is very far advanced, intellectual demonstrations are uninforming for them; and, if they impede the working of influences which advance this softening and humanising process, they are even noxious; they retard their development, they impair the culture of the world. . . . Old moral ideas leaven and humanise the multitude: new intellectual ideas filter slowly down to them from the thinking few; and only when they reach them in this manner do they adjust themselves to their practice without convulsing it. It was not by the intellectual truth of its propositions concerning purgatory, or prayer for the dead, or the human nature of the Virgin Mary, that the Reformation touched and advanced the multitude: it was by the moral truth of its protest against the sale of indulgences, and the scandalous lives of many of the clergy.

Colenso's work, therefore, cannot be justified on the ground that it informs the little-instructed many unless it does so in such a manner as to edify them. That it fails to afford this edification Colenso himself seems aware, for he speaks of the need *"to fill up the aching void* which will undoubtedly be felt at first." And for the "comfort and support of troubled minds under present circumstances" he provides only his own commentary on the Epistle to the Romans, two chapters of Exodus, some noble words of Cicero, the truths revealed to the Sikh Gooroos, and a Hindu prayer.[19]

Nor is Colenso's work more successful in informing the few than in edifying the many. It was for the instructed few, in fact, rather than the uninstructed many that he intended the arithmetical demonstrations that, as Arnold presents them, produced the following results:

"Allowing 20 as the marriageable age, how many years are required for the production of 3 generations?" The answer to that sum disposes (on the Bishop's plan) of the Book of Genesis. Again, as to the account in the Book of Exodus of the Israelites dwelling in tents —*"Allowing 10 persons for each tent (and a Zulu hut in Natal contains on an average only 3½), how many tents would 2,000,000 persons require?"* The parenthesis in that problem is hardly worthy of such a master of arithmetical statement as Dr. Colenso; but, with or without the parenthesis, the problem, when answered, disposes of the Book of Exodus. Again, as to the account in Leviticus of the provision made for the priests: *"If three priests have to eat 264 pigeons a day, how many must each priest eat?"* That disposes of Leviticus. Take Numbers, and the total of first-borns there given, as compared with the number of male adults: *"If, of 900,000 males, 22,273 are first-borns, how many boys must there be in each family?"* That disposes of Numbers. For Deuteronomy, take the number of lambs slain at the Sanctuary, as compared with the space for slaying them: *"In an area of 1,692 square yards, how many lambs per minute can 150,000 persons kill in two hours?"* Certainly not 1,250, the number required: and the Book of Deuteronomy, therefore, shares the fate of its predecessors. *Omnes eodem cogimur.*[20]

Colenso, as A. O. J. Cockshut observes, did "answer the question, what is the value of the Bible as a mathematical treatise?"[21] But in his unawareness that the educated few had long

known what he himself had only recently discovered, he failed
to answer the questions Arnold asked:

What follows from all this? What change is it, if true, to produce in
the relations of mankind to the Christian religion? If the old theory
of Scripture Inspiration is to be abandoned, what place is the Bible
henceforth to hold among books? What is the new Christianity to be
like? How are Governments to deal with national Churches founded
to maintain a very different conception of Christianity?

It is questions like these that must be answered if the higher
culture is to be informed but that Colenso "never touches with
one of his fingers."[22]

Against Colenso's work Arnold places the *Tractatus Theologico-Politicus* of Spinoza, to whose "positive and vivifying
atmosphere" he had taken himself "with profit" as early as
1850.[23] Unlike Colenso, Spinoza wrote in Latin, the language
of the instructed few, and therefore made impossible any dis-
turbance of the uninstructed many. Even for the members of
the higher culture who shared the prejudices of the multitude,
moreover, he prefaced a warning not to read his book. Unlike
Colenso, again, Spinoza "was moved to write, not by admiration at the magnitude of his own sudden discoveries, not by
desire for notoriety, not by a transport of excitement, . . . but
because, grave as was the task to be attempted, and slight as
was the hope of succeeding, the end seemed to him worth all
the labour and all the risk." Where Colenso loves to dwell
among verbal problems that are to him "a sort of intellectual
land of Beulah" and would devote folios to the sums in Ezra
"should God, in His providence, call him to continue the
work," for Spinoza "the interesting question is, not whether
the fanatical devotee of the letter is to continue, for a longer
or for a shorter time, to believe that Moses sate in the land of
Moab writing the description of his own death, but what he is
to believe when he does not believe this." The doctrine presented by Spinoza is not, to be sure, the doctrine of any Christian church; but he was neither a member nor a minister of any
church:

When he claimed for Churchmen the widest latitude of speculation in religious matters, he was inviting Governments to construct a new Church; he was not holding office in an old Church under articles expressly promulgated to check "disputations, altercations, or questions." The Bishop of Natal cries out, that orders in the Church of England without full liberty of speculation are an intolerable yoke. But he is thus crying out for a new Church of England, which is not that in which he has voluntarily taken office. He forgets that the clergy of a Church with formularies like those of the Church of England, exist in virtue of their relinquishing in religious matters full liberty of speculation. Liberal potentates of the English Church, who so loudly sound the praises of freedom of inquiry, forget it also.

Before the tribunal of literary criticism, however, Colenso is condemned not because his personal position is false, but because his work, like Ichabod Wright's translation of Homer, has no justification for existing:

When, in 1861, he heard for the first time that the old theory of the verbal inspiration of Scripture was untenable, he should, instead of proclaiming this news (if this was all he could proclaim) in an octavo volume, have remembered that excellent saying of the Wise Man: If thou hast heard a word, let it die with thee; and be bold, it will not burst thee."[24]

II

Lady de Rothschild told Arnold that she "thought the Colenso article too strong,"[25] and Arnold was at first inclined to agree. "The tone . . . is a little sharper than I could wish," he confided to his mother, "but the man is really such a goose that it is difficult not to say sharp things of him. I get an opportunity of saying a good word of Stanley, Keble, and one or two other friends, and of giving a rap over the knuckles to one or two who are not friends."[26] Later, however, he was "pleased with this performance . . . and glad of the opportunity of saying what [he] had to say,"[27] because, as he explained to the archbishop of York, the article had been primarily aimed not at Colenso, who was merely a "blunderer" and "an innocent," but at those "Liberal potentates" who were exploiting him: "if it had not been that a certain section of Liberals was making capital out of Colenso, and that this section is, in my opinion, far more able and disposed to damage the cause of true culture, which is the same as the cause of true religion, than Recordism is, I should have left Colenso's book unspoiled."[28]

This is why it will not do simply to dismiss "The Bishop and the Philosopher" as a "flagrantly unreasonable onslaught"[29] or as "supercilious ridicule."[30] For despite the *argumentum ad hominem* occasionally directed at Colenso, who would hardly have accepted an obscure bishopric had he desired notoriety, to do so is to take Arnold both too seriously and too lightly: on the one hand to miss the irony of his vivacities, nowhere more felicitous than here, and on the other hand to ignore the gravity with which he viewed the religious crisis of his time. To level the charge of unfairness, moreover, is to confuse the issue. To his contemporaries no less than to Arnold—and contemporary testimony is almost unanimous on this point—Colenso's work was "ruthlessly negative."[31] Indeed, if the question of fairness must be raised, one should submit that a century after its publication, the slender little volume appears very much as Arnold first described it. Though earnest and doubtless of some historical importance, it remains a naive, pedestrian, and unintelligent piece of biblical criticism, moving from a portentous introduction ("Most gladly would I have turned away from all such investigations as these, if I *could* have done so,—as, in fact, I did, until I could do so no longer"[32]) to such trivial conclusions as that the camp of the Israelites was too large for the observance of the Levitical law to carry out dung daily, or that whereas in the wilderness the people were supplied with manna, no provision seems to have been made for feeding their cattle. But the real issue is neither the merit of Colenso's work nor Arnold's justification in condemning it. Rather, it is Arnold's presentation of a doctrine that rests on a number of debatable and not wholly consistent assumptions.

Of these the most obvious concerns the distinction between the little-instructed many and the much-instructed few. The distinction is perhaps less invidious than it might at first appear, for it reflects a major problem that an expanding democracy posed for the Victorian age. At the same time, however, it was clearly anachronistic, as Mill had already pointed out and as James Martineau would later argue in defending one of his own books:

So long as for certain subjects Latin remained the literary language of Europe it was easy to address a selected audience by writing *ad cleros* in Latin, *ad populum* in the *vernacular* tongue. But now that every book must be accessible to every reader, the choice lies between total suppression or free utterance of conviction. I cannot see that we are entrusted with any right of suppression when once profoundly convinced of a truth not yet within others' reach.[33]

This dilemma faced by the biblical critic had been epitomized in an encounter between Mark Pattison and John Henry Newman soon after the publication of *Essays and Reviews*. At first terrified that Newman would condemn his contribution to the volume, Pattison was relieved when Newman distinguished between "speculations broadcast upon the general public . . ., unsettling their faith without offering them anything else to rest upon," and "theological speculation . . . addressed to learned theologians." But on reflection, Pattison immediately saw the hollowness of the distinction: if one writes in Latin "he will remain unread; and if he publishes an English dissertation any one who can buy the book may read it."[34] Nor was Newman's distinction in total accord with a passage from his own *Essay on the Development of Christian Doctrine* (1845) that had expressed an even graver objection. Commenting on Locke's definition of love of truth as the refusal to entertain a proposition with greater assurance than proof of it warrants, Newman had protested that such a view

cut off from the possibility and the privilege of faith all but the educated few, all but the learned, the clear-headed, the men of practised intellects and balanced minds, men who had leisure, who had opportunities of consulting others, and kind and wise friends to whom they deferred. How could a religion ever be Catholic, if it was to be called credulity or enthusiasm in the multitude to use those ready instruments of belief, which alone Providence had put into their power?[35]

The distinction between the few and the many is open to yet another objection. In denying that religious books are justified in seeking to inform the uninstructed, Arnold declares that the masses are incapable of attaining knowledge and truth "in the full sense of the words" (which does not explain why a book may not attempt partial enlightenment) and must be "softened and humanised" in preparation for enlightenment. It is not clear precisely how this softening and humanizing process achieves the desired result or who directs it, but Arnold's basic point remains unaffected: he is objecting in part to the timing of Colenso's work. It is the same point Newman would later make in his *Apologia*:

In reading ecclesiastical history, when I was an Anglican, it used to be forcibly brought home to me, how the initial error of what afterwards became heresy was the urging forward some truth against the prohibition of authority at an unseasonable time. There is a time for every thing, and many a man desires a reformation of an abuse, or the fuller development of a doctrine, or the adoption of a particular policy, but forgets to ask himself whether the right time for it is come.[36]

The right time, according to Arnold, is after moral ideas have had a leavening effect on the multitude. But exactly when has this leavening effect been accomplished? Were the masses still raw when Colenso began publishing his study of the Pentateuch, but humanized a decade later when Arnold published *Literature and Dogma*? Granting the point, however, by what means do intellectual ideas reach the masses after moral ideas have done their work? Arnold later attempted an answer when he declared that Spinoza and Galileo left their speculations "to filter down gradually (if true) into the common thought of mankind.''[37] But the all-important parenthesis begs the question. How does one verify Spinoza's statement, "The Bible contains much that is mere history, and, like all history, sometimes true, sometimes false," unless there is a Colenso to examine the historicity of the Pentateuch? And, finally, just how are these intellectual ideas to be adjusted to the life of the˘ multitude "without convulsing it"? Presumably in this instance by an affirmative, constructive approach to the biblical problem. But how may this approach be made until after some destructive work has been completed? Was Arnold's work in biblical criticism possible without, for example, Strauss's?

The question is further complicated by the fact that Arnold is objecting not only to the timing of Colenso's work, but also to his assuming prerogatives that, as a clergyman in the Church of England, he has surrendered. This was precisely the position of the *Guardian*, which in December 1862 accused Colenso of dishonesty in retaining his bishopric:

It is high time that amiable and conscientious persons such as he is, cease to deceive themselves by the shallow talk with which he closes his preface about the Church "representing the religious life of the nation" and "requiring to protest against all perversions of the truth, etc." The Church of England is a religious society which takes pledges as to the tenets of her office bearers before she commissions them. In truth no religious society can be carried on at all except on some such plan as this. It is not open to an honourable man to accept her places of influence and dignity and then to employ these advantages in abandoning the very principles on which she is founded.[38]

The following February, forty-one bishops addressed a letter to Colenso in which they said that "the inconsistency between the office you hold and the opinions you avow is causing great pain and grievous scandal to the Church."[39]

At the opposite pole was John Stuart Mill, who in his inaugural address at St. Andrews several years later was to argue:

If all were to desert the Church who put a large and liberal construction on its terms of communion, or who would wish to see those terms widened, the national provision for religious teaching and worship would be left utterly to those who take the narrowest, the most literal, and purely textual view of the formularies. . . . Almost all the illustrious reformers of religion began by being clergymen, but they did not think that their profession as clergymen was inconsistent with their being reformers.[40]

Among these reformers was Bishop Tait of London, the "Liberal potentate" whom Arnold had rapped over the knuckles and whose vacillation concerning *Essays and Reviews* had elicited an angry rebuke from Frederick Temple:

Many years ago you urged us from the University pulpit to undertake the critical study of the Bible. You said that it was a dangerous study, but indispensable. . . . Such a study, so full of difficulties, imperatively demands freedom for its condition. To tell a man to study, and yet bid him, under heavy penalties, come to the same conclusions with those who have not studied, is to mock him. If the conclusions are prescribed, the study is precluded.[41]

It was again the indecisive Tait who, having expressed concern about Colenso's first volume, found himself quoted in the preface to the second:

As to free inquiry, what shall we do with it? Shall we frown upon it, denounce it, try to stifle it? This will do no good, even if it be right. But after all we are Protestants. We have been accustomed to speak a good deal of the right and duty of private judgment. It was *by the exercise of this right, and the discharge of this duty*, that our fathers freed their and our souls from Rome's time-honoured falsehoods.[42]

A. P. Stanley agreed. In the *Edinburgh Review* of April 1861, he had deplored the idea that "truth was made for the laity and falsehood for the clergy—that truth is tolerable everywhere except in the mouths of the ministers of the God of Truth—that falsehood, driven from every other corner of the educated world, may find an honoured refuge behind the consecrated bulwarks of the sanctuary."[43] And although he read Arnold's Colenso paper "with great interest—great admiration," he was "evidently annoyed," Arnold wrote to his mother,

that I should treat any amount of freedom of speculation as unorthodox for an English clergyman, and particularly annoyed by my touch at Tait. But when in a conservative country like this shall we ever get the Church of England enlarged so long as her authorities keep crying out uncontradicted that there is room for all in her at present, and perfect liberty of thought and speech—which there is *not*. I asked him in my answer why Tait should be at London House rather than John Mill, except because he had consented to serve the State as a public instructor on terms of less ample liberty than John Mill would demand.[44]

If this is true, then Colenso is presented with only a fictitious choice when he is required either to edify the many or to instruct the few, for he is not entitled to the freedom of speculation enjoyed by an isolated thinker like Spinoza. Indeed, Arnold said, a clergyman in the 1860s could be in a sound position only by abstaining altogether from "dealing with speculative matters" or by confining himself "to such matters as Stanley does" or "to pure edification." To write "for or against Colenso," on the other hand, put him "inevitably in a false position."[45] With "The Function of Criticism at the Present Time" behind us, we can see the point toward which Arnold is moving—the necessity for disinterestedness if there is to be fruitful inquiry. But how is this ever to be achieved in religious matters? "It may be time," Arnold suggests, "for the State to institute, as its national clergy, a corporation enjoying the most absolute freedom of inquiry."[46] Meanwhile, apparently, the Colensos must remain silent, and it is not clear why the state would institute reform unless they spoke out, as Colenso continued to do, declaring that he intended "to fight the battle of liberty of thought and speech for the clergy."[47]

There is one final objection to the thesis advanced by "The Bishop and the Philosopher." Its major pronouncements are made not in the name of Matthew Arnold, but in the name of "literary criticism." Arnold speaks merely as a "humble citizen" of the "Republic of Letters." Not he, but this Republic determines whether a religious book edifies the many or informs the few. This elaborate fiction contains a patent contradiction, of course, for after disclaiming any intention to subject Colenso's work to specialized criticism, the Republic of Letters ridicules him for having only recently discovered inconsistencies in the Pentateuch that the educated few had long since been aware of. But the principal difficulty is the delegation to literary criticism of power to pass final judgment from a position of magisterial anonymity. Aside from the immense pretensions of this claim, there is its obvious impossibility. Literary criticism is an abstraction and as such is as incapable of judging Colenso's book as it is of writing it.

III

Much of the doctrine presented by "The Bishop and the Philosopher," therefore, is tentative, imprecise, in the air. And here it might have remained had it not been for the response of the periodical press and for Arnold's sensitivity to his critics. His conscience, to be sure, "a little smote" him, he later confessed, "with having been . . . too purely negative and intellectual on such a subject,"[48] and it is this penitent spirit that helps account for the somewhat altered tone in his anonymous review of Robert Willis's translation of the *Tractatus Theologico-Politicus*, published in the *London Review* of December 27, 1862. Here Colenso is still an object of ridicule, but the irony is more restrained: in Spinoza, Arnold says, the reader will find, "if not so much arithmetic, at least a more interesting strain of criticism." Even Colenso's claim to free inquiry escapes censure: "Recent events . . . have powerfully called public attention to critical examinations of Scripture." And, finally, in condemning Willis's incompetent translation, Arnold seems excessively aware of his negative position in the review: "we have been compelled to perform a task which is revolting to us, and . . . we find ourselves with these hangman's hands."[49]

Still, it was the public outcry against "The Bishop and the Philosopher" and not Arnold's pangs of conscience that contributed most to modifying his thesis. The points at issue were early defined in the *Spectator* of December 27, which protested that a distinction between truth that edifies the many and truth that instructs the few implies that these truths "do not *command* the mind at all, or they would not permit you to shelve them so quietly in these mental cupboards," and it assumes that you can "decide, in God's place, what truth is fitted for the common herd, and what for your intellectual aristocracy." Such a distinction is "absolutely counter" to the spirit of Christianity, for it advocates "a reserved esoteric teaching for the few, and a purposely alloyed gospel for the many." Although Colenso's book is misleading and does not contribute to an understanding of the revelation contained in the Bible, he is nevertheless "far nearer to the frame of mind of a servant of the truth, with his energetic, critical arithmetic, than Mr. Arnold, with his aristocratic forbearance from injuring the prejudices of the multitude." There can be but one conclusion to a faith like Arnold's, the *Spectator* said in a comment foreshadowing its attitude toward the apostle of culture in the late sixties: the intellectual aristocracy will soon wish

> to live and lie reclined
> On the hills like Gods together, careless of mankind.[50]

The next issue of the *Spectator* continued the attack on Arnold's position with a long, incoherent letter from Frederick Denison Maurice,[51] that deeply spiritual but sometimes unintelligible divine[52] who had been driven by the controversy into an agony of soul-searching. Torn between his friendship with Colenso, who a decade earlier had defended him against the charge of heresy, and his utter disapproval of Colenso's work, with its "quantity of criticism about the dung in the Jewish camp, and the division of a hare's foot,"[53] Maurice chose to remain publicly silent. But, as he later explained, he felt compelled to write to the *Spectator* in protest against Arnold's doctrine. It "threatened to make human letters, exclusive, not humane," he said; it left "the vulgar only religious feelings which need not have any basis of truth"; and it "asserted for Spinoza and other illustrious men an isolation . . . which . . . they must have lamented as their bitterest calamity."[54]

Maurice's reticence about Colenso was responsible for the spread of the controversy the following week to the *Examiner*, which Arnold regarded as "the organ of the regular English liberal of the Miss Martineau type."[55] An outraged correspondent identifying himself as "Anti-Esotericus" wrote to complain that Maurice had given Arnold's article undeserved praise. The distinction between instruction and edification, he remarked sarcastically, was a "recondite subtlety" that became, when stripped of "all the solemn pomp and parade" with which it was presented, only "a coarse and clumsy distinction." Even so, however, it failed to conceal the fact that Colenso provides both. He instructs by "explaining to those who do not know it that the Pentateuch is not to be read as an authentic history, but as a narrative full of divine instruction in morals and religion," and he edifies by presenting "to those who do know it, but who dissemble their knowledge, . . . an example of honesty and truthfulness."[56]

The following week the *Examiner* itself entered the controversy with what Arnold described as a "furious" middle article denouncing "the jesuitical doctrine that truths of religion are for a select circle of *cognoscenti*, and that the vulgar are not to be disturbed in possession of convenient fictions tending to the support of an irrational faith." A doctrine so distinguishing between the few and the many—by the latter, according to the *Examiner*, Arnold means "pigs"—explains "the displeasure with which Professor Arnold's article . . . is

spoken of by liberal men of all shades of religious opinion."[57]
In the same issue of the *Examiner* was a letter from another
correspondent objecting to Arnold's "unfairness to Bishop
Colenso" and to the "dishonesty in his treatment of the question" and lamenting that "a son of Dr. Arnold" should be
among "the bigots" who persecuted "the public expression
of opinion."[58] A week later this theme was taken up and developed at length in a second letter from Anti-Esotericus:

> Can it be possible that a son of Dr. Arnold can belong to those
> timid pseudo-liberals who seek to divert attention from their own
> suspected latitudinarianism, or to excuse their pusillanimous reticence,
> by vilipending the productions of men who do not hesitate to im-
> peril their prosperity, and almost their subsistence, rather than burthen
> their consciences with what would be, as regards their own sense of
> the truth, a *suppressio veri?*[59]

Within the privacy of personal correspondence the liberal
reaction to "The Bishop and the Philosopher" was still more
angrily expressed. A. V. Dicey, the well-known jurist, said
bluntly that Arnold had "acted in an unworthy way."[60] Colenso, feeling hurt and somehow betrayed that his friend Alexander Macmillan should have published the article, protested
that it was "flippant and conceited."[61] J. A. Symonds agreed
with A. O. Rutson that it was "abominably bumptious, swag-
gering, & illiberal," and Sir Edward Strachey was sufficiently
"fired up" about it to write to the *Spectator*. But the stir it had
created, Symonds maliciously added, was precisely what was
wanted by the "egotistical" Arnold with his "contemptible
selfconsciousness."[62]

Meanwhile the controversy had reached the *Saturday Review*, which Arnold thought "civil" and promising of "actual
friendliness"[63] because of its concession that "there is a great
deal more than conceit or arrogance in this claim of the educated few." The doctrine as a whole it rejected as invalid, however, first because the spread of education has made writing
for the few impossible, and second because the requirement

either to instruct the few or to edify the many is "a mere arbitrary canon." Furthermore, the paper thought, the distinction
is a fundamentally mistaken one, advocating a culture of the
few which is "very superficial, and does the nation very little
good."[64]

The article in the *Saturday Review* was apparently the cause
of a shrill and confused denunciation of Arnold published
two weeks later in the *London Review*, which described the
Saturday as a pretentious journal that liked to think of itself
as representative of the "instructed few." If Arnold's principles were carried out, it said, a typical issue of the *Saturday*
would contain "three or four articles and one or two reviews,
written in crabbed Latin, promulgating frightful heresies for
the instructed few," and if Arnold was right "that in the matter of religious belief the great mass of mankind ought to be
guided entirely by their feelings, and by the authority of the
few who happen to be highly instructed, and that they have
nothing to do with any direct evidence of the truth or falsehood of their opinions," then Christianity was "a great mistake" and the Reformation "a piece of impertinence."[65]

The *London Review* was not alone in directing attention
to Arnold's heterodoxy, although its significance was interpreted in various ways. The *Nonconformist*, on the one hand,
saw in his being no "suspiciously orthodox critic" support for
its own pronouncement that Colenso's was "the most ignorant, stupid, and impertinent book that we ever read."[66] *John
Bull*, on the other hand, caustically noted that if the gospel of
Spinoza that Arnold praised was not the good news brought
by the angels of scripture, the shepherds to whom they
brought it were after all not among the "instructed few."[67]
And when the *English Churchman*'s description of Arnold's
article as "judicious" elicited from a surprised correspondent
the objection that Arnold was really "recommending us to
take the avowed infidel Spinosa as our great oracle in these
perplexing investigations," the paper explained with embar-
rassment that it had intended only a literary judgment: "Had

we entered fully into the theological consideration, we should have expressed as little satisfaction with it."[68]

Such was the reaction of the press to "The Bishop and the Philosopher." Despite its almost unanimous disapproval, however, Arnold enjoyed support from David Masson, the editor of *Macmillan's Magazine*, who had "strongly" approved the article;[69] from Alexander Macmillan, the head of the publishing firm, who thought that Arnold had written an "admirable paper" about a book that would not "serve any useful purpose";[70] and from "many serious people, Dissenters and churchmen," who had "understood the drift" of the article and were "greatly pleased with it." Yet following his usual practice, Arnold kept a close eye on the response in the periodicals, planning an answer but waiting as long as he could so "that as many adversaries as possible [might] show [him] their hand."[71]

IV

The answer was not at all what Arnold's critics might have expected. It was so different, in fact, that he rightly believed the newspapers would "not quite know what to make of this last position of [his]."[72] Ostensibly, it was a review of the first volume of *Lectures on the History of the Jewish Church*, by A. P. Stanley, whom Ruskin once praised for getting on "more easily" than Colenso "by consummate tact, and uttering his heresies in the least startling manner."[73] His book, Arnold declared, "meant for all the world to read," both edified and informed and was thus welcomed by one who "had been reproached with denying to an honest clergyman freedom to speak the truth" and "misrepresented as wishing to make religious truth the property of an aristocratic few, while to the multitude is thrown the sop of any convenient fiction."[74] Here the true nature of the article is disclosed: it is a defense of the thesis by which Colenso was condemned, and as such it is one of Arnold's most skillful polemical works. Where the former article was ironic and supercilious, the latter adopts a solemn

tone befitting the religious issue and scrupulously avoids ridicule. Where the former seemed deliberately designed to provoke attack, the latter conscientiously seeks to mollify. And
where the former rested on assumptions regarded as absolute
truths, the latter is both more modest and more moderate,
explaining and qualifying what earlier was imprecisely
stated. At the same time, however, Arnold still fails to clarify
his doctrine completely, and he so retracts as to leave it in
some essentials as inconsistent as before.

The most apparent of his modifications concerns the distinction between the few and the many. Wishing to remove the
offensive implications of this dichotomy, Arnold now speaks
of the few not as dangerous freethinkers who enjoy a special
privilege, but as a group who seek the ideal life through the
intellect, and of the many not as the vulgar multitude who
should remain in ignorance, but as a group who seek the ideal
life through religion. Yet this is not the distinction with
which Arnold began, a distinction between levels of enlightenment rather than ways of life; and although it removes a
major cause of objection, it involves Arnold in further difficulties, for it eventually forces him to make still another division, this one tripartite. There are now the few, the "educated
minority," and the "least-instructed." The few, Arnold explains in reply to Maurice's "remarkable letter" (one of the
few touches of irony he allowed himself in the article) and to
the *Saturday Review*, "are not a great class, but a few individuals" who live in an "austere isolation" from which they "address an imaginary audience of their mates." Obviously this
is an altogether different group from the "educated Europe"
that Colenso had at first failed to inform. And the "educated
minority," far from demanding only instruction, now "ask
and need to be edified" when "they enter the sphere of religion."[75] Thus the original doctrine that a religious book must
either inform the instructed few or edify the uninstructed
many has become meaningless.

If this is so, then on what grounds is Colenso still to be

condemned? Arnold's answer takes him into yet another distinction, one that grows out of his distinction between the sphere of pure speculation and the sphere of religion. Each sphere has ideas proper to itself, and what is true in one may be false in another—when, for example, an idea is taken from the sphere of speculation and placed in the sphere of religion without being harmonized with ideas already there. It was because Colenso's work failed to effect this harmony that he was censured. We can see that Arnold is moving toward one of his favorite themes—the distinction between absolute and relative truths—but here it is too loosely stated to be persuasive. He suggests, for instance, that Spinoza's statement, "The Bible contains much that is mere history, and, like all history, sometimes true, sometimes false," has meaning on both the absolute and the relative level. But surely this is not so; unless we alter the generally accepted meanings of its key words, the statement is either true or false on the only level on which it can be read. Nor is it more accurate to say, as Arnold does, that Galileo's statement that the earth moves would have become a falsehood in spite of its absolute truth if it had been applied "so as to impair the value of the Book of Joshua for the religious life of Christendom."[76] Arnold intends, of course, to distinguish between truths of science and truths of religion, but the relative truth of Galileo's statement nevertheless depends not on the biblical use to which it is put, but on the answer to the question, "Moves in relation to what?"

Arnold would probably have protested that he spoke in a literary rather than in a scientific sense, that the judgment of Colenso's work was made by literary criticism and not by a specialized scientific criticism. Yet even here his method is inconsistent, failing to define precisely the role of literary criticism. He admits, for example, that criticism does not determine whether the few are justified in living "an existence separate from that of the mass of mankind." But no sooner has he said this, as E. K. Brown pointed out,[77] than he removes the qualification by describing "this purely intellectual life, when really followed, as justified so far as the jurisdiction of criticism extends, and even admirable." Again, Arnold confesses that literary criticism "too readily falls" into ridicule. But if it is capable of so erring, how was it able to assume an air of infallibility in ridiculing Colenso? Or again, we are told that "literary criticism takes no account of a doctrine's novelty or heterodoxy."[78] But this is clearly false, for the whole point of its condemnation of Colenso was that he failed to reconcile novel, heterodox ideas with the ideas the masses already possessed. In short, the powers of literary criticism are now less extensive than they were at the outset; but in theory they are still awesome and in practice ill defined, and in their imperfect application, they suggest not so much the absolute authority of an anonymous force as the fallibility of an individual critic.

There remains, finally, the central question posed by Arnold's original doctrine—how the masses are ever to be enlightened if the Colensos are to be silenced. At first he answers with the argument of "The Bishop and the Philosopher": a speculative thinker like Spinoza or Galileo simply leaves his intellectual ideas "to filter down gradually." But we soon discover that the doctrine has been altered by an important addition. The religious reformer, Arnold now says, utilizes ideas that "are in the world; they come originally from the sphere of pure thought; they are put into circulation by the spirit of the time."[79] Here, in his first public use of the term *Zeitgeist*, Arnold explains how a work such as Colenso's may be mistaken because it is premature. But this early treatment of the idea lacks both system and completeness, creating as many problems as it solves. By having the impersonal force of the *Zeitgeist* supplant the human agency of the speculative thinker, Arnold approaches a deterministic philosophy in which human effort counts for little, and by apparently eliminating all human agency after the ideas are conceived, he fails to explain how they pass from the realm of pure thought into the world.

Despite its flaws, however, Arnold's position was manifestly stronger than it had been before. Two of the weekly newspapers that had opposed him, the *Examiner* and the *London Review*, were silenced by the article, and another paper, the *Englishman*, thought it "excellent."[80] The *Saturday Review* even published what was tantamount to a confession that it had been convinced.[81] "Say what they will," Arnold wrote with obvious satisfaction to his mother, "the character of Colenso's book is now pretty well marked, and no clergyman will write quite in that strain again."[82]

But several of Arnold's critics were not so readily persuaded. One was Maurice, who spoke out once more against what he considered the most objectionable part of Arnold's thesis—the claim of omnipotence for literary criticism. In a personal letter to R. H. Hutton, editor of the *Spectator*, Maurice warned that it was the function of the clergy "to preserve men from substituting the intellectual discerner, the man of religious instincts and impulses, the exalted critic, for the Living God."[83] And in a letter published by the *Spectator*, he confronted the central issue of the controversy when he declared that literary criticism

may become a frightfully irresponsible power. Mr. Arnold certainly will not let the multitude control it; nor have I any desire for such a court of appeal. The men of intellectual ideas . . . are too much out of the sphere of ordinary existence to exercise any practical jurisdiction. . . . The literary critic must then be omnipotent, if there is not a real judge higher than he is. If I am appealed to as a clergyman, I must speak as one. I must say distinctly I think there *is* a higher judge than the Critic.[84]

The *Reader*, which to Arnold was a "paper of the *Mauritians*,"[85] was equally dissatisfied with the role he had assigned to literary criticism. Although Arnold thought the paper "favourable" because of its praise for his having "brought out with telling force the need of a *positive* Gospel," the notice as a whole stressed his clinging "to shreds and remnants of his old *poco-curante* creed of intellectualism": he still distinguished between those who were permitted to treat the religious life with absolute freedom and those who were not. But, the *Reader* objected,

> either that religious life is a lie, when it proclaims that there is "one Lord, one faith, one baptism, one God and Father of us all," or it is a truth. If it be a lie, it can furnish no worthy standard to a criticism which searches after truth. If it be a truth, then the existence of these "sublime solitaries," who are above all religion, is simply impossible, and the "literary criticism," which claims to be an indifferent arbiter between religion and them, has no ground to stand on.[86]

A more severe critic was William Rathbone Greg, an essayist and acquaintance of the Arnold family who a decade earlier had questioned religious orthodoxy in *The Creed of Christendom*. Though his reply was "very civil" and "without any vice at all,"[87] it was the longest and most searching of the contemporary answers to the Colenso articles. Arnold had already attempted a reply to some of the objections Greg raised, but, as Greg recognized in calling the review of Stanley "a singular aggravation of the offence" of the first article, his answer was still inadequate at a crucial point—the argument that the *Zeitgeist* alters, apparently without man's aid, the current ideas of the world. "But what is Time save an abstraction," Greg asked, "unless it means the sum of influence exerted on the general mind by some scores of writers like Dr. Colenso! How could 'Time' operate if all Colensos are to be condemned to everlasting silence?" And turning on Arnold his own weapon of ridicule, Greg ironically observed that Arnold seemed to think new ideas would be produced "by some undescribed mental effluvia, some subtle intellectual emanation, homeopathic, and therefore at once harmless and penetrating."[88]

V

After the publication of the second Colenso paper, Arnold had insisted that "no amount of noise or faultfinding [would] induce [him] to add another word."[89] Perhaps as a result of Greg's answer, however, his resolution was broken, and he was to return again and again to the attack on Colenso. But before a reply to Greg could be made, there remained an unfinished letter Arnold had intended to write to the *Times* in January. He completed it shortly after the appearance of Greg's article but did not publish it until December, and then in *Macmillan's*, where the two previous papers had appeared, even though it had "too much of the brassiness and smartness of a *Times* article."[90] Entitled "A Word More About Spinoza," this third article prompted by the Colenso controversy was in part a reply to Maurice's first letter to the *Spectator*, and by implication a reply to journals like the *English Churchman* which had been scandalized by praise of the infidel Spinoza.

Maurice had misunderstood Arnold's purpose in writing about Spinoza, which, as Arnold explained to his mother, had been "rather to modify opinion about him than to give it a decisive turn in his favour."[91] But Maurice implied that Arnold had carefully slanted his account in order to strengthen the thesis that love of God was the basis of Spinoza's teaching and the end of his life, and he had further maintained that although as a Hebrew Spinoza brought to Goethe and Lessing an assurance not dreamed of in their philosophy, the demand for a universal humanity created by the French Revolution now made his "negations . . . obsolete" and "his naked absolutism incredible."[92] Arnold concedes that the form of Spinoza's principal work is "repellent," that his seemingly "rigid dogmatism" is alien to modern philosophy, and that as a speculative work the *Tractatus* is to a certain extent "in the air," lacking a base and supports. He admits, too, that Spinoza's ideal of the intellectual life is not the Christian's ideal of the religious life, and that between the two "there is all the difference which there is between the being in love, and the following, with delighted comprehension, a reasoning of Plato." But Maurice's explanation that Spinoza appealed to Goethe because he was a Hebrew Arnold dismisses as "fanciful," and in reply to Maurice's contention that Spinoza's doctrines are no longer adequate, Arnold insists that by "crowning the intellectual life with a sacred transport, by . . . retaining in philosophy, amid the discontented murmurs of all the army of atheism, the name of God, Spinoza maintains a profound affinity with that which is truest in religion, and inspires an indestructible interest."[93]

Of the papers he wrote on Colenso and Spinoza, Arnold sought to preserve only "A Word More About Spinoza," which appeared as "Spinoza" in the first edition of *Essays in Criticism* and as "Spinoza and the Bible" thereafter. He never publicly acknowledged his anonymous review of Willis's translation of the *Tractatus* and never republished "Dr. Stanley's Lectures on the Jewish Church." Later he worked portions of "The Bishop and the Philosopher" into the reprinted piece on Spinoza, perhaps in response to the criticism of the *Pall Mall Gazette* that the essay seemed "very abrupt and incomplete without the tract that was originally its counterpart."[94] But the reprinted portions of "The Bishop and the Philosopher" contained no reference to Colenso, and the essay as a whole was never republished by Arnold, presumably because Colenso's appeal from his deposition by the bishop of Cape Town was pending at the time *Essays in Criticism* was being prepared for publication.[95] After reversal of the decision by the Privy Council gave Arnold the freedom to republish the essay in a subsequent volume, the occasion that had elicited it had long since passed.

Yet Arnold did not allow either the controversy or his role in it to be completely forgotten. In a footnote to *Essays in Criticism*, he said that although his "dislike to all personal attack and controversy" caused him to abstain from reprinting the Colenso articles, he was nevertheless compelled to declare his "sincere impenitence for having published them." The preface to the volume, moreover, resumed the ridicule of Colenso, depicting him as "that favourite pontiff of the Philistines," and the hare's stomach (an allusion to his much-disputed argument that the dietary laws in Leviticus err in naming the hare as an animal which chews its cud) as the "English Caabah, or Palladium of enlightenment."[96] And several years later, in *Culture and Anarchy*, Colenso once more became the object of ridicule when Hepworth Dixon appeared as "the Colenso of love and marriage—such a revolution does he make in our ideas on these matters, just as Dr. Colenso does in our ideas on religion."[97]

Even as late as the seventies, Arnold continued to refer to the controversy when he and Greg again exchanged words. With the republication in 1868 of Greg's essay, which one reviewer thought a "fatal blow" to Arnold "as a guide acceptable to the public,"[98] Arnold was prompted in the preface to *Culture and Anarchy* to allude rather brusquely to Greg as one with whom he differed about edification. Four years later, after the publication of *Literature and Dogma*, Greg twitted Arnold for censuring Colenso and then doing "precisely the same thing [as Colenso] in a far more sweeping fashion, and in a far less tentative and modest temper."[99] Nettled by this reproach, Arnold replied in the introduction to *God and the Bible* that although he had "no wish to revive a past controversy," he would repeat his conviction that Colenso's book undermined religious faith and in its place offered only a "comically insufficient" substitute. If Greg, "who took up arms" for Colenso, failed to understand this, it was because his own work in biblical criticism had the same fault.[100]

VI

These exchanges with Greg, of course, were but trivial offshoots of a long controversy. Of central importance, however, was the redefinition of criticism to which Arnold had been driven by the replies to his Colenso articles and which he reached in "The Function of Criticism at the Present Time," an essay that grew directly out of the controversy and is the most significant product of it.

"The Function of Criticism" begins where "The Bishop and the Philosopher" had begun—with a contrast between the critical spirit on the Continent and the lack of it in England. Answering the objection that his contrast had implied an overestimate of the critical faculty and an underestimate of the creative, Arnold now attempts to demonstrate the interdependence of the two faculties. Creative effort of the highest kind is not at all times possible, he says, but depends upon a certain current of ideas that sustain and enliven the creative faculty—a current of ideas such as was present in Greece during the age of Pindar and Sophocles and in England during the age of Shakespeare, but absent from the England of the Romantic poets. Here again is the theme of the *Zeitgeist*, the inexorable spirit of time that not only sweeps away old ideas and brings in new, but also determines that the literature of one period is to be great, as in the Renaissance, and that of another premature, as in the early nineteenth century. But Arnold's treatment of the *Zeitgeist* has undergone an important evolution. The pure abstraction of the Time Spirit has been replaced by a human agency, the critical power, which establishes "a current of fresh and true ideas" that makes creative epochs possible.[101] Thus the doctrine originally advanced in the review of Stanley's *Lectures* has been modified in at least three ways. Arnold now explains how ideas are put into circulation; he makes human effort rather than a deterministic force responsible for their circulation; and he shows the critical effort to be a positive and affirmative force allied with the *Zeitgeist* and providing more than a negative judgment of Colenso, but contributing directly to the birth of creative periods.

Without this critical effort to prepare for it, the creative effort of a period inevitably fails. This is why Byron is "so empty of matter, Shelley so incoherent, Wordsworth . . . so wanting in completeness and variety." But why, with the French Revolution preceding it, was the Romantic movement so barren of ideas? Arnold's answer takes him back once again to the thesis he had developed nearly two years before. The French Revolution originated in the world of ideas, in the world of pure reason, whose prescriptions are of "absolute, unchanging, . . . universal validity." But these ideas were given "an immediate political and practical application." They were brought "abruptly into the world of politics and practice" in an attempt "violently to revolutionize this world to their bidding." Here was the "grand error" of the French Revolution, which violated the principle that force is the legitimate ruler until right is ready, and that right is not ready until we have "attained [a] sense of seeing it and willing it." The two worlds of which Arnold speaks are not the same as the realm of speculation and the realm of religion of which he had previously spoken—the world of pure reason is Plato's, and the world of practice is the pragmatic Englishman's, the Puritan's, the Philistine's—but the distinction he draws has clearly evolved from the earlier one. His use of it, however, has a validity that was formerly lacking. Although still insisting that the ideas of one world must not be confused with those of the other, Arnold makes a less rigorous, a less neat distinction between these ideas than he had made before, and he declines to argue by the relaxed means of easy paradox. That an anomaly is objectionable in the sphere of politics he admits, but this is not to say that an idea may be true in one sphere and false in another. Nor does he maintain that the ideas of the French Revolution were falsified by their application. On the contrary, the point is both more simple and more convincing: that the world of ideas gives us one view, the world of practice another; that, for example, the British Constitution may from the practical side appear to be "a magnificent organ of progress and virtue," but from the speculative side "a colossal machine for the manufacture of Philistines." The original doctrine is further strengthened and clarified by the elimination of the troublesome requirement to "harmonize" the ideas of one sphere with those of the other. The formula, "Force till right is ready," retains the demand for a stable adjustment of ideas at the same time that it avoids imposing a kind of intellectual censorship, and it recognizes the need for state action at the same time that it allows for the enlightenment of the masses in preparation for the rule by right.[102] Arnold thus preserves the essential grounds for his contention that Colenso failed to edify, but removes what was untenable and objectionable.

The new distinction between the world of ideas and the world of practice permits Arnold to make still more refinements on his original doctrine. It enables him, first of all, to continue to distinguish between the few and the many, but without becoming involved in difficulties of logic. The few reappear as those with a critical frame of mind and a desire "to see the object as in itself it really is"—hence a more realistic, a less exclusive division than earlier, providing a category to which more than the solitary philosopher may aspire. The many, on the other hand, are those who "will never have any ardent zeal for seeing things as they are," who are satisfied by "very inadequate ideas"—hence an apparently less ignorant, less potentially dangerous group than before, and one more capable of partial enlightenment. From his previous description of the few, moreover, Arnold takes the two preeminent characteristics that he ascribes to criticism: curiosity, the "love of a free play of the mind on all subjects, for its own sake," and disinterestedness, the steadfast refusal "to lend itself to . . . ulterior, political, practical considerations about ideas." They recall, of course, the isolated thinker, like Spinoza, who lives in the realm of pure speculation and regards the ideal life as "an eternal series of intellectual acts," and who does not himself transport these ideas into the world, but leaves them to filter down and to adjust themselves, through an agency other than his, to the life of mankind. The critic Arnold describes, however, has a purpose and a usefulness that the philosopher lacks. His life is not one of austere solitude, and where the philosopher seems to dwell in a kind of lotus land of indifference, the critic is moved by a profound sense of responsibility. What is more valuable still, Arnold's emphasis on disinterestedness, the attitude of objectivity that he failed to define adequately when he first condemned Colenso, provides an effective response to those who had reproached him, a liberal, for attacking Colenso, another liberal. If the critic is to have a free play of the mind, Arnold insists, he must keep aloof from all party considerations, from "all questions of practical consequences and applications."[103] We may infer, then, that Arnold's censure of Colenso is to be applauded precisely because it opposed political pressures and the liberals' denunciation of him condemned because it violated a fundamental canon of criticism.

At the same time that he assumes this advantage over his critics, Arnold repeats his censure of Colenso, though in more restrained and defensible terms. He emphasizes Colenso's good intentions and, in a portion of a footnote withdrawn after 1865, makes an obvious attempt to placate feelings by saying that Colenso's "subsequent volumes are in great measure free from the crying fault of the first" and that "he may perhaps end by becoming a useful biblical critic." As the judgment of Colenso becomes milder, furthermore, its basis grows stronger. Arnold returns, to be sure, to his rigid and oversimplified distinction between truth of science and truth of religion, repeating his objection that Colenso strengthened the masses' confusion of the two, and replying to the *Spectator* that "the ignorant are not informed by being confirmed in a confusion." But he is both more flexible and more accurate when he declares also that Colenso's work "reposes on a total misconception of the essential elements of the religious problem, as that problem is now presented for solution." The essence of the problem is to put "a new construction" upon biblical data, "taking them from under the old, traditional, conventional point of view and placing them under a new one."[104] This is more precise and meaningful than pages of talk about the few and the many, or edification and instruction, and more persuasive in indicating Colenso's failure—

a failure to see the religious problem as "it really is" and thus a notable failure as criticism.

It is a failure, too, not simply *as* criticism, but as *judged* by criticism. This brings Arnold to his principal objective in "The Function of Criticism at the Present Time"—to develop the concept of criticism that had been rather pretentiously but imperfectly formulated in "The Bishop and the Philosopher." It is true, of course, that he does not develop this concept consistently and logically throughout the essay, for he speaks of criticism now in one sense and now in another. Sometimes he uses the word in a philosophic context, to designate a view of things that may be described as realistic or scientific; sometimes in a literary context, to distinguish critical from creative works; and sometimes in a political or religious context, to refer to a method of reconstructing traditional but outmoded ideas. But throughout the essay, Arnold moves in general toward a comprehensive definition of criticism that is both more modest in its claims than was the anonymous and omnipotent judge of Colenso, and yet more deserving of the authority delegated to it. He tends to speak of criticism not as an abstraction of absolute power, but as a certain attitude of mind; not as a force fully realized, but as an endeavor, an effort, an attempt; not as an arbiter of all things intellectual, but as a goal, an aim to be achieved. Thus while he can still declare authoritatively that Colenso's work is "of no importance whatever" to criticism, he can also speak more tentatively of "the attitude which criticism *should* adopt."[105]

The definition of criticism eventually reached by Arnold evolves from an account of the functions criticism serves (significantly, in the original title the noun *function* was pluralized) and the qualities it possesses. At first its purpose is simply "to establish an order of ideas" and "to make the best ideas prevail." Here, in alliance with the *Zeitgeist*, is the sifting process performed by criticism—taking the ideas that have come from the speculative thinker and verifying or rejecting them. To this initial function several attributes are later added: intellectual curiosity, disinterested objectivity, a cosmopolitan desire "to know the best that is known and thought *in the world*." Here is the sense of Europe "as being, for intellectual and spiritual purposes, one great confederation," a mature form of that sense of the "educated Europe" at whose tribunal Colenso was ridiculed. It is characterized, finally, by the ambition to propagate this best that is known and thought. Here is its missionary zeal, radically different from the philosopher's indifference to the fate of his ideas because of the masses' incapacity for them. But Arnold does not leave the concept of criticism here. In reply to the reproaches of his adversaries in the Colenso controversy (notably Maurice) that he had claimed too much for criticism, he now claims even more than he had previously, making of it nothing less than a kind of religion. Criticism as thus interpreted provides all that Colenso provided in reminding Protestantism of its pretensions to a "rational and intellectual origin," but it provides more, for it is concerned with man's total being—with the intellectual part, which previously seemed to belong exclusively to the few, and with the emotional part, which seemed to belong exclusively to the many. It is able, furthermore, to place the "ideal imperfection" of man's practice in juxtaposition with "speculative considerations of ideal perfection" and so lead man "towards perfection, by making his mind dwell upon what is excellent in itself, and the absolute beauty and fitness of things."[106] This is still an immense claim for criticism, but as an answer to the objection of Maurice that Arnold wished to substitute the "exalted critic" for the "Living God," it fully justifies the authority given to it.

"The Function of Criticism at the Present Time" was the most notable result of the Colenso affair, but it was not the only one. The controversy also provided Arnold with a central symbol. Several years later, when his *New Poems* were published, Mrs. Colenso expressed to her friend Lady Lyell a wish to see them, although, she added, *"The Saturday Review* says that a horror of Bishop Colenso is one of the articles of his faith." Yet she knew that the same might have been said of the *Saturday* itself. It "seems to make a point," she wrote, "of sneering at Colenso in every month's [*sic*] issue. 'Except in an age of Philistinism or general want of sensibility, no such book as his could have been published.' "[107] The *Saturday Review*, of course, was not often in such complete accord with Arnold. Its diagnosis of the ills of the time suggests, therefore, that the critic who was one of its favorite targets had already struck some blows of his own in his assault on the bastions of Philistia.

CHAPTER FIVE

Philistinism and *Geist*

. . . . the obstinate, and now contemptuous, aversion to all energy of thinking is the mother evil, the cause of all the evils in politics, morals, and literature, which it is my object to wage war against . . . .— Coleridge to Southey, 1809

It's a part of solid English sense not to think too much; to see only what may be of practical use at the moment.—Decoud in *Nostromo*

To judge is to see clearly, to care for what is just and therefore to be impartial,—more exactly, to be disinterested . . . .—Amiel

. . . a University training is the great ordinary means to a great but ordinary end; it aims at raising the intellectual tone of society . . . . It is the education which gives a man a clear conscious view of his own opinions and judgments . . . . It teaches him to see things as they are . . . .—Newman

The true liberal endeavours to effect as much good as he can, with the means which he has at command; but he would not extirpate evils, which are often inevitable, with fire and sword. He endeavours, by a judicious progress, gradually to remove glaring defects, without at the same time destroying an equal amount of good by violent measures. He contents himself in this ever imperfect world with what is good, until time and circumstances favour his attaining something better.—Goethe

In November 1863, a month before the publication of the last of his Colenso papers, Arnold wrote to "K" that he thought

in this concluding half of the century the English spirit is destined to undergo a great transformation; or rather, perhaps I should say, to perform a great evolution . . . . I shall do what I can for this movement in literature; freer perhaps in that sphere than I could be in any other, but with the risk always before me, if I cannot charm the wild

137

beast of Philistinism while I am trying to convert him, of being torn
in pieces by him; and, even if I succeed to the utmost and convert him,
of dying in a ditch or a workhouse at the end of it all.[1]

The crusade against Philistinism that is described in this somewhat melodramatic passage had begun the previous June
with the lecture on Heinrich Heine. There, parting company
both with George Eliot, who had depicted Heine as "only a
poet" and neither "a hero" nor "a solemn prophet,"[2] and
with Carlyle, who had slighted him in his emphasis on the
romantic writers of Germany, Arnold had insisted on Heine's
significance as "a brilliant soldier in the Liberation War of
humanity" and as "the most important German successor and
continuator of Goethe in Goethe's most important line of activity," that of service in the same war. For some critics, of
course, this is to misread both Heine and Goethe.[3] But to
Arnold the importance of each was his engagement in that
struggle of the modern spirit to which he had devoted his inaugural lecture and of which Frank Newman and Bishop Colenso seemed singularly unaware. The great voice of this
spirit in the nineteenth century was Goethe's, giving expression to the desire to be freed from outmoded institutions and
beliefs, and its Moloch was Heine, counseling "open war" in
"a life and death battle with Philistinism."[4]

With his love of France because of her "accessibility to
ideas" and his hatred of "*genuine British narrowness,*" Heine
was to Arnold a "Paladin of the modern spirit." And in
searching for an English equivalent for Heine's *Philister*
to designate a stupid but stubborn enemy of light, Arnold
seized on the word *Philistine*, introduced it at "the very head-
quarters of Goliath," and pointed to the dangerous procedure
of a people who have always acted

by the rule of thumb; what was intolerably inconvenient to them they
have suppressed, and as they have suppressed it, not because it was
irrational, but because it was practically inconvenient, they have seldom in suppressing it appealed to reason, but always, if possible, to

some precedent, or form, or letter, which served as a convenient in-strument for their purpose, and which saved them from the neces-sity of recurring to general principles. They have thus become, in a certain sense, of all people the most inaccessible to ideas and the most impatient of them; inaccessible to them, because of their want of familiarity with them; and impatient of them because they have got on so well without them, that they despise those who, not having got on as well as themselves, still make a fuss for what they them-selves have done so well without.

To be sure, Arnold admitted, the English regard for the prac-tical side of things had led to prosperity and liberty, whereas in Germany the regard of a chosen few for the ideal side had led to the dictatorial rule of Bismarck. But Philistia

is not the true promised land, as we English commonly imagine it to be; and our excessive neglect of the idea, and consequent inaptitude for it, threatens us, at a moment when the idea is beginning to exer-cise a real power in human society, with serious future inconveni-ence, and, in the meanwhile, cuts us off from the sympathy of other nations, which feel its power more than we do.

With this as his text, Arnold began his series of epistles to the Philistines, urging them to acquire *Geist*.

A second epistle was delivered the following November when Arnold lectured on Joubert, whom he presented as "a French Coleridge."[5] Like Coleridge, who made a "con-tinual instinctive effort . . . to get at and to lay bare the real truth of his matter at hand," Joubert had "an ardent impulse for seeking the genuine truth on all matters [he] thought about, and a gift for finding it and recognising it when it was found." And again like Coleridge, who made this intellectual effort "in a country where at that moment such an effort was almost unknown . . . and where ordinary minds were . . . habit-uated . . . to regard considerations of established routine and practical convenience as paramount," Joubert was a child of light in an alien age. He thus provided an instructive contrast to Macaulay, that "great apostle of the Philistines" whose efforts were directed toward the mastery of rhetoric rather than the search for truth. But whereas the reputation of one would fade, Arnold predicted, that of the other would last; for although living "in the Philistine's day, in a place and time when almost every idea current in literature had the mark of Dagon upon it," Joubert was one of the few who "never bowed the knee to the gods of Canaan."

After an interruption of the epistles with the lecture on "Pagan and Medieval Religious Sentiment," Arnold resumed them in June 1864 with "The Literary Influence of Academies."[6] Beginning and ending with satiric references to Macaulay's smugness in praising English literature for its greatness, he developed the thesis that the English were preeminently characterized by "energy and honesty, not an open and clear mind, not a quick and flexible intelligence." The faults from which their literature suffered were therefore precisely those that are prevented by an intellectual center and authority such as academies afford: orthographical antics, eccentric judgments, provincial style, extravagance, and lack of balance; in short, freaks and violence that are affronts to taste and reason.

But the definitive attack on Philistinism was reserved for "The Function of Criticism at the Present Time," which Arnold wrote as an essay for Bagehot's *National Review*, intending it to introduce *Essays in Criticism*, and delivered as a lecture in October.[7] Ostensibly a reply to comments he had made in the second of the Homer lectures, and in reality (as we have seen) a defense of his position in the Colenso controversy, it is inseparably related to the lectures immediately preceding it. Although the Philistines themselves are specifically alluded to only twice, they and their attitudes—their disbelief in the existence of an absolute and universal order of reason, their zealous desire to effect practical and immediate reforms, their insularity and extravagant love of self, their lack of critical judgment, their hideous institutions—are present throughout. There is the *Times*, which might any day declare a decimal coinage to be an absurdity; there is the member of the Parliament who considers an anomaly unobjectionable; there are Charles Adderley and John Roebuck, who eulogize the Anglo-Saxons as "the best breed in the whole world" and pray that England's "unrivalled happiness may last"; there is Frances Power Cobbe, whose *Religious Duty* reminds one of the British College of Health—"the grand name without the grand thing"; and there is the English Divorce Court, "an institution which neither makes divorce impossible nor makes it decent." Arnold found the essay "very troublesome" to write and at first feared that what he had said would "give offence," blaming a "horrible cold and sore throat" for "a *nuance* of asperity in [his] manner . . . which need not have been there" and which he was determined to "try and get rid of . . . in correcting the proofs."[8] Yet the lecture itself "went off very well," he later reported to Lady de Rothschild, promising her that "parts of it [would] make [her] laugh when [she read] them."[9]

Another of his readers, however, was less amused. He was James Fitzjames Stephen, an old critic of the Arnold family. A month after its November publication, he attacked the lecture in a review that was of central importance in shaping the course of Arnold's social and political criticism for the next several years.

I

Fitzjames Stephen, the distinguished jurist and elder brother of the more famous Leslie, was once characterized by Charles Eliot Norton as "burly and broad-shouldered in mind as in body."[10] At Cambridge, where he was "an indolent, slovenly, undistinguished undergraduate," he was known variously as "the Gruffian," "the Giant Grim," and "the British Lion." Lacking in aesthetic appreciation, sentiment, and affability, he thought *Robinson Crusoe* the ideal novel because "it could be read without a tear from beginning to end," praised Hobbes's *Leviathan* for laying down the "proper principles

of rigidity and ferocity," and, as a recent critic has wittily observed, "was inclined to believe that life would be tolerable
but for its enjoyments." His most noted book, *Liberty, Equality, Fraternity*, an attempt to rescue the pure utilitarianism of
Bentham from the "sentimental deviationism" of Mill, was,
as this same critic has remarked, the work of a man who as a
child "had refused to see anything dreadful about guns, and
who thought hell-fire the securest sanction of morality."[11] Although Norton believed that Stephen had "one of the clearest and strongest of solid English intelligences," with a
mind of "almost brutal force and directness,"[12] R. H. Hutton
considered him "narrow";[13] his own cousin, A. V. Dicey, objected to his "always trying to show somebody else's error";[14]
and George Eliot found "extremely repulsive" his "tone towards much abler thinkers."[15] Sir Thomas Farrer even diag-
nosed a disease that he called "Fitzjames-Stephenism," describing its symptoms as "arbitrary ways and autocratic habits
of mind, leading to lust for dominion, pride of race, and the
cult of force as the essence of life," and its opposite qualities as "true self-regard, humanity, justice to inferiors, sympathy, and Sermon-on-the-Mountism."[16] Arnold would have
concurred in the diagnosis. "Fitz-James [*sic*] Stephen," he
wrote to Goldwin Smith many years later, "is not worth
much, though he has a style of vigour."[17]

An indefatigable journalist whose work, it has been said,
was part "pot-boiling," part "escapism," and part compulsion
("If I were in solitary confinement," he confessed on one occasion, "I should have to scratch newspaper articles on the
wall with a nail"),[18] Stephen had tangled with Arnold more
than once in the past. His review of *Tom Brown's School-
days* for the *Edinburgh Review* in 1858—which conceded Dr.
Arnold's virtues but depicted him as a man of "intense and
somewhat impatient fervour" who "saw all kinds of evil
with such keenness . . . that he was hardly capable of forming
a cool judgment on its extent or intensity"[19]—so annoyed
Arnold that he came to think of it as the origin of "Rugby

Chapel."[20] The following year Stephen wrote for the *Saturday Review* "a very clever and long answer" to Arnold's pamphlet, *England and the Italian Question*; and although this time he was so "civil" that "no one [could] complain of his tone,"[21] Arnold did not soon forget the criticism. In "The Literary Influence of Academies" five years later, as Frederic E. Faverty has noted,[22] he replied to Stephen's objection to his defense of Louis Napoleon by pointedly using it as an illustration of the provinciality into which "that old friend of all of us," the *Saturday Review*, occasionally fell:

And the same note may not unfrequently be observed even in the ideas of this newspaper, full as it is of thought and cleverness: certain ideas allowed to become fixed ideas, to prevail too absolutely. I will not speak of the immediate present, but, to go a little while back, it had the critic who so disliked the Emperor of the French. . . . it is a note of the provincial spirit not to hold ideas of this kind a little more easily, to be so devoured by them, to suffer them to become crotchets.[23]

Arnold was thus not unprepared for Stephen's "long, elaborate attack" on "The Function of Criticism at the Present Time," due partly, he said, to Stephen's "being Colenso's advocate, partly also to his ideas being naturally very antagonistic" to his own. He recognized, too, that Stephen "meant to be as civil as he could," even if his civility took the somewhat unusual form of sending his wife to call in a gesture of amity. But despite the fact that " 'the judicious' seem[ed] inclined to be very staunch to [him], in all the warfare [he had] to go through," Arnold knew that Stephen was attacking him *"au fond,"*[24] and he suspected "that dear old K half sympathised, in her heart, with a great deal of" what he had said.[25]

The attack, entitled "Matthew Arnold and His Countrymen,"[26] is aimed at a critic so bent upon demonstrating the inferiority of the English to the French that for Stephen he not only has "taught himself to write a dialect as like French as pure English can be" but also, "like his French models," has developed "quick sympathies and a great gift of making telling remarks" but "hardly any power of argument." There is, for example, Arnold's condemnation of Colenso, whom he treats as "a mere Philistine of rather a contemptible kind"; or there is the passage about Wragg: "Criticism ought to show that Wragg should have been called (say) Fairfax; and that, instead of saying 'Wragg is in custody,' the brutal journalist should have said, 'And so, on that cold November night, the door of Nottingham gaol was shut behind our sinful sister.' " But what essentially vitiates Arnold's thesis, Stephen argues, is that he overlooks two vital considerations: first, that in their practical efforts the English are for the most part pursuing a philosophy that both understands and rejects the philosophy Arnold accuses them of neglecting; and, second, that whereas Arnold himself distinguishes between the spheres of practice and theory, he repeatedly objects to "practical measures on theoretical grounds."

Arnold's entire essay, according to Stephen, assumes the truth of a "transcendental theory of philosophy" that has been "utterly denied" by the most influential English thinkers since the days of Hobbes. Thus the member of Parliament who had no objection to anomalies was speaking empirically and meant only that political institutions exist to promote human welfare and that experience alone can show which institutions achieve this result. Far from being enemies of light, Stephen declares, the English as a whole are the most logical people in the world, translating abstract principles into concrete action, as in the policy of free trade, the reform of the criminal code, and the enlightened governing of India. Arnold, by contrast, "is like a man who says to a painter or a sculptor, 'What a gross Philistine you are to pass your time in chipping at the hideous stone, dabbling with that nasty clay, or fiddling about with oil-paints and canvas! Why do you not at once rise to the sphere of pure reason, and produce, as I do in my dreams, statues and pictures of eternal and absolute beauty?' " Yet Stephen finds the conclusive proof of Arnold's incapacity for logical reasoning not here, but in his comment that "to count by tens is the easiest way of counting," where his language is imprecise (he should say "to take as your unit an established base of notation" instead of "to count by tens" and add the qualifications, "ten being given as the base of notation" and "except for numbers under twenty"), and his conclusion a *non sequitur* (the simplest way of counting does not necessarily determine what system of coinage should be adopted).

The frailty of Arnold's logical powers was equally evident to Stephen in the inconsistency between his pretended separation of theory and practice and his actual judgment of the one by the other. In condemning the Divorce Court, for example, Arnold deals with a practical matter that is not properly his concern until he has "a theory which will fully explain all the duties of the legislator on the matter of marriage." Similarly, he censures Colenso for writing "*ad populum*," whereas by his own doctrine he "ought to sit on a hill retired, and argue high about a new synthesis of the four Gospels, and care nothing for practice." And in addition to being inconsistent, he perversely argues "that it was a crime against literary criticism and the higher culture to attempt to inform the ignorant."

In his conclusion, Stephen struck a note that was to become the dominant one in criticism of Arnold during the sixties. Alluding to a scene in 1 *Henry IV* that was to be frequently evoked, he portrayed Arnold as an affected and fastidious critic of his countrymen, too dainty to engage with them in the necessary but unpleasant work of eradicating the evils of the time:

With all his ability, he sometimes gives himself the airs of the distinguished courtier who shone so bright and smelt so sweet when he had occasion to talk with Hotspur about the prisoners. He is always using a moral smelling-bottle, like those beloved countrymen, who, at foreign *tables d'hôte*, delight to hold forth on the vulgarity of "those English."

II

Stephen's attack reminded Arnold of his brother Edward's rationalization that those who did "not go his way" did not "reason." Yet he was convinced that his procedure was the most effective he could adopt, even though it might cause, "now and then, a little explosion which fidgets people."[27] Several days before the publication of the attack, in writing to his mother about a middle class commission to which he had not been appointed and which was "full of people who [had] declared themselves beforehand against State-intervention," he had said that "this, like all else which happens, more and more turns me away from the thought of any attempt at direct practical and political action, and makes me fix all my care upon a spiritual action, to tell upon people's minds, which after all is the great thing, hard as it is to make oneself fully believe it so."[28] In the same manner, Stephen's article served to reenforce the belief that his "sinuous, easy, unpolemical mode of proceeding" was "the best way of proceeding if one [wanted] to get at, and keep with, truth" and that "only by a literary form of this kind being given to them [could] ideas such as [his] ever gain any access in a country such as [England]." Thus "from anything like a direct answer, or direct controversy," he would "religiously abstain." But at the same time he would "take an opportunity of putting back this and that matter into its true light" if he thought Stephen had "pulled them out of it"; and within days after the appearance of the article, he had "the idea of a paper for the *Cornhill*, about March, to be called 'My Countrymen.'"[29]

Because of more pressing work, however, "My Countrymen" was delayed for a year, not appearing until 1866. In January, the month following the attack, Arnold was occupied with the publication of *Essays in Criticism*; in February, with research for the first of his lectures on Celtic literature; and in March, with preparations for his study of secondary education on the Continent.[30] But the delay in writing "My Countrymen" did not prevent a prompt answer to Stephen. *Essays in Criticism*, on the contrary, provided an opportunity, and in its preface as well as in footnotes to individual essays, Arnold replied both to him and to a number of other critics.

The preface, Arnold thought, was "done with that *light hand*" that both he and Frederick Locker-Lampson had "such an affection for."[31] Written with a similar preface of Renan in mind, as R. H. Super has noted,[32] it opens with a glance toward the staff of the *Saturday Review*, and toward Stephen in particular, as Arnold declares that, although several of the essays were "much criticised at the time of their first appearance," he will refrain from answering his critics:

. . . it is not in my nature,—some of my critics would rather say, not in my power,—to dispute on behalf of any opinion, even my own, very obstinately. To try and approach truth on one side after another, not to strive or cry, nor to persist in pressing forward, on any one side, with violence and self-will,—it is only thus, it seems to me, that mortals may hope to gain any vision of the mysterious Goddess, whom we shall never see except in outline, but only thus even in outline.

Just as Frank Newman's erudition was a handicap and Arnold's less exacting scholarship an advantage, so now is the stringent logic of Stephen a weakness and the more flexible method of Arnold a virtue. The point is made explicit in a second paragraph, excised when the *Essays* were republished in 1869:

I am very sensible that this way of thinking leaves me under great disadvantages in addressing a public composed from a people "the most logical," says the *Saturday Review*, "in the whole world." But the truth is, I have never been able to hit it off happily with the logicians, and it would be mere affectation in me to give myself the airs of doing so. They imagine truth something to be proved, I something to be seen; they something to be manufactured, I as something to be found. I have profound respect for intuitions, and a very lukewarm respect for the elaborate machine-work of my friends the logicians.

Their "fine showy edifice," Arnold says, is like a pyramid of eggs in which the only fresh one, now hidden and forgotten, is the original intuition.

The response to the other of Stephen's principal objections is still lighter and more amusing. Returning to the central theme of the Oxford lectures when he describes the age as one of "dissolution and transformation," Arnold notes the *Saturday Review*'s assertion that this work is completed and that the English, having "searched all anchorages for the spirit," have "finally anchored" themselves, "in the fulness of perfected knowledge, on Benthamism." This consummation not only consoles the spirit, he admits, but also accounts for a phenomenon he observed the previous summer during his daily travels in a railroad near which a celebrated murder had recently occurred. Although he had no anxiety for himself because, as the *Saturday Review* recognized, he was a transcendentalist, he was nevertheless concerned for his fellow passengers, many of whom belonged to that middle class which was responsible for "all the great things which have ever been done in England." But far from being troubled, they preserved a "passionate, absorbing, almost blood-thirsty clinging to life" that puzzled Arnold until he read the *Saturday Review*'s "touching explanation": "traversing an age still dimmed by the last mists of transcendentalism," these were ardent disciples of Bentham who wished only "to be spared long enough to see his religion in the full and final blaze of its triumph"; and instead of being on their way toward some commonplace bourgeois activity, they were perhaps "on a pious pilgrimage, to obtain from Mr. Bentham's executors a sacred bone of [their] great, dissected master."

But the *Saturday Review* was not the only weekly that Arnold made the object of his banter in the preface. There was also the *Guardian*, "an eminently *decorous* clerical journal" that found "thoroughly distasteful and disquieting" his "tendency to say exactly what [he thought] about things and people."[33] Almost two years earlier, in a review of John Conington's translation of *The Odes and Carmen Seculare of Horace*, the *Guardian* had praised the "singular modesty" and "thoughtful and courteous discretion" of the author and pointedly contrasted his desire "to justify the course which he has himself pursued" with that of Arnold in his Homer lectures: "to assail the system of others."[34] This represented a reversal of the *Guardian*'s position, for two years previously it had supported Arnold in the debate with Newman and had gone so far as to assert that he "would scarcely attempt to teach Mr. Newman common sense," which would be "harder work even than translating Homer."[35] After 1863, however, the paper repeatedly opposed Arnold, at first because of his vivacities and later because of both his apparent levity and his unorthodox doctrine. In its review of *Essays in Criticism*, for example, it was to ask:

What is the unsatisfactory element in Mr. Arnold as a writer? Why, with his great gifts, is he of little or no weight as a teacher? Why do his criticisms occasionally cause intense disgust? What is the defect in his powers of amusing which makes them soon annoying to minds of refinement and intelligence?

And then it answered its own questions:

He seems to enjoy demolishing, or trying to demolish, a contemporary. He indulges in expressions which fix like arrows in the living flesh, and rankle there. . . . The University of Oxford . . . has been annoyed at seeing one of its Professors stepping forward from his professorial chair to tread so heavily on duly graduated toes; and many of her members, who are no reactionists, have wished that they could have back, in the place of Mr. Arnold's rather too searching criticisms, the good old-fashioned harmless Latin Essays which . . . were heard perhaps by a couple of Bedels, and read by nobody at all.[36]

Eight years later the *Guardian*'s position was unchanged. Referring in its review of *Literature and Dogma* to Arnold's seeming contempt for those who held to traditional Christian beliefs, it said that since his influence was "an unwholesome one," it cared little "that he should act in a manner which must inevitably tend to lessen that influence."[37]

Joining the *Saturday Review* and the *Guardian* in Arnold's preface was a third weekly, the *Examiner*, which in December 1864 had published a long letter from one Joseph Hemington Harris, a prolific correspondent and author of theological tracts who, under the pseudonym "Presbyter Anglicanus," deplored a recent speech in which Disraeli had given his most memorable performance as defender of the faith. Speaking in the Sheldonian Theatre at Wilberforce's invitation, Disraeli had denounced religious liberalism to a delighted audience, describing Colenso as one of those "who appear to have commenced their theological studies after they had grasped the crosier, and who introduce to society their obsolete discoveries with the startling wonder and frank ingenuousness of their own savages," and Maurice as one of those "nebulous professors, who seem in their style to have revived chaos, and who if they could only succeed in obtaining a perpetual study of their writings would go far to realise that eternal punishment to which they object."[38] The wit of these passages was lost on Presbyter Anglicanus, whom Arnold understandably identified with the Anti-Esotericus who nearly two years earlier had in the same journal criticized his position toward Colenso. The identification was all the easier to make, moreover, because of Harris's inability to enjoy Disraeli's "contemptible joke." It was "one of the most ominous signs of the time," he said gravely, and "must fill all sober-minded men with astonishment and dismay" that an "assembly of Englishmen and Christians . . . could listen in uproarious merriment to a Parliamentary leader while he asserted that the vilest iniquity would be well compensated by a forced perusal of the writings of Frederick Denison Maurice. The juxtaposition of the two ideas involves a horrible blasphemy."[39]

With this letter, which clinched his claim to be "one of our modern leaders of thought," Harris joined the host of Philistines whom Arnold was preparing to slay with a single shot from his sling. Among his fellow victims were Ichabod Charles Wright, whose indignant defense of the right of his translation to exist had appeared almost simultaneously with Stephen's article; Colenso, "that favourite pontiff of the Philistines"; the *Guardian*, "whose own gravity [was] so profound that the frivolous [were] sometimes apt to give it a heavier name"; both Stephen and the editor of the *Saturday Review*; a newcomer, the *Daily Telegraph*; and a regiment of minor figures. Arnold began the attack with a characteristic maneuver: asking a question only to withdraw it after firmly implanting it in the reader's mind. He would not ask Wright whether Elizabeth Wragg had found John Roebuck's speech a comfort, lest the *Guardian* should put "a harsh construction upon [his] innocent thirst for knowledge, and again [tax him] with the unpardonable crime of being amusing." Nor would he ask Presbyter Anglicanus whether "to some of his remote ancestors, . . . long before the birth of Puritanism, . . . some conception of a joke must . . . have been conveyed," for the coming east wind proclaimed "the earnest, prosaic, practical, austerely literal future" when the world would be the Philistines': "then, with every voice, not of thunder, silenced, and the whole earth filled and ennobled every morning by the magnificent roaring of the young lions of the *Daily Telegraph*, we shall all yawn in one another's faces with the dismallest, the most unimpeachable gravity. No more vivacity then! My hexameters, and dogmatism, and scoffs at the Divorce Court, will all have been put down."

The library of this future was to be a plain building like an enlarged British College of Health, "the grand name without the grand thing." Inside was the English Kaaba or Palladium of enlightenment, the hare's stomach, an organ which Colenso had made the center of controversy when he pronounced the Levitical reference to the hare chewing its cud to be erroneous. Around the bleak room were such leaders of humanity and philosophy as "our intellectual deliverer Mr. James Clay," a political aspirant and enemy of classical education who had found in the second stanza of Gray's "Ode on a Distant Prospect of Eton College" neither Latin nor Greek, but "pure, unadulterated, exquisitely tender English feeling—a feeling the ancients had not; . . . and they never produced such a stanza."[40] And there was even the editor of the *Saturday Review*, "with the embarrassed air of a late convert": "Many a shrewd nip has he in old days given to the Philistines . . .; but in his old age he has mended his courses, and declares that his heart has always been in the right place, and that he is at bottom, however appearances may have been against him, staunch for Goliath and 'the most logical nation in the whole world.' "

The ostensible purpose of the preface was not, however, to slay Philistines. It was, instead, to plead that they attack Arnold alone rather than implicate the university he served as professor of poetry. The plea, of course, is a pretext for the justly famous coda of the preface, with its familiar features of the Arnoldian landscape. Like the perpetually flowing Oxus or the elm tree of "Thyrsis," the Oxford Arnold evokes is a symbol of permanence in an impermanent world: a symbol of eternal beauty and truth, a timeless voice calling one toward the goal of perfection. She is the lovely city of towers, the adorable dreamer, the queen of romance whose centuries-old struggle against Philistinism makes his own warfare seem like the apparition of a day.

III

In footnotes to the 1865 volume, Arnold permitted himself more direct and detailed answers to the critics of his essays. The longest of these, added to "The Function of Criticism at the Present Time" in response to Stephen's attack, were later withdrawn.[41] The first, concerning Arnold's use of decimal coinage as an illustration of universal reason, expressed gratitude to Stephen for his "counsels about style" but then, after reducing his suggestions to a meaningless statement, declared a preference for simple language to language of "exact accuracy" and "philosophic propriety." Later, in a more serious vein, Arnold explained his point: that France had one monetary system because the "mass of Frenchmen" felt the force of "purely rational, intellectual considerations" sufficiently to legislate in accordance with them, and England another because its system was already established and the English were too practical to trouble themselves "about its intellectual aspect."

In a second footnote to "The Function of Criticism at the Present Time," Arnold answered Stephen's charge that in condemning the Divorce Court he had violated his own doctrine by objecting on theoretical grounds to a practical measure, which was not properly his concern until he had fully explained the legislator's duties concerning marriage. On the contrary, Arnold replied, this was precisely the kind of "invasion of the practical sphere" to which he was opposed. What he advocated was "taking a practical measure into the world of ideas, and seeing how it look[ed] there." The present court looked hideous in the world of ideas because it was not the result of any thoughtful consideration of marriage but was merely a means of allowing the rich the anomalous privilege of divorce. Furthermore, if his "practical critic" were to compare the Catholic idea of marriage as indissoluble with the Protestant idea of it as terminable, Arnold concluded, he would likewise regard the court as "strangely hideous."

Arnold also replied to his critics in two footnotes to another of the essays, "The Literary Influence of Academies."[42] One was in answer to the *Saturday Review*'s objection that in describing Addison as provincial because of his commonplace ideas, Arnold had ignored "the astonishing platitudes of French Academicians of the second order."[43] Arnold's reply, recalling the theme of the *Zeitgeist* in his earlier complaints

to Clough about the Victorian age as compared with the Elizabethan, is that Addison was more than a second-rate writer
but achieved less than his talent promised simply because of
the atmosphere in which he lived. The absence of an academy
tended to tell upon him as it later tended to tell upon Macaulay.

The other note was in response to criticism of the interpretation Arnold had placed on Renan's remarks concerning
J. W. Donaldson's Latin treatise, *Jashar*, and Charles Forster's
elaborate philosophy of history evolved from parallels to the
little and great horns of the he-goat mentioned in Daniel.
Both were the work of Englishmen, Arnold had represented
Renan as saying, and thus one should be "surprised at no
extravagance." Shortly after the appearance of "The Literary
Influence of Academies" in the *Cornhill*, the *Daily News*
published a nasty anonymous attack that Arnold attributed
to Goldwin Smith, who was at the time, one recalls, a man of
"bitterness and strife." He was without equal, John Morley
thought, "in the way of pungent controversy,"[44] but he was
also without "a real sense of justice," as A. V. Dicey remarked,[45] and without control of the "talent for sarcasm" that
Disraeli caricatured in *Lothair*.[46] He was personally on amiable terms with Arnold, praising him after his death for pierc-
ing "the hide of Philistinism with the silvery shafts from his
bow."[47] But there were temperamental differences between the
two that led to frequent encounters. Smith thought Arnold
"destitute of originality and therefore of sympathy with mental independence,"[48] and Arnold thought Smith capable of
"the funereal solemnity of an undertaker" and afflicted by
"irritations and envyings" that were injurious to the spirit.[49]

Arnold, Smith said, had completely misinterpreted Renan,
who simply meant that Donaldson's work had been universally condemned—in England as well as on the Continent, he
pointed out. But the true source of his eruption was not this
essay by Arnold but an earlier one: "The Bishop and the
Philosopher." When Arnold condemned Colenso and praised
Stanley, Smith declared, betraying his real target, it

never occurred to him as relevant or important that in hard knowledge of Hebrew and in power of grasping a critical issue, Bishop Colenso's works may surpass Dean Stanley's by as much as M. Rénan's philology surpasses Mr. Forster's. Even now, the essay in the *Cornhill* betrays certainly ignorance, apparently indifference, whether M. Rénan's judgment is well or ill grounded in reality. This is the original sin of English nature, and specially of the school of which Mr. Arnold is so brilliant a defender, this indifference to literary or religious truth (as distinct from ornament or use), which asks not what is true, but who has said it, or, as in the present case, how has it been said?

Among the primary duties of an academy, Smith concluded sharply, might be to "suggest to gentlemen of a jaunty air and on good terms with the world, that the profoundest issues on which the human mind is employed may after all involve truths, duties, and consequences, too important to be settled by compliments to friends, or by encomiums, however merited, on grace of style."[50] Arnold was hardly more guilty of misrepresentation than Smith of excessive severity, but in any event the lameness of his answer—he still believes that "there is a shade, a *nuance* of expression," in Renan's comment that implies what he said it did—is an apparent concession of error. He was not to forget Smith's reproach, however, and a year later he would attempt to turn the tables on him.

IV

Some two months after the publication of *Essays in Criticism*, Arnold wrote to Lady de Rothschild that if he republished the volume he would "leave out some of the preface and notes, as being too much of mere temporary matter."[51] The decision had apparently been reached at least two weeks earlier, when he told his mother that "the Essays [were] of too grave a character to tack much matter of an ephemeral kind permanently to them."[52] Accordingly, in preparing the volume for a second edition four years later, Arnold suppressed approximately half of the preface and omitted altogether the footnotes concerning decimal coinage and the Divorce Court.

But topicality was only one of the reasons for excision. There was also a question of taste, about which there were differences of opinion. Although Lady de Rothschild and John Duke Coleridge were "greatly taken with it," Arnold was right in believing that his "own family, from their training and their habits of thinking and feeling, would not find [the] preface to their taste":[53] when he read it to a brother and sister "they received it in such solemn silence that [he] began to tremble,"[54] and he told his mother that he felt sure it "would not exactly suit" her either.[55] Among the reviewers there was the same divided opinion. The young Henry James thought the preface manifested an amiability that was "a strong proof of [Arnold's] wisdom": it "admirably" reconciled "smoothness of temper with sharpness of wit."[56] The *Examiner* agreed that it had been "written in buoyant spirits" and "with delightful good humour,"[57] and the *Westminster Review* called it an "amusing . . . quiverful of stinging, if not absolutely poisoned arrows, shot right and left at reviewers, system-mongers, and the fat-headed respectable public in general, winding up with an eloquent appeal to Oxford."[58]

The *Pall Mall Gazette*, on the other hand, considered the preface a "whimsical and petulant" essay that seemed to suggest that "half the vivacity of the nation was expended in jesting about hell, or writing hexameters hard to scan."[59] R. H. Hutton, quoting in the *Spectator* the passage beginning, "Yes, the world will soon be the Philistines'," wondered whether there was not in it "just a grain of fatuity—'of that failure in good sense which comes from too warm a self-satisfaction' "—for which Arnold had criticized A. W. Kinglake.[60] The *North British Review* found the same passage "affected," with "a straining after humour which is very dismal."[61] The *London Review* called the preface "a piece of idle and incoherent chatter,"[62] and the *British Quarterly Review* declared that much of it was "a wanton outrage upon the amenities of literary warfare, and serves no purpose but to show how sensitive is the author himself, and yet how utterly indifferent to the feelings of others."[63]

Arnold's humor received an unexpectedly appreciative notice, however, from the *Saturday Review*,[64] whose "altered tone" he thought was the "best justification of the Preface."[65] The reviewer, whom internal evidence shows to be Fitzjames Stephen, described *Essays in Criticism* as "an excellent little volume," with a preface that

> is a curiosity, coming as it does from a man who has suffered many things from many reviewers, and is determined to be no better, but rather to become worse, and to go on not only repeating, but even exaggerating, the sins for which it was their painful duty to take him to task. Like the early Christians exposed to wild beasts in the arena, Mr. Arnold has been baited by reviewers. . . . His attitude in the midst of this storm of censure is almost as peaceful as that of Daniel in the den of lions, seated, as the showman observed, on his three-legged stool and reading the *Times* newspaper. He returns blessings for curses. . . . The only objection to Mr. Arnold's Preface is that it is too goodnatured. There is no pleasure in hitting a man who will not hit you back again.

Replying in kind to Arnold's civility, Stephen obligingly answered his ironic inquiry about the fate of Elizabeth Wragg by informing him that she was still in custody, awaiting trial the following month.

On the question of whether Elizabeth Wragg should be called something else Stephen was willing to concede, but on the questions of decimal coinage and the Divorce Court he was unyielding. The English retained their duodecimal system, he argued, because

> the Decimal Coinage Commissioners proved, on purely theoretical grounds, that it is a more convenient one than the decimal system. The "mass of Frenchmen" no doubt trusted the opinion of some Commission of their own, and the difference between the two countries is a difference of theory. This is the very point which we tried to establish, and which Mr. Arnold is apparently quite unable to understand. . . . To say that "we are too practical a people to trouble ourselves about the intellectual aspect" of the question is really to talk without a meaning. In proportion as people are practical they act in a reasonable manner.

Stephen, of course, was right, as Arnold recognized by withdrawing the footnote in 1869.

In response to Arnold's further comments on the Divorce Court, Stephen observed that since a court that must deal with adultery cannot be "ornamental," the question was whether the present court was "more hideous than it ought to be." That depended, he said, on the theory that determined legislation concerning marriage, and unless Arnold could state such a theory, he had "no right to condemn the existing court." Since he was apparently unable to make even "a statement of general principles," however, one suspected that he knew "little or nothing about jurisprudence" and simply felt "pleasure in using vague and big phrases." It was no reproach to him "to be a man of taste and not a man of thought," Stephen concluded, "but he ought not to deny to the whole English nation the power of thinking, merely because their thoughts do not happen to be expressed in a way which suits his taste." Stephen was again clearly right, and the result was the withdrawal in 1869 of a second long footnote.

V

Soon after the publication of *Essays in Criticism*, Arnold left for the Continent as a member of the Schools Inquiry Commission, remaining abroad until November. It was his second such mission, for in 1859, as an assistant commissioner to the Newcastle Commission on elementary education, he had spent some five months examining the schools of France, Switzerland, and Holland. The immediate product of this study was *The Popular Education of France*, published in the spring of 1861, shortly after its appearance as an official report, and including an introduction, later entitled "Democracy," written specifically for it. More clearly than anything else he wrote during the sixties, the introduction showed that the arena in which he sought to charm the wild beast of Philistinism extended far beyond Oxford.

Arnold took great pains with the introduction,[66] which went slowly because "much tact" was needed "as to how much and how little to say."[67] He began cautiously, in an obvious effort at conciliation. He was aware of the widespread jealousy and suspicion with which the state was regarded in England and of the conviction that only that power which was absolutely necessary should be granted to it, and this opinion he would not now question unless he believed there had been changes that removed the reasons once supporting it. Sweeping changes had, in fact, occurred as a result of the irresistible force of the modern spirit, manifested in the democratic movement and in the decline of the aristocracy's influence on the political life of the nation and on the spirit and character of the people. Under these altered circumstances, action by the state—"the organ of the national reason," "the nation in its collective and corporate character"—might now be salutary rather than dangerous. It could be salutary by answering the needs of a middle class that, despite its proud claim to need no help, wanted personal dignity, ideas, and culture. It could provide for this class, whose culture was "narrow, harsh, unintelligent, and unattractive," schools with a public character that conferred on them "a greatness and a noble spirit." In short, with the influence of the middle class increased and that of the aristocracy lessened, it might help the English avoid the fate of becoming Americanized.

Arnold's thesis encountered much of the hostility he had anticipated and carefully sought to overcome. Although recognizing that his "considerable experience as an inspector of schools . . . entitled [him] to a respectful hearing" and conceding that the "conciliatory tone of his essay [would] mitigate the opposition his views [were] sure to excite," the *Athenaeum* nevertheless concluded that he was a "theorist" and "bureaucrat" whose "darling engine of social improvement, State-Action, means a Government commission with a circumlocution office attached."[68] The *Edinburgh Review* agreed, declaring that his report "betoken[ed] a propensity to adopt the bureaucratic spirit of continental administration to a degree which [was] painful and repugnant to the mind of every liberal Englishman."[69] The *Eclectic Review* spoke of his "beaureaucratic [*sic*] despotism" as a cure worse than the disease,[70] and the *Inquirer* said that in his concern that English institutions not be Americanized he had forgotten that it was "still more needful to guard against Germanising or Gallicising them."[71] The *Literary Gazette*, straining for an appropriate allusion, even depicted him as a Ulysses captivated by the Gallic seductress, state action:

Oh, fair French vision! more alluring than the Siren, and too tempting for our wise and travelled Ulysses! Bind him to the mast, for Ulysses is no longer wise. Stop up the ears thrilling with the fascinating promises of "despotic beneficence," and row this ship of ours out of sight and hearing of a shore more perilous to crew and cargo than any peril possible.[72]

If his critics regarded state action as a remedy worse than the illness it was intended to cure, Arnold himself believed a worse remedy to be another (and ironic) result of the work by the Newcastle Commission—Robert Lowe's Revised Code of 1862. Among the commission's recommendations had been that a portion of public aid to elementary schools should be transferred to local rates and, in order to motivate teachers to emphasize the fundamentals of reading, writing, and arithmetic, should take the form of a capitation grant dependent on the number of pupils who could pass an appropriate examination. Seizing on this recommendation, Robert Lowe, vice-president of the Committee of Council on Education and an advocate of the principles of free trade in education as well as in commerce, proposed a revised code of "payment by results," which in essence would have reduced all aid to this single capitation grant. Although it possessed a certain appeal for the economy minded, the new plan aroused a prolonged controversy that eventually elicited from Arnold an anonymous article of protest and several letters to the press.

The article, entitled "The Twice-Revised Code" because of concessions Lowe later announced he was willing to make, was in a style very much different from that of *The Popular Education of France*. Whereas in the one Arnold had "sincerely meant to be conciliating and persuading," in the other, written at some risk to his professional future, he wished "to sum up the controversy . . . and to have the last word," a purpose that led him into a "lively" and "vivacious" manner and a sharpness, much of it aimed at Lowe, that he had not allowed himself in the official report. But despite these differences in tone, the same point of view lay behind the two works. As Arnold had earlier urged state action for the enrichment of middle-class culture, so now he argued against the Revised Code because of its restriction of the state's role to a mechanical one. It was "the heaviest blow dealt at civilisation and social improvement in [his] time," he declared in a rare hyperbole. When opposition mounted, he was pleased that its opponents took his own ground: "that the State has an interest in the primary school as a *civilising agent*, even prior to its interest in it as an *instructing agent*";[73] and in each of the first three letters that he contributed to the controversy, he insisted that the principle of rewards on which the Revised Code was based represented a fallacious notion of the state's responsibility to popular education.[74] After the dispute flared up again late in 1865 over the so-called conscience clause, he confidently predicted that the idea of the state's duty to education would prevail despite all the "regulation claptrap" uttered in its opposition; and in answer to the *Pall Mall Gazette*'s criticism of his concept, he described the state as the embodiment of the "deeper life" of the nation to which George Wither had referred in his *Vox Pacifica*.[75]

The debate on the Revised Code was, in effect, an interruption for Arnold, but with the partial defeat of Lowe on the issue of payment by results, he was able to resume his task of reporting to the English on his 1859 mission and to turn his attention from elementary to secondary education, which he thought an even "more urgent matter."[76] The result was *A French Eton*, published in *Macmillan's Magazine* in three installments between September 1863 and May 1864. After devoting the first number to an account of the Toulouse Lyceum and the Sorèze College, he reached in the second the central question: how England could provide comparable schools for the middle and professional classes, schools whose public nature conveys those "influences which expand the soul, liberalise the mind, dignify the character." Here, where prejudices were so strong that "prodigies of persuasion and insinuation" were required to prevail against them,[77] Arnold gave the same answer he had given in *The Popular Education of France*: "For public establishments modern societies have to betake themselves to the State; that is, to *themselves in their collective and corporate character.*" Some things, he agreed, the state had better leave alone. But education was not one of them.[78]

Reaction to this second installment was sharply divided. On the one hand the *Spectator* hoped that the plan Arnold suggested would gain sufficient support to "beat down the opposition alike of sectarian feeling and of that horror of State interference which in England so often interrupts an otherwise rapid progress,"[79] and the *Museum and English Journal of Education*, though critical of his "uncompromising and undiscriminating attack upon all private schools," nevertheless said categorically that "State education [was] a greater necessity than State police or a standing army."[80] The *Nonconformist*, on the other hand, was predictably hostile. Despite "all his experience," it declared, Arnold had "not comprehended public feeling in this country on such a matter" and knew "little of the force of the opposition to State-education, or of its deepest roots."[81]

After the completion of the first two numbers of *A French Eton*, Arnold wrote to Richard Cobden, whose support he wished to gain but who had indicated that his primary interest was in the lower class, that "one must look, as Burke says, for a power or *purchase* to help one in dealing with such great matters, and I find it nowhere but in an improved middle class." What was needed, he explained, was "to open their mind and to strengthen them by a better culture . . .; we shall then have a real force to employ against the aristocratic force and a moving force against an inert and unprogressive force, a force of ideas against the less spiritual force of established power, antiquity, prestige, and social refinement."[82] In the final installment, therefore, Arnold reiterated his belief, against the *Athenaeum*'s objection,[83] that the culture of the aristocracy had declined and that the middle class thus found itself in the center of the intellectual life of England. But before it could assume the role previously played by the class it had supplanted, before it could meet the demands made by the modern spirit, it would have to perfect itself; it would have to become "cultured, liberalised, ennobled, transformed." And there was no surer means for effecting this transformation, Arnold once again concluded, than the public establishment of schools that were cheap and accessible to all.[84]

The periodical notices of *A French Eton* were on the whole more appreciative than those of *The Popular Education of France* but equally cool toward Arnold's view of the state. The *Athenaeum* said that although he had profited from criticism of the earlier volume, Arnold continued to build "up a beautiful system of State-education" without "reference to practical difficulties" or "the actual needs of society."[85] The *Educational Times* described him as belonging "to a small class of rigid State educationists" and reassured its readers that there was little danger of the state's "taking upon itself the . . . burden of educating our Middle Classes, who are so well able to take care of themselves."[86] The *Westminster Review* flatly denounced state support as a *deus ex machina* and "one of the worst pitfalls to which a wholesome national life can be exposed."[87] Harriet Martineau, in the most intelligent review the book received, pointed out that "the State is an abstraction, wholly unavailable for use, till it is embodied in an agency." And even if this agency could be found, she said, there was still the obvious question of why it should be sought: "If the State is ourselves, there is nothing that it can do for us that we cannot do for ourselves, by going to work in the same way, or a better."[88]

VI

Later, in *Culture and Anarchy*, Arnold would attempt to answer these objections by defending his concept of the state more fully. But in the meanwhile he had before him the long-deferred task of writing "My Countrymen," which he completed soon after his return to England after nearly seven months abroad. It was thus an altogether different essay from the one originally planned, being less a reply to Fitzjames Stephen than a report to his countrymen on their position in world affairs. The impressions Arnold had brought home with him from the Continent were sufficiently disturbing to cause concern: clusters of provincial English tourists huddled together, insulating themselves from European currents of thought; encomiums in the press on the death of Palmerston, who had found his country the first power in the world and left her the third; the depressing conviction that there was "a real, an almost imminent danger of England losing immeasurably in all ways, declining into a sort of greater Holland, for want of . . . ideas, for want of perceiving how the world is going and must go, and preparing herself accordingly." Haunted by this conviction, Arnold wrote "My Countrymen" out of a new resolve to do all he could, and in every way, "to prevent its coming to pass."[89]

A measure of the change "My Countrymen"[90] underwent before its completion is the difference between the facetious opening, recalling the playful banter of the 1865 preface, and the ominous body of the essay itself, where there is a touch of both the ironic wit of Heinrich Heine and the patriotic fervor of Lemuel Gulliver. Arnold begins in a characteristic manner, confessing ignorance about the transcendental system that Stephen accused him of embracing but that in reality is quite beyond the strength of "a mere dabbler in these great matters." Yet he has been justly rebuked. He recognizes now that the newspapers have answered his pleas for better schools with a torrent of rhetoric in praise of the middle class; and as a result he is humbly penitent, vowing to meddle no more with practice. Nevertheless, he sees no harm in trying to continue to see things as they are. And to see them as they are is to see that foreign opinion of England is not the same as England's opinion of herself.

The discrepancy between the two views is dramatized by means of a device Arnold first employed in "My Countrymen" and later refined in letters to the *Pall Mall Gazette*—a dialogue between "certain foreigners," who would become the Arminius of *Friendship's Garland*, and Arnold himself, as naive and ineffectual a defender of England as Gulliver in the presence of the king of Brobdingnag. The foreign friends, who speak in a voice with a distinctly Arnoldian ring, declare that England is not what she was forty years ago, when she knew the way the world was going. But now she is unprepared for the work demanded by a new age, work requiring not force and energy, but intelligence. The age of aristocracies has passed, they say; nations now rise or fall depending on the intelligence of the middle class. And in intelligence the English middle class, with its narrow and repulsive religion and its barbarous culture, is absolutely lacking. When Arnold, aghast, produces a recent speech of Robert Lowe by way of protest, the answer is equally brutal: "Allow us to set clap-trap on one side." Rhetoric will get you nowhere, Arnold's friends inform him; only transformation will. "Unless you change," they warn, using his own language, "unless your middle class grows more intelligent, you will tell upon the world less and less, and end by being a second Holland."

The liveliness of Arnold's manner in "My Countrymen" was calculated to attract attention, and the sharpness of his criticism to invite comment. It was thus no surprise that the essay proved to be something of a sensation when it appeared in the *Cornhill* for February 1866, Arnold having correctly predicted that there would "be a good deal of talk about" it. Reaction ran the gamut from enthusiastic endorsement to angry denunciation, the two extremes roughly reflecting political lines. Carlyle "almost wholly approve[d]"; Sir James Shuttleworth thought the paper "timely and true";[91] Robert Lytton (Owen Meredith), who applauded Arnold's "combat with the Goliaths of Philistia," called it "admirable" and told Browning of his gratitude for "the courage and felicity with which [Arnold] has uttered what I and many others whose 'heart burned within us' have long felt."[92] To the *London Review* the paper was "striking" and "provocative of wholesome thought";[93] to the *Sunday Times* it was "excellent" and "powerfully-written";[94] to the *Court Circular* it was "capital" and "of more real value, perhaps, than anything that has appeared in the *Cornhill* for a long time."[95] The *Press* described the essay as a "gem" and Arnold as "this most thoughtful of living essayists" who was "always original and suggestive" and whose "paradox [was] preferable to other men's common-place."[96] The *Westmorland Gazette and Kendal Advertiser* said that he had "done good service in setting before braggart Mr. Bull the picture which he throws upon the retina of the continental eye."[97] And the *Edinburgh Evening Courant*, which noted with pleasure that the testimony Arnold brought from abroad was "eminently honourable to our old Toryism," used the essay for making a series of attacks on John Bright and middle-class policy.[98]

Other journals, while willing to concede a certain element of truth in "My Countrymen," were nevertheless inclined to agree with those members of Arnold's family who did "not quite like it."[99] The *Illustrated Times* called it "capricious" and said there was "something cold and alien" about Arnold's manner.[100] The *Illustrated London News* thought he had caused "needless irritation," presenting "many unpleasant truths . . . with an intense enjoyment exceedingly well calculated to defeat the object he professes to have at heart."[101] The *Spectator* described him as "an intellectual angel" and, in a comment anticipating a prevalent attitude toward Arnold later in the sixties, declared that

there is far too much of the Epicurean gods about him to inspire any sympathy. The dogmatism which is natural to the temperament of the earnest practical zealot is in him perverted into alliance with the temperament of the calm, purely contemplative thinker. . . . He prefers contemplating blankly the gulf between him and the uncultured people he pities. He exults in the intellectual paces which he displays before them, and [in] the beauty and delicately graduated variety [to] which they are simply blind. He is almost supercilious in his disdain for their clumsy and heavy tread. "Let them that be filthy be filthy still," is too accurate an expression of his grand unconcern.[102]

In a lighter vein, the *Examiner* published an amusing parody in which the writer recorded a conversation he had overheard in a railway carriage between a Frenchman and an English gentleman named Sampson, who left in sorrow after learning that England had "sunk in the opinion of the world to— let us see—to the fourteenth place: after Turkey"; and the Frenchman, upon being told by the writer that everything he had said was "exquisite, absolute, unmitigated Bosh," delightedly exclaimed, "Aha, I have then been talking *du Boche* all my life without knowing it!"[103]

The *Saturday Review*, on the other hand, took a sterner position. The writer, presumably Fitzjames Stephen, said that "if any one seriously doubts whether England is a great nation and is doing a great work in the world," he should look not "at the phrases which happen to be fashionable in French or German society" but at a few facts: that "England is the only great European country which enjoys political freedom to its full extent," that "England is the only great country in which the religious controversies of the day . . . have taken a practical form," and that England "is labouring honestly and vigorously to use its power for the good" of the people of India whom it rules. If after looking at these facts "you still sneer at the general result," the review concluded pointedly, "and still fail to see the lines of greatness and majesty through the dust and sweat and noise and turmoil which obscure what they develop, you despise human life itself."[104]

Of all the critics of "My Countrymen" Arnold attempted an immediate answer to only one—the author of two long letters to the *Pall Mall Gazette* pseudonymously signed "Horace."[105] The writer, who identified himself as "a subject of Napoleon III., a writer in French newspapers and reviews, a friend of England and the English, and a Liberal," was in reality, Arnold believed, "a woman I know something of in Paris, a half Russian, half English woman who married a Frenchman." Regardless of the author's identity, however, Arnold thought little of the first letter, although he contemplated "a short and light letter by way of reply" after the second appeared.[106] His motive was apparently the conviction that since Horace professed to be one of those foreigners who were allegedly disdainful of England, he had, in questioning the accuracy of Arnold's report on Continental opinion, disputed the very basis for his indictment.

The chief purpose of the first letter was to comment on a double irony in Arnold's thesis: that in disparaging political liberty he derided precisely the feature of English life to which France pointed as an example; and in praising the strong government, boulevards, and theaters of France, he overlooked her despotic prefects, conscription, and "inward humiliation." Indeed, Horace said in a pungent metaphor, "the savoury odour of our Imperial pottage" seems so to have penetrated into Arnold's nostrils that he is "ready to exchange [his] birthright for it." This is why "one loses all patience" when he blandly describes "the great wrongs of France as the 'inconveniences' of her system, while deploring the state of his own free country, which does not 'understand ideas.' "

The answer to such criticism, Horace concluded, was simple: had he written "My Countrymen" in France, he "would have brought down upon him . . . a thundering *avertissement*—supposing . . . he had found an editor foolhardy enough to publish it, and a printer willing to risk his license by printing it."

In his second letter, published three days later, Horace argued that the unfavorable picture of England's middle class that Arnold drew was the inescapable result of the political freedom it enjoyed: mediocrity could make itself more loudly heard in a free than in an enslaved society. Yet in actual fact, the English *bourgeois* was not inferior to his French counterpart, who rarely received a letter, whether from Islington or Camberwell; lived in a hideous house with a flowerless garden behind it; read only a newspaper excluding politics and devoted to scandal; and practiced not a narrow, repulsive religion but a narrow, repulsive irreligion. Arnold had derived his notions of England's foreign reputation, Horace said, from Victor Duruy, the minister of public instruction; and thus he had "been smiting his Philistines with the jawbone of a Minister." But he had obviously received a misleading impression, for England had given to Europe "her example, her political experiences, and her practical teachings," and if she continued to protect her liberties, she would "be fully entitled to the good-will and gratitude of the friends of freedom all over the world."

Arnold's reply, which appeared three days later as "An Explanation" in the *Pall Mall Gazette*,[107] effectively illustrates his skill in turning adverse criticism to his own advantage. Horace, he says, confirms what his foreign friends told him —that whereas the Continent could see its shortcomings clearly enough, England could see only what redounded to her own honor and glory. He admits that Horace is probably right in his account of the French *bourgeois*, but he can look at France with "inexhaustible curiosity and indulgence" because the French "faults are not ours, so we are not likely to catch them; their merits are not ours, so we are not likely to become idle and self-sufficient from studying them." He does not wish his countrymen to become "the café-haunting, dominoes-playing Frenchmen, but rather some third thing, neither the Frenchmen nor their present selves." His only point of difference with Horace, then, is that Horace desires political freedom for France, and he desires knowledge of how to use this freedom in England. But the French having "lost their tails," Horace wants to talk of nothing but tails. Arnold rejoices that England has not lost hers and sees no danger of her doing so. The human economy, however, "takes in other things as well,—hearts, for instance, and heads." In the one the English are not deficient, "but in heads there is always room for improvement." And this is why he has sought to convert the middle class, for whom, he says in a phrase pointing toward the thesis of his concluding lecture at Oxford, he wishes "to work out a deliverance from the horrid dilemma in which 'Horace' and others try to fix us;—liberty and Philistinism, or else culture and slavery."

VII

After the appearance of his reply to Horace, Arnold wrote to his mother that he "was glad to have [had] an opportunity to disclaim that positive admiration of things foreign, and that indifference to English freedom, which have often been imputed to me, and to explain that I do not disparage freedom, but take it for granted as our condition, and go on to consider other things." The other things that he wished to turn to were his educational report and the last of his lectures on Celtic literature. And although the readers of his answer to Horace were "much taken with" it, he was glad "to leave irony and the Philistines."[108]

Four months later, however, he was lured back to the pages of the *Pall Mall Gazette* by a letter that Goldwin Smith had written to the *Daily News*[109] toward the end of the Austro-Prussian War, when English opinion of Prussia was under-

going a change that Arnold attributed to the base desire for a
strong Germany to curb France. He had not forgotten Smith's
stinging rebuke a year earlier, with its implication that Fran-
cophile deference was behind his indictment of Philistinism;
nor was he unaware of Smith's distrust of Napoleon III and
hence his hostility toward France. The letter was well suited,
then, for the ironic purpose to which Arnold put it when he
introduced to the English public Arminius, a descendant of
Voltaire's von Thunder-ten-Tronckh and one of the party of
foreign friends whose views had been recorded in "My Countrymen." When Arminius is shown the letter by Smith, whom
he identifies as a "fanatic," he asks in the blunt fashion that
will be his hallmark, "But pray what is to unite Germany
and England against France?" Earlier in the year, in the Celtic
lectures he published, Arnold had said that the "bent" of the
time was toward "science," toward "knowing things as they
are"; and throughout the lectures he had emphasized that in
this trait the Germans were preeminent.[110] Now Arminius answers his own question by declaring that nations are no longer
drawn together by a common liberalism or a hatred of despotism. What unites or divides them is *Geist*—intelligence, the
opposite of "Ungeist." "The victory of 'Geist' over 'Ungeist,'"
he says, is "the great matter in the world. The same idea is at
the bottom of democracy; the victory of reason and intelligence over blind custom and prejudice." This is why German
Liberals have a sympathy for France that they do not have
for England, where *Geist* is a real force "only in a few scat-
tered individuals."[111]

   Arnold's return to the *Pall Mall Gazette* was greeted with
the usual disapprobation of his family, who preferred his
"graver" to his "gayer manner." Yet he thought the letter had
been "a great success."[112] It was having "all the effect [he]
could have wished," he told George Smith a week after its
publication, "and a second might possibly do harm."[113] Even
as he wrote this, however, two articles were appearing that
would change his mind.

Smith had already answered the letter in the hospitable pages of the *Daily News*,[114] ridiculing Arnold's advocacy of *Geist* and correcting his account of Continental affairs. Arnold was wrong, he said, in his interpretation of altered opinion toward Austria, which was "the mere incarnation of military force" and "nothing but a great army of mercenaries, treading civilization under its hoofs"; he was shockingly wrong in describing the French emperor as a "representative of French Democracy"; and he was wrong about Liberal opinion regarding a strong Germany, which was "the best and the only guarantee for peace and good feeling" between France and Germany. Smith's answer had sufficient effect on Arnold to persuade him to alter several passages when he republished the letter in *Friendship's Garland*, where he excised the description of Napoleon III as "that firm believer in democracy" and the statement that England desired "France and Germany to tear one another to pieces," and softened the attitude of European Tories toward the French emperor from one of hatred to one of "no real love."

Three days later, the *Illustrated Times* referred with approval to Smith's reply, agreeing that Arminius was "utterly wrong" in his account of English opinion concerning Germany.[115] But what apparently overcame Arnold's reluctance to publish more letters was a satiric middle article in the *Spectator*, written in the manner of the *Examiner*'s parody of "My Countrymen" and anticipating in several respects the more famous parody by Frederic Harrison of the concluding lecture at Oxford. Sarcastically describing Arnold as "our greatest intellectual seer" and "the only pure intellect in England," it recorded a conversation on a railway carriage between a pale, elderly gentleman who was Arnold's disciple and a vigorous young man who was skeptical about the new doctrine Arnold preached. "If Geist means Napoleonism," he said, "Geist means enlightened absolutism to my mind,—anything but democracy. This is the sort of thing that puzzles a poor fellow so about your 'great teacher' and his Geist. I am not sure Geist means anything in the world except what a poetical sort of fellow, with a good deal of French culture, and a high-trotting intellectual pace, chooses to smile upon." But the elderly gentleman, "in a sort of ecstasy," corrected him: "It hath not been given to the carnal mind to judge the operations of Geist. Geist is at once imperial and democratic. Geist is her own interpreter. Geist is justified of her children." At this point, however, the conversation was interrupted as the train reached its destination and the passengers left the carriage, the pale gentleman making "a half-reverential bow" over the *Pall Mall Gazette* containing Arnold's letter, and the youth impatiently muttering to himself, "Damn Geist!"[116]

Arnold's reply, dated twelve days after the first letter, was in the form of correspondence from Arminius himself, complaining that his English friend had "rushed into print with an idea or two he picked up from me . . . and . . . made rather a mess of it." Yet he was aware that Arnold was "a poor creature" at argument, and having a sincere regard for him, he willingly came to his aid. There was urgent need to help, moreover, for he wrote in the immediate aftermath of the Hyde Park riots, reminded of the comment Goethe had made on the anarchy of his own age: "There is no earnestness to approach the Whole, no willingness to do anything for the sake of the Whole." The French had faith in *Geist* even though they were perhaps not "solid enough," Arminius said. But the English had no sense of it at all, regarding culture as moonshine and seeking to develop the life of the nation "by rioting in the parks, abolishing church-rates, and marrying a deceased wife's sister."[117]

VIII

Two more letters followed during the second week of August, the first from Arnold, expressing injured feelings that Arminius had chosen to speak directly to the English rather than through him and ironically exacting vengeance by dismissing his talk of *Geist* as a "tissue of nonsense" and "vague

declamatory trash"; and the second from Arminius, deploring Arnold's "blind adoration of everything English" and
his "incapacity for arguing."[118] But neither of the letters attracted the attention that was received by the letter Arnold
wrote the following month to Hugh Owen, declining an invitation to read a paper at the Eisteddfod. With perhaps too
gracious a return of the compliment the Welsh had paid him,
he replied that the moment had come for "the greater delicacy
and spirituality of the Celtic peoples" to help combat the vulgarity, coarseness, and unintelligence of the English Philistine, faults that threatened England's growth even more than
the "helplessness" of her aristocracy and the "rawness" of her
lower class.[119] For some readers, the letter was the final insult
Arnold had heaped upon a long-suffering nation; and after
its publication in the *Pall Mall Gazette* on September 5 and
the *Times* a day later, it was roundly denounced by a press
Arnold had repeatedly ridiculed in delivering his message of
Geist.

The *Times*, which one of Arnold's friends in "My Countrymen" had called "a gigantic Sancho Panza,"[120] scornfully
dismissed Arnold's letter as an "effusion" and "arrant nonsense," and the Eisteddfod as "one of the most mischievous
and selfish pieces of sentimentalism which could possibly be
perpetrated" and "a foolish interference with the natural progress of civilization and prosperity."[121] It was equally blunt
when "Talhaiarn," the Welsh bard who had opened the Eisteddfod, wrote to protest that "neither an Act of Parliament
nor all the wisdom, wit, and ridicule of *The Times* will put
down the passion of the Welsh people for their national institution and their loving fondness for their old language."[122]
In reply, the *Times* described Arnold's letter as an "extraordinary illustration" of the follies of glorifying everything Welsh
and encouraging the use of the Welsh language, and concluded with some helpful advice to its correspondent: "The
best service 'TALHAIARN' could do his countrymen would
be to drop his outlandish title and to refuse ever to talk Welsh
in Wales."[123]

But a more celebrated denunciation of the Eisteddfod and of Arnold's letter appeared in the *Daily Telegraph*,[124] which had held a central position in English Philistinism since the preface to *Essays in Criticism*. On the same day as the initial attack by the *Times*, it published a "savage" fourth leader written by a young assistant editor named James Macdonell, who was driven by an "aggressive eager nature," as his sister-in-law described it, and a resentment of Arnold's "high-and-mighty airs."[125] With ponderous sarcasm, he complained that Arnold "has long been telling us that we are a nation of vulgar, illiterate boors. . . . But when . . . we have asked the elegant JEREMIAH what he would have us do to get souls and get 'Geist,' he has contented himself with a few Delphic utterances, in which our darkened understandings have failed to see a glimmer of meaning." At last, however, the prophet has spoken out unmistakably. The Eisteddfod, "a grand national debauch" where the Welsh sing ballads, talk patriotism, and eat leeks, is to be England's deliverer, "so that the garden of British Philistinism shall yet blossom as the rose with culture, and 'Geist,' and MATTHEW ARNOLDS." Although Macdonell agreed that this was a consummation devoutly to be wished, he nevertheless requested

a sight of the prophet's credentials. From what place does he hail? What has he done that he should put on airs, and proclaim himself so immensely holier than other men? The answer is simple: he is the high-priest of the kid-gloved persuasion. He has what used to be called a "mission"; that is, he has come to this earth to preach the gospel of urbanity and to wage war against emphasis.

In carrying out this mission, Macdonell said, he has commanded his disciples to go to France and Germany, and after their "native rudeness" has been "softened" by the "urbane atmosphere" of the Continent, they are to return home and "regularly buy two-penny worth of second-hand culture."

This, Macdonell admitted, was "a mighty result." Yet, more in anger than in sorrow, he wondered whether the result was altogether desirable:

When "Geist" is a little more common in these islands, a nation of MATTHEW ARNOLDS may be tolerable. Till that day, we may be permitted to offer up a fervent prayer for deliverance from such a visitation. Vulgarity, we agree with our superfine friend, is far from pleasant; but vulgarity, we may be permitted to add, can assume more forms than one. It can speak the language of the study as well as of the street; it is none the less repulsive because it employs the words of culture; and sometimes—even in the case of Professors of Poetry—it can take the form of self-conceit. Airs may be put on in a fashionable magazine as well as in a fashionable park. A literary coxcomb is quite as offensive to a cultured taste as the kind of coxcomb who is more common. Nor, we would add, is it surprising that personal vanity should sometimes find vent in rebuking the vanity of nations. A little arrogance is no doubt pardonable in a JEREMIAH denouncing the sins of a people; but the assurance must first of all be given that the JEREMIAH is real. The time has not come for recognising as a JERE-MIAH the man who can pen pretty verses, turn pretty sentences, and express pretty sentiments. There is no analogy, we would remind Mr. ARNOLD, between a prophet and a fop.

After reading these "inhuman attacks" on him Arnold determined to "do penance in a little preface" when he published the Celtic lectures in a single volume.[126] Before that time arrived, however, he found occasion for several satiric rejoinders. Arminius returned in November to the pages of the *Pall Mall Gazette* so "immensely tickled" by the *Daily Telegraph*'s description of his "artless and obscure" friend that he was in a mood for reconciliation following their three months' estrangement. But about British Philistinism he was as caustic as ever. The *Times*, he said, was "the well-to-do Philistine," in whose oracle there must be "no uncertain sound . . ., no faltering, nothing to excite misgivings or doubts"; and the *Daily Telegraph* was "the rowdy Philistine," having like Elkanah Settle a boisterous style and a prose incorrigibly lewd.[127]

The immediate reason for the return of Arminius was a speech by John Bright concerning Irish land tenure and alluding to the Prussian reforms of Stein, which Arnold thought he could explain to the readers of the *Pall Mall Gazette*.[128]

When he was amusingly answered by an Irish squire and diligent student of "the wit and wisdom of Arminius," raising further questions about Prussian and Irish tenants,[129] he wrote a second letter, replying in kind.[130] But a more basic response to the first of the letters was a middle article in the *Standard*,[131] declaring that the system Arnold described "could not be carried out in the British empire without tyranny of a kind that we have done with six hundred years ago," and voicing again the objection to Arnold's ironic manner and his gospel of *Geist*:

. . . if Mr. Arnold has a fault, it is that he is somewhat over-exquisite in his critical part—that he holds himself too high above the heads of the poor herd who are the objects of dissection. He is a little too eager it may be to prove to us, miserable denizens of Philistia, how very low we are in the scale of humanity. He flouts us, perhaps a little too often, with our lack of *Geist*. He carries his own superior culture a little too loftily, and beats us with it sometimes too unmercifully. Worms will turn if trodden on, and in revenge it is no wonder that Mr. Arnold's victims should discover in his own too violent and frequent repudiation of Philistinism something which betrays that he, too, is of the children of Gath. The very emphasis with which he declaims against *Un-geist* compels us to inquire into his own claims to be our instructor. We may admit our own want of intellect; we may be all given over to Philistinism, provincialism, and other peculiar English vices; but we desire to know what is the new Gospel which Mr. Arnold has undertaken to preach, and what is his claim to preach it thus vociferously in season and out of season.

Arnold believed that his first letter had been "successful," making "the knowledge of Stein's land reforms *popular*, which was no easy feat." After his reply to the Irish squire, therefore, he let the matter drop, having been assured by both Browning and John Duke Coleridge that it was "impossible to over-rate the effect" his letters produced. But there was still the "penance" to do for his letter to Hugh Owen, a promise he fulfilled the following May (1867) when he completed an introduction to the Celtic lectures that he was "pleased with."[132]

A year earlier Arnold had concluded the last of the Celtic
lectures with the passage that moved the principal of Jesus
College to exclaim, in Milton's words, that the angel had
ended. The English, Arnold said, summarizing the message
he had repeatedly delivered since the lecture on Heine, were
becoming aware that they had "sacrificed to Philistinism culture, and insight, and dignity, and acceptance, and weight
among the nations, and hold on events that deeply concern[ed them], and control of the future." But they could not
conquer their "hard unintelligence" by storm. It had to be
"suppled and reduced by culture, by a growth in the variety,
fulness, and sweetness of [their] spiritual life; and this end
[could] only be reached by studying things that [were] outside of [them]selves, and by studying them disinterestedly."
The benefit to be derived "from knowing the Celt and things
Celtic" lay precisely here, he went on to say in the introduction, resuming the theme where he had left it the previous
May. And it was Hugh Owen's appreciation of his insistence
on this benefit that had led him to extend the invitation Arnold declined in a letter that he now skillfully defends.

In replying to Owen, he confesses, he naturally "enlarged
on the merits of the Celtic spirit and of its works, rather than
on their demerits." Yet both in the letter itself and in the
lectures, he clearly pointed out the dangers against which the
Celtic glorifiers should guard. "The sooner the Welsh language disappears as an instrument of the practical, political,
social life of Wales," he said, "the better; the better for England, the better for Wales itself." The *Times*, however, "prefers a shorter and sharper method of dealing with the Celts,"
and in disposing of them it "most severely treated" him as
well. For himself he has little concern, accustomed as he is to
such attacks and to the Corinthian style of leading articles.
But "these asperities of the *Times*," he says, characteristically
turning a personal attack on himself into an issue of broad
implications, suggest the reasons for England's difficulties with
Ireland. Might not the English traits extolled by the *Times*,

he asks, "have a better chance of making their way among the poor Celtic heathen, if the English apostle delivered his message a little more agreeably?" The Englishman, with his "boundless faith in machinery," expects the Welshman to be automatically drawn to him, seemingly unaware that people are united not by mechanical but by spiritual ties, and articles like those in the *Times* reflect this "want of sympathy and sweetness in the English nature." If he is to grow, therefore, the Englishman cannot rest satisfied with Goldwin Smith's "eloquent" view of England as "the favourite of Heaven" or with the claptrap of the *Times*. On the contrary, Arnold concludes, with the most devastatingly ironic use he ever made of a biblical allusion, he must "leave the dead to bury their dead, and . . . go on unto perfection."[133]

Arnold might well have been pleased with the introduction, which the periodical reviewers praised with a unanimity they had not shown toward the preface to *Essays in Criticism*. The *Westminster Review* thought that he "was entirely in the right" and that the *Times* had demonstrated "the most narrow prejudices and the worst spirit of bigotry."[134] The *British Quarterly Review* said that whereas the articles in the *Times* were "rough" and "obtuse," *On the Study of Celtic Literature* was a "surpassingly beautiful . . . lay sermon of high and important moral urgency."[135] The *Spectator* agreed that he was "absolutely just" in his reply to the *Times* and declared that the volume contained the most valuable criticism he had yet written: "His attacks upon Anglo-Saxon Philistinism have all been vigorous, and many of them just, but they have had all the defects of purely destructive criticism; they have irritated, without suggesting adequately how we could learn to be better. But in these lectures Mr. Arnold shows us not only where we are wrong, but why we are wrong."[136]

The four-year campaign against Philistinism had thus come to a close with Arnold neither torn to pieces nor dying in a ditch. But there was still before him the self-imposed mission of helping to transform England, of making more compelling the idea of the state to which he had often referred, and of pointing the way more clearly toward the perfection of which he had spoken. The mission had gained new urgency, moreover, by agitation concerning the Second Reform Bill, arousing old fears of a nation torn by anarchy. In the meanwhile, Arnold's "constant companion" had been Bishop Wilson's *Maxims of Piety and of Christianity*,[137] and these, together with his deepened appreciation for the imaginative qualities of the Celts, made apparent that more than *Geist* was required for transformation. As he was preparing, then, for his final Oxford lecture, delivered a month after the completion of the Celtic introduction, he was led irresistibly to consider sensitivity to beauty as the necessary complement to clarity of mind. Taking his text from Swift, he would speak on sweetness and light, and in doing so would create still another controversy.

CHAPTER SIX

The Apostle and the Enemies of Culture

Something inherently mean in action. Even the Creation of the Universe disturbs my Idea of the Almighty's greatness . . . .—Coleridge

Action is consolatory. It is the enemy of thought and the friend of flattering illusions.—Conrad

. . . He who gave our nature to be perfected by our virtue, willed also the necessary means of its perfection.—He willed therefore the state —He willed its connexion with the source and original archetype of all perfection.—Burke

. . . the culture of the individual is dependent upon the culture of a group or class, and . . . the culture of the group or class is dependent upon the culture of the whole society to which that group or class belongs.—T. S. Eliot

That to every parish throughout the kingdom there is transplanted a germ of civilization; that in the remotest villages there is a nucleus, round which the capabilities of the place may crystallize and brighten; a model sufficiently superior to excite, yet sufficiently near to encourage and facilitate imitation; this, the unobtrusive, continuous agency of a Protestant church establishment, this it is which the patriot and the philanthropist, who would fain unite the love of peace with the faith in the progressive amelioration of mankind, cannot estimate at too high a price.—Coleridge

Some six months before the Tories dished the Whigs and took their historic leap in the dark, Frederic Harrison replied in the *Fortnightly Review* to the now famous thesis of Robert Lowe that the franchise should be denied to the working class because of its moral and intellectual unfitness for the responsibility of suffrage. Harrison, a thirty-five-year-old barrister, Comtist, and friend of the laborer, answered that the sole reason for extending the franchise was "that the existing House of Commons performs its task ill" and "by the proposed change it will perform it better." The "658 well-bred gentlemen" of the House of Commons were "no tyrants," he said. But with "the absolute control over this nation, boundless opportunities, credit, and prestige, no difficulties, and no antagonists," they had succeeded only "in duping their people, in degrading their political tone, in stifling public activity." Zealous "for little but their personal ambitions and class privileges," they had employed two decades of unlimited power to create a host of grievances:

> no national education, no efficient poor-law, no reorganized army, no law reform, no contented Ireland; the ancient iniquity of game-laws unabated, the laws of landlord and tenant, of master and servant unredressed; men who care for public good wearied out or hunted down, till no man is so desperate as to venture to force anything through this jungle of obstruction; practical improvements untouched from very despair of their ever becoming practicable.

These sins of omission did not in themselves justify extension of the franchise, Harrison admitted. But they illustrated the evils that were perpetuated by Robert Lowe's "cant about culture" and the man of culture, who in politics was "one of the poorest mortals alive," unrivaled in his pedantry and lack of judgment. The "best part" of the working class, on the other hand, was of all classes the most able to exercise political power because of its "sense of justice," "openness and plainness of character," and "practical knowledge of social misery." It had, in short, "the brightest powers of sympathy, and the readiest powers of action."[1]

Harrison came to regret the intensity of his reply to Lowe, who later wrote a fantasy based on the Comtian view of history that his critic thought "the only thing on Reform worth reading." But regret did not imply a change of political purpose. On the contrary, as Maurice Cowling has noted, Harrison was a determined Positivist who advocated "a fundamental revolution" by which a Comtian polity would supplant a "Venetian" one. And in his correspondence he was even more inflammatory than in print. The "Liberal M.P.'s," he said privately, were "a pack of curs" who did not understand that "strong measures, processions and physical force" were essential if Gladstone was to be "dragged out" of his shell.[2]

Harrison's article appeared at a time when Arnold's final lecture at Oxford was "forming itself" in his mind.[3] The lecture he eventually delivered was in part the essay on "Culture and Its Enemies" that he had intended for the *Cornhill* early in 1867.[4] But before he could complete this essay, repeatedly deferred because of the pressure of other duties,[5] Harrison gave new point to the debate between culture and its enemies. For one thing, he offered a direct challenge to the thesis of "The Function of Criticism at the Present Time," where the concept of culture had been adumbrated. In ridiculing the "cant about culture," Harrison denied its role as a propagator of "the best that is known and thought in the world." His contempt for the indecisive man of culture ran counter to the first essential element of disinterestedness, the "love of a free play of the mind on all subjects, for its own sake"; and his impatient demand for practical, immediate answers to practical, immediate problems ran counter to the second element, the steadfast refusal to yield to political or practical considerations. His anger with those in authority, his advocacy of a complete transfer of political power, his appeal for far-reaching changes in English society—all struck at the belief in "force till right is ready." Harrison's method, moreover, was for Arnold as objectionable as his message. Based upon an elaborate and ingenious philosophic system, it was a rigidly logical method whose very rigidity precluded discovery of solutions to the problems with which it dealt. Already alarmed by the Hyde Park riots of the preceding summer, Arnold could thus hear in Harrison only the inflammatory voice of one crying out in the wilderness of Comtian thought.[6]

Even before delivering his concluding lecture, Arnold found occasion, in the second of two letters on compulsory education which he wrote to the *Pall Mall Gazette* in April, to portray Harrison as "that powerful young publicist, . . . furbishing up a guillotine" and evoking "a Jacobinical spirit."[7] Then, in the lecture itself, he assigned him a still more subversive role as culture's principal enemy. Here Harrison was represented in the very first paragraph as a writer whose "systematic and stringent manner" epitomized the hostile view of culture. Later he appeared in the foremost ranks of those who wished to lead a new political power in "the ways of Jacobinism." And at the conclusion, he was said to have written an article that so "hisses" with "fierce exasperation" that it demanded the reminder, "where bitter envying and strife are, there is confusion and every evil work."[8]

In this final lecture, delivered on the afternoon of June 7, Arnold placed against the Jacobinism of Harrison the culture of Oxford. Before a sympathetic and "very crowded audience"[9] steeped in the university's "sentiment . . . for beauty and sweetness," he declared that culture is quite different from what its enemies suppose it to be, a mere dabbling in classical literature. It is, on the contrary, the love and pursuit of intellectual and ethical perfection. On one level, it has its origin in "a desire after the things of the mind simply for their own sakes and for the pleasure of seeing them as they are," and on a higher level, in "the noble aspiration to leave the world better and happier than we found it." On this higher level it can now act effectively, because the period of intellectual delivery that it needs in order to flourish is at hand. When thus liberated, culture has a goal even beyond that of religion: it strives for the inward, general, and harmonious development of the human personality. Culture is thus an indispensable corrective to the fragmentary view of life embraced by those who do not know it or who misunderstand it. Unlike its enemies, it proclaims a view of perfection that unites the two qualities of beauty and intelligence, of sweetness and light.[10] "Gt. applause at the end," Mrs. Arnold noted with pleasure in her diary that evening, "& altogether very successful."

I

When "Culture and Its Enemies" appeared unchanged in the July *Cornhill*, however, it was less enthusiastically received. The first to attack was the *Morning Star*, a "vile" paper and "true reflexion of the rancour of Protestant Dissent in alliance with all the vulgarity, meddlesomeness, and grossness of the British multitude."[11] In an article that Lord Strangford called "simply absurd"[12]—a retaliatory leader prompted by Arnold's criticism of John Bright, brother-in-law of the *Star*'s former editor and an influential figure in the paper's management—it denounced the lecture as being "founded from beginning to end on the most absurd and obvious misconception," and echoing "here and there some nonsensical sneers" of "blockheads," "cads," and "small Tory scribblers." Having been in the society of "pedants" and "prigs," the paper said, Arnold wrote in "a very small, sneering, and unworthy style of criticism."[13]

The *Star*'s attack was followed several days later by a sarcastic third leader in the *Daily Telegraph* describing Arnold as a snob who boasted of teaching "the gentlemen of England" but not the "sons of tradesmen"; as an obscurantist who condemned the political party that had long fought for the spread of education—and hence of culture—but praised the university that had resisted it; and as a fastidious fop whose "gentle limbs," too tender for battle, were clothed in "a flowered dressing-gown." Toward this "elegant creature" the *Telegraph* felt only the disgust of Hotspur.[14]

The article in the *Daily Telegraph* was amiability itself, however, compared with the *London Review*'s "outrageous"[15] attack on Arnold's "monotony of nonsense" and eruption into "cultivated hysterics": "For Mr. Arnold does not shriek, he only squeaks. He could do nothing so ungentleman-

ly as to shriek. He uses his throat for the purpose of jump-
ing down it, rather than uttering anything worth listening to."
With even more ponderous sarcasm than that employed by
the *Daily Telegraph*, it depicted Arnold as "an intellectual
fop" who

> plumes himself upon being what he calls a Liberal, whilst all the
> time he is the most illiberal of men. . . . He writes with white kid
> gloves on, and his sweetness is that of eau-de-Cologne. A powerful
> intellect he would call a vulgar one. . . . Burns was a very great man,
> I dare say, but he was not at Oxford, and we all know that he had a
> very bad French accent. Such is the general tone of Mr. Arnold's crit-
> icisms. There is an air of "Plato and rose-water" about him, but a
> great deal more rose-water than Plato.

Hence Arnold's "outburst" against John Bright, who

> is something more than a classical scholar, a spinner of fine phrases,
> and a minor poet: he is a doer and a worker. To him, and such as
> he, do we owe the inestimable boon of cheap bread, of free trade,
> and of open labour markets, without which our brethren must have
> ever remained in poverty with all its accompanying evils. These are,
> we know, far too material matters for the consideration of such a
> transcendentalist and superlatively fine thinker as Mr. Matthew Ar-
> nold. He has never lost an opportunity of sneering not only at the ma-
> terial wealth of England, but at everything else which has raised us
> above other nations. When we look back upon his writings, we do
> not forget that he has sneered at our Protestantism, sneered at science,
> and when he could find nothing else, sneered at English surnames. In
> his present essay he has probably reached his climax.

Yet the paper gratefully noted that an answer to Arnold's
lecture had been provided by the recently opened London College, which intended to produce valuable members of society and not "intellectual dandies" exhibiting "their little
rococo minds for the admiration of young ladies or of old
women—of both sexes."[16]

Meanwhile there had been sectarian criticism of the lecture. The *Illustrated Times* cautioned the public "to watch

and distrust" Arnold, who was "a most insidious ally of the party of centralisation, whether in religion or in politics."[17] More responsibly, the editor of the *Nonconformist*, Edward Miall, published a long front-page protest against the misrepresentation of its motto, "The Dissidence of Dissent and the Protestantism of the Protestant religion," which had been taken from Burke to show the paper's twofold purpose: "to deliver religious life as embodied in the churches from the overruling and corrupting influence of Civil Governments, and to uphold the rights of private judgment against sacerdotal tyranny." After a defense of Nonconformists that "touched" Arnold,[18] Miall concluded by reproaching him for his injustice to them:

> If Nonconformists are narrow and inadequate in their ideal of human perfection . . . it ill becomes an Oxford Professor, lecturing at Oxford, to tax them with their deficiency. For two hundred years they have been shut out from that University by the exclusive and jealous spirit of the Establishment, and from whatever sweetness and light it is supposed to diffuse. Why select the victims of its meanness and intolerance as an illustration of one-sidedness, when the cruel monopolist to whose injustice it should be attributed is suffered to escape? Why ridicule the stunted proportions and deformities which have been the result of hard usage, and not rather denounce the narrow and inadequate ideal of the Establishment which deliberately and persistently inflicted them? Man of culture and poetry as Mr. Matthew Arnold is, he has not showed himself free from the vice of the system in connection with which he was trained. His sympathies are with the oppressor, not the oppressed. . . .[19]

Another Nonconformist paper, the Leeds *Mercury*, was less restrained. In an angry leading article devoted largely to name-calling, it described Arnold as a victim of "social dyspepsia," "pretensions and self-conceit" who despised earnestness and expressed his "refined and gentlemanly" views in sneers.[20]

The *Spectator*, on the other hand, thought the lecture was the most compassionate and least supercilious of Arnold's addresses to his countrymen. But it objected to his heterodox thesis that the love of perfection goes beyond religion. Echoing the doctrine of "unconsciousness" advocated by Carlyle and Mill, it declared that sweetness and beauty are the products "not of conscious yearning after sweetness and beauty, but of the moral and religious submission of our will to the inspiration of a divine love." The fatal weakness in Arnold's culture, the paper said, is that it "really has no direct moral authority over us."[21]

The complaint of the *Spectator* was later developed more fully in what Arnold told his mother was "the best answer to [his] lecture from a Puritan point of view that [he had] seen."[22] In a brief notice on July 12, the Aberdeen *Free Press* said that his advocacy of culture, though "remarkable" and "able," was needlessly unjust to religion;[23] and in a long review the following week it argued that despite his "insight," "freshness of thought," and "eloquent pleas for ideas," Arnold's solution to the problem of attaining human perfection was inadequate because of his failure to take "conquest" into account:

Human nature has risen through culture, but culture has been maintained and advanced . . . through conquest; through conquest over passion and appetite within us—through conquest of external nature —through abiding conflict with the passion, vice, self-seeking, which have ever been so rife, and still continue rife, in the world. . . . "Sweetness and light" . . . are elements of culture, but they will fail unless there be also the element of conquest. The element of poetry is noble and potent. But the puritan element is not less essential, has a function at least as indispensable and as noble. It is now the fashion to decry the Puritans, and Mr. Arnold, in a way not worthy of him, falls into the fashion and leads it. The Puritans, doubtless, did not reach perfection; but Puritanism brought into the national life and character higher elements than had entered it before. . . . Mr. Arnold is unjust towards Puritanism, because inappreciative of its true place and function. . . . The Puritans are no more to be judged by the standard of Virgil and Shakspeare than Shakspeare and Virgil are to be judged by their standard. . . . There is the poetry of life, but there is also the battle of life. . . . The race has needed its reformers, and its martyrs, no less than its singers—Huss, Luther, and Knox, no less than Virgil, Goethe, and Shakspeare.

Without the indispensable "Puritan element," the paper concluded, culture would be only "a nerveless, pampered dilettantism, without conscience, without noble impulse, and without any real stimulus to progress."[24]

Among Arnold's few supporters was the *Globe and Traveller*, which published a third leader enthusiastically endorsing his views.[25] But the Liverpool *Daily Post* was right in predicting that these views were "too novel to be popular,"[26] and as the summer faded into autumn the controversy continued. By September it had reached America, where the *Nation* published a letter from a correspondent contrasting the useless life of the man of culture, who "has simply crammed his head with knowledge, none of which ever comes out to give 'sweetness and light' to mankind," with the fruitful labors of manufacturers, merchants, and artisans. Commenting on the letter in the same issue of the *Nation*, E. L. Godkin agreed that Arnold's man of culture was a critic cloistered from the everyday world of reality, and Arnold himself a "faultfinder" who "absolutely declined all responsibility as to remedies."[27] Later in the autumn, the *Westminster Review* seized the occasion of the publication of *New Poems* to express relief at returning to an Arnold without "that air of coxcombry and insolent impertinence to others which he so affects in prose."[28] But the *Eclectic and Congregational Review* found the fop even in the verse. Although Arnold is "a poet of grief" who "sees and feels really the sadness and sorrow of things," it said, he "never seems to go to a funeral without a lace pocket-handkerchief to absorb the lachrymatory distillations."[29]

A more intelligent response than this stale repetition of old charges was made by Henry Sidgwick, then a young Trinity Fellow and later a "favourite" of George Eliot[30] who occupied with distinction the Chair of Moral Philosophy at Cambridge.

In what Arnold thought was a "clever" article in *Macmillan's Magazine*,[31] he described the lecture as overambitious, "because it treats of the most profound and difficult problems of individual and social life with an airy dogmatism that ignores their depth and difficulty"; vague, because in it Arnold "is speaking sometimes of an ideal, sometimes of an actual culture, and does not always know which"; and perverse, because it ignores the antagonism between self-development and self-sacrifice, culture calling for the one and religion for the other. Sidgwick's thesis was the seemingly paradoxical one that there is too little culture in Arnold's account of both religion and culture. If he possessed more of the sweetness he praises, Sidgwick said, he would not be contemptuous of the forms in which religion exists; and if he possessed more of the intellectual curiosity he advocates, he would not be led into a superficial, inadequate conception of religion that ignores its true power. The same applies to Arnold's treatment of culture. If he were the spokesman for an ideal culture, he would not be guilty of Pharisaical smugness, and he would recognize the faults by which culture in its present state is weakened—the lack of enthusiasm, the absence of sympathy with the common people, the incapacity for action. And if Arnold were to distinguish between ideal and actual culture, he would realize that the aim of ideal culture is not to promote a fastidious development of the individual but to answer the needs of humanity. One feels little sympathy, Sidgwick concluded in what by now had become a cliché, "with a cheerful modern liberal, tempered by renouncement, shuddering aloof from the rank exhalations of vulgar enthusiasm, and holding up the pouncet-box of culture betwixt the wind and his nobility."[32]

Three months later appeared the wittiest of the replies to "Culture and Its Enemies," Frederic Harrison's "Culture: A Dialogue," which so amused Arnold that he laughed until he cried.[33] The two speakers in the dialogue are Harrison, in the role of a belletristic trifler who talks airily as Arnold's disciple, and Arminius, the Prussian whose brusque manner he effectively exploits for a satiric purpose. The basic irony of their dialogue derives from the embarrassing questions that Arminius, in the *Pall Mall Gazette* the friend of Arnold but now his critic, asks of Harrison, in reality Arnold's opponent but now his ostensible disciple who, in defending his master's position, so undermines it as to make it indefensible. To add point to this dialogue on culture, both Harrison and Arminius are endowed with an inexhaustible fund of literary allusions from which they draw with ludicrous results. Through their exchange Harrison attempts to achieve a serious objective, which is to show that Arnold's description of culture is so hopelessly vague, his conception of culture's function so all-embracing, and his reasoning so completely unsystematic that he is often speaking of little more than a meaningless abstraction; that he so emphasizes mere refinement and a critical attitude of mind as to have a pernicious effect in social, political, and religious spheres; and that he flagrantly misrepresents Comtism, which is directly opposed to Jacobinism and which has, in fact, many of the aims Arnold himself ascribes to culture. At the end of the dialogue, after Harrison has patiently explained to the obtuse Prussian that in culture there is "harmony, but no system; instinct, but no logic; eternal growth, and no maturity; everlasting movement, and nothing acquiesced in; perpetual opening of all questions, and answering of none; infinite possibilities of everything; the becoming all things, the being nothing," Arminius begins to pace the room, muttering to himself:

> But I remember when the fight was done—
> .   .   .   .
> And telling me the sovereign'st thing on earth
> Was parmaceti for an inward bruise.[34]

With the publication of Harrison's satire, the controversy flared up once again in the daily and weekly press. The *Morn-*

ing Star gleefully noted that Arnold had been given "a Roland for his Oliver,"[35] and the *Saturday Review*, which in an earlier issue had said that Arnold's lesson was "just the lesson which, in an age and country like our own, men have the least inclination, and the greatest need to learn,"[36] now leaned more sympathetically than before toward the man of action as opposed to the man of culture. Reformers like Harrison, the *Saturday* asserted, believe "there are certain definite evils to be eradicated. And it is because Mr. Arnold will not lend a hand to the humble operation of uprooting them, that they grow impatient with him, and want to know what he means by all his contemplation."[37]

II

From early summer Arnold had been planning a sequel to "Culture and Its Enemies," under the title, "Anarchy and Authority." He originally conceived of it as a single essay for the August *Cornhill* in which he would "say several things which need[ed] to be said in accompaniment to what" had been said in the lecture. But "Culture and Its Enemies" elicited so many replies that he postponed the article, first to autumn and then to winter, in order "to gather up all the murmurings into one and see what they [came] to."[38] This procedure created problems of its own, however, for the early numbers of the "Anarchy and Authority" series were in turn attacked by the periodical press and thus called for further sequels. The ultimate result was that Arnold wrote not one but five essays, published in the *Cornhill* during the winter and summer months of 1868.

By November 1867, when he seems to have begun the first of the essays, all of his critics had declared themselves and he could see what their murmurings came to. It was, essentially, that he had not succeeded in freeing the word "culture" from its traditional associations with the cloistered and ineffectual man of letters,[39] and that in his role as apostle of culture he too closely resembled the foppish lord who infuriated Hotspur. More specifically, the murmurings came to four basic objections. There was first the complaint that Arnold's concept of culture was impractical, encouraging a skeptical, critical frame of mind that led to paralysis of action. A second objection was that he wrote from the viewpoint of a cultivated, privileged, and overfastidious person who was contemptuous of the common man and concerned with his own refinement rather than with the urgent needs of humanity. From religious and sectarian journals in particular came a third criticism, that he was indifferent to the sterner side of morality, hostile to conventional faith, and unjust to Puritanism. And, finally, it was said that his entire case for culture was vitiated by confusion and the absence of logical, systematic thought.

Arnold had earlier written to his mother, after the appearance of the review in the Aberdeen *Free Press*:

. . . What you say about the Aberdeen paper is very true and it gives me pleasure that you see it: if one writes on one side, people will have it you are blind to all other sides . . . . But something of what Papa did as against the Evangelicals—an enlarging of the idea of religion . . . —is the great want of our spiritual and intellectual life of England at present. . . .[40]

If he was both to answer the critics of "Culture and Its Enemies" and to enlarge "the idea of religion," therefore, Arnold had four not entirely consistent tasks to perform in the "Anarchy and Authority" series. He had first to show that culture was of great practical value, even while requiring an attitude of disinterestedness. He had then to explain how the individual could not successfully pursue his own perfection without at the same time striving for the perfection of mankind as a whole. He had further to soothe the hurt feelings of the Dissenters and, if not to allay the fears of all the orthodox, at least to demonstrate how culture complemented religion and how, in revealing the errors of Protestantism, it was religion's friend rather than enemy. And once again, while simultaneously suggesting that he was a more orderly thinker than he had pretended to be, he had to argue that the flexibility demanded by culture could in fact achieve more useful results than could the rigidity by which the systematic philosopher was bound.

In the first of the essays, later entitled "Doing as One Likes," Arnold's primary purpose is to meet the objection that he preached a doctrine of inactivity. He will try his "very best," he announces at the outset, "to drive at practice as much as [he] can," and this he attempts to do by insisting throughout on the practical benefits to be derived from culture. It proves its value, first of all, in showing that "random and ill-regulated action" is "a practical mischief," and that to remain aloof from it is "in real truth the most practical line our endeavours can take." It suggests the idea of the state, a center of authority checking the unrestrained exercise of freedom, and thus provides "a practical benefit." It explains that this center of authority can be neither the aristocracy nor the middle class, neither of which possesses light, and that it cannot be the working class, whose potential is still unknown. Finally, in this dilemma, with on the one hand the need for authority and on the other the apparent impossibility of finding it because of the jealousy between classes and the inadequacy of each, culture conceives the idea of one's "best self," of rising above class to the state as a whole and finding in it the center of authority. This solution, of course, is less "practical" than Arnold pretends, for, as Lionel Trilling has pointed out, it raises enormously difficult questions in politics, ethics, and epistemology.[41] But by circuitous reasoning (culture is enabled both to suggest the idea and then, because it is a study of perfection, to develop the capacity to overcome the problems created by the idea), Arnold passes over the difficulties for the moment and concludes with the triumphant assertion that "our poor culture, which is flouted as so unpractical, leads us to the very ideas capable of meeting the great want of our present embarrassed times!"[42]

III

To the periodical press, however, this was a rhetorical flourish comprising something less than total victory. The *Illustrated London News* remained unconvinced, declaring that Arnold still had a "really effeminate horror of simple, practical, common-sense reforms, aiming at the removal of some particular abuse."[43] The *Daily Telegraph* insisted that his entire argument rested upon an elaborate fiction. Everything that he "feels about 'culture, sweetness, and light,'" it said, "is felt by every educated man; but he speaks as if there were between this great trinity and our middle and working classes an antagonism which does not really exist." Before the Reform Bill of 1832, the *Telegraph* continued, the middle and working classes opposed state interference because political power was concentrated in a single class, but since then "the true idea of 'the State,' as the central embodiment of the permanent will of the people, has made way amongst thinkers."[44] The *Illustrated Times*, on the other hand, thought that Arnold frankly avowed "the doctrine of a 'Central Infallibility' in a new shape."[45] And the *Daily News*, finding Mill more to its taste, preached on a text from *On Liberty*:

The alternative is between a man's doing, under safeguards and checks which reserve the same liberty for others, what he likes, and his doing what some one else, probably not one whit wiser than himself, likes. In the interest of that culture which absorbs Mr. ARNOLD'S worship, it is better that there should be an infinite variety of experiments in human action; first, because as the explorers multiply the true track is more likely to be discovered, and secondly, because the diversity of individual character requires for its highest culture specialities of treatment. No doubt, the common reason of society ought to check the aberrations of individual eccentricity. It can only do so by its action on the individual reason, and it will do so in the main sufficiently if left to this natural operation. Mr. ARNOLD will make the State the organ of the common reason. He may make it an organ of something or other, but how can he be certain that reason will be the quality which will be embodied in it?

According to the *News*, Arnold would let the state determine what was in agreement with right reason and should therefore be allowed, and what was in conflict with it and should therefore be prohibited. "In other words," it concluded, "the tyranny of majorities and oppression of minorities is the last issue of the doctrine of culture."[46]

Arnold sought to answer these objections in the February installment of "Anarchy and Authority," entitled "Barbarians, Philistines, Populace" in the second and subsequent editions of *Culture and Anarchy*.[47] But the overall strategy of the essay was determined by Frederic Harrison's ridicule of his unsystematic thought. In the first "Anarchy and Authority" paper, Arnold had already replied, in an amusing passage later excised when the series was republished as a volume, to the complaint that he had misrepresented Comtism. When speaking of "abstract systems of renovation applied wholesale," he explained, he had meant "such things as Comte dating a preface the 15th of Dante, 66th year of the Comtian era, instead of the 30th of July, 1854; dating an appendix the 22nd of Moses, a circular the 27th of Aristotle."[48] Yet however absurd the results to which a system of thought may lead, Arnold is now unwilling to pass as the unsystematic thinker Harrison's satire had made him out to be. This is the obvious reason for his attempt to create the illusion of order and system in what is made to appear a careful classification of English society into Barbarians, Philistines, and Populace, and at the same time the reason for his repeated and ironic disclaimer of being a systematic thinker: "From a man without a philosophy no one can expect philosophical completeness"; "it seems neglectful, and a strong instance of that want of coherent philosophic method for which Mr. Frederic Harrison blames me, to leave the aristocratic class so much without notice and denomination"; "this humble attempt at a scientific nomenclature falls, no doubt, very far short in precision of what might be required from a writer equipped with a complete and coherent philosophy, yet, from a notoriously unsystematic and unpretending writer, it will, I trust, be accepted as sufficient."[49] By this method, of course, Arnold hopes to have it both ways: through the illusion created by his three-fold classification to appear to have a kind of logical system such as Harrison demanded, and through his disclaimer of system to retain the flexibility on which he himself had insisted.[50]

This retention of flexibility becomes of particular value when Arnold turns from Harrison to the more recent criticism of the *Daily Telegraph*. In reply to its accusation that he had created a fictitious condition of anarchy and of hostility to state intervention, Arnold now broadens his account of the lawless expression of individual freedom to include not only the rowdy's hooting and threatening and smashing as he likes, but also (and here he returns to the thesis of "The Literary Influence of Academies") intellectual aberrations as well: the Nonconformist's faith in the literary judgments of the *British Banner*, Hepworth Dixon's admiration for the military might of the Mormons, Frederic Harrison's praise of the Populace. Here, even more than in the political agitation of the previous years, Arnold implies, is the need for a central authority to check affronts to right reason.

But opposing the establishment of this central authority, he says, are two powerful and widespread doctrines. One, "a peculiarly British form of Atheism" preached by the *Times*, holds that a best self and right reason are nonexistent or at least impossible to ascertain. Quoting from two recent articles in the *Times*[51]—one excusing the failure to suppress the Fenians on the grounds of the sanctity of individual liberty, and the other expressing doubt that the conflict of interests and the jealousy between classes that are inherent in the British system can ever be overcome—Arnold comments that here indeed is "the iron and inexorable solemnity of tragic Destiny."[52]

In contrast to this fatalism is the second doctrine, "a peculiarly British form of Quietism" taught by the *Daily News*.

Its endorsement of Mill's belief in "an infinite variety of experiments" and its complacent view that a "natural operation" will prevent eccentricity are to Arnold the expression
of an "excessive reliance on an over-ruling Providence." More
important to the development of his thesis, however, was the
doubt expressed by the *News* that right reason would be embodied in the state. In confronting this doubt, Arnold finally extricates himself from the circuitous logic that in the previous essay had confused the whole issue of the relationship
between the best self and the state. We cannot be certain, he
admits, that the state will embody reason, nor can we ever
attain a condition of perfection. But there is between the individual and the state a reciprocal relationship that may benefit both. The state being the collective nation and therefore
bearing great authority, the more of our best self contributed
to it the greater its authority, and in turn the stronger its check
upon our expression of the "natural taste for the bathos."
Like Carlyle and Ruskin before him, Arnold argues that liberty to act wrongly is not liberty at all. Far from being a denial
of freedom (and here Arnold indirectly responds to a list
of suppressions that the *News* had sarcastically implied he
would have advocated), the state's restraining the Reverend
W. Cattle from Papist-baiting and Charles Bradlaugh from
railing-breaking is in truth their liberation from false freedom, for in showing them the irrationality of their actions,
the state may in time bring "their individual reason into harmony with right reason."[53]

IV

The second installment of "Anarchy and Authority," which
attracted less attention than the first (so little, in fact, that
the *Morning Star* could say only that "we have tried hard to
see the humour of this newest essay of Mr. ARNOLD'S, and
. . . we really don't see it"[54]), was followed four months later
by an essay that included all of the present chapter on "Hebraism and Hellenism" in *Culture and Anarchy*. It was in-

tended as a reply in part to Henry Sidgwick's complaint that his conception of religion was shallow and his view of its relationship to culture distorted, and in part to the objection of the Aberdeen *Free Press* that he ignored the importance of "conquest." Arnold's response, quite simply, is to invert the criticism: to argue that England's present difficulties derive from the preponderance of Hebraism (by which he means the Hebraic-Christian tradition in general and Puritanism in particular) over Hellenism (by which he means culture or, as he had previously designated it, criticism). The aim of both, he says, is human perfection. But they pursue this aim in different ways: Hebraism by its emphasis on doing rather than thinking—on right conduct, obedience to the will of God, and strictness of conscience—and Hellenism by its emphasis on intelligence, spontaneity of consciousness, and seeing things as they are. Yet neither represents the whole law of human development, for each is but a contribution, and its value in a certain period of history depends upon the specific needs of the time. Christianity, for example, was a rebirth of Hebraism as an expression of man's spiritual impulses and was therefore a necessary reaction to the moral indifference of the pagan world. The Renaissance, on the other hand, was a rebirth of Hellenism as an expression of man's intellectual impulses, which had been repressed during the Middle Ages. Since the Renaissance, the predominant current in Europe has been Hellenistic, whereas in England it has been Hebraic.

This cyclical view of history, in which England is once again outside the main stream of thought, recalls the thesis of "The Function of Criticism at the Present Time." But Arnold now accounts differently for England's isolation. In an exposition that relies largely on erroneous racial theories of the day,[55] and to whose "scientific" basis he appeals possibly in answer to Sidgwick's objection that he had not "mastered the elements of the problem,"[56] Arnold argues that the English, though of Indo-European stock and logically belonging to the movement of Hellenism, have, in fact, a strong affinity to the Semitic race, which is manifested primarily in the Hebraizing tendency of Puritanism. As a consequence of Puritan predominance in England, the central stream of the Renaissance as a triumph of Hellenism was blocked, and a minor stream in the form of the Reformation, which purged and renewed Hebraism, gained the ascendancy. Thus for more than two centuries, while the central current of European progress has been an intellectual one, the central tendency in England has been a moral one. The result of this disruption of the natural order of development has been confusion and a need for authority; and the remedy is to be found not in a greater emphasis upon Hebraism, as Sidgwick supposes, but in a return to the central movement of Hellenism.

The argument is continued in the next number of "Anarchy and Authority," where Arnold turns specifically to Sidgwick's contention that fire and strength were more needed than sweetness and light. This reflects, he answers, the great fault of Puritanism—its belief in an *unum necessarium*, its inclination to develop a single side of man's nature without regard to the harmonious perfection of his total personality. Hellenism may lack the moral strength and earnestness of Hebraism, but whereas Hebraism is prone to the baneful error "of cutting our being in two," Hellenism insists on "the development of the whole man." If there is danger in Hellenism, consequently, there is even graver danger in the exclusive predominance of Hebraism. This danger Arnold finds illustrated in Puritanism's literal, mechanical reading of St. Paul and, more strikingly, in the case of a Mr. Smith whose explanation for his suicide, the result of his laboring "under the apprehension that he would come to poverty, and that he was eternally lost," epitomizes a mechanical concern with business and a mechanical conception of salvation. It is this concern with one object to the exclusion of all other objects, this inversion of values and confusion of means and ends, that Hellenism can correct. Such, indeed, has been its function throughout history, as evidenced by St. Paul's letting his

consciousness play freely around Hebraism's fixed and mechanical rule of conduct, and by the Greek attitude toward
freedom as of value only in reference to an ideal of complete
perfection. What is most needed at the present time, therefore, is Hellenism, "making a stream of fresh thought play
freely about our stock notions and habits."[57]

Of these stock notions, Arnold says, none seems more de-
finitively an expression of wisdom than the proposed disestablishment of the Irish Church. Yet it is precisely this issue
that becomes for him the means both of showing culture's
value to religion and of answering the Nonconformists' complaint that he had misunderstood their intellectual position
and scorned their sectarianism. The Liberal effort to disestablish the Irish Church, he argues, has been motivated not
by what is reasonable and just, but by a Nonconformist antipathy to church establishments that is based solely on a mechanical reading of Scripture. As a result, the very ends the
measure was intended to effect have been defeated, for the
Liberals have lost the opportunity to gain the good will of the
Irish, and they have sought to destroy the advantages of common and traditional worship services that the Established
Church affords. Arnold thus adroitly turns the tables on
Miall's protest that he had misrepresented the purpose of the
Nonconformist. By illustrating the harmful effect of Nonconformist doctrine on governmental policy, he places in ironic
light the stated purpose of Nonconformists "to deliver religious life . . . from the overruling and corrupting influence
of Civil Government." And by distinguishing between speculation and worship—the first a private matter no more successful outside the Establishment than within, but the second
a public matter successful only where it is collective and national—he seeks to show the fallacy in Nonconformist determination "to uphold the rights of private judgment against
a sacerdotal tyranny." In Arnold's account of both the Establishment and the Nonconformists, moreover, there is a parallel suggesting his effort to appeal to both. Just as the Estab-

lishment is outside the main current of Hellenism, so are the Nonconformists outside the current of the Established Church. The solution to the predicament of each is to be found in culture.

Thus all roads lead to culture. In saying this, Arnold also pleads guilty to Harrison's accusation that he had engaged in semantic jugglery. "We will not stickle for a name," he concedes, "and the name of culture one might easily give up"[58] —a concession that now makes rather pointless the earlier debate with Bright and Harrison over the meaning of the word. But at the same time, Arnold insists—in reply to those critics who had accused him of preaching a doctrine of refined inactivity and of antagonizing the believers in action—that by whatever name we call it, culture shows that the ills of the time are to be cured not by the attempt to remove certain specific evils, but by the free play of the consciousness around those fixed notions that are the cause of the difficulty.

V

The critics of "Anarchy and Authority" placed less value on the free play of the mind. The *Globe* thought Arnold was simply "getting dull" and "beginning to write like a Philistine."[59] The *Illustrated London News* said that his thesis seemed "to be that under present circumstances it is inexpedient to do anything in particular"; and echoing a recent article by James Macdonell that had described Arnold as "the down-encradled darling of the revolutionary boudoir" and his culture as lisping "in silvery tones Respectability's frantic shout,"[60] it added that his "refinement [was] degenerating into languid superciliousness."[61] In a more substantial review contrasting Arnold with Carlyle, the *Spectator* declared that the "*tendency* of Mr. Arnold's teaching is to delay all action till we have got not only a distinct right step or two before us, but a wide field of clear survey round us,—and this, we maintain, is not only to obstruct right action, but to obstruct intellectual sight." A "single practical step, taken in the light," it concluded, "will produce more light for the future than any amount of pains in bringing 'a free play of consciousness' to bear on the ultimate conditions of the question."[62]

Nevertheless, in the concluding number of the series, Arnold once again argues for the superiority of "a free play of consciousness" to any "single practical step" and in so doing provides his final answer to the persistent charge that he made no effort to solve specific problems. Having taken in the previous installment two measures of the Liberals—the disestablishment of the Irish Church and the Real Estate Intestacy Bill—and shown how they illustrated a mechanical policy less effectual in securing real reform than would be a critical examination of the problems involved, he now resumes his thesis with a consideration of two other Liberal measures—the attempt to legalize marriage to a deceased wife's sister and the policy of free trade. In each of the four instances, the Liberal case is condemned as having faulty motives and harmful results. The attempt to disestablish the Irish Church derives from Nonconformist antipathy to the Establishment and leads to the alienation of the Irish. The Real Estate Intestacy Bill, based on the belief that a man's children have a right to equal shares of his property and designed to break up the aristocracy's almost exclusive possession of land, is, in fact, unsanctioned by the existence of natural rights and is, in effect, less beneficial than the recognition of the harm that wealth causes to a privileged class and to the Philistines, for whom it establishes a false ideal. The proposal to legalize marriage to a deceased wife's sister follows the example not of "the race which invented the Muses, and chivalry, and the Madonna," but of the people "whose wisest king had seven hundred wives and three hundred concubines." The Liberal policy of free trade, finally, intended to increase the wealth of the nation, fails to enable the poor man to eat cheap bread but succeeds in increasing the number of poor men who want to eat it. Thus all four instances show, Arnold declares in a sentence containing the essence of *Culture and Anarchy*, "that our main business at the present moment is not so much to work away at certain crude reforms of which we have already the scheme in our own mind, as to create, through the help of that culture which at the very outset we began by praising and recommending, a frame of mind out of which the schemes of really fruitful reforms may with time grow."[63]

But a more significant function of this concluding installment of "Anarchy and Authority" is to provide Arnold's final answer to one of the most damaging of all the charges leveled against the doctrine of culture—that in its delicacy and fastidiousness it was contemptuous of the common man and of the men of action who attempted to help him. To answer this charge had become a matter of compelling importance to Arnold during the previous winter, when he had been subjected to a series of attacks by a "raw and intemperate Scotch youth" named Robert Buchanan.[64] Arnold had fared rather well in Buchanan's mildly satiric "Session of the Poets," published in September of 1866,[65] but after their meeting at the Grant Duffs' later in the autumn, when Arnold listened without enthusiasm to Buchanan's poetry,[66] he was treated less leniently. Buchanan apparently suspected him of writing some anonymous reviews of his verse,[67] and he may have been annoyed by criticism contained in Arnold's correspondence with him.[68] Besides, as Arnold knew, the recent death of his father had caused a crisis in his life that led to his "going off his centre, poor fellow."[69]

Arnold seems to have become aware of Buchanan's enmity toward him through the pages of the *Spectator*. By coincidence the same issue contained both a review of Buchanan's *David Gray, and other Essays, Chiefly on Poetry* (1868) and a notice of the second installment of "Anarchy and Authority," which it described as "full . . . of an intellectual scorn for unintellectual persons."[70] This "very bad service" that the paper had done him caused Arnold real concern. "It is not at all true," he protested to his mother, "and it sets people against one."[71] But the *Spectator* was less severe than Buchanan, who had attacked him in two of the essays in *David Gray*. One of these, a curious hodgepodge of imaginative insight, juvenile idealism, and sheer nonsense entitled "The Student, and his Vocation," advances the thesis that the vocation of the Student (a kind of solitary prophet who unpretentiously helps mankind, as distinguished from the noisy person who seeks glory) is to capture the attention of the masses and through "true love for the species" point the way to eternal truth. Arnold fails in this vocation, according to Buchanan, because he is an egotistical prattler who lacks "the mysterious and god-like quality of love for the species." In fact, a remarkable passage asserts, Arnold's selfish asceticism and alarmist fears of anarchy are in direct conflict with the philoprogenitiveness of God, who "would *swarm* the earth with beings. There are never enough. Life, life, life,—faces gleaming, hearts beating, must fill every cranny. Not a corner is suffered to remain empty. The whole earth breeds, and God glories."[72]

Another essay in *David Gray*, "On My Own Tentatives," finds Arnold equally unsatisfactory in his literary criticism and poetry. "I have been doing my best [in three volumes of poetry]," Buchanan writes, "to show that actual life, independent of accessories, is the true material for poetic art"; for "the further the poet finds it necessary to recede from his own time, the less trustworthy is his imagination, the more constrained his sympathy, and the smaller his chance of creating true and durable types for human contemplation." His "greatest opponents," on the other hand, have been men of "literary culture" like the "distinguished living critic" who reminded him "that if one, while going to the life, chooses a subject which is naturally poetical, one's chances of the best poetical success will be increased tenfold." The distinguished critic is, of course, Arnold, who loses "all his grace" when he tries in his poetry to touch "the solid ground of contemporary thought," Buchanan says, and "his utterance becomes the merest prose."[73]

Buchanan's comment became the source of a warm exchange with the *Spectator* when the reviewer of *David Gray* called it "a blunder." Pointing to those poems by Arnold in which there is an "ever-recurring, never exhausted lament over the extinction of faith in the educated classes of modern society," he declared that in such lines as

> Wandering between two worlds, one dead,
> The other powerless to be born,

there is the cry of "fate-stricken men" that Buchanan had praised in the work of the earliest English poets.[74] The following week Buchanan replied in a long, acrimonious letter disclaiming "once and for ever" the "reviewer's fancy that the lazaretto crying of Mr. Matthew Arnold is to be confounded with the heart-wrung utterance of 'fate-stricken men,'" and describing Arnold as both "a thin egotist, faintly inflated with intellectuality," and "a trifler, a theorist, who has only half lived, and therefore sees only one side of human life and thought." The editor's laconic response—"Mr. Buchanan does not understand . . . Mr. Arnold, and should not criticize what he does not understand"[75]—served merely to anger Buchanan into writing another letter, this one protesting that although he fully recognized "the merits of Mr. Arnold as a *dilettante*," he had been concerned only with indicating where Arnold "had subsided into . . . self-inflated egotism and retrograde perfection."[76]

Despite the support he enjoyed from the *Spectator*,[77] Arnold felt it imperative to answer Buchanan, who not only had said what many readers thought, but in doing so had attracted attention in three successive issues of an influential weekly. The opening for an answer, moreover, was provided by Buchanan's reliance on "Divine philoprogenitiveness"—another form of the belief in an overruling Providence that the *Daily News* had confidently proclaimed and of the conviction, eloquently expressed by the *Times*, that mere population was in itself an ineffable good. Here was Arnold's opportunity to answer the persistent charge that he was without social conscience. Against Buchanan's delight in the multiplication of the human species, accordingly, he sets a dismal picture of the residents of an East London district: "children eaten up with disease, half-sized, half-fed, half-clothed, neglected by their parents, without health, without home, without hope." At the root of the problem, Arnold argues, are the Hebraic notion that reproduction is the chief end of man and the Liberal notion that population is an absolute proof of a nation's prosperity. To dispel both notions is essential, for "to bring people into the world, when one cannot afford to keep them and oneself decently and not too precariously, or to bring more of them into the world than one can afford to keep thus, is . . . by no means an accomplishment of the divine will or a fulfilment of Nature's simplest laws." The passage vindicates Arnold's previous claim that culture is motivated by "the noble aspiration to leave the world better and happier than we found it" and suggests how "culture, or the study of perfection, leads us to conceive of no perfection as being real which is not a *general* perfection, embracing all our fellow-men with whom we have to do. . . . So all our fellow-men, in the East of London and elsewhere, we must take along with us in the progress towards perfection, if we ourselves really, as we profess, want to be perfect." Whereas Arnold had at first seemed to be referring primarily to the individual when he spoke of a "general and harmonious perfection," he now clearly has reference to the whole of society; and the clarification is his most effective reply to the critics who had said he was unconcerned about the masses and who had described him as a fop with a refined eudaemonism for his philosophy and a pouncet-box for his olfactories.[78]

VI

The conclusion of the "Anarchy and Authority" series was acknowledged by the periodical press with expressions of relief. The *Oxford Chronicle and Berks and Bucks Gazette* thought that the essays, though "thoughtful," were "somewhat cynical."[79] The consistently hostile *Illustrated London News*, which described the series as "the laborious apology of a fastidious man for labouring at nothing else," said that Arnold was "an intellectual Pharisee" who was contemptuous of both "insignificant persons whom he singles out by name" and "every one who conceives that good may be effected by Act of Parliament."[80] And the *London Review* published another outrageous attack in which it denounced Arnold as a "balcony-philosopher" engaging in "negative criticism," prescribing a "course of inaction," and inviting everyone to "depart with him into the land of intellectual lotos-eating."[81]

Some two months later, in October 1868, Arnold began preparations for publishing "Culture and Its Enemies" and the five numbers of "Anarchy and Authority" in a single volume. In November he started writing a preface to the volume, but the death of his eldest son made him unable to continue in the vein of persiflage in which he had begun, and for a while he "thought [he] had no heart to chaff any one any more." Later, however, as he got into the preface the challenge of controversy raised his spirits, and he was "led, here and there, to chaff [his] enemies."[82] Chief among these were Huxley, who had facetiously accused him of inventing Bishop Wilson and then quoting repeatedly from his own creation; W. R. Greg, whose criticism of his position in the Colenso matter had been reprinted in 1868; and Oscar Browning, an "indiscreet, unreliable, egotistical, extravagant, resentful"[83] assistant master at Eton who had just published an unscrupulously distorted review of *Schools and Universities on the Continent*[84] and to whom Arnold now replied with some of his sharpest irony.

But Arnold's chief purpose in the preface was to placate the Nonconformists, whose offense at his earlier remarks concerning them had never been removed. It is indicative of his skill in accomplishing this purpose that William Smith, the editor of the *Quarterly Review* and likewise the victim of Arnold's irony (for he had published the review that was not only an irresponsible attack on Arnold's work but also an immodest advertisement for his own schoolbooks), shook hands with Arnold after reading the preface and "forgave [him] all [he] had said about him[self] and the *Quarterly*, which . . . was a great deal, for the sake of the truth and usefulness of what [Arnold] had said about the Nonconformists."[85] Arnold's thesis is that because they have developed one side of their being at the expense of all the other sides, the Nonconformists "have become incomplete and mutilated."[86] And because they have remained outside the Establishment, disappearing into hole-and-corner groups, they suffer from provincialism and a lack of totality. The solution is to bring them within the Established Church, allowing them to continue with their own form of church discipline but insisting on their general and harmonious perfection. Thus culture once again proves to be the friend of those who have been its enemies.

Yet, as a whole, the reviewers did not so regard it. The *Daily News* said that the book "abounds in personal criticisms expressed with all the licentious freedom of a court jester" and "shows clearly how much anarchy of thought may co-exist with pretensions to the highest culture."[87] The *Morning Star* declared that Arnold had spoiled his argument for culture "by associating it with a fanatical defense of that exceedingly poor creature, the connection between Church and State."[88] William Kirkus in the *Fortnightly Review* objected that the doctrine "not only aims at perfection, which is good, but seems incapable of acting at all, even for the removal of admitted wrongs, *until perfection is attained*, which is mischievous and anarchic."[89] The *Spectator* thought that in political economy he was "absolutely at sea," having "a vague impression that the blind pursuit of free trade produces an accumulating pauperism" and "that the thing to be taught is apparently Malthusianism."[90] To his mother, who liked the book so little that he did not send her a copy of it, he confessed that it was "the theme of much blame and little praise."[91] And to Grant Duff he wrote: "A Colonel Baird, a cousin of Mrs. Arnold's, has forwarded to the India Board a memorandum on the unsavoury subject of *Earth-closets*. . . . You will have seen, with the pleasure and amusement of a true friend, all the earth closets lately emptied on my head for my Culture and Anarchy Essays."[92]

Some of the flaws in *Culture and Anarchy* for which Arnold was criticized—excessive topicality, oversimplification in argument, vagueness of definition, and so on—were almost inevitable in the kind of serial publication from which the volume evolved; and they are an inseparable part of that general thinness in his concept of culture of which T. S. Eliot was later to complain.[93] Yet *Culture and Anarchy* is properly read not as a definitive essay in political and social criticism, but as a part of a continuing controversy in which Arnold engaged for well over a decade. After its completion, he at first expressed pleasure to "have done with this social-political writing for some years."[94] He plunged into a projected work on Greek poetry, glad to be employed "in a line which [took him] quite away from all the questions in which [he had] had so much controversy, and on which it would be easy to say too much and go on too long,"[95] and determined to "leave all [his enemies] untouched for a year or two at any rate, however much they [tore him]."[96] But neither the nature of the controversy nor the pressure of the political events behind it would allow Arnold to remain silent for long; and by early summer of 1869, he was once again chaffing his enemies when, after an absence of more than two years, Arminius reappeared on the pages of the *Pall Mall Gazette*.

The occasion for his return was the serious illness of Mrs. Bottles, whose imminent death raised the question that had been dealt with in one of the Liberal measures Arnold had criticized in the concluding number of "Anarchy and Authority"—Thomas Chambers' bill to legalize marriage with a deceased wife's sister. In April it had passed its second reading, and now it received endorsement as an "admirable bill" from the young lion of the *Daily Telegraph* to whom Arnold satirically ascribed his letter. By this time, of course, Arminius had dropped Arnold "entirely" and "taken up with a much younger . . . and a much better-dressed man, with whom he [was] pursuing researches concerning labour and capital." But the Prussian's absorption with Harrison, who had conquered him with his witty dialogue on culture, enabled Arnold to answer another of his critics, George A. Sala. An indefatigable correspondent for the *Daily Telegraph* and the embodiment of its vulgarity, Sala had described Arnold in the most recent of his volumes as a "shallow and conceited sciolist" who had invented the term *Philistine* "in order to insult writers whose minds and views were broader than his."[97] The *Telegraph* itself provides the amusing answer to this sneer through its Paris correspondent, who, when Arnold asks whether anyone will think Bottles a man of "delicacy" if he marries his wife's sister, nostalgically recalls hearing the word in his "fresh, enthusiastic youth" before he knew Sala.[98]

Two months later, amidst a chorus of applause at the passage of another measure that had been criticized in the "Anarchy and Authority" series—Gladstone's Irish Church Bill —Arnold wrote again to the *Pall Mall Gazette*, this time signing his own name and affecting despondency because of "the universal disgust" with which his argument for "cultivated inaction" had met. Now chastened by his past errors, the result of his having no "systematic philosophy," he offered to expiate for them by lending his support to Thomas Chambers. But in his role as mock convert, he also noted ironically what the unregenerate Arnold had predicted: that the Irish Church Bill was passed not because the Liberals had allowed their minds free play on the issue, but because the antipathy to establishments was a stock notion among those who held political power.[99]

Another year passed before Arnold resumed his correspondence with the *Gazette*, shortly after the outbreak of the Franco-Prussian war had summoned Arminius back to the

Continent. In his farewell to England, the Prussian once again exhorted Matthew Arnold's countrymen to get *Geist* and to emulate the example of Germany in elevating "*a whole people through culture.*" Two other letters that Arnold had written were not published, presumably for the reason he gave to the editor: the events of the time were "too great and too earnest" for his "ironical" and "chaffy" manner to be suitable. But the following November, three more letters appeared, the last of them an account of the death of Arminius by the *Daily Telegraph*'s young lion. Writing in the characteristic style of his paper, he reported that in his final moments Arminius had managed to send a parting message to Frederic Harrison—"Tell him to do more in literature,—he has a talent for it"—and to utter a dying prayer: "God bless *Germany.*"[100]

Harrison was not pleased, however, by this linking of his name with a benediction on Germany, and in December he sent to the *Pall Mall Gazette* a letter that was in part a second parody of Arnold, reproaching him both for his political views and for his apparent levity in dealing with grave matters. "Under the distinguished patronage of his Grace the Grand Duke of Geist," Harrison wrote, "I should like to say a few words about this war. Seriously, I have little mind to jest. This whirlwind of blood we live in, this life-struggle of a noble people, calls for something more, I think, than lettered badinage." And he went on to ask why the Prussian cause retained "the goodwill of intelligent, peaceable, liberal men" in spite of "the outrageous pretensions of Germany to supremacy in arms," "the yet more sinister designs of Bismarck," and "the still rising flood of destruction around us."[101]

The death of Arminius had left Arnold without an appropriate means for reply, but in the dedicatory letter to *Friendship's Garland*, written the following February, he used a recollection of the Prussian to conclude his debate with Harrison. In the course of a general conversation the previous summer, Arminius had opposed Harrison when, resum-

ing the role he had first played in Arnold's work as the inflammatory spokesman for Jacobinism, Harrison began "to
harangue, with his usual fiery eloquence, on the enervation of
England, and on the malignancy of all the brute mass of us
who are not Comtists." On the contrary, Arminius had curtly
answered, the real danger of England lay in its "surfeit of
clap-trap." And in this same letter, which contained verbal and
thematic echoes of the concluding lecture at Oxford nearly
four years earlier, Arnold gives his final answer to its critics:
an ironic promise to the *Daily Telegraph*, edited by that "great
austere toiler" who had rebuked him for remaining aloof from
the "dusty arena of political life," that he will not always
be an Ishmael but will ally himself "to some of those great
Liberal movements which,—however Arminius might choose
to call them petty aimless activities . . .—seem . . . highly
productive of enjoyable excitement and honourable importance to their promoters."[102]

VII

If this was rather frivolous tilting with his opponents, the
reason was that Arnold had been elsewhere engaged in a
more serious answer to the critics of *Culture and Anarchy*.
Despite all that he had said in reply to their objections, two
remained that he wished to deal with further. One, the
complaint of Puritanism and Nonconformity, concerned the
question of the relationship between the Dissenters and the
Established Church. The other, the complaint of religious orthodoxy as a whole, concerned the more general question of
the relationship between culture and religion.

Some ten months after the publication of *Culture and Anarchy*, Arnold had written to his mother, apropos of his having lunched with Henry Allon, a leading Independent minister of London and editor of the *British Quarterly Review*,
that he hoped to "do something to win" the Dissenters.
"The feeling of the harm their isolation from the main current of thought and culture does in the nation," he explained,

"a feeling that has been developed in me by going about among them for years, is the source of all I have written on religious, political, and social subjects."[103] That he had not yet won them, however, was evident from the *British Quarterly*'s review of *Culture and Anarchy*, which had said in part:

Mr. Arnold tells Dissenters that no large-minded, thoroughly-cultivated men have sprung up among them, because of their separation from establishments; that these establishments bring those who are educated under their influence into connection with national life, and thus tend to the harmonious perfection of their whole being. As our author will not allow us to quote "a genius" who, says he, is always delivered from the class to which he belongs by birth, it is hard to disprove the assertion. He is scarcely fair thus to disparage those who, by religious scruples which had little to do with the question of establishments *per se*, have been forcibly excluded, not only from the Universities, but from every higher school in the kingdom, and who have had to extemporize their entire system of education for themselves, who have, nevertheless, shown in almost every department of knowledge, art, energy, and literature, that they had aspirations after the perfection of being, and have been able to achieve something answering to that desire.

Although the reviewer thanked Arnold for his "wise reproof" and "sharp blows," he was still convinced that there was "more 'sweetness and light' in [the free churches] than can be possibly procreated by societies which draw hard and fast lines around themselves, and array themselves with infallible decisions, indelible orders, and exclusive privilege."[104]

A more serious complaint by Arnold's critics, and one that troubled him more deeply than his contemporaries were aware, concerned the apparently subordinate role to which he assigned religion. In the spring of 1872, when the *British Quarterly* published an article by R. H. Hutton praising his poetry but giving pain by its "remarks on his religious principles," Arnold wrote to Allon:

As to praise of my poetry, I have indeed more than cause to be, as you say, satisfied: perhaps, as one advances in life, purely literary respects and literary praise seem to be not quite so much as they did when one was younger and had not in one's own circle those to whom they are comparatively indifferent, and with whom religious respects far outweigh them. It so happens that I live chiefly with those to whom the remarks on the religious tendencies, or rather on the want of them, in my poetry, will give more distress than the commendation of the poetry, much of it, as poetry, will give pleasure.[105]

Hutton, of course, was not alone in his criticism of Arnold's religious views. In the autumn of 1867, for example, an old friend, J. C. Shairp, had protested that whereas Arnold made religion "an ingredient in culture," religion was one of those things that were "ultimate ends in themselves" and thus refused "to be employed as means"; and if culture made "its own idea of perfection the end and religion the means, [it] would degenerate into an unhealthy artificial plant."[106] The *Tablet* said that "if either Hellenism or Hebraism (in its noblest sense) is to be sacrificed, we should prefer to sacrifice Hellenism and cling to Hebraism."[107] The *Morning Star* more bluntly declared that Arnold's "entire lack of avowed dogmatic faith" made him a guide unacceptable "to the public."[108]

Of all the criticism on this point, none was more penetrating than that of the *London Quarterly Review*. In reading Arnold, it said, one could not "resist the conviction that, whatever his own view of the Christian revelation may be, it does not at all resemble that of a man who recognises its exclusive Divine efficiency, and the objective reality of its alleged supernatural facts. We cannot imagine what can remain in Christianity for Mr. Arnold except a *caput mortuum* of bewildering and powerless legends. What, in such a case, can Hebraism avail to correct man's moral weakness, and to sustain his faltering purpose against the assaults of temptation?" The answer, according to the reviewer, is that Arnold accommodates his concept of culture to the weakness of man "by deposing the moral from the grand and far excelling eminence which it has hitherto occupied, and placing it on a level with the intellectual. Hebraism and Hellenism are made to stand side by side as equal and component forces necessary to bring about human perfection." The "obvious tendency" of such a doctrine is "to lessen our reverence for moral excellence, and to weaken the force of conscience." More seriously still, the doctrine gives little or no attention

to any supreme authority on morals such as exists in Divine revelation. That is right which commends itself to the cultivated mind as allowable, or expedient, or conformable to nature. The prevailing sentiment of cultured people thus becomes the sole standard of morals. We need not stay to show how shifting and uncertain such a standard must be, nor how surely it would be continually reduced. The path of virtue, while still retaining its name, would become more and more easy and pleasant, until at last, human desires, attended by self-satisfaction and the approving smiles of the cultured, unchecked by such old-world things as conscience and revelation, would roam over all the ground left undisputed by the dread of unpleasant temporal consequences.[109]

These, then, were two fundamental criticisms of *Culture and Anarchy* that could not be ignored. Arnold had to demonstrate more convincingly than before the need to bring the Dissenters within the Establishment, and he had to explain more fully the moral sanctions of a culture that embraced religion. The two tasks would require of him most of the decade that followed.

CHAPTER SEVEN

The Bible and Its Interpreters

These principles I believe to be irrefragable; that a Church Establishment is essential to the well-being of the nation; that the existence of Dissent impairs the usefulness of an Establishment . . .; and that to extinguish Dissent by persecution being both wicked and impossible, there remains the true, but hitherto untried way, to extinguish it by comprehension.—Dr. Thomas Arnold

Freeborn . . . thought theology itself a mistake, as substituting . . . worthless intellectual notions for the vital truths of religion.—Newman, *Loss and Gain*

My whole instinct in matters of religion is towards reconstruction; to quote your favourite Epistle to the Hebrews, *"the removing of those things that are shaken, as of things that are made, that those things which cannot be shaken may remain."*—Angel Clare to his father in *Tess of the d'Urbervilles*

The man of science has learned to believe in justification, not by faith, but by verification.—T. H. Huxley

A consciousness of the worth of the morally beautiful and good could be attained by experience and wisdom, inasmuch as the bad showed itself in its consequences as a destroyer of happiness, both in individuals and the whole body, while the noble and right seemed to produce and secure the happiness of one and all. Thus the morally beautiful could become a doctrine, and diffuse itself over whole nations as something plainly expressed.—Goethe

Several days before the Irish Church Bill was finally passed in July 1869, expressing what he thought was the victory not of reason but of Nonconformist antipathy to church establishments, Arnold predicted to his mother that the Dissenters would "triumph, as I was sure they would. But I am equally sure that . . . I am doing what will sap them intellectually, and what will also sap the House of Commons intellectually, so far as it is ruled by the Protestant Dissenters; and more and more I am convinced that this is my true business at present."[1] He had begun this true business the previous year in the conclusion to the third number of "Anarchy and Authority," where he had cited Puritanism's interpretation of St. Paul as a striking illustration of its tendency to seize on "the one thing needful." It had taken such terms as *grace*, *faith*, *election*, and *righteousness*, he said, terms used by Paul in trying to analyze "some of the most delicate, intricate, obscure, and contradictory workings and states of the human spirit," and employed them "in an isolated, fixed, mechanical way, as if they were talismans." By thus Hebraizing, taking "Paul's writings as something absolute and final," Puritanism had given his terms a "false and misleading" sense that was a "monstrous and grotesque caricature" of his meaning.[2]

This was to be the theme of the two essays on St. Paul that Arnold contributed to the *Cornhill* when he resumed the subject in the autumn of 1869. Meanwhile, however, two events occurred that helped to determine the course his criticism was to take. In the same year Renan published in *Saint Paul*, the third volume of his *Histoire des origines du christianisme*, an account of the Apostle as an arrogant, self-intoxicated, and inflexible man who scorned reason, eulogized folly, and embraced an absurd transcendentalism. Neither saint nor *savant*, and inferior to both Francis of Assisi and the author of the *Imitation*, he was a man of action who most resembled Luther, with whom he shared a violence of language, restless energy, and fanatical attachment to an idea espoused as if it embodied absolute truth. Paul was for Renan the father of the subtle Augustine, the arid Aquinas, the sombre Calvin, the crabbed Jansen; and the end of his reign, now at last in sight, was cause for rejoicing.[3] It was thus to Renan, obviously, that Arnold alluded when he later told Ernest Fontanès, a French minister with whom he corresponded about religious matters, that in dealing with Paul he had been led to write "en homme de lettres mécontent de la très mauvaise critique littéraire qu'on appliquait à un grand esprit."[4]

But biblical exegesis on the Continent produced another work that Arnold also read in the summer of 1869 and found more to his taste—Édouard Reuss's *Histoire de la théologie chrétienne au siècle apostolique.* Like Renan, Reuss viewed thaumaturgy through the eyes of a modern, declaring in his preface that science, "no longer satisfied with theories and abstractions, such as were accepted in the past century," insists that historical investigation be placed "upon the solid basis of facts studied in detail and verified by the light of criticism." But unlike Renan, he saw in Paul "a quick and cultivated mind," "an ardent and deeply sensitive soul," and "a brilliant imagination worthy of a son of the East." And unlike the Puritans with their mechanical reading of scripture, he recognized that Paul's original thought had been "torn and mangled" by schoolmen who had turned his "few very simple principles" into a "ponderous bulk of dogmatism" through their failure to comprehend that because of the meager religious vocabulary he had inherited, he was forced to concentrate "a whole world of ideas in a single word." By *faith*, for instance, he meant becoming "one with Christ, living by His spirit, and according to His will, instead of following the impulses of . . . carnal affections," and by *resurrection*, "the awaking now to the new spiritual life in Christ." In none of his writing was there mention of the "legal contract" that scholasticism was to make of the theory of vicarious atonement. Redemption was accomplished for Paul simply because "the old man is become dead by mystical communion with the death of the Saviour, and not because God, like a common creditor, is satisfied by receiving the payment due to Him."[5] To his entire reading of Pauline doctrine, Reuss brought a reverence and liberalism inevitably appealing to the son who thought of himself as continuing the work of Dr. Thomas Arnold. The book, Arnold wrote to his mother, was one "papa would have delighted in."[6]

I

The first of Arnold's two articles on St. Paul[7] opens with a contrast between Renan, who disparaged both Paul and Puritanism, and Reuss, whose careful and impartial explication of Pauline doctrine suggests that it is Puritanism that should be disparaged and Paul who should be exalted. The contrast necessarily invites the Puritan to make a return upon himself, in Arnold's familiar phrase, and ask whether he has properly understood Paul. For Puritanism, Arnold argues, has translated into scholastic and scientific language what in Paul is figurative and imaginative; it has made primary what in Paul is secondary. Whereas Puritanism exists solely for the sake of belief in "a sort of magnified and non-natural man" proceeding in a manner minutely described but impossible to verify, Paul bases everything on the ruling impulse of Hebraism—the desire for righteousness, for obedience to the universal moral order. Whereas Puritanism attaches chief importance to sanctification and regards righteousness as its outward sign, thereby encouraging its adherents to look for "strokes of magic" rather than to exert themselves, Paul elevates right conscience to the position of preeminence. And whereas Puritanism begins with an appeal either to man's fears (as in Calvinism) or to his hopes (as in Methodism), Paul begins with an appeal to reality and experience. Whereas the one is rationally unsatisfying, therefore, the other is scientifically valid.

Less than a month before the appearance of this first paper on Paul, the *Noncomformist* published "a bitter article" on his poetry that caused Arnold concern about his relationship with the Dissenters. The total impression produced by the two volumes of *Poems* (1869), the reviewer said, was "displeasing." Almost every state they depicted was "one of continuous and unrelieved mental distress"; nor was it a noble distress, but merely "the outcry of a weakness that shrinks from decisive effort." The love poems treated illicit, light, or prurient desires, and the other poems substituted "wild emotionalism" for true passion. As a whole, the poetry suffered from the fatal defects that Arnold had "no higher inspiration" than trust "in the individual man," continually railed "at the meanness of the age," and combined a culture and disgust that were "miserable" furnishings for art. "These faithless, hopeless, all but loveless poems," the reviewer concluded, "show what we may expect if Christian art should ever become Pagan; not the freshness, the passion, the delight of early Grecian culture, but more than the trouble, the misanthropy, and the self-scorn of its later days."[8] As a result of the review, Arnold feared, "the Protestant Dissenters [would] more and more feel that it [was] war between [them], and that what [he was] doing [struck] at the very root of their influence and power."[9]

After the publication of the paper, however, he was less concerned. "The Protestant dissenters are reading my Cornhill article very much," he wrote to his mother a week later; "but at this crisis it will not, I see, do me any harm with them." It was "opportune," he thought, reaching Nonconformists when an "extraordinary movement of unsettling [was] taking place among them," and thus was received with "extreme indulgence."[10] The reviews were indeed surprisingly moderate, replying in essence that if Paul sought righteousness, so, too, did Puritanism. The *Nonconformist* conceded that Puritans had "often laid themselves open" to reproaches like those of Arnold but asserted that they placed "the pursuit of goodness before that of happiness," insisted "that to be blessed a man must first be holy," and did not "neglect, any more than Paul did, to point out the consequences of sin."[11] The Baptist *Freeman*, acknowledging that Arnold had "infused as much 'sweetness' as possible into what [would] be very offensive to many," nevertheless reminded him that righteousness occupied "the fundamental place in the Puritan's theology as in Paul's."[12] The *English Independent* relied heavily on sarcasm, portraying Arnold as engaged in a tournament with "the most famous champions of Christendom" and waiting "to receive the crown of sweetness and light"; but at the end it returned to the same innocuous note: "If any one word were chosen to express the characteristic of Puritanism, it would be RIGHTEOUSNESS."[13]

In the second of the two articles,[14] half of which he had written before notices of the first began to appear, Arnold continues his emphasis upon Paul's "scientific" advantage over Puritanism. Whereas the essence of one, he says, lies in theological terms like *calling, justification,* and *sanctification*— words derived from Paul without a true understanding of his meaning—the essence of Paul's teaching lies in his own experience of faith ("a holding fast to an unseen power of goodness") and of resurrection ("a rising, in this visible earthly existence, from the death of obedience to blind selfish impulse, to the life of obedience to the eternal moral order"). Puritanism has thus sophisticated "religion of the heart into theories of the head," and "the heavy-handed Protestant Philistine" has seen "in Paul's mystical idea of man's investiture with the righteousness of God nothing but a strict legal transaction." But science, Arnold predicts, will gradually dissolve "the materialism of popular religion," and then the real doctrine of Paul will "arise out of the tomb" where it has lain for centuries and "edify the church of the future."

Arnold thought it "not worth while" to send his mother the "lucubrations" he had received, though he did forward newspaper clippings to show "how entirely" he had "reached the special Puritan class [he] meant to reach."[15] The response there was predictable, repeating the objections voiced earlier to the first of the articles. The *Nonconformist* thought it strange "that it should be left to Mr. Arnold in this nineteenth century, to discover that the most active and intelligent part of Christendom, that which has certainly done most for human liberty and progress, has utterly mistaken the teaching of the great Apostle, and that not on some secondary and subordinate point, but on the essential doctrines of its system."[16] The *English Independent*, in another review of strained metaphor and tedious sarcasm, concluded that Arnold could hurt only himself by his "attempt to dress up the doctrine of salvation by faith in Christ as a true Saviour . . . in the technical formulae of ultra-Calvinism, and under that caricature to charge it as a sectarian peculiarity upon Puritanism, when in fact that doctrine is not only the singly possible result of an honest interpretation both of Paul's writings and of those of all Christ's Apostles, but is the creed of 'Puritans' in common with all the churches of Christendom, with one insignificant exception."[17] A more personal protest was expressed in "a letter from Archdeacon Stopford, a prominent Irish Evangelical and a subscriber to the Cornhill from the beginning, discontinuing the magazine because he [would] not let such pestilent doctrine come into his home."[18]

But from other sources there was reassuring praise. In November Henry Allon told Arnold that although "his leading brethren" among the Dissenters thought he "was hard upon Puritanism as distinguished from Anglicanism, there was but one voice among them of admiration for the articles and of assurance of the good they would do."[19] Archbishop Tait's chaplain, William Henry Fremantle, also wrote "to express his agreement and satisfaction" with the articles "and his sense of the good they [were] calculated to do."[20] Whether or not he had rendered Paul's "ideas with perfect correctness," Arnold told his mother, there was "no doubt that the confidence with which these people regarded their conventional rendering of them was quite baseless, made them narrow and intolerant, and prevented all progress." In a third paper, "Puritanism and the Church of England," he would "show how the Church, though holding certain doctrines like justification in common with Puritanism, ha[d] gained by not pinning itself to those doctrines and nothing else." This "concluding and *ecclesiastical*" article, he hoped, might "do something to win" the Puritans, who had cut themselves off "from the main current of thought and culture . . . in the nation." Then he would leave the subject.[21]

"Puritanism and the Church of England,"[22] intended "to clear away offence or misunderstanding," is a diplomatic answer to the implied charge that Arnold had unjustly singled out the Puritans for criticism. Not ill will, he replies, but respect made him speak as he did, for his one desire is to comprehend them within the Church and thus prevent the waste —not only to themselves but to the nation as a whole—caused by their separation. He addresses the Puritans because theirs are separatist churches founded on doctrines taken to be the complete gospel, whereas historic churches like the Church of England, neither existing nor separating for such doctrines, have a collective life and a potential for development greater than that of separatist churches. The Church of England has demonstrated this potential in the past by consistently resisting Puritan attempts to impose a strict definition of its tenets of predestination, original sin, and justification; and the probability of continual growth follows from its very nature as a national church, with its greater freedom of mind allowing the "gradual exhibiting of the full sense of the Bible and Christianity, which is essential to religious progress."[23] The source of this expansion lies not within the Church, however, but outside—in the operation of the *Zeitgeist*, creating a movement of ideas to which the Church must remain open and receptive. The proper sphere of the Church, then, is moral and practical, not metaphysical, and hence separation is never justified on intellectual grounds. Nor are the Puritans justified in their defense that they too preach righteousness, for the righteousness they espouse too often resembles the stern vindictiveness of the early Jews,[24] and in reality they combine religion and politics in "a fractious mixture." Rather than proclaim their own righteousness, they should unite with the Church in a moral endeavor made all the stronger by their union.

Almost immediately after the appearance of "Puritanism and the Church of England" in the February *Cornhill*, Arnold began preparing the three articles for publication in a single volume, making extensive revisions and additions[25] that "much fortified and improved" the treatise and introducing it with a preface that cost him "much pains" but that he thought Alexander Macmillan would read "with pleasure."[26] Later entitled "Modern Dissent,"[27] the preface is still another attempt to meet objections to Arnold's treatment of Puritanism. To the complaint that the doctrine he condemned was characteristic not only of separatist churches but of much of Christendom, in particular the Evangelical party within the Church of England, he replies that the Evangelicals avoid mixing politics with religion, do not separate for the sake of opinions, and leave themselves open to development. And to the *Nonconformist*'s satiric wonderment that it should have been left to him to discover a new religion and found a new church, he makes a similar response: neither is his discovery new nor, even if it were, is the establishment of a new church justified. The thesis he advances is merely the work of the *Zeitgeist*. It is therefore not something fixed and rigid, like Puritanism, which must now "execute an entire change of front" and present "a new reason for its existing," but the product of a natural growth and thus capable of further development.

II

St. Paul and Protestantism, the first of Arnold's works to see a second edition within a single year, attracted such attention that by the spring of 1871 J. N. Simpkinson could write in the *Edinburgh Review*, "Newspapers, journals, magazines, reviews, pamphlets, speeches, have been full of replies to it, ranging from gentle remonstrances and deprecatory apologies to the fiercest and most unsparing retorts."[28] So varied were the responses, in fact, that Arnold "ended by not much attending to any of them, but saying . . . with St. Paul, 'He that judgeth me is the Lord.' "[29] In general, however, critical reaction followed ecclesiastical lines. On the one hand, spokesmen for the Church of England deplored his interpretation of Pauline doctrine but endorsed his view of Nonconformity, whereas on the other, the Dissenters insisted that he misunderstood both Paul's doctrine and their own. Thus Simpkinson, fulfilling the intention of the editor, Henry Reeve, to review the book "in a sense of strong agreement and approval,"[30] declared that although Arnold had insufficiently "set forth the essence of Christian doctrine" the *Edinburgh* was "in substantial agreement with him rather than with the best and most successful of his opponents."[31] R. W. Church in the *Quarterly Review* said much the same thing: "our differences with Mr. Arnold, both as to the respect due to Calvinistic and Arminian theology, and as to the tenableness of that view of St. Paul which he would put in their place, do not affect the question, which he has handled with so much temperate wisdom and with so strong a grasp, between the Church and Nonconformity."[32] The *Christian Observer*, an Anglican journal, thought that Arnold had "deliberately suppressed the objective truths of our religion," but it thought also that his "strictures on the present attitude of Dissenters towards the Established Church" were merited if severe.[33] And in a review Arnold found amusing, the *Guardian* improved "the occasion against the Dissenters"[34] by regretting "that they should appear to display so much keener an interest in defending themselves than in resisting what to most Christians would appear like attacks on Christianity itself."[35]

Among the Dissenters to whom the *Guardian* had reference was the reviewer for the *British Quarterly*, an organ of the Congregationalists, who said that Arnold was guilty of "an animus against Nonconformity which is even passionate in its intensity and reckless in its blindness," and "so intensely loving in his Christianity, that in the name of love he can vituperate those who will not love as he does, with a vehemence that O'Connell might have envied."[36] The *Nonconformist* agreed, declaring that *St. Paul and Protestantism* had revealed "where Nonconformity may expect to find its most bitter and unrelenting foes";[37] and a Methodist minister concluded his long answer to Arnold in the *London Quarterly* by saying of him, "From all such expositors of the holy Apostle, we are, by himself, commanded to 'turn away.' "[38] In more temperate language but with equal firmness, A. S. Wilkins, a distinguished young graduate of St. John's whose Nonconformity had disqualified him for a fellowship at Cambridge, replied that "it is impossible for honest men to consent to accept formularies, which they believe naturally and legitimately lead to the errors against which they feel most bound to protest."[39]

Of all the replies to *St. Paul and Protestantism,* the ablest was that by the respected Independent minister in Birmingham, R. W. Dale,[40] who "had humour enough," his son later said, "to relish Mr. Arnold's self-confidence as an exponent of the inner secret of the devout life."[41] But toward Arnold's account of Nonconformity he showed less indulgence. The real secret of Puritanism, he protested, was to be found not in any theological doctrine, but rather "in the intensity and vividness with which it has apprehended the immediate relationship of the regenerate soul to God." It thus belongs to the main stream of the Protestant movement, "the supreme force" of which is "spiritual, not ethical." When Luther preached justification by faith after the religious life of Christendom had been crushed for centuries under a "vast mechanical system of 'means of grace,' " he preached "a most vital spiritual fact" that "brought men face to face with God Himself." Neither the authority nor the organization of the church, Dale insisted, had anything to do with the efficacy of this direct relationship between man and God:

No recognition or assistance from without is necessary for the validity of its ecclesiastical acts, the efficacy of its sacraments, or the acceptableness of its worship. It is enough that He, the Lord of the Church, is with His disciples, and that they have received the Holy Ghost. . . . That the right of appointing a man to be its spiritual teacher should vest in a patron, and be a marketable commodity, that it should be the privilege of any Minister of State, appears too monstrous to require discussion.

Arnold's argument that free development takes place within rather than outside the church was likewise unimpressive to Dale, who in reply pointed to the growth of Calvinism after its repression, the rise of Methodism, and the Oxford Movement. And the portrayal of Nonconformists exercising a "watchful jealousy" moved him to ask the indignant question with which he concluded:

> When farmers are refused a renewal of their leases because they are Nonconformists, when the day-school is closed against a child on Monday because it was at the Methodist Sunday-school the day before, when in the settlement of great properties it is provided that no site shall be sold or let for a Dissenting chapel, and that if a tenant permits his premises to be used for a Dissenting service his lease shall be void, can Mr. Arnold wonder that we are "watchful?"

The restraint and balance of Dale's review account for its eventual emergence as the central response to *St. Paul and Protestantism*, praised by both those who admired Arnold's book and those who denounced it. What Dale had done, essentially, was to remove the debate from a partisan arena and focus attention on Arnold's real target—not Nonconformity, but doctrines that nearly all of Christendom held in common. This was why Simpkinson as well as Wilkins could speak of the review as deserving a respectful and attentive reading, and why the *Guardian* could describe it as a "really powerful defence."[42] Whatever doctrinal or ecclesiastical differences might separate them, Anglicans and Dissenters alike came to agree that Arnold's "new religion of the Bible," as it was to be called, was either impossible or inadequate, or both. Leslie Stephen, for example, while assenting to much of Arnold's thesis, considered "totally fallacious" the assumption that "popular Christianity can be gradually purified of its accretions and transformed into a religion of mildness and sweet reasonableness with no earthly admixture."[43] R. H. Hutton complained that the definition of God as "a stream of tendency" made the Pauline gospel unintelligible.[44] Even Simpkinson conceded that on some points, such as those dealing with Paul's concepts of faith and resurrection, Arnold's book "deserve[d] the blame it ha[d] met with."[45]

Arnold had long since recognized that reviews of the book had given a distorted impression of his objective, and that he himself had helped to make what was primary—Paul's doctrine—secondary to the question of Puritan dissent. In preparing a second edition in the fall of 1870, accordingly, he sought to right matters by placing "Puritanism and the Church of England" after the two essays on "St. Paul and Protestantism," which had followed it in the first edition. This new arrangement, as R. H. Super has noted, was an answer to criticism in the *Academy* and the *Athenaeum* that the volume had appeared to be written "backwards."[46] Yet it was also an expression of Arnold's realization that his "expostulation with the Dissenters ha[d] rather diverted attention from the main essays." Although "convinced" that "the general line" he had taken toward the reading of Paul and the New Testament had "a lucidity and inevitableness about it which [would] make it more and more prevail,"[47] he had nevertheless been brought by his critics to an increasing awareness of opposition to this "general line." If it was to prevail he would have to concern himself less with dissent than with doctrine.

At the same time two other forces were at work shaping the sequel to *St. Paul and Protestantism*. Throughout the sixties Arnold had insisted on the need for intelligence, employing a variety of terms to express what England lacked and for want of which she might decline into a second Holland: criticism, *Geist*, Hellenism. But the startling defeat of France by Germany in 1870–71 prompted a reexamination of the needs of the moment that was to be reflected in his later and altogether different emphasis on conduct, righteousness, Hebraism. In January 1871 Arnold attributed the fall of France "to that want of a serious conception of righteousness and the need of it, the consequences of which so often show themselves in the world's history, and in regard to the Graeco-Latin nations more particularly." Within a few weeks he was expressing the wish that "the present generation of Frenchmen [might] pass clean away as soon as possible and be replaced by a better one,"[48] and in a review of *La Réforme intellectuelle et morale de la France* the following year, he reprimanded Renan for failing to see that the absence of "conscience, self-control, seriousness, steadfastness" among his countrymen was "simply fatal."[49] A more pressing issue than the political and ecclesiastical one of dissent, Arnold concluded, was a religious and spiritual one, the resolution of which would determine national survival. To preserve the Bible as an indispensable support in this critical struggle would require removal of the superstructure of miracle and dogma that had been erected upon it so as to leave secure the moral foundation beneath.

But the new claim of Hebraism did not mean the displacement of Hellenism. It meant, rather, that a different and in some ways more significant role was to be assigned to it. In June 1870, after hearing Lord Salisbury at the dedication of Keble College speak both "of the great future for physical science" and of the need "for retaining and upholding the old ecclesiastical and dogmatic form of religion," Arnold described him as "a dangerous man" because of his ignorance of "the immense work between" religion and science "which is for literature to accomplish." Later that fall he cited the conflicting impulses and demands of the time that called for "methods of insight and moderation": while Swinburne was making his irresistible appeal to the undergraduate with his pagan poetry and Huxley to the working man with his scientific approach, religious dogmatists were insisting on a narrowly sectarian education.[50] At such times, Arnold was to argue, literary tact was essential as a reconciling influence, bridging the gap between science, which disproved the miraculous but left nothing in its place, and theology, which had a genius for abstruse reasoning but was unable to prove its assertions.[51] The role of letters, in short, was the same as it had been when it rescued Homer from the pedantry of Newman and the Pentateuch from the arithmetic of Colenso. It was to save the Bible from the onslaughts of a secular age by showing that it should be read as literature, not as dogma.

III

The central argument of *Literature and Dogma*[52] is that the *Zeitgeist*, by shattering traditional beliefs in miraculous occurrences, plenary inspiration, and a personal God, has demonstrated the insecurity of doctrines based on assumptions incapable of proof. The masses, accordingly, have turned from the Bible. If it is to be preserved as the most important of all books of religious instruction and edification, therefore, a basis for it must be found in something that can be verified rather than assumed. It is impossible, of course, to restore it to the position it once held. But by placing upon it "the right construction," one may find "a real experimental basis" that will endure. And this is the work of culture, which perceives that biblical language is "fluid, passing, and literary, not rigid, fixed, and scientific."

The language of the Bible is the language of a people who had neither talent for abstruse reasoning nor interest in metaphysics. Unlike the bishops of Winchester and Gloucester, moreover, they had no inclination to do something "for the honour of Our Lord's Godhead." But no people ever felt so strongly that conduct, by Arnold's reckoning, "is three-fourths of life and its largest concern," and "that succeeding, going right, hitting the mark in this great concern, [is] *the way of peace*, the highest possible satisfaction." Having thought long and deeply about this fact of life, they concluded—with a leap from the empirical to the metaphysical that Arnold seems to have ignored—that there was a power beyond themselves that had made obedience to the moral order the law of human behavior. To this power they assigned various names, but by all of them they meant "The Eternal not ourselves which makes for righteousness." This was descriptive language *"thrown out* at a vast object of consciousness" that, while not fully grasped, was nevertheless clearly understood, through personal experience, to be a force that "made for the great concern of life, *conduct."*

The original perception of Israel, then, was that *righteousness tendeth to life!* It was a true and invaluable perception, but it was not to endure. In the six centuries following the age of David and Solomon, it suffered many shocks: the questioning of Job, the skepticism of the author of Ecclesiastes, the despondency of Malachi. As a whole, the Hebrews lost sight of the fact that the promises made them were promises made to righteousness, not promises accepted mechanically because made to a chosen people. When they were sent into captivity, perplexed and angry that a privileged race should suffer, they looked for a miraculous change to restore their fallen fortunes; and after their return to Jerusalem, they were disappointed not to find the immediate renewal of the empire of David and Solomon that their prophets had foretold. Out of these conditions arose the Messianic hope, an invasion of *Aberglaube*—belief beyond that which is certain and verifiable—into the faith of a people who had previously based all their belief on what they could experience.

The Messiah who eventually appeared was not the Messiah who had been anticipated. But his being altogether different was the reason for his incomparable significance. The religion of the Hebrews had become a matter primarily of national and social conduct, of executing duties "peculiarly capable of a mechanical exterior performance, in which the heart has no share." What was needed was more inwardness and more feeling—a personal religion, in brief, and a fuller description of righteousness. And this was precisely what Jesus provided. To religion he reapplied emotion and to righteousness he restored the sanction of happiness. Religious life began anew, as he came with a method of inwardness (which called for repentance) and a secret of self-renouncement (which brought peace) working in and through an element of mildness, the conjunction of the three creating the total impression of his "sweet reasonableness."

Once again, however, the truth that righteousness leads to happiness suffered a dangerous accretion of *Aberglaube*. The disciples and reporters of Jesus were incapable of fully understanding and conveying his message. Uncritical, prone to error, far beneath him, they misinterpreted his words and thereby imputed miracles to him. In the prophecies of Isaiah and Jeremiah and in the Book of Daniel, they found what they believed were predictions of his coming, for he spoke of himself as the Messiah, the Son of Man, the Son of God. Seeing thaumaturgy in all that he did, they twisted the words he uttered while healing one possessed of an unclean spirit and made of the cure a miracle instead of the result of moral therapy. When he used the language of popular *Aberglaube*, translating it into the sense of a higher ideal, as in the statement, "The hour is coming, and now is, when the dead shall hear the voice of the Son of God, and they who hear shall live," he was imperfectly understood to prophesy his physical resurrection. And, finally, with the passing away of the first generation without the Advent that he had supposedly foretold for it, his followers looked to a later time for which it had certainly been foretold, and thus encouraged Christianity to fix its attention on the future and on the miraculous, and to rest "the proof of Christianity, not on its internal evidence, but on prophecy and miracle."

Like Spinoza, whom he earlier praised for being unconcerned with disproving biblical miracles, Arnold has no interest in pursuing the rationalistic methods of the Tübingen school. It is enough for him to assert that the *Zeitgeist* "is sapping the proof from miracles" and that "the human mind, as its experience widens, is turning away from them." More than this, he thinks, cannot be said, for whatever one may be-

lieve about the affirmative demonstrations of miracles, a negative demonstration is impossible, and a rationalistic explanation, an attempt to explain supernatural events as distortions
of real events, is futile, leading to more difficulties than it
solves. That miracles do not occur, however, mankind has become more and more convinced, and this being so, one can
perform no greater service than to make the Bible independent of them.

How, then, does one relieve Jesus of responsibility for the
erroneous belief that he performed miraculous acts? Arnold
answers by saying that he was over the heads of his reporters,
who could and did make mistakes.[53] But how, in the report
of Jesus, do we distinguish between what is his and what is
his reporters'? Arnold admits that it is extremely difficult always to know what Jesus said and what he did not say, but he
believes that the Fourth Gospel, which had been disparaged
by Baur, Strauss, and Renan, has "such eminency and value"
precisely because of the certainty with which the Aryan metaphysics of the author can be distinguished from the doctrine
and discourses of Jesus. "The moment Jesus speaks, the metaphysical apparatus falls away, the simple intuition takes its
place; and wherever in the discourse of Jesus the metaphysical apparatus is intruded, it jars with the context, breaks the
unity of the discourse, impairs the thought, and comes evidently from the writer, not Jesus."

Yet despite his addition of miracles and metaphysics to the
words of Jesus, the author of the Fourth Gospel, like the other
early followers, still knew that to believe in him was to accept
and practice his method and secret. As Christianity spread,
however, increasing emphasis was placed on miracle and legend, until eventually the supernatural came to be regarded
as the essential belief and its elements to be formulated in
various creeds. Arnold refuses to describe this as "a degrading
superstition." It is rather "extra-belief and fairy-tale, produced by taking certain great names and great promises too
literally and materially"—like the Protestant doctrine of jus-

tification, which imagines a kind of magnified Lord Shaftesbury who sends his son to deal with a race of offenders and who is related to a third Lord Shaftesbury, working quietly and efficiently in the background. The real objection to such a doctrine as a basis for conduct is "that it is *not sure*; that it assumes what cannot be *verified*." And when this is discovered, the danger is that "the whole certainty of religion seems discredited, and the basis of conduct gone."

IV

No other book by Arnold gained so wide an audience as did *Literature and Dogma*. Published in February 1873, after serial publication in the *Cornhill* had presumably been discontinued by Leslie Stephen because of Arnold's heterodox thesis,[54] it reached a fourth edition within a year, was soon translated into French, and, following a fifth edition, appeared in a popular edition that was reprinted sixteen times during the next forty-one years. Corresponding to this wider audience was the most extensive coverage Arnold had ever been given by the periodical press, both in England and in America and on the Continent as well. In the number of words written, the reply to him easily surpassed the book itself.

The response to *Literature and Dogma*, as one might suppose in view of the unsettled religious beliefs of the time, was even more varied than that to *St. Paul and Protestantism*, ranging from blanket condemnation to surprise that Arnold should attempt anything so remarkable as salvaging the Bible. At one extreme was the Roman Catholic *Dublin Review*, which expressed its contempt by consistently misspelling Arnold's given name, referring to his "ignorance," "insolence," and "imbecility," and concluding that his book was "so evidently childish both in thought and execution, that it might be harmlessly left to amuse the nursery."[55] Another Catholic journal, the *Tablet*, felt compelled "to expose the impertinence of coming forward in the interests of Christianity to upset Christianity, and the vanity of one who professes to reconstruct it."⁵⁶ Protestant journals were in general less acerbic but equally firm in defending religious orthodoxy. The *Congregationalist*, which found in Arnold "no Christian element at all" but only "utter scorn . . . of every principle of the Christian creed," declared that "Christianity is a supernatural system or it is nothing."⁵⁷ The Methodist *London Quarterly Review* denounced his thought as "chaotic confusion" and his book as one "which ought to be left to enjoy an ephemeral triumph over its own class of congenial spirits, and then disappear."⁵⁸ The *British Quarterly* vented its customary hostility in the assertion that the book's "wild imaginations and hopeless conclusions are a sufficient antidote to all that Mr. Arnold has previously written."⁵⁹

Sharply contrasting with these views were those expressed in journals without ecclesiastical affiliation. The *Scotsman*, for example, said that no illustration could "give an adequate idea of the subtlety and beauty of the current of thought which flows on from beginning to end of the book," described it as a volume "to be kept permanently beside one" and an education in itself, and declared that its union "of courage, power, and beauty [were] certain to give it a permanent place in English literature."⁶⁰ A short notice in the *Westminster Review* spoke of it as an "excellent antidote," "healthy" and "substantially correct," to "mischievous identifications of religion with absurd dogmas."⁶¹ Llewelyn Davies, one of the four reviewers singled out for praise in *God and the Bible*, called it "a book of rare moral and intellectual force, original in the greatness and directness of its aim."⁶² Albert Réville, whose review Arnold particularly appreciated,⁶³ said that his "theological adversaries, far from reproaching him with what they think his impieties, should congratulate him on his efforts," for his book was "powerfully conceived," "boldly written," and "penetrated with the great need that the present age feels for a religious renovation that, without breaking with the past, will do justice to the progress accomplished by the general intelligence."⁶⁴ From Holland also came an even stronger endorsement. L. W. E. Rauwenhoff, a Dutch theologian who advocated religion without metaphysic, gave to Arnold's aim of making religion independent of dogma his complete and enthusiastic support.[65]

At the opposite extreme from the *Dublin Review* was a curious notice of the fifth edition of *Literature and Dogma* written for the *Nuova Antologia di Scienze, Lettere ed Arti* by a young Italian liberal, Angelo de Gubernatis, whom Arnold later described as "perhaps the most accomplished man" of his nation.[66] The book, Gubernatis said, would have been impossible in Italy, where one could find ascetic writers prepared to extol the Bible for its perfection, and Voltairian writers intent upon demolishing it completely, but never a serious university professor writing an entire volume to prove that it could be better interpreted than it is. In Italy the Bible was regarded as a sacred text for priests, a book full of obscenity[67] and contradictions for unbelievers, a historical document to be used with great care by scholars, and a collection of lovely excerpts of Oriental poetic eloquence for literati; but it never had been and never would be a rich source of inspiration for everyday living. In England, on the other hand, the Bible was beginning to be discussed by people like Arnold who had an exaggerated notion of the moral, political, and religious importance of the Old Testament. It was strange indeed to find him, with all his conviction and ingenuity, struggling on such treacherous ground beneath cloudy skies, attempting to build a new world from the Bible alone—as if Plato had founded his *Republic*, Gubernatis remarked scornfully, on a text of Hesiod.[68]

Met by such conflicting reactions to *Literature and Dogma*, Arnold might well have reached the same conclusion he had come to after the publication of *St. Paul and Protestantism* —that God alone was his judge. It was months, however, before he saw a review of the book. Only three days before its appearance, he left for Italy, not "to fly from the evil report of it," as Huxley had said facetiously,[69] but rather to recover from a succession of domestic sorrows. Early in 1872 his second son had died—the third such loss he had suffered in four years—and by the end of the year, according to Charles Eliot Norton, he looked "troubled and worn," and his grief-stricken wife seemed "broken by calamity."[70] Understandably, therefore, Arnold left instructions that "*no* reviews should be sent" to him, since the book was "sure to be much attacked and blamed."[71] Even on the Continent he was unable to escape comments on the work, hearing about it everywhere he went; but presumably he did not read notices of it until after his return. Then, in less than a year, characteristically, he determined "to pass in review the principal objections" brought against it.[72] The result was a series of seven articles published in the *Contemporary Review* from October 1874 through September 1875 and then republished, together with a preface, as *God and the Bible*.

V

The "main objections" to *Literature and Dogma*, Arnold wrote to James Knowles, editor of the *Contemporary*, had "been two: one, to its refusal to affirm a personal God; the other, to its use of the Fourth Gospel."[73] The title he eventually gave to his reply, the least felicitous of the compound titles he was fond of giving to his books, thus denotes the central criticism of the previous volume and suggests the two major topics of its successor: the existence of God as proved by miracles, metaphysics, and experience (the concern of the first three chapters), and the biblical canon, in particular the Fourth Gospel (the concern of the final three chapters). The area Arnold chose for defending *Literature and Dogma* was strictly defined, therefore, excluding or but slightly touching a number of objections, such as that his reading of scripture was arbitrary and impressionistic, that his assumptions regarding the miraculous begged the question, that his logic proved faulty and his definitions inadequate, and that he made of Jesus only a charming, humanistic teacher and of Christianity a mere system of ethics. But by so choosing the objections he would answer, Arnold gained an immense advantage over his critics.

These critics, he implies, are of two sorts, both inimical to real Christianity. On the one hand are those who have hurled at him the charge of being anti-Christian and anti-religious but who deserve, so grotesque is their travesty of religion, to have hurled at them in return the retort of Polycarp to his execrators: "Away with the atheists!" And on the other hand are Liberals who wish to hasten the death of Christianity, reproach him for writing as an advocate of the Bible, and (according to one of the most diverting of Arnold's vivacious eruptions) seem inclined to make rejection of the Fourth Gospel a part of their creed, together with disestablishment and marriage with a deceased wife's sister. Between these two extremes, Arnold pursues what appears inescapably to be the right course—positive, constructive, religious, and essentially conservative.

The audience for whom *God and the Bible* is intended is likewise restricted, and with comparable advantages. Arnold addresses not those "still striving to be content with the received theology," not the "frivolous" upper class or the "raw" lower class in their "religious insensibility," not Catholics or Liberal secularists with their virtual ignorance of the Bible. He writes, rather, for those who are both religious and intellectually serious but who in their dissatisfaction with dogmatic Christianity have turned from the Bible as well—those, in short, for whom *Literature and Dogma* was intended. Yet the "grave objections" brought against that book have "puzzled and shaken" the many readers it has enabled "to use and enjoy the Bible, when the common theology, popular or learned, had almost estranged them from it." This is patent fiction, for if Arnold's readers had previously renounced belief in a personal God, they were unlikely to be further disturbed by the replies of his critics, and most of them were almost certainly unaware that his use of the Fourth

Gospel had encountered "grave" objections, one of the most significant of which came from a critic writing in Dutch. But the strategy is a skillful one, allowing Arnold to suggest that in answering his critics he seeks not to satisfy a polemical urge, but only to aid the "baffled, distressed, and bewildered" reader of their criticism.[74]

This reader, like Arnold himself, is but a plain, simple person. For him learned discussions are irrelevant; he wishes only to have the facts presented to him and then be allowed to reach his own conclusion. Fair- and open-minded, unbiased and attentive, he is the judge to whom Arnold constantly appeals. But in addressing him, Arnold writes not as a Tübingen professor who, with a scholarly reputation at stake, devises ingenious schemes of great vigor and rigor and sacrifices fact to theory; nor does he write as one holding a brief for traditional theology because he has an interest in preserving it. He is, rather, the disinterested critic, intent only on seeing the Bible as it really is; and here he has qualities ideally suited for the task. On the one hand, his notorious lack of philosophical principles and inaptness for abstruse reasoning enable him to confess unashamedly his failure to understand Descartes' famous utterance, with the result that he is led to an analysis that shows how unsatisfactory such language is. And on the other hand, his implied critical tact, as on the matter of the internal evidence of the Fourth Gospel, allows him to settle questions where positive evidence is lacking and literary criticism is thus all-important, just as with Frank Newman he had previously settled similar questions.

On one point alone does Arnold make any substantial concession to his critics—the use of personalities in his parable of the three Lord Shaftesburys and in his repeated references to the bishops of Winchester and Gloucester. That in the one instance he had been guilty of sacrilege and in the other of unpardonable irreverence most of his reviewers were agreed. The Manchester *Guardian* said that "the repeated mockery of 'the triune Lord Shaftesbury' displeases at first and disgusts at last."[75] W. J. Courthope declared in the *Quarterly Review* that "to jest on a matter which, to nine-tenths of his countrymen, is a matter of religious belief" placed him on a level with Charles Bradlaugh.[76] The *London Quarterly Review* predicted that the "parody of the three Lord Shaftesburys [would] remain, so long as the writings of this author are read, the foulest opprobrium . . . that modern theological literature can be charged with."[77] A. P. Stanley thought the passage "dangerous and regrettable,"[78] and Fitzjames Stephen even warned that it was "really actionable."[79]

In *God and the Bible* Arnold defended the illustration by declaring that he was unable to treat the "legend" and "fairytale" of popular religion with solemnity. But because of the happiness the fairy tale had given, because of the beauty and pathos it contained, he thought it should be regarded indulgently. And this was precisely what he had done in the parable[80]—a defense difficult to reconcile with his reproach of Colenso a decade earlier for asserting that although the Book of Exodus is fiction, its writer is not culpable because he intended no deception. Yet Arnold continued to believe that the "parable had the advantage of fixing sharply" in his reader's mind what he meant, and when he finally excised it in preparing the popular edition of 1883, as E. K. Brown remarked,[81] he made clear that he acted solely in deference to Lord Shaftesbury, whom he admired and to whom it had given pain.[82]

To criticism of his comments on the two bishops, which the *Guardian* in particular had found "insulting,"[83] Arnold was more amenable, eliminating a number of them from the fifth edition (1876) of *Literature and Dogma*. In the introduction to *God and the Bible*, however, he defended the passages. Although he spoke there with some restraint, he said, about the bishop of Winchester, Samuel Wilberforce—Huxley's opponent in a celebrated debate at Oxford and the victim of a fatal accident in the summer of 1873—Arnold nevertheless felt compelled to say that Wilberforce's signal addiction to claptrap disqualified him either for helping in the present religious crisis or for entering the kingdom of God.[84] And the bishop of Gloucester, C. J. Ellicott—Disraeli's unsuccessful choice for the archbishopric of Canterbury about whom Lord Granville had once asked, "Is he *really* such a fool as he seems to me?"[85]—was similarly addicted and thus in danger of suffering the same fate.[86]

VI

If Arnold had offended his readers by engaging in personalities when speaking of bishops, he had offended them in precisely the opposite manner when speaking of God. Several years later their reaction was satirically suggested by an exchange between Mr. Luke and Lady Grace, in Mallock's *New Republic*, which epitomized the chief issue between Arnold and orthodox opinion:

"Quite so," said Mr. Luke, not waiting to listen, "towards that great Law—that great verifiable tendency of things—that great stream whose flowing such of us as are able are now so anxiously trying to accelerate. There is no vain speculation about creation, and first causes, and consciousness here, which are matters we can never verify, and which matter nothing to us—"

"But," stammered Lady Grace aghast, "Mr. Luke, do you mean to say that—but it surely must matter something whether God can hear our prayers, and will help us, and whether we owe Him any duty, and whether He is conscious of what we do, and will judge us—it must matter—"

Mr. Luke leaned forwards towards Lady Grace, and spoke to her in a confidential whisper.

"Not two straws—not that," he said with a smile, and a very slight fillip of his finger and thumb.

Lady Grace was thunderstruck.

"But," again she stammered softly and eagerly, "unless you say there is no personal—"

Mr. Luke hated the word *personal*; it was so much mixed up in his mind with theology, that he even winced if he had to speak of personal talk.

"My dear Lady Grace," he said, in a tone of surprised remonstrance, "you are talking like a Bishop."[87]

Those who were more articulate than Lady Grace sought to controvert Arnold on the question of a personal God by adopting in general one or more of three positions: they attempted to give evidence to support belief in a personal God, chiefly that of the testimony of Jesus; they argued that only when one believed in a personal God did religion become meaningful; and they pointed out that Arnold's "stream of tendency" was in fact no more verifiable than a personal deity.

Among the ablest of the critics taking the first position was Llewelyn Davies, who devoted nearly half his twenty-page review to considering the question of belief in God. Although admitting that man's language was anthropomorphic and inadequate, Davies argued that faith in a "Father," "the object of man's devotion and gratitude," was "altogether *natural*" and verified by "experience, conscience, emotion." Jesus, moreover, witnessed to such a God, for he "spoke with authority as knowing the Father, and reported fatherly purposes of God towards men, and because he announced an unseen Kingdom, a Kingdom of hearts and inward lives, to be really established on the earth, . . . men were drawn to him"—far more than if he had said only that "self-control leads to happiness."[88] John Tulloch, who gave to the question almost the whole of his article on Arnold's "amateur theology," agreed:

If Christian theology teaches that "God is a person," it is not merely that any bishops have thought or reasoned so, but because all the revelations of the Divine, "the not ourselves," in history and in human life, have pointed towards this conclusion. When men were athirst for the Divine, and could not find it in such mere stoical conceptions of order and righteous power as Mr. Arnold . . . tenders for our acceptance, then the words of Christ revealed to them a living Father —not merely a Power making for righteousness, but a divine Person loving righteousness and hating evil.

The existence of such a God, Tulloch said, was certain if not "scientifically" verifiable:

Religious facts are not facts of the same nature as the properties of fire or water, and you cannot certify them in the same manner. . . . They are none the less true on this account. They yield an experience of their own which is their sufficient evidence. And taking religious experience as our guide, can there be any doubt that the personality of God is a fact to it as sure as the fact that fire burns, although not after the same manner sure? It *proves itself within* the spiritual sphere.[89]

A subtler line of argument was followed by Albert Réville, "a pastor at Rotterdam and one of the best French writers going," as Arnold had once identified him,[90] who developed the position that the religious life is dependent on belief in a personal God. Describing Arnold as "decidedly too much afraid of the idea of the personality of God," he distinguished between calling God "a person" and speaking of a "personal" God:

By a personal God one understands not a person like you or me, but a God possessing in a far higher degree than mere human persons that consciousness and intelligence which, within the limited circle of our experience, are only possessed by personal beings. It is in vain to ask, how we can verify the fact that God possesses them. In the first place I should answer that the experimental study of the universe discloses too many ends, aims, and harmonious coincidences for it to be rationally possible to deny conscious intelligence to the sovereign mover of that "stream by which all things fulfil the law of their being." But I should say further: As soon as you tell me of a "power not ourselves which makes for righteousness," the first question that inevitably presents itself to my mind is: Is this power conscious, intelligent, that is to say personal? or is it blind, unconscious, impersonal?

If the latter, Réville said, "I cannot feel for it that sacred emotion which raises morality to the rank of religion." It was here, he thought, that Arnold's "meagre . . . conception of the Deity" made itself most felt: "Morality deals with concrete, practical life, such acts as conscience commands; religion is the sentiment, the emotions which man experiences in the presence of the Absolute." And for the same reason Arnold provided an inadequate account of the ministry of Jesus, who preached not an abstract notion of a moral force but "a feeling, intense and pure, of the living God"—a religious feeling possible only "in relation to a God who possesses,—granted in an indescribable degree,—but still really possesses those perfections of existence to which the conscience, the intelligence, the power of loving in man are but feeble approximations."[91]

Réville's argument, like that of Davies, went through many variations in the English periodicals but remained essentially the same. Thus the *Saturday Review* complained at length that although Arnold provided new insights and perspective, he did not afford a basis for a reasoned faith, his method leading only to a vague, indefinite religion and to the unhelpful conception of God as an influence.[92] The *Christian Observer* declared that the "cardinal defect" of his "religious system" was "the exclusion from it of the doctrine of the personality of the Deity."[93] Writing on "dogmatic extremes" in the *Contemporary Review*, John Tulloch sadly observed that the "special feature" of the time was "the dogmatism of a new philosophy and culture, whose watchword is the denial of that Divine Personality which has hitherto been supposed to constitute the pith of all religion."[94]

Of all the journals, the most insistent on this point was the *Spectator*, which had said in its review of the first of the two *Cornhill* installments of *Literature and Dogma* that Arnold's "power which makes for righteousness" was "incapable of generating emotion unless we attribute to it thought and will and love; and if we attribute that to it, there is no pretence for excluding even the idea of personality." Pointing to Arnold's admission that his "scientific" definition of God was inadequate and less proper than a description such as "Clouds and darkness are round about him," it argued that if the method of personification was more proper and adequate, it should also be more exact[95]—to which Arnold replied by comparing Wordsworth's description of the earth as "the mighty mother of mankind" with the geographers' description of it as "an oblate spheroid."[96] This distinction failed to satisfy the *Spectator*, however, and in the first of its two articles on the complete *Literature and Dogma* it continued the debate:

Wordsworth did not either produce, or intend to produce, the effect of making us *trust* in the Earth as if she were a person who could answer our appeals. The word "Mother" was for him a metaphor the drift of which every one understands without warning against over-interpretation. The writers of the Old Testament did both produce, and intend to produce, the effect of making men trust in God as a living being who would answer their appeals.[97]

The following week the *Spectator* concluded that "the great object" of Arnold's book was "to cut away from the Old and New Testaments the very foundation of their faith, to give us a Christianity 'in the air,'—a subtilised morality adrift from the only anchor of the human affections,—a living God."[98]

Like a number of other papers, the *Spectator* also hinted that Arnold's "stream of tendency" was no more capable of verification than the personal God of whom they spoke. But none of them pursued the implication so fully as did Henry Dunn, former secretary to the British and Foreign School Society who earlier had objected to Arnold about the religious views expressed in his poems on Empedocles and Obermann. In a pamphlet entitled *Facts, Not Fairy-Tales* Dunn remarked that an impersonal power making for righteousness was not only a "poor exchange . . . for a heavenly Father" but in fact no more certain: "I can no more be *sure* that this '*not ourselves*,' supposed to be around us, makes for righteousness than that he thinks and loves. The whole thing may be a fairy-tale." If the one can be experienced, Dunn argued, so can the other. And if the experience of a loving God is a limited one, so, too, is the experience of a power making for righteousness: "Multitudes in all parts of the world have had no such experience. In them selfishness is predominant, and the light is darkness."[99]

Later critics pressed still further the argument that Arnold's "not ourselves" rested as much on metaphysical assumptions as did the God of popular religion. Thus in 1876 William Knight, professor of moral philosophy at St. Andrews, posed the obvious question when he asked, how do we know the "eternal not ourselves" is eternal except "by an *à priori* process, which the new philosophy would disown?" All of man's "experience of 'tendency' in the direction of righteousness," he said, "is personal. Observation of the results of human action, and consequences of wrong-doing and of righteous conduct respectively, shows that certain causes, set in motion by ourselves or by others, issue in certain subjective effects." Furthermore, if there is "a stream of tendency not ourselves that makes for righteousness, there is also a stream of tendency not ourselves that makes for wickedness."[100] Eight years later, writing in the *Contemporary Review*, H. D. Traill summarized the case against Arnold:

> As long ago as the appearance of the first edition of "Literature and Dogma," it was pointed out by many of its critics that its proposed basis of religion had really no more scientific certainty, was no more verifiable than that which it was designed to replace; and some such critics . . . went so far as to say that it actually added to the difficulties that it pretended to remove. The "Eternal Power," the "something not ourselves," and "the making for righteousness," are each of them, it was urged, conceptions no more directly given in consciousness than that of a "Personal God." Nothing is given in consciousness but the subjective fact of certain impulses; and the other so-called "certainties" are simply so many conjectures explanatory of the fact. We do not *know* that the impulses in question proceed even from an external Power, still less from an eternal one, or that, if they do, that Power makes for righteousness alone and not for unrighteousness also. We do not know this, these critics said, and there is no possible means of ascertaining it. So, they concluded, there are three unverifiables, not one unverifiable. . . .[101]

VII

An "incurable heretic" on the question of a personal God, as he described himself to Charles Appleton, editor of the

Academy,[102] Arnold devoted the first three chapters of *God and the Bible* to answering these objections by his critics. In the first of these, the title of which, "The God of Miracles," misleadingly implies a greater reliance on miraculous testimony than the reviewers in general showed, he begins by recalling how in *Literature and Dogma* he had attempted to restore use of the Bible by insisting that it required belief only in that which could be verified, and that its language was literary, not scientific. This, he says in answer to Davies's assertion that the bishop of Gloucester merely used the approximate language Arnold himself admitted to be the most suitable language to use in speaking of God, is why the bishop should make clear that he means "to talk, not science, but rhetoric and poetry"—in which case one's only criticism would be that "it is bad rhetoric and poetry, whereas the rhetoric and poetry of Israel is good." But the bishop and others who employ this language "mean it for science; they mean it for a more formal and precise account of what Israel called poetically 'the high and holy one that inhabiteth eternity;' and it is false science because it assumes what it cannot verify."[103]

The objection to speaking of God as a person who thinks and loves, Arnold repeats, is that we have no experience on which to base such a belief. Taking a position that is essentially what Huxley defined as agnostic, he declares in reply to Réville that he neither professes to have discovered God to be an impersonal power nor denies to Him conscious intelligence. And, he says in commenting on a statement in the *Edinburgh Review* regarding Strauss's *Der alte und der neue Glaube*,[104] he does not assert God to be a *thing*. All he maintains is that "men do not know enough about the Eternal not ourselves that makes for righteousness, to warrant their pronouncing this either a person or a thing." Arnold concedes to Réville that although his stream of tendency is more certain than the God of popular religion, it may appear to be less satisfying. But in a rhetorical question that evades the point of Réville's distinction between morality and religion, he asks "the plain reader" whether it is not a mistake to think of God as a person when we have no experience to justify our doing so.[105]

The primary support for belief in "a magnified and non-natural man," Arnold implies by the title of his first chapter, has been the miraculous. The critics of *Literature and Dogma* had, of course, objected to his denial of miracles, but they had objected even more to what they considered to be his flippant treatment of the supernatural. Chief among these was the *Guardian*, which listed several works mentioned in a previous issue as worthy of study on the subject of miracles (the *Summa Theologiae* of Aquinas, Dean Mansel's contributions to *Aids to Faith*, Canon Mozley's *Bampton Lectures*, and Newman's *Essays on Miracles*) and declared that while some readers might be satisfied with Arnold's "airy tone of assurance" in dismissing the miraculous, others demanded "solid replies to solid treatises."[106] Arnold's reply is precisely the same one he had made in *Literature and Dogma*: "To engage in an *à priori* argument to prove that miracles are impossible, against an adversary who argues *à priori* that they are possible, is the vainest labour in the world." But the modern spirit having come increasingly to an awareness that "miracles are untrustworthy," the important question—the question he had directed at Colenso years earlier—was what was to become of religion now that they could not be relied on. This was the question that he was seeking to answer—"to have done with all this negative, unfruitful business, and to get to religion again;—to the use of the Bible upon new grounds which shall be secure."[107]

No more certain to Arnold than the God of miracles is the God of metaphysics, which he examines in the second chapter. He turned to it with obvious relief, for the first of the essays in the *Contemporary* had "made many people very angry," he wrote to Knowles; and in the second part, which he thought "not bad," he had been able to adopt "an easier and lighter tone than was possible for the first part." He continued to believe that the central question was "between not having the Bible studied and prized at all, in some ten years time, or having it studied and prized with new ideas and on new grounds." Yet he would gladly avoid controversy: "I really *hate* polemics," he added, "and I should not wonder if there was some unpleasantness for you, too, in the Contemporary being made the vehicle for them."[108]

The second chapter, more than half of which is spent in reducing the Cartesian proposition to "I think, therefore I breathe,"[109] is concerned with demonstrating the semantic difficulties—the vagueness and ambiguity—of metaphysical language about the being of God. Only when he has shown these does Arnold turn to the argument of his critics, principally Henry Dunn, that a personal God is as capable of verification as his enduring power. Here Arnold begs the question, repeating his contention that man's experience teaches him that happiness is inextricably related to conduct (an assertion that ignores Dunn's remark that much of mankind has no such experience), and declaring that our experience of the God of righteousness is essentially different from our experience of a God who thinks and loves (an assumption that his critics had insisted was incapable of proof). Nor is he more convincing in his answer to the objection that his description of God as the *Eternal* goes beyond experience into metaphysics. Whereas the word involves a metaphysical concept in one sense, he says, in another (that which is lifelong) it does not. Everything the Hebrews learned from their own experience and from the experience of their fathers led them to believe "that righteousness was salvation, and that it would go on being salvation from one generation of men to another" —"the only sound sense in which we can call the law of righteousness, or the law of gravitation, or any other law . . . eternal."[110] It is a passage like this which explains Jowett's comment that in his arguments based on the meaning of words Arnold was guilty of "a most Philistine sort of fallacy."[111]

The law of righteousness that Israel experienced, Arnold

admits, was eventually personified into "a human agent that feels, thinks, loves, hates." But this was to confuse the realm of experience with the realm of metaphysics, and Arnold declines to invest the "Eternal not ourselves" with personal attributes, just as he refuses to concede that proof of its existence requires evidence other than empirical. With equal ease he rejects both the ontological argument (the concept of a perfect circle, he says, may derive not from the existence of one but from imagining a circle "rounder" than any found in experience) and the teleological (a watch implies a watchmaker only because we know that men make watches). Metaphysical arguments for the existence of a personal deity, Arnold concludes, are in reality supported by belief in the miraculous. But while arguments from miracles are dismissed with "tenderness" because of the "comfort and joy" they have given, metaphysical arguments, which have neither convinced nor pleased anyone, are dismissed with "sheer satisfaction."[112]

Since all of this is a "joyless task of learning what not to believe," Arnold willingly turns in the third chapter to what is affirmative and fortifying. Here he gains the additional advantage of selecting as his principal antagonist a reviewer for the *Westminster* who had attacked *Literature and Dogma* for reasons altogether different from those of orthodox critics, accusing Arnold of finding not too little in the Bible but too much.[113] The reviewer was apparently not Walter R. Cassels, the author of *Supernatural Religion*, as Arnold at first conjectured,[114] but he resembled him in his mastery of the relentlessly negative, heavy-handed, and mechanical methods of German criticism.

The thesis the *Westminster* reviewer attempts to develop is that the power making for righteousness that Arnold professes to find in the Bible derives altogether from an arbitrary and distorted reading of the Old Testament. Far from being such a power, he argues, the God of Israel ("a barbarous or semi-barbarous people . . . in a very early stage of civilization") was "a purely personal God" who had "none of the remorseless impassibility of a law" but altered his purposes in response to prayer or sacrifice. He was "more patriotic than righteous," loving his friends and sanctioning the extermination of enemies "by any means, however immoral"; and his followers were distinguished not by righteousness but by "intense devoutness" and "blind obedience." Although from time to time there were prophets with "more spiritual insight" who "caught glimpses of a higher righteousness than that of the law," the reviewer insists that these were "reformers and poets who in no way affected Israel's habitual inclination to equate righteousness with ceremonial observance. With the call of Abraham, he admits, an important step forward was achieved, the element of love being introduced to modify the "abject fear" of earlier worship. But after this "no substantial progress was ever made," and between the "imperfect morality" of Israel and the "ideal religion" Arnold ascribes to it—one "in which morality is all in all"—an unbridgeable chasm remains.

Criticism of this kind, Arnold replies, assumes that people "must be rigidly consistent, must show no conflicting aspects, must have no flux and reflux, must not follow a slow, hesitating, often obscure line of growth." Israel's concept of an eternal power making for righteousness evolved in a "loose and wavering" manner, to be sure, but it nonetheless evolved and endured. Whereas the Hellenic concern for morality degenerated into the "religious solemnity" of a courtesan's portraying Venus emerging from the sea, the Hebraic concern grew "into an enthusiasm, turbid, passionate, absorbing and all-pervasive, to *bring in everlasting righteousness.*" The "glorifications of righteousness" by the prophets and psalmists, which the *Westminster* reviewer dismissed as exceptional rather than characteristic utterances, became a central part of the religious life of the nation. Even Israel's shortcomings testify to the force of its concern with righteousness, as in the confession, "I called mine own ways to remembrance, and turned my feet unto Thy testimonies," which Arnold quotes again and again in rhetorical answer to the reviewer's argument that Israel's God was a magnified man of human passions and imperfections, and its religion largely one of fear and ceremony.[115]

And how does one account for "this native, continuous, and increasing pressure upon Israel's spirit of the ideas of conduct and of its sanctions"? Arnold replies "by supposing that Israel had an intuitive faculty, a natural bent for these ideas; that their truth was borne in upon him, revealed to him." Here, of course, is the same inconsistency to which his critics previously pointed. If Israel derived its ideas of righteousness through revelation, it did not derive them empirically; and if it derived them by means of an intuitive faculty, it had a metaphysical bent that Arnold denied it possessed. But Arnold insists that he puts "aside all the preternatural" and gives only a "natural" explanation, which "is yet grander than the preternatural one." And then, having it still a third way, he adds that even if one rejects the notion of intuition or special bent, there is still left the fact that cannot be accounted for—"a religion insisting on the idea of righteousness with an energy and impressiveness absolutely unparalleled."[116]

This is why it "does not matter two straws," Arnold says in answer to Courthope's complaint in the *Quarterly Review* that an "enduring power" raised a metaphysical question,[117] whether we assign the origin of "moral perceptions to intuition, or to education, or to evolution and inheritance." And as if to show how little it matters, he suggests yet another source for Israel's ideas of righteousness: they came not from revelation, or intuition, or chance, but from "a feeling" for religion. What is important is that religion is "morality touched with emotion," that it is equally religion whether it has arisen from one source or another, that in Israel morality appears most touched with emotion, and that Israel was therefore "endued with most bent for religion."[118] Such an argument makes unnecessary either an F. H. Bradley to demolish it or Arnold's own admission to distaste for logic.

Nor is he more persuasive in answering the objection of Charles Secrétan[119] that the idea of a power making for righteousness is neither experiential nor capable of verification. A Swiss theologian at the Academy of Lausanne, Secrétan agreed that it was necessary "ramener l'enseignement religieux à des vérités susceptibles d'une démonstration expérimentale, attendu que le siècle où nous vivons n'en admet pas d'autre." But, he asked,

le secret de Jésus-Christ, que le bonheur se trouve dans le sacrifice et qu'il s'y trouve uniquement, mais la foi de l'ancien peuple à l'existence d'un suprême pouvoir qui assure l'avantage à la justice dans le cours des choses humaines, ces hautes doctrines sont-elles donc réellement des notions expérimentales, tellement que chacun soit en état de les vérifier? Le Dr. Arnold l'affirme; or, qui ne voit, qui ne comprend aussitôt que les propositions contraires expriment seules la vérité du fait? La réalité d'une puissance ou d'une loi suivant laquelle l'ordre de justice tendrait à prévaloir dans l'histoire des peuples et des individus: tel est le propre objet de la foi, laquelle se fonde si peu sur l'expérience qu'elle est éprouvée et affinée par les démentis que l'expérience lui prodigue chaque jour.

Arnold lamely replies that it "is easy to dispute" the experiential truths of which he speaks, but, again begging the question, he declares that "on the whole, they prove themselves, and prevail more and more." If one is unable to accept this as adequate proof, "for him *Literature and Dogma* was not written."[120]

He is more convincing in response to Secrétan's criticism that the "fond de ses idées est d'un kantien beaucoup plus que d'un empirique" and that because of his confusion he is led into a dilemma he never resolves: if we have eudaemonism as motivation and conscience as authority, how are we to reconcile the two? "Nous le demanderions volontiers à l'auteur," Secrétan tartly remarked, "si ses dédains pour la logique étaient moins prononcés." Arnold answers that a careful distinction is to be made between *pleasure* and *utility,* which connote "low and false views of what constitutes happiness," and *joy* and *happiness*, which do not. And quoting the testimony of Augustine, Pascal, Barrow, and Butler to the truth that man seeks happiness as his highest goal, he insists that "joy and happiness are the magnets to which human life inevitably moves." When one rejects this truth, as do the theologians of the Unitarian school who most loudly oppose eudaemonism, he makes "a fatal error" and becomes the victim of "sterility in religion."[121]

This characteristic stress on joy is the focal point of Arnold's reply to R. H. Hutton, who, in reviewing the first installment of *God and the Bible* as it appeared in the *Contemporary*, raised the old issue of a personal God when he said that "if the personifying language about God is mere poetry, it seems to us quite impossible to say where the poetry of the Bible ends and its serious meaning begins." Referring to Arnold's comparison of "the personifying language of the Bible about God, with the personifying language of Wordsworth about Nature," he asked "where it appears that Wordsworth seriously inculcates prayer to Nature, or treats distrust in the promises of Nature as a sin, or addresses her in the matter-of-fact, down-right, eager mood of real expectation and confidence so common in the Psalms"; and he concluded that it was "very nearly impossible for a rational man to assert that the authors of the Bible used the personal language about God in any less serious and profoundly convinced sense than that in which they spoke of the secrets of man's moral experience."[122] Arnold's reply to the first of these strictures is that we know the Bible is to be read literally when it speaks of righteousness as salvation, and figuratively when it speaks of God as talking, thinking, and loving, because in the one instance the writer is on ground of experience where we can follow him, and in the other he is not. In response to the second objection, he quotes Wordsworth's "Nature never did forsake the heart that loved her" and refers, as an example of language that "treats distrust in the promises of Nature as a sin," to Butler's recognition of a "course of life marked out for man by na-

ture, whatever that nature be." Israel, he says, "had an irresistible intuition" that "virtue is the law man is born under" and
thus broke "into joy."[123]

The replies to Secrétan and Hutton virtually conclude the
first half of *God and the Bible*, the remainder being only a
series of answers to miscellaneous criticism of little or no importance. The fatuous comment by the *Westminster* reviewer
that Arnold should not speak of the "secret" of Jesus since
Jesus made no secret of it himself receives the obvious answer:
the word suggests the special truth that Jesus proclaimed, not
something he sought to conceal. To the criticism that he supposes Jesus to have achieved actual cures in exorcising unclean spirits, when the Jewish thaumaturgists are also represented as being successful, Arnold replies that because there
are charlatans one must not assume there are no genuine physi-
cians. The *Westminster Review*'s assertion that it is absurd to
speak of Jesus as the son of a power making for righteousness
is countered by the statement that the Bible "never speaks of
the Eternal as a natural law, but always as if this power lived,
and breathed, and felt." Finally, Courthope's questions—
"How . . . can it be verified that righteousness is alone possible by the method of Jesus? Was there no righteousness in
the world before the Christian era?"[124]—are answered, Arnold
declares, by the passage in the Fourth Gospel in which Jesus
says, "Before Abraham was, I am."[125]

VIII

If the quotation fails to answer the reviewer's questions, it
at least serves its apparent purpose of bringing Arnold to the
problem with which he deals in the second half of *God and
the Bible*: the authenticity of the Fourth Gospel. His reliance
in *Literature and Dogma* on the sayings of Jesus reported in
this gospel had been sharply criticized in at least two quarters,
the Continental critics and the English reviewers under the
influence of the Tübingen school. L. W. E. Rauwenhoff regarded it as one of the weakest parts of the book.[126] Albert

Réville said that the use he made of the Fourth Gospel was "extremely arbitrary," contrasting "strangely with his advanced views on the general subject of Biblical interpretation" and suggesting that "he had lost sight of the formidable arguments brought by contemporary criticism against the historical character of the words attributed to Jesus in this gospel."[127] The author of a brief notice in the *Westminster Review*, questioning Arnold's assigning to Jesus himself the discourses recorded in the Fourth Gospel, declared that nothing was more certain than that "these discourses proceed from an unknown writer."[128] Frank Newman made the same point in more daring language: the gospel, he said, "abounds with utterances which most sound minds would call impiety or insanity from any human prophet, however holy and eminent."[129]

Yet this was scarcely fundamental criticism of *Literature and Dogma*, as much of the criticism had been, and why Arnold should have devoted half of *God and the Bible* to answering objections that left his central argument unaffected is not clear. The explanation may lie simply in an interest in the Fourth Gospel that had been stimulated first by his father and later by the controversy over its authenticity. Dr. Arnold, according to Frank Newman, "rested the main strength of Christianity on the gospel of John," which he regarded "as abounding with smaller touches which marked the eye-witness, and, altogether, [as] the vivid and simple picture of a divine reality, undeformed by credulous legend."[130] Other scholars, however, were less confident; and when Renan summarized the controversy in 1867 he divided opinion on the subject into four clearly defined categories. Orthodox opinion, wholly untenable from the viewpoint of rational criticism, he said, held that the gospel was written by the Apostle John, the son of Zebedee; that all of its statements are true; and that the discourses it records were actually spoken by Jesus. A second opinion, that of Ewald, in some respects of Reuss and others, and of Renan in the first edition of the *Vie de*

Jésus, was that the Fourth Gospel, though it may have been revised and retouched by his disciples, is in substance the work of John, that the facts regarding Jesus are direct traditions, and that the discourses are often free compositions expressing only the manner in which the author conceived the mind of Jesus. A third opinion, now endorsed by Renan, was that the gospel, not the work of the Apostle John but attributed to him by some disciple about the year 100, has discourses that are almost entirely fictitious, but narrative portions that contain valuable traditions ascending in part to the Apostle John. A fourth opinion, the "radical" view of Baur, Strauss, Réville, and others, was that the gospel is in no sense the work of the Apostle John; that neither the facts nor the discourses recorded in it are historical; that it is a partly allegorical product of the imagination; and that the purpose of the author, writing in approximately the year 150, was not to recount the actual life of Jesus but to propagate the idea he himself had formed of Jesus.[131] In 1874 this radical view was adopted by Walter Cassels in his popular and widely discussed *Supernatural Religion*; and when he dismissed the gospel as having "no real historical value,"[132] he raised anew the whole question of its authenticity.

The question of the validity of the Fourth Gospel, Arnold says, like the question of the date, authorship, and manner of composition of any portion of the Bible, is not essential to the reader of *Literature and Dogma*. The method, the secret, the mildness and sweet reasonableness of Jesus are adequately depicted in the Synoptics, and they remain even if we lose the Fourth Gospel. Why, then, should the reader whom Arnold is ostensibly addressing be concerned with textual criticism? Simply because man naturally desires knowledge, Arnold replies, and especially knowledge about a document that has been the subject of widespread and heated discussion and that has been for Christendom, as Luther described it, "the true head-gospel."[133]

But two obstacles hinder a sound evaluation of evidence

concerning the gospel canon. One of these, notably present in England, is the tendency to answer biblical questions in the manner most convenient to traditional theology. The other exists primarily in Germany, where theories of "great vigour and rigour"[134] are regularly propounded by a body of specialists intoxicated by their subject and "carried away by theorising." Arnold seeks to avoid both errors, of course, and thereby gains a strategic advantage over his two sets of critics, English and Continental. Convinced that his reader merely desires "the fair facts of the case," he is "determined to reject nothing because it does not suit us," "to let the facts about the Gospel-Canon fairly and simply speak for themselves," and to proceed as he would "in a literary inquiry where we were wholly disinterested." Proceeding in this manner, and assisted by the author of *Supernatural Religion*, who had employed an exhaustive methodology only to reach the same answer, Arnold arrives at precisely the conclusion he had stated in *Literature and Dogma*: that the record we have of the life and sayings of Jesus has passed through half a century or more of oral tradition and through more than one written account.[135]

When he confronts the problem of Johannine authorship, however, Arnold speaks with an assurance that invites the same objection he made to Baur: he settles issues by personal inclination rather than by the necessary laws of literary criticism. The gospel in its present form, he concludes, is not the work of John, because the writer is manifestly not a Jew. But the texts Arnold adduces in support of this conclusion are capable of more than the single construction he places upon them. The reference to the Jewish passover in 2:13, for example, may not be comparable to an Englishman's describing the Derby as "the English people's Derby," but may, rather, express the writer's conviction that the feast has been superseded by the messiahship of Jesus. The introduction of John the Baptist in a manner different from that in which he is introduced by Jewish writers may reflect opposition to sectarian claims that would exalt him over Jesus. The descriptions of Caiaphas as "high priest that year" and of Bethany as "beyond Jordan" may not be mistakes that a native would never have committed; the one may simply mean that Caiaphas was high priest at that time, and the other presumably refers to a town about which speculation would be more certain if its site, now vanished, were known.[136]

Yet the question of Johannine authorship is not essential to Arnold's position. What is essential is to establish a connection between John and the Fourth Gospel and to disprove the claim that the sayings of Jesus recorded in it are late inventions and thus spurious. Here Arnold is vindicated by twentieth-century scholarship, which in its tendency to accept both Johannine authorship and an early date for the composition of the Gospel has largely repudiated the radical view of the Tübingen critics.[137] Following the tradition that speaks of the request made by John's friends that he give his recollections and of a revision subsequently made of his account, Arnold conjectures that in his old age John was asked by the elders of Ephesus to give to the world his collection of *logia*, "sayings of the Lord," and incidents in the Lord's life that had not previously been published. The presbytery of Ephesus then provided a redaction, probably the work of a Greek Christian who was a literary man as well as a theologian. It was in existence as early as the first quarter of the second century, for it is quoted by Basileides, who flourished about 125—a date very close to the date now assigned to the Fourth Gospel and a quarter of a century earlier than the date assigned by the Tübingen school.[138]

But the Tübingen critics rested the strength of their case against the Fourth Gospel on internal rather than external evidence. It was the work not of John, they said, but of a superb artist and a profound thinker who freely invented. To Arnold, on the contrary, it was nothing of the kind. Reviewing the evidence in the final chapter of *God and the Bible*, he cites a number of flaws that militate against the Tübingen view: awkwardly combined *logia*, jolts in the narrative, misunderstanding of Jesus' true meaning, the admission of comments that run counter to the author's alleged bias against Jews, and the absence of an imaginative intellect that could deal with Jesus as Plato dealt with Socrates.[139] In his illustrations of these flaws, Arnold is not always convincing: he sees as artistic failure, for instance, what may be only difficulty of interpretation at the beginning of the tenth chapter; he reads as incongruous in John 4:6 a word that apparently has a wider range of meaning than he gives to it; and, characteristically, he accuses the writer of misinterpreting what is intended to refer to spiritual rebirth as applying to physical resurrection.[140] But Arnold's central argument nevertheless remains unaffected. The internal evidence of the Fourth Gospel points not to the conjectural artist of the Tübingen school but to a Greek Christian who edited with imperfect success the separate *logia* he had before him.

If the gospel is a redaction, then, how are the authentic words of Jesus to be distinguished from the words of the editor? "Where the *logia* are suited to the character of Jesus," Arnold replies, "they come from Jesus. Where they are not, there we have the theological lecturer merely expanding a theme given by Jesus, developing or thinking that he develops it." The essential point to recognize is that the gnomic sayings, a form of speech natural to Semitic people, are Jesus' own, and the long, repetitious discourses are the work of the Greek editor. When this distinction is made, "the Fourth Gospel comes out no fancy-piece, but a serious and invaluable document, full of incidents given by tradition and of genuine 'sayings of the Lord.' "[141]

IX

In the conclusion to *God and the Bible*, Arnold returns to the central argument of *Literature and Dogma*—that the Christian believer must abandon reliance on miracle, understanding the supernatural elements of the Bible to be "poetry

and legend," and take "hope in presence of the religious prospect thus profoundly transformed." His hope derives from the
simple fact that this altered view of Christianity is but the view
of the religion Jesus really wished to establish. Interpreting
the parable of the unprepared wedding guest to be the sentence Jesus himself passed on popular Christianity, which
misunderstood and materialized his religion, Arnold declares
that he stamped it, "even from the very moment of its birth,
as . . . ignorant and transient, and requiring all who would be
truly children of the kingdom to rise beyond it."[142]

Readers were rather inclined to say the same of *God and the
Bible*, which attracted less attention than *Literature and Dogma* but still encountered the old objections to Arnold's manner and the substance of his argument. Archbishop Tait, for
example, described the first of the *Contemporary* installments
as "a marvellous piece of conceit" and said that Arnold "pa-
tronise[d] the Bible in the most easy and good-natured
way."[143] The *Church Quarterly Review*, commenting on Arnold's paradoxical desire "to see the fruits of religion flourish and abound, while he applie[d] the axe of his criticism to
the roots of the tree on which they grow," was convinced that
"his position and influence" had been "decidedly weakened."[144] The *Westminster Review* sarcastically observed that,
far from lacking the "vigor and rigor" of the Germans, Arnold could "select, reject, accept, restore, suppress, divide, and
join, with the best professor of them all."[145] And Albert Réville, in a review epitomizing the general reaction, declared
that although there was a certain "moral grandeur" in Arnold's stoutly defending his theory with "imperturbable serenity against the objections of every kind which, from the
most opposite camps, crash in upon it like converging artillery
fires," it was nevertheless "a pity that so much ability and science, so much literary art and moral vigour, should be utterly
wasted . . . and should finally produce only one of those curious fruits which we examine attentively for their strangeness
but never so much as wish to taste, so clear is it that we cannot
even pierce the rind with our teeth."[146]

Undaunted by this response, Arnold began in 1876 to publish the first of the five articles that reappeared the following
year as *Last Essays on Church and Religion*. Three of these—
the two addresses on "Bishop Butler and the Zeit-Geist" and
"A Last Word on the Burials Bill"—have only a peripheral
connection with his earlier work in biblical criticism, but two
others are significantly related.

The first of these, the address on "The Church of England"[147] which he delivered at Sion College to the London
clergy, is in part a continuation of his attempt to comprehend
the Dissenters within the Establishment. More important,
however, it is his most meaningful statement regarding the
role of the Church. This role, he says, is to promote goodness;
but goodness as he now defines it is more than the narrow
morality that seemed to comprise the righteousness of which
he previously spoke. It is, rather, the love of perfection that
he had once made the aim of culture. The Church, Arnold declares, cannot continue to be the stronghold of the privileged
—the aristocratic and propertied classes—but must bring itself
into accord with what is both the popular ideal and the ideal
of Christianity—an "immense renovation and transformation
of things, a far better and happier society in the future." Arnold took "great pains" with his remarks, which cost him
"some horrid days in the preparing," and although neither
James Martineau nor Henry Allon liked what he said about
the Dissenters,[148] he was able to "carry" his audience with
him in an address that "went off very well."[149]

The other essay, "A Psychological Parallel,"[150] returns to
the subject of thaumaturgy that is central to all of Arnold's
biblical criticism. The parallel he draws is between the belief
of St. Paul in the physical resurrection of Jesus and the belief
of Sir Matthew Hale in witchcraft. In neither case is there un-
truthfulness or lack of intelligence, but simply acceptance of
what seems plausible. To say that Paul shared the mistaken
beliefs of his time, therefore, is neither to reject him nor to
condemn him on moral grounds, just as to criticize orthodox
theology is not to dismiss Christianity or to raise moral ques-

tions regarding belief, but rather to seek a firm, intellectual basis for religious faith. The revolt against popular Christianity, then, is not moral but intellectual. "And no moral advantages of a doctrine can avail to save it, in presence of the intellectual conviction of its want of conformity with truth and fact."

Before sending "A Psychological Parallel" to the *Contemporary*, Arnold wrote to Knowles that he hoped it would be his "last theological paper." "I shall always be grateful to you," he added, "for the valuable stage you have given me, to strut and fret my little theological hours upon." But he intended now "to return to literature proper and to [his] old place the *Cornhill*."[151]

It was not to be his last theological paper, and he was to publish only once more in the *Cornhill*. Yet the following year, in the preface to *Last Essays on Church and Religion*, he repeated his promise of a return to literature. The volume, he said, concluded his attempts to deal with those religious and ecclesiastical questions that he neither had entered upon with pleasure nor left with reluctance. He knew, too, "what offence [his] handling of them [had] given to many whose good-will [he valued], and with what relief they [would] learn that the handling [was] now to cease." Here, however, he allowed himself an escape clause. In a passage foreshadowing the famous quotation that introduces "The Study of Poetry," he declared that in returning to literary criticism he was in reality returning to the field where "the transformation of religion" could alone be accomplished—through "the qualities of flexibility, perceptiveness, and judgment, which are the best fruits of letters."[152]

The problem, Arnold said, was to transform the popular mind, to cure its "grossness of perception and materialising habits," and not to seek a remedy by retaining a materialistic religion that corresponded to those habits. The partisans of popular religion, on the other hand, believed that they could make their own terms and save what could not be saved. Citing two reviews of *Literature and Dogma*, one by Gubernatis, already quoted, and the other by Challemel-Lacour,[153] a writer and politician who was to succeed Renan in the Académie française, Arnold pointed to the contrast between the reception of his book in England, where it was regarded as revolutionary, and that on the Continent, where it was considered reactionary. The "whole force of progressive and liberal opinion on the Continent" had decisively pronounced against Christianity, he said, and liberal opinion in England would eventually decide against popular Christianity. The danger was that it would decide against Christianity as well.[154]

This was why it was essential to insist on what he called "the *natural truth* of Christianity," which rested on the proposition that conduct is a considerable part of life, if not at least three-fourths, to which figure Challemel-Lacour had objected. The secret of Jesus' teaching was his recognition that obedience to man's higher self brings happiness, and obedience to his lower self, misery. Nor is obedience to the higher self simply a matter of self-interest. Answering by implication Secrétan's charge of eudaemonism, Arnold finds true happiness to reside only "in a kind of impersonal higher life, where the happiness of others counts with a man as essential to his own."[155]

It is here, he thinks, that the criticism of Maurice Vernes,[156] the last critic of *Literature and Dogma* whom he answered directly, goes awry. A Protestant liberal and student of comparative religion, Vernes had granted that

l'idée de justice, tendant au bonheur, est mise en relief par le judaïsme avec une force particulière; mais il n'est necessaire de remarquer que cette justice est inséparable d'une rémunération materielle en cette vie et qu'elle apparaît très-rarement distinguée d'un privilège conféré à la nation juive, peuple élu de Jéhova, aimé de lui à l'exclusion des autres nations et objet de ses faveurs quand il ne transgresse pas la loi divine.

Nor was the Messianic hope essentially different: "prétendre, comme le fait M. Arnold, que le développement de l'idée messianique est en contradiction avec la pensée intime du judaïsme, c'est rejeter les résultats les plus certains d'une saine exégèse." Indeed, "M. Arnold écarte les textes, nombreux et décisifs à mon sens, qui donnent au 'royaume de Dieu' une signification positivement messianique."

The question, Arnold replies, is which of the two possibilities is the more likely: that Jesus was misunderstood by his followers, or that he was the supernatural personage they imagined him to be. The "more reasonable Jesus," he says, answering his own question in the same way he had earlier answered it, is "the more real one." And this real Jesus "will continue to command allegiance," he concludes, and "Christianity will survive because of its natural truth." Old forms of worship will remain only as poetry, but Christianity itself will continue as the indispensable bulwark to the major part of life that conduct comprises.[157]

X

Despite its title, *Last Essays on Church and Religion* was not Arnold's farewell to the religious questions of the day. Again and again in the late seventies—as in "Equality," "Irish Catholicism and British Liberalism," and "The French Play in London"—he returned to both the ecclesiastical and the theological issues with which he had dealt, criticizing Puritanism for its narrowness and urging the transformation of popular Christianity. He continued to be regarded with suspicion by the Dissenters, and when in 1883 there was the possibility that Gladstone would appoint him to the Charity Commission, R. W. Dale wrote to Henry Allon that if "Gladstone wanted—wch. every one knows he does not want—to select a man who wd. be exceptionally offensive to Nonconformists, Mr. Arnold wd. be the man."[158]

It was not until the following year, however, that his religious views again aroused public controversy. The occasion was a speech that he delivered after the unveiling of a mosaic at St. Jude's Church in the East End of London. After expressing compassion for what he called "the sacrificed classes" of the city's slums and praising the vicar of the parish for his efforts to raise their level of life, Arnold warned that culture was ineffectual without religion. But the religion he spoke of was a Christianity purged of the supernatural.[159]

When the speech gained wide publicity on the pages of the *Times* and the *Pall Mall Gazette*, R. H. Hutton seized the opportunity to make another attack on Arnold's "transformed Christianity,"[160] and the *Guardian* sharply rebuked both the vicar for having invited a speaker who denied the existence of a personal God and Arnold for having referred "with a gentle sneer to the East London Mission and its attempt to help the poor by presenting to them the 'preternatural and miraculous' aspect of 'popular Christianity.' "[161] The following week the *Guardian* was answered by a correspondent protesting that Arnold did not deny the existence of a personal God but merely said that the question could not be answered, to which the editor bluntly replied that if this was what he believed, he could not be called a Christian.[162] Yet the matter was not to be so easily resolved, and three more letters to the paper appeared in quick succession.[163]

This obscure controversy, as Fabian Gudas has pointed out, was apparently the inspiration for Arnold's final essay devoted to the central religious problem of the age. Entitled "A Comment on Christmas" and published in the *Contemporary Review* for April 1885,[164] it begins with a reference to criticism of Arnold, presumably expressed in a letter, for continuing to read the Bible even though he denied that miracles occur. The argument of such a critic, he observes, is that one should either take the Bible and recommend it with its miracles, "or else leave it alone, and let its enemies find confronting them none but orthodox defenders of it like [himself]." But unable to accept either of the alternatives thus offered him, Arnold answers his critics, including the *Guardian*, to whose leading article of the previous year he alludes, by depicting the incarnation as a legend, though a legend that does homage to the Christian virtue of purity.[165]

Two years later Arnold republished "A Comment on Christmas" in the popular edition of *St. Paul and Protestantism*, for which he wrote a new preface. There he commented on the work of the *Zeitgeist*, which had made his criticism of some Puritan doctrines to seem now "almost a waste of labour." But he observed also that "mankind's familiar fancies of miracle, blood, bargain and appeasement" still obscured the real Jesus.[166]

A decade earlier he had written to Grant Duff in much the same vein. Replying to his friend's praise of his version of Isaiah, he said that his gratitude was all the greater because "the labour of mine which you commended was one which I undertook with a good deal of hope, and which has produced very little result. But I more and more learn the extreme slowness of things, and that though we are all disposed to think that everything will change in our lifetime, it will not. Perhaps we shall end our days in the tail of a return current of popular religion, both ritual and dogmatic. Still, the change, for being slower than we expected, is not the less sure."[167]

If in some respects the prophecy has proved true—if on the whole Arnold speaks more immediately to the twentieth century than does either Frank or John Henry Newman, for example—then it was again Grant Duff who, of all his contemporaries, most succinctly appraised his biblical criticism. On April 11, 1889, after attending a meeting in the Jerusalem Chamber concerning the Arnold Memorial Fund, for which nearly £7,000 had already been subscribed, Grant Duff returned home and that evening recorded in his diary his reflections about the day's activities:

How strange amidst all its revolutions is the continuousness of England! Here were we assembled in a room which was historical long before Shakespeare, and made world-famous by him—to do what? In the very place in which the Westminster divines had set forth in elaborate propositions the curious form of nonsense which was Christianity to them, to do honour to a man who, standing quite outside their dogmas, had seen more deeply into the heart of the matter than all of them put together.[168]

CHAPTER EIGHT

The Humanist and His Adversaries

To poor Dorothea these severe classical nudities and smirking Renaissance-Correggiosities were painfully inexplicable, staring into the midst of her Puritanic conceptions: she had never been taught how she could bring them into any sort of relevance with her life.—George Eliot, *Middlemarch*

Mr. Swinburne's ideal poet is an impassioned rhapsodist, standing on a lofty sea-lashed rock, with his hair streaming to the wind, communing with the mighty forces of nature, and pouring forth wild musical words in praise of the eternal truths of liberty, fraternity, and equality.—Arthur Tilley

. . . I . . . wish that my children might be well versed in physical science, but in due subordination to the fulness and freshness of their knowledge on moral subjects.—Dr. Thomas Arnold

To speak of Emerson as [Arnold] does among the friends and worshipers of the American seer requires an heroic temperament.—*Andover Review*

. . . the closest connexion between Great Britain and Ireland is essential to the well-being, I had almost said, to the very being, of the two kingdoms.—Burke

The promise of a return to literary criticism that Arnold made in the preface to *Last Essays on Church and Religion* was fulfilled even before it was announced, for in January 1877 he published anonymously "A French Critic on Milton." Thus, quietly and inconspicuously, as E. K. Brown noted,[1] he withdrew from the social, political, and religious controversies that had engaged his chief attention during the preceding decade and a half; and when he declined the following month to be considered for the Poetry Chair, he made clear that a fundamental reason was his desire to avoid the "odious" and "intolerable" row that would result from the inevitable raising of the religious question.[2] In the eleven years remaining to him, he again devoted his energies to literature, editing selections from Wordsworth and Byron and producing essays on English and Continental writers from Samuel Johnson to Tolstoy. With greater leisure and freedom than he had long enjoyed, he indulged his taste for the theater, insisting as strongly on the need to organize it as he had earlier insisted on the need to organize secondary education, and found unexpected pleasure in reading novels, which he had once regarded as a form of opium.

Leaving the turbid waters of controversy for the purer air of letters, Arnold entered on a period freer of partisan abuse, of attack and rebuttal, than any he had experienced since the publication of his first volumes of poetry. His major work had been accomplished, and he was to strike out in no new directions; the titles of his final books—*Mixed Essays, Irish Essays and Others, Discourses in America*—betrayed their heterogeneous concerns and the absence of a unifying thesis. Nearly all the famous slogans and phrases had been coined, the central ideas developed, the principal objections of his critics answered as fully as they ever would be. Disraeli told him early in 1881 that he "was the only living Englishman who had become a classic in his own lifetime."[3] Two years later John Duke Coleridge described him in America as "the most distinguished Englishman living."[4] Meeting him presumably for the first time in February 1880, Hardy thought he gave the impression that he had "made up his mind upon everything years ago, so that it was a pleasing futility for his interlocutor to begin thinking new ideas, different from his own, at that time of day."[5]

Nevertheless, these last years were different, in emphasis if not in basic principles, for they represent Arnold's emergence from his long preoccupation with the religious problems of the age, with the issues of political and ecclesiastical Dissent as well as with the questions of faith and morality. These concerns would recur, to be sure, as in the celebrated attacks on the French worship of the great goddess Lubricity. But they recede into a secondary position as Hellenism reappears to displace Hebraism from the forefront, though this time with the aesthetic sense clearly given an importance equal to that of intelligence.

The voice of humanism, in short, speaks out more and more decisively. Arnold returns to the poetry of Wordsworth and, like Mill after his spiritual crisis, finds it "delightful." On his first visit to America he is most struck by "that buoyancy, enjoyment, and freedom from constraint which are everywhere," by the "universal enjoyment and good nature" that he finds. T. H. Green, the historian, tells him "that the more he looks into Puritanism, and indeed into the English Protestant Reformation generally, the worse is his opinion of it all." More revealing still, Arnold writes to his friend Fontanès in 1881 that the future lies with those who perceive that "man feels himself to be a more various and richly-endowed animal than the old religious theory of human life allowed, and he is endeavouring to give satisfaction to the long suppressed and still imperfectly-understood instincts of this varied nature." A revolution both inevitable and salutary, he continues, is taking place against "the sombreness and narrowness of the religious world." Expressed in various forms—in the "growing desire for . . . amusement and pleasure"; in "the wonderful relaxation, in the middle class, of the old strictness as to theatres, dancing, and such things"; and especially in the "awakening demand for beauty, a demand so little made in this country for the last century and more"—it shows "that whoever treats religion, religious discussions, questions of churches and sects, as absorbing, is not in vital sympathy with the movement of men's minds at present."[6]

I

The first fruit of Arnold's renewed humanism was the essay on Falkland,[7] published in March 1877 on the occasion of the proposal to erect at Newbury a monument to a famous casual-

ty of the Civil War. Unlike Milton, whom two months earlier he had depicted as having defects characteristic of "the
whole Puritan party to which he belonged" and intellectually
and poetically injurious—"asperity and acerbity, . . . want of
sweetness of temper, of the Shakspearian largeness and indulgence"[8]—Falkland was for Arnold a "phenomenon of an
amiable Englishman." He was "the sweetest-mannered of
men" and a "martyr of sweetness and light"—a "martyr of
lucidity of mind and largeness of temper, in a strife of imperfect intelligences and tempers illiberal." Showing "reason and
moderation" from the outset, he was alone among his party
to speak against the impeachment of Strafford "with unfair
and vindictive haste." Although he disliked Laud's "heat, fuss-
iness, and arbitrary temper," he refused to agree to his impeachment. When he was pressed to take office under the
Crown he was reluctant to comply, for he feared that if he accepted, Charles "would require a submission which he could
not give." Possessing almost every quality of the hero—"rank,
accomplishment, sweet temper, exquisite courtesy, liberality,
magnanimity, superb courage"—he finally added the trait—
a sense of fatality—that crowned his "irresistible charm."

Set against the Falkland of Arnold's essay are the Puritans,
"with their temper, their false, old-Jewish mixture of politics
with an ill-understood religion." Both at home and abroad
their victory was a disaster. Under them the nation fell first
into anarchy and then into "the bad and false system of government of the Stuarts," and in foreign affairs they were strong
rather than wise. The Puritan conception of righteousness,
moreover, was so "grossly imperfect" and "false" that "it led
straight to moral anarchy, the profligacy of the Restoration,"
and later, among the middle class where religion survived,
to "a narrowness, an intellectual poverty, almost incredible"
and to "that character of their steady and respectable life
which makes one shiver: its hideousness, its immense ennui."
One cannot be certain, Arnold concludes, that English political liberty is the result of the Puritan triumph, and by no

means certain that "the England of to-day is the best imaginable and possible result from the elements with which we started at the Renascence."

A month after its appearance, Arnold's essay was bitterly assailed by Goldwin Smith,[9] writing in that acerbic manner which distinguished him as well as those he defended. He began with the usual barbed pleasantry: "Those who subscribe to the Falkland testimonial are collectively set down by Mr. Arnold as the 'amiable'—those who do not subscribe as the 'unamiable.' Few, we trust, would be so careful of their money and so careless of their reputation for moral beauty as to refuse to pay a guinea for a certificate of amiability countersigned by Mr. Matthew Arnold." This was followed by the characteristically sarcastic comment that of Pym's existence Arnold "has shown himself conscious by once mentioning his name." And once again there was the propensity for the *argumentum ad hominem* and for the exhumation of dead and irrelevant issues:

Falkland's paramount regard for truth would have extended to all his fellow-men as well as to himself and his own intellectual circle. He would never, we are confident, have advised any human being to separate religion from truth; he would never have suffered himself to intimate that truth was the property of a select circle, while "poetry" was good enough for the common people; he would never have encouraged thousands of clergymen, educated men with sensitive consciences, to go on preaching to their flocks from the pulpit, on grounds of social convenience, doctrines which they repudiated in the study, and derided in the company of cultivated men; he would never have exhorted people to enter from aesthetic considerations a spiritual society of which, in the same breath, he proclaimed the creeds to be figments, the priesthood to be an illusion, the sacred narratives to be myths, and the Triune God to be a caricature of Lord Shaftesbury, multiplied by three.

But Falkland, according to Smith, was not the man "of extraordinarily serene and well-balanced mind" whom Arnold portrays. He was, on the contrary, "rather excitable and impulsive." His proposal to have the charges against Strafford formally drawn up by a committee not only indicated his belief that the grounds for impeachment were adequate, but also revealed an "almost fatuous" notion that Strafford would have respected such a formality. Speaking in favor of the Bishops' Bill, he "violently denounced Laud as a participator in Strafford's treason," and there is no "positive proof" that he refused to concur in Laud's impeachment. In the most questionable act of his life, one that Arnold passes over with "a graceful literary movement," he became secretary of state four days after Charles's attempt to seize the Five Members and thus "assumed a certain measure of responsibility . . . for a proceeding which . . . rendered civil war inevitable."

Smith's real purpose, however, was not to criticize Falkland but to defend the Puritans, whom he accuses Arnold of mowing down with "some trenchant epithet." Reminding him of the portrait of Colonel Hutchinson, he says that "Lucy Hutchinson is painting what she thought a perfect Puritan would be; and her picture presents to us, not a coarse, crop-eared, and snuffing fanatic, but a highly accomplished, refined, gallant, and most 'amiable,' though religious and seriously-minded gentleman." Without Puritan morality, according to Smith, the Renaissance "would have probably been like the life of Lorenzo—vice, filthy vice, decorated with art and with elegant philosophy; an academy under the same roof with a brothel." He admits that "the Puritan Revolution was followed by a sacerdotal and sensualist reaction," but he insists that "the Puritan party still remained the most moral and respectable element in the country" and that the reaction was "not altogether the condemnation" of the Puritans' strict morality but "partly the weakness of humanity."

When Arnold republished the essay on Falkland, as E. K. Brown has indicated,[10] he made two small revisions that were apparently a concession to Smith's criticism. He admitted that Clarendon's praise of Falkland was "a little excessive," and he qualified the statement that Clarendon's touch "is simpler than in the *History*" by adding the clause, "where in his memoirs he speaks of Falkland."[11]

But in his detailed reply to Smith, Arnold was less disposed to be conciliatory. The answer, contained in the essay on "Equality"[12] that he published in March 1878, depicts Smith as a writer who, despite his "eloquence and power," is "too prone to acerbity," too much "a partisan of the Puritans." To the reader, then, he appears biased and ill-tempered, lacking the first requisite of the critic—disinterestedness—and consequently defenseless against Arnold's invitation, "Let us go to facts." The facts as Arnold presents them are that the Puritans "had not the spirit of beauty"; it was their Parliament that ordered that the masterpieces of Italian art assembled by Charles be either sold or burned. Nor had they urbanity or amenity; in a typical display of bad manners in controversy, Milton answered an anonymous opponent with the remark that he did not intend "to dispute philosophy with this pork, who never read any." And even in Smith's choice of "the most favourable specimen he can find" of the Puritan type, one can still point to "where this type deflects from the truly humane ideal." Relating from Mrs. Hutchinson's memoirs[13] the story of her husband's discovery of notes concerning infant baptism and the crisis they precipitated—the pregnant Mrs. Hutchinson's inability to reconcile them with scripture; her husband's troubled study of "all the eminent treatises on both sides, which at that time came thick from the presses"; the invitation of ministers to a dinner discussion of the problem; and all with the ultimate result that the infant was not baptized—Arnold says that the solemn way in which the Hutchinsons confronted their dilemma reminds one of "the conversation which reigns in thousands of middle-class families at this hour, about nunneries, teetotalism, the confessional, eternal punishment, ritualism, disestablishment." These are the concerns of "the Puritan type of life"; and in "the long winter evenings of Toronto," Arnold wryly observes, Goldwin Smith has perhaps had some experience with them. But this Puritan type of life, he declares in a series of trenchant phrases that he would repeat again and again in the following years, offers "a religion not true, the claims of intellect and knowledge not satisfied, the claim of beauty not satisfied, the claim of manners not satisfied."

II

A year after his answer to Smith, Arnold began the first of several polite debates with Swinburne, with whom he had enjoyed an amicable relationship ever since Swinburne's glowing review of *New Poems* in 1867.[14] The ultimate source of their debates was difference of opinion concerning the nature of poetry; the immediate source, disagreement over Victor Hugo. In his essay on Renan (1872), Arnold had said that one found "something of a bathos in [the] challenge to Germany to produce a living poet to surpass" Hugo,[15] and in the essays on George Sand (June 1877) and "A French Critic on Goethe" (January 1878), he had ridiculed Hugo's pretensions, describing him as "half genius, half charlatan" and expressing astonishment at a list of the world's great poets that would include his name.[16] Later, in a passage subsequently deleted from the essay on Wordsworth (July 1879), he publicly criticized Renan—as he had criticized him privately[17] —for giving exaggerated praise to Hugo before the French Academy, quoting as a corrective the judgment of Goethe that "*Hernani* was an absurd composition." And the following month, in "The French Play in London," he took unmistakable aim at Swinburne when he challenged the view of a new generation for whom Hugo was "a great poet of the race and lineage of Shakspeare." Hugo, like Scott, was for Arnold "a great romance-writer"; and, like Pope, he had "an admirable gift for versification." But he did not have "the distinctive spirit of high poetry." With all his gifts, he was fatally restricted by a form, the rhyming alexandrine, that was incurably artificial and inflexible—"a form radically inadequate and inferior, and in which a drama like that of Sophocles or Shakspeare is impossible."[18]

Swinburne had always regarded Arnold as an unreliable critic of French poetry, and behind his attitude toward Hugo he further detected the malevolent influence of Sainte-Beuve, whom he "never appreciated," according to Gosse, and to whom he "owed little or nothing."[19] Consequently, in *A Study of Shakespeare*, on which he was working at the time the essays on Wordsworth and "The French Play in London" appeared, Swinburne described Hugo as "the common lord and master of all poets born in his age—be they liege subjects as loyal as myself or as contumacious as I grieve to find one at least of my elders and betters, whenever I perceive —as too often I cannot choose but perceive—that the voice is the voice of Arnold, but the hand is the hand of Sainte-Beuve."[20] Arnold acknowledged Swinburne's gift of the book with the flattering comment that he followed his work "with interest and often with keen pleasure" and with the request that Swinburne think "mercifully" of him when he now and then blasphemed Hugo.[21] Whereupon Swinburne responded by sending him a copy of *Songs of the Springtides*, which included the "Birthday Ode for the Anniversary Festival of Victor Hugo" crowning him "Our Father and Master and Lord"[22] —an extravagance that to Arnold was as great in one direction as the "violent sonnet"[23] occasioned by the monument in Westminster Abbey to a son of Napoleon III and condemning A. P. Stanley to "Scorn everlasting and eternal shame"[24] was in another. Swinburne added that Arnold's "kindly acknowledgment" of his book on Shakespeare had encouraged him in his work of conversion "in spite of all despair on that subject" and referred him to his article, "Victor Hugo: 'Religions et Religion,' " where he had "taken up the glove flung down" to him and suggested that Goethe's judgment of *Hernani* was as worthless as Voltaire's of *Hamlet*. Arnold calmly replied that while Swinburne's ode had "force and eloquence," Hugo himself lacked the "charm and accent of a poet";[25] and he continued to ridicule the belief that this "half genius, half charlatan" was "a sublime poet."[26]

At the same time that he was attempting to convert Arnold to the cause of Hugo, Swinburne was also seeking to engage him in debate about Collins and Gray. The occasion was Ward's *English Poets* (1880), introduced by Arnold's essay on "The Study of Poetry," which proclaimed Gray the "poetical classic" of his age. In the essay on Gray himself, Arnold was more qualified in his praise, conceding that "Collins has something of the like merit," but he insisted nevertheless that Gray was "alone, or almost alone . . . in his age."[27] Previously, in his review of Arnold's poems, Swinburne had questioned the passage in the essay on Maurice de Guérin in which Arnold, speaking of the inadequacy of the heroic couplet, asserted "that the English poet of the eighteenth century whose compositions wear best and give one the most entire satisfaction,—Gray,—does not use that couplet at all." He reminded Arnold of Gray's "admirable fragment" in the ten-syllable couplet ("Hymn to Ignorance"), a reminder that led Arnold to change "does not use" to "hardly uses," and objected to his placing Gray above Collins, who of everyone in his age seemed to Swinburne to have "most in him of the pure and high and durable spirit of poetry. The overture of his 'Ode to Liberty' is worthy of Coleridge or Shelley; Gray's best ode by its side is somewhat hard and thin."[28] In the later essay on Collins, which Gosse arranged for him to contribute to Ward's anthology, Swinburne repeated his claim for Collins's superiority, a claim based on a characteristic preference for the poet of lyric gift and republican sympathy: he was the first English poet after Milton "to reannounce with the passion of a lyric and heroic rapture the divine right and the godlike duty of tyrannicide."[29]

Two years later, in his life of Gray written for the "English Men of Letters" series, Gosse pointedly described Arnold's essay as "by far the best account of Gray, not written by a personal friend," and rebuked Swinburne for being "deeply and extravagantly unjust to the greater man" in "his ardour to do justice to Collins." The two poets, he said, were alike in having the "gift of clear, pure, Simonidean song." But whereas "Collins was simply a reed, cut short and notched by the great god Pan," in Gray the song "seemed merely one phase of a deep and consistent character, of a brain almost universally accomplished."[30] As an expression of his indebtedness, Gosse sent a copy of the book to Arnold, who acknowledged it in a letter telling of the "satisfaction" it had given him:

"Simonidean" is the right word to express the note struck by Gray— you could not have taken a better. Collins, at his best, strikes the same note, and perhaps we must own that the diction of Collins in his Ode to Evening is more Simonidean, more pure, than Gray's diction—but then the Ode to Evening has not the evolution of Gray and of Simonides—like the rivers of central Asia, it loses itself in the sand. As to the Ode to Liberty, to speak of it as Swinburne does is really to talk nonsense.[31]

The following year, in the essay on Emerson, Arnold again insisted on the "grand superiority" of Gray's poetry, employing the same analogy when he said that although the "Ode to Evening" was purer in diction, it was "like a river which loses itself in the sand, whereas Gray's best poems have an evolution sure and satisfying."[32]

The final expression to the differences in poetic principles that separated Arnold from Swinburne was given in "Wordsworth and Byron" (1884), an essay partly inspired by a passage in Arnold's "Wordsworth" that Swinburne interpreted as "a courteous and friendly challenge."[33] Arnold had asserted that whatever is concerned with the question of "how to live" is a moral idea, whether uttered by Milton in *Paradise Lost*, or Keats in the "Ode on a Grecian Urn," or Shakespeare in *The Tempest*.[34] If Swinburne was right in thinking this directed at him, Arnold would have had in mind the opening paragraph of the essay on Baudelaire (1862) or such passages as that in *William Blake* (1868) in which Swinburne, defending the art for art's sake position, argued for a distinction between artistic and ethical concerns and asked to "hear no more of the moral mission of earnest art," and that in his essay on Hugo's *L'Année Terrible* (1872) in which he repeated his argument and asserted categorically that the "rule of art is not the rule of morals."[35]

Swinburne replied that Arnold's comment on Keats's ode suggested the harmful effect of theological study on the literary critic: " 'A criticism of life' becomes such another term or form of speech as 'prevenient grace,' or 'the real presence,' or 'the double procession of the Holy Ghost.' " Although conceding that a "certain criticism of life" was unquestionably present in the best work of some poets, he found it incomprehensible that the phrase could be interpreted to include Keats, "the most exclusively aesthetic and the most absolutely nonmoral of all serious writers on record," and he denied that such criticism enhanced the value of poetry. The two essential poetic qualities, he said, were "imagination and harmony," the presence of which, even without the support of ethical concern, made "the best and highest poetry."[36]

But Swinburne's real target in the essay on Wordsworth and Byron was not, of course, Arnold's comment on Keats. It was, rather, his praise of Byron at the expense of Shelley. Here Swinburne was modifying his stance, for in previous years he and Arnold had exchanged compliments while praising a poet they both admired. The preface to Swinburne's edition of Byron for Moxon's *Miniature Poets* (1866) had begun with a handsome reference to Arnold's comment in the essay on Heine about the neglect of Byron[37] and had gone on to speak of "the splendid and imperishable excellence which covers all his offences and outweighs all his defects: the excellence of sincerity and strength."[38] In his own essay on Byron (1881), Arnold returned the compliment by quoting from the passage and praising Swinburne for having so isolated and described, "with the instinct of a poet," the distinguishing power of Byron.[39]

At the conclusion of his essay, however, Arnold had made a prediction that for Swinburne was "sheer paradox"—namely, that Wordsworth and Byron would come to be regarded as the preeminent English poets of the nineteenth century. The issue here, as H. J. C. Grierson has observed in a lucid explanation of why Arnold should have been simultaneously drawn both to Wordsworth as the poet of soul and Byron as the poet of actuality, is "the ever-recurring one of the relative values in poetry of technique and inspiration, art and life."[40] It is the same issue that divided Swinburne and Arnold in their appraisals of Hugo, Gray, and Collins, and the same that eventually gained succinct and celebrated utterance in literary name-calling: Swinburne was "a sort of pseudo-Shelley," Arnold said, and so invited the obvious retort that he was "a sort of pseudo-Wordsworth."[41]

III

In the meantime, Arnold had engaged in more significant debate with an opponent for whom he had greater affection and respect—Thomas Henry Huxley. Their differences, in fact, were so tempered by friendship, as William Irvine noted, that the two men offered "the happy spectacle of antagonists who never fully realized how deeply they were at variance."[42] They enjoyed the kind of easy relationship that made possible the exchange of their own works as well as jokes about Bishop Wilson, and in 1872 Arnold could say of Huxley that there were "few indeed among those with whom I have become acquainted in these later and colder years of life for whom I feel, and have felt from almost the first meeting with him, such affectionate liking and regard." After the publication of *Literature and Dogma*, he wrote Huxley that it was "always pleasant" to feel himself in sympathy with him, adding that he was confident there was "a strong ground of sympathy" between them; and four years later, when sending him a copy of *Last Essays on Church and Religion*, he said that there were "few people to whom I send my things with so much pleasure, though I know you cannot always agree with me."[43]

Superficially there was considerable sympathy between them so that from one point of view Fred G. Walcott is justified in describing their debate as "nothing more than an amicable clarification, the shoring up of a basic agreement."[44] Throughout his Oxford lectures, as in those on Celtic literature, Arnold had emphasized that the tendency of the times was toward science, toward knowing things as they are. He rested the central argument of his religious and biblical writings on the assumption that the modern, scientific spirit demanded a verifiable basis for belief. In his report of 1876 to the Committee of Council, he proposed that "some knowledge of the facts and laws of nature" be made a required part of elementary education, and in a similar report two years later he declared "that an entire ignorance of the system of nature is as gross a defect in our children's education as not to know that there ever was such a person as Charles the First."[45]

But neither Arnold's deferential attitude toward Huxley nor his general agreement with him could obscure a fundamental difference. Disagreement was apparent, for example, in the passage in *Schools and Universities on the Continent* in which Arnold had said that whereas the study of letters, concerned with "the operation of human force, of human freedom and activity," heightens "our own force and activity," the study of science, concerned with "the operation of non-human forces, of human limitation and passivity," "tends rather to check it."[46] He had thought Lord Salisbury dangerous because he was ignorant of the immense task of reconciling science and religion, which was for literature to accomplish, just as he had thought Huxley's appeal to the working man a call "for methods of insight and moderation."[47] In the introduction to *Literature and Dogma*, he had drawn the battle lines with his reference to the "notorious" revolt of the friends of physical science "against the tyranny of letters,"[48] and later, in "A Speech at Eton" in May 1879, he had narrowed them when he defined education as knowing "the best which has been thought and said in the world" and declared that "of this *best* the classics of Greece and Rome form a very chief portion, and the portion most entirely satisfactory."[49]

The following year Huxley replied to the challenge when he delivered an address in Birmingham at the opening of Sir Josiah Mason's Science College, where the absence of any provision for "mere literary instruction and education" presented him with the opportunity to answer the "Levites in charge of the ark of culture and monopolists of liberal education." Quoting from the "epistles to the Philistines," which had been written by the "chief apostle of culture," he questioned the central assumption of Arnold's thesis—that literature alone could provide an adequate criticism of life. On the contrary, Huxley argued, "an army, without weapons of precision and with no particular base of operations, might more hopefully enter upon a campaign on the Rhine, than a man, devoid of a knowledge of what physical science has done in the last century, upon a criticism of life." The advocates of an exclusively literary education, he said, had committed two errors of great consequence. They had ignored the part played by science in disproving beliefs implicitly accepted by those who had contributed to the best that has been thought and said, as a result of which the modern world was more widely separated from the Renaissance than the Renaissance was from the Middle Ages; and they had forgotten that this best that has been thought and said was inseparable from the scientific conceptions that helped to shape it, so that knowing "the best thoughts and sayings of the Greeks" required knowing also "what they thought about natural phenomena." We could not pretend to be inheritors of their culture, Huxley declared, unless we were convinced, as the best of them were, that "the free employment of reason, in accordance with scientific method, is the sole method of reaching truth."[50]

Soon after delivery of the lecture, Huxley sent Arnold a

copy of it, and on the twenty-first Sunday after Trinity (for which the gospel text was a favorite passage from Matthew recounting the story of the improperly attired wedding guest and ending with the warning that many were called but few chosen), Arnold replied:

> What you say of me is abundantly kind, and God forbid that I should make such a bad return as to enter into controversy with you: but I will remark that the dictum about knowing "the best that has been known and said in the world" was meant to include knowing what has been said in science and art as well as letters. I [remember] changing the word *said* to the word *uttered*, because I was dissatisfied with the formula for seeming not to include art, and a picture or a statue may be called an *utterance* though it cannot be called a *saying*: however I went back to *said* for the base reason that the formula runs so much easier off the tongue with the shorter word. But I never doubted that the formula included science.[51]

The second sentence is a damaging admission that he had given more care to euphony than to accuracy, and the other two sentences are not altogether convincing, for Huxley could have pointed to several passages in Arnold's writings that seemed to exclude scientific knowledge—the scornful remark in the preface to *Culture and Anarchy*, for example, that Cornell University seemed "to rest on a misconception of what culture truly is, and to be calculated to produce miners, or engineers, or architects, not sweetness and light."[52] Still, the fundamental issue was not a semantic one, as Arnold made clear in his answer two years later.

The occasion Arnold chose for his reply was the Rede Lecture, which he delivered at Cambridge in July 1882 and published the following month in the *Nineteenth Century*.[53] Inviting his "crowded audience"[54] to consider whether the "brisk and flourishing" movement to oust letters in favor of science should prevail, he began by undermining the enemy's position: when he spoke of knowing ancient Greece, he said, he meant "something more than a superficial humanism, mainly decorative," but "knowing her as the giver of Greek art, and the guide to a free and right use of reason and to scientific method, and the founder of our mathematics and physics and astronomy and biology." But having thus clarified—and in reality broadened—his own position, Arnold returned to the dialectic method both he and Huxley employed in an argument that tended to represent literature and science as irreconcilable opposites. His irony became sharper and his mock humility more pronounced: whereas the partisans of science had an "ability and pugnacity" that made "them formidable persons to contradict," he himself adopted a "tone of tentative inquiry, which befits a being of dim faculties and bounded knowledge." Responding in kind to Huxley's criticism that the advocates of literary education failed to acknowledge the role of science, he declared that the advocates of science failed to consider "the constitution of human nature." And in a passage that is the humanistic counterpart to the question he had posed twenty years earlier for Colenso—if the old theory of plenary inspiration is untenable, what then?—he said that after we are told that our "ancestor was 'a hairy quadruped furnished with a tail and pointed ears, probably arboreal in his habits,' there will be found to arise an invincible desire to relate this proposition to the sense in us for conduct, and to the sense in us for beauty"; and this science does not do.

But does literature do it? Arnold's answer is a variation on the argument he used in *Literature and Dogma* and *God and the Bible*: an appeal to experience. He "cannot tell" and he is "not much concerned to know" how literature engages the emotions; the important thing is that it does. Experience shows that it has "the power of refreshing and delighting us," of "fortifying, and elevating, and quickening, . . . of wonderfully helping us to relate the results of modern science to our need for conduct, our need for beauty." If driven to a choice between humane letters on the one hand and science on the other, he would prefer the student who is ignorant of the moon's diameter but knows that "Can you not wait upon the lunatic?" is a bad paraphrase of "Can'st thou not minister to a mind diseased?," to the student who knows the moon's diameter but thinks the paraphrase a good one. It is because literature calls out men's "being at more points," makes "them live more," that Arnold is confident of its future, and particularly confident of the future of Greek literature. The "admirable symmetry of the Greeks," he says in a passage reminiscent of the 1853 preface, "is just where we English fail, where all our art fails." Someday the Englishman will recognize this deficiency and turn to Greece and its *symmetria prisca*, acknowledging that his "hairy ancestor carried in his nature . . . a necessity for Greek."

IV

In the same letter in which Arnold called Grant Duff's attention to the Rede Lecture, he also mentioned another of his essays, "A Word About America,"[55] where he had trusted himself so successfully to his "flair" that when Henry James was asked to write a reply to it, he answered that he could not, "it was so true, and carried him so along with it."[56] Treating the theme of equality with which he had dealt four years earlier, Arnold referred to the numerous letters he had received from America, inviting him to come there and see the kind of civilization he had praised. But "with the best will in the world," he said, "I have never yet been able to go to America, and probably I never shall be able." Within little more than a year he was there for the first of his two visits.

Arnold took with him two completed lectures: the Rede Lecture, "Literature and Science," which he had revised for an American audience and was to deliver so often in response to the "perfect craze in New England for hearing it" that he was eventually bored with it; and "Numbers," which he had designed for New York and written at a cost of labor that had "nearly broken [his] heart" and which became popular after the first inaudible performance, adding "remnant" to the Arnoldian slogans that were on everyone's tongue. But with a third lecture, that on Emerson, he had unique difficulty. He was unable to write a word of it until after his arrival in America, where he was subjected to a dismaying and "blaring publicity" that occupied almost all his time;[57] and as he prepared to deliver it in Boston he remarked, with some prophetic truth, "I only trust that I may get through the first half of it without being torn to pieces."[58]

Arnold had great respect for Emerson, and in the inevitable comparison between him and Carlyle—Emerson had died in April 1882 and Carlyle a year earlier—it was Emerson who emerged as the more enduring influence. "I always found him of more use than Carlyle," Arnold wrote to "K," "and I now think so more than ever."[59] In the lecture itself,[60] moreover, Emerson joined still more distinguished company—that of Newman and Goethe—and his voice, Arnold recalled, was to the Oxford undergraduate "as new, and moving, and unforgettable" as the voices of the others.

Before he reached the end of the lecture, however, Arnold gave to some of his audience the impression that he had come not to praise Emerson but to bury him. Emerson was not a great poet, or a great writer, or a great philosopher, he declared, devoting somewhat less than half the seventy pages of printed text to surrendering "to envious Time as much of Emerson as Time can fairly expect ever to obtain." Only then, having "cleared the ground," did he state the importance of Emerson's worth. He was "the friend and aider of those who would live in the spirit," and herein lay his immense superiority to Carlyle. Where the one perversely abandoned the search for happiness as an illusory aim, the other contemplated "the happiness eternally attached to the true life in the spirit" and thus offered to England "cheerfulness and hope" and to America "serenity" and "elevation."

Emerson's daughter wrote Arnold "a charming note" telling him "that she found not a word in the lecture . . . to give her pain"; both "his family and literary executor [were] perfectly satisfied" with it;[61] and the *Nation* even described it as "a great success" and "a beautiful and delicate piece of criticism, such as no other Englishman or American, save perhaps Lowell, could have produced."[62] Yet for some of Emerson's admirers Arnold's praise was so faint as to be almost imperceptible. Referring to the comment that Emerson was a friend of those who would live in the spirit, the *Literary World* asked, "What Matthew Arnoldese is this? Did we not say that Arnold had no faith? He is forever pulling down. And the present is only a new instance of an iconoclastic habit which is his second nature."[63] The Reverend Mr. Bartol asserted that the "critical telescope" Arnold had brought with him was "of insufficient power to take an observation of Emerson,"[64] and several weeks later a writer in the *Critic* reported that New England would "have none of Matthew Arnold," that the "lecture on Emerson ha[d] utterly destroyed him in the sight of the good people of that quarter of the globe," and that they "absolutely refuse[d] to buy his works, not withstanding [sic] the new and cheap form in which they ha[d] appeared."[65] A correspondent for the Boston *Transcript* was further annoyed that Arnold had gone "out of his way and forced circumstances for an ill-natured fling at Hawthorne [in the statement that *Our Old Home* was "the work of a man chagrined"], thereby showing himself in no whit superior to the average English tourist who crosses the seas of which Great Britain is the reputed mistress, accepts the hospitality and homage of the truly literary guild of Boston and Cambridge, and goes home and patronizes or abuses us."[66]

Arnold himself was "satisfied" with the lecture, believing that Emerson would also have approved and predicting that it would "be liked in England, and [would] help [Emerson's] fame there." Rather than agree with those who objected to his "not having praised Emerson all round," which would have been "impossible," he felt that he had "given him praise which in England [would] be thought excessive, probably."[67] Consequently, before the lecture was published in *Macmillan's*, according to E. K. Brown,[68] he made "here and there" in the "revise" from which he read "incidental qualifications" of his praise, adding to the statement that there was no passage in Emerson that had become a familiar quotation the requirement that it be familiar not only to his American admirers but to all readers of English poetry, and inserting a tentative "I think" to the description of Emerson's *Essays* as the most important prose written in English during the century. But Arnold was not insensitive either to criticism of the lecture or to the feelings of his audience. In Concord he delivered one of his other lectures, not wishing "to stand up in [Emerson's] town as a critic of him,"[69] and eventually, as Brown indicated, both softened his criticism and heightened his praise, as when he modified with "almost" the assertion that Emerson's prose style was sometimes unsound in a manner "impossible to a born man of letters" and referred to him as a "beautiful" as well as "rare spirit."

For the next three months, Arnold delivered lectures and addresses in relentless succession, appearing both in Canada and in the major cities of America. Except for Baltimore, where he spoke during the Christmas season, his audiences in the East were generally large and appreciative. But those in the Middle West were small,[70] a kind of counterpart to the increasingly vexing (if also more amusing) nature of the petty harassment with which the newspapers had pursued him ever since his arrival. A Detroit paper, he reported, compared his reading from his manuscript to "an elderly bird pecking at grapes on a trellis," and an evening paper in Chicago described him as having "harsh features" and "supercilious manners" and wearing "ill-fitting clothes."[71] Not surprisingly, when Arnold, in one of his last public appearances before sailing on the *Servia*, expressed to the Authors Club his gratitude for the "unbounded kindness" with which he had been received in America, he was careful to distinguish between the literary class, which had given him its support, and the general public and the press, which would always, he said, seek to impose their "preferences upon a man of letters."[72]

Within little more than a month, as if to fulfill his prophecy, Arnold became both the victim of a journalistic hoax and the object of some sharp criticism. Having discovered that the Chicago *Tribune* was pirating his foreign news, Melville Stone, editor of the Chicago *Daily News*, decided to lay a trap with what purported to be an account of an article written by Arnold about his Chicago visit and contributed to the *Pall Mall Journal*. By a prearranged plan it was printed in one copy of the New York *Tribune*, which made its way to the Chicago *Tribune*'s correspondent and hence to the *Tribune* itself, and when it appeared on April 7 it "created a sensation." The *Daily News* feigned innocence by interviewing those whom Arnold had allegedly criticized and reporting their angry replies,[73] and in its editorial response the *Tribune* declared that it was "unlucky for everybody that Matthew Arnold came to America at all," described his visit as "a failure," "a social disappointment," and even "a vexation to a degree that strained the limits of courteous toleration," and complained that his most "conspicuous" failure was in Chicago: "Had he not been gratuitously entertained while here, had not his expenses been paid for him, his lecture profits would hardly have paid the board bills of the apostle of sweetness and light, his family, and the dog."[74]

When the *Daily News* finally disclosed the hoax, explaining that the article was as fictitious as the journal in which it had allegedly appeared, the *Tribune* tried to reverse itself. But there remained an unpleasant memory of Arnold's visit that was reflected in several negative appraisals of the impression he had made. The *Literary World* thought that on the whole the tour had been a failure, citing as evidence both the criticism made of Arnold while he was in America and "the flavor of the apocrypha . . . growing up since his return home."[75] Edwin P. Whipple wrote caustically in the *North American Review*, "Now the Almighty may very properly condescend to the human beings he has created; but he is the only being who has a right to condescend,—except, it seems, Mr. Matthew Arnold; and the latter uses the privilege at times in a fashion which makes us regret that the exception was made in his favor."[76] Four years later the *Nation*, which had more than once defended Arnold from his detractors, concluded that his lecture tour "was a mistake, and added nothing to his fame. He had no preparation for that sort of work, and was evidently very ignorant of the special needs of the audiences for which he sought, and very ill fitted to encounter the sort of treatment that American newspapers deal out to literary and scientific men who do not please their taste."[77]

V

In his last essay published during his lifetime, "Civilization in the United States," Arnold took notice of the treatment he had received from American newspapers, describing them as the chief barrier to attaining the distinction and sense of elevation that America lacked. But the immediate product of the American visit, "A Word More About America," is concerned less with America than with another country— Ireland. Arnold had earlier shown his interest in the Irish question by editing Burke's papers in 1881 and writing several articles of his own, most notably "Irish Catholicism and British Liberalism" (1878) and the two parts of "The Incompatibles" (1881). It was Gladstone's announcement late in 1885 of his plan for home rule, however, that aroused the "apprehensions"[78] which made Ireland Arnold's chief concern in the final years of his life.

By this time he had long since suffered the first of the severe chest pains that indicated a heart condition ultimately fatal. But though occasionally oppressed by a feeling of "old age, poverty, low spirits and solitude,"[79] he continued to believe that "the chief good, that which above all makes life worth living, is *to be of use*."[80] One of his last essays begins with "the excellent advice"[81] of Ptolemy that almost twenty-five years earlier he had quoted to "K" on her birthday: "As you draw near to your latter end, redouble your efforts to do good."[82] Poetic inspiration had also long since deserted him;

yet it was "something to be of use in prose," he wrote to Charles Eliot Norton, "and by coming out from time to time as the organ of 'the body of quiet, reasonable people' " he believed he did "some good."[83] With growing disapproval of Gladstone and disenchantment with the Liberal party, he had come increasingly to see the Irish problem as the area in which to redouble his efforts.

On his return from the American tour, Arnold brought with him a conviction that provided the theme of "A Word More About America" and eventually underlay his entire treatment of the Irish question—that the "political sense" in America was "sounder" than that in England. Where America had successfully solved the political and social problem, he said, and where the American people, with almost Sophoclean vision, saw things "straight" and "clear," England was still groping for the path it should take, and the Englishman of the eighties was no better than the Philistine of the sixties whom Arnold had ridiculed. Nowhere were English uncertainty and blindness more evident than in the policy toward Ireland, about which there was no "clear vision of the great, the profound changes still to be wrought before a stable and prosperous society" could arise there. The solution to the problem, Arnold maintained, basing his argument on analogy with the American division of state and federal powers, was not to make Ireland separate and independent, but rather to provide provincial legislatures that would control local affairs but would not endanger the unity of the Empire.[84]

Arnold's analogy was false, as a reader of Lawrence Hammond's definitive study of Gladstone and Ireland[85] is forced to conclude, and his appraisal of Gladstone both inaccurate and unjust. With truer vision than his critics possessed, Gladstone found appropriate historical analogy not in the American Civil War, but in the nationalist movements of Europe; and far from seeking personal or party advantage, he courageously devoted himself to winning approval for the unpopular idea that the only means of retaining Ireland in the

Empire was to grant its demands for home rule, now inseparably connected with national pride and a sense of its past history. But his most eminent contemporaries in science and
letters were united with Arnold in opposing him. When he introduced his Home Rule Bill on April 8, 1886, Arnold described the action as the "nadir" of Liberalism, fulfilling his
direst predictions about the Liberal party and revealing Gladstone as "a dangerous minister." During debate on the bill
immediately prior to his second American visit, Arnold renewed his attack with a letter to the *Times*, repeating his
analogy with America in the reminder that "the North did not
give the South a national Parliament." And two months later,
after the bill had been defeated and the Conservatives had
won the general election that followed, he wrote from America a second letter to the *Times*, inconsistently praising England for having "more of solid political sense than any other
country" and comparing Gladstone to a "desperado burning
his ship" or a "gambler doubling and trebling his stakes."
Rather than have the support of "the civilized world," he said,
Gladstone was supported in America by only one person "of
high intelligence and wide knowledge" whom Arnold had
met—E. L. Godkin, the Irish editor of the *Nation*.[86]

Early the following year, before Parliament had met, Arnold contributed a second article to the *Nineteenth Century*,
declaring that the Conservatives had risen to their "zenith"
through "the great power of quiet reasonable opinion in England" and could remain there only by granting the Irish due
control of their local affairs and denying the demand for a separate Parliament. Four months later, in a third paper, "Up to
Easter," he defended his role of commentator by saying that
although his political intrusions caused irritation to others and
gave little pleasure to him, it was important that he speak out
as a "plain reasonable" person (that same impartial observer
who several years before had settled the questions concerning
the Fourth Gospel). Expressing satisfaction with the work of
the Conservatives thus far, he predicted that if they could

bring order to Ireland and solve the problems of local government and land reform, they would be extended the power necessary to effect these measures.[87]

Before he could write another paper, Arnold was finally challenged by E. L. Godkin, answering the letter about American opinion of home rule that he had sent to the *Times* a year earlier. "Go where you will in the United States," Godkin asserted, "you will find that popular feeling, however ignorant about the facts of the case, runs in favour of the Irish, and the farther west you go, the stronger it will be."[88] Seizing the opportunity such an answer gave him, Arnold replied in "From Easter to August" that sentiment in America favored Ireland because American society was still "in an early and simple stage" and had not yet developed that corporate sense which revealed the dangers of home rule. And in response to Godkin's questioning the statement that he was the only American "of high intelligence and wide knowledge" whom Arnold knew to support Gladstone's policy, he invoked an anonymous arbiter reminiscent of the jury that two and a half decades earlier had condemned Colenso—the "highly instructed and widely informed Americans" who, together with their European counterparts, comprised "the civilized world" opposing Gladstone.[89]

In the meanwhile, Arnold had received a reply from the last of the critics whom he was to live to answer publicly— Goldwin Smith. Several years before, after their friendship had been renewed when he was Smith's guest in Toronto, Arnold described him in "A Word More About America" as a man of "singular lucidity and penetration" whom, despite his bitterness toward the Church, he would have most wished to see in Parliament during the previous decade.[90] Smith replied in a personal letter that he was "no longer fierce for Disestablishment" and explained the real direction of his bitterness: "Not against the *Church*, but against the *Toryism* which a Liberal was always encountering in elections, and the Cretinism which goes with ritualism and of the dangerous character of which I think you are hardly aware." Pleased that Smith desired "Church reform rather than Church abolition,"[91] Arnold eventually used his "admirable" letter in the essay on "Disestablishment in Wales," where he turned to another of the issues that he had said the Conservatives would have to deal with successfully in order to continue in power. Although conceding that the Welsh Nonconformists had a grievance, he cited Smith's remarks to support his thesis that the security of the Church of England had already been weakened by disestablishment in Ireland and would be further weakened by disestablishment in Wales.[92]

Shortly before beginning work on "Disestablishment in Wales," Arnold had delivered at Hull an address that became the last of the essays he published during his lifetime—"Civilization in the United States." The subject was "very ticklish,"[93] he told Lady de Rothschild. But at the end of "A Word More About America," he had promised to say something further about it; and whereas his first visit had shown him the success of America in solving the political and social problem, the second had shown him its failure in solving the human problem. The "capital defect of life" in America, he wrote Grant Duff from Massachusetts in the summer of 1886, was that "compared with life in England it [was] so uninteresting, so without savour and without depth."[94] With this as his theme, Arnold returned to the idea that had been central to almost everything he had written during the preceding thirty-five years, from the 1853 preface on. Civilization, he said, "is the humanization of man in society," the fulfillment "of the true law of human nature." Its realization is the achievement of the interesting—that which is elevated and beautiful, and the absence of which in America was betrayed by its restless citizenry, its art and architecture, its political leaders, and most of all its newspapers. Elevation and beauty are not everything, Arnold conceded. But, he added, closing with a favorite peroration—the same that had concluded *A French Eton* and *God and the Bible* and the prefaces to *On the Study of Celtic Literature* and *Culture and Anarchy*—they are indispensable to attaining "a renovated and perfected human society on earth,—the ideal society of the future."[95]

CONCLUSION

When in *God and the Bible* Arnold treated the evidence relating to the Fourth Gospel, he commented on the all-importance, in weighing such matters, of "sound judgment and common sense, bred of much conversance with real life and with practical affairs," and contrasted these with "the intemperances and extravagances" of German critics "which men versed in practical life feel to be absurd." He went on to say that Goethe—"the greatest poet of modern times, the greatest critic of all times"[1]—seemed "to have strongly felt how much the discipline of a great public life and of practical affairs had to do with intelligence." In "a remarkable passage," Goethe had suggested that culture was "but a higher conception of political and military relations." And in "a more remarkable sentence still," he had added that whenever "the French lay aside their Philistinism, they stand far above us in critical judgment." What Goethe had meant, Arnold explained, was "that in France the practical life of a great nation quickened the judgment, and prevented fumbling and trifling."[2]

To no writer of his time does the passage apply more appropriately than to Arnold himself, whose "voice of civilized reason," as Douglas Bush has recently said, "still speaks to us more directly" than does the voice of any of his contemporaries.[3] One reason for his enduring significance, of course, is the extraordinary variety of his concerns and interests, the extraordinary number of points at which he touched his age —as poet, educator, and literary, political, social, and religious critic. Arnold himself testified to his need for variety of activity as well as to his sense of a worldly element in his temperament, and he was aware that the two drives were com-

297

plementary. Prone to low spirits and indolence, he experienced renewal from the diversity of his interests and exhilaration from combat with his critics; rather than dissipate his energies, therefore, they gave balance and vitality to his work. He spoke most frequently, as in the encounters with Newman and Colenso, not as a scholar who had devoted his life to the subject, but as a man of letters who knew something of the world at large, who was acquainted as poet and critic with the views of "educated" Europe and as school inspector with the everyday life of England and the Continent. He had, moreover, the talent of the man of affairs for seizing the opportunities his critics afforded him to sharpen his ideas and refine their expression, and the tact, when his position had been solidified as fully as possible, to tamper with it no further but to move on to other matters.

The movement from one encounter to another, however, is marked by a continuity of purpose that may be described as Arnold's attempt to see things as they really are. Emphases shift, to be sure, and specific aims vary. But in all his polemical engagements, his central objective is to correct distorted, illusory, provincial ways of thinking and by so doing help to shape not only the literature but the social, political, moral, and religious life of his time as well: in the fifties, to counteract the excesses of Romanticism, with its undisciplined exuberance and subjectivity, by emulating a poetry of nobility and grandeur; in the sixties, to purge the middle class of its Philistinism and prepare it for assuming its responsibilities as the ruling class of the future; in the seventies, to provide a solid basis for Christian belief that cannot be swept away by the *Zeitgeist*; and in the eighties, to find in a new humanism the means of fulfilling the inherent longings—aesthetic, intellectual, spiritual—of mankind.

The various controversies in which Arnold engaged are thus parts of a continuous chain. Behind the Homer lectures is the same attraction to the Greek world that produced the 1853 preface, and behind the ridicule of Colenso is the same protest against pedantic mutilation of great books that led to the criticism of Newman. The attack on the bishop of Natal heralded a campaign against Philistinism that elicited a series of related works: several of the *Essays in Criticism,* the introduction to *On the Study of Celtic Literature,* and all of *Culture and Anarchy* and *Friendship's Garland. Literature and Dogma* was as clearly a sequel to *Culture and Anarchy* as *God and the Bible* was a sequel to *Literature and Dogma,* and although Arnold's turning away from biblical and theological criticism in the late seventies suggests a certain discontinuity, there is throughout the work of his final decade a persistent theme that expands on an earlier argument: that neither Puritanism, nor aestheticism, nor science can meet the demands of humanity for a full and harmonious development.

If the language in which Arnold delivered these messages to his contemporaries was vulnerable, as Frederic Harrison wittily showed, to the criticism that it was too abstract, too remote from the realities of life to be meaningful, so too was his position vulnerable—as attested by reviewers who likened him to Hotspur's foppish lord—to the criticism that he was aloof from and even indifferent to the authentic concerns of nineteenth-century England. The famous *Vanity Fair* caricature, portraying a sneering Arnold as he grandly proclaims, "I say, the critic must keep out of the region of immediate practice," and the equally celebrated Beerbohm cartoon of the puzzled niece's questioning— "Why, Uncle Matthew, oh why, will not you be wholly serious?"—are but two expressions of the belief that Arnold sought to be serenely detached from his age and could never be trusted to speak earnestly about its concerns.

He was, on the contrary, deeply immersed in the life of his time, anxious both about the issues it faced and his own role in meeting them. The texture of his prose, as R. H. Super's edition has decisively demonstrated, is made up to a remarkable degree of allusions to contemporary persons, places, and

events. While for the present-day reader these may sometimes seem obscure and trivial, they at least convey a sense
of immediacy and reality that witnesses to Arnold's involvement in his age. Similarly, his controversies reveal not an
aloof writer, but one very much concerned with the criticism
of his work and eager to answer it: in a brief preface to the
1854 *Poems*, a fourth lecture on Homer, an article contrasting Stanley's biblical criticism with Colenso's, an essay de-
fining the function of criticism, a long defense of the concluding lecture at Oxford, a series of theological works, and so
on. That he was sensitive to criticism is frequently evidenced
—by his concern, for example, over the charges that he was a
fastidious critic scornful of the common man, and that he expressed in his poetry the views of an infidel or atheist—but
that he was indebted to his critics is also evidenced by the
quotation from Burke that he chose as an epigraph for *Essays in Criticism*, declaring that conflict obliges the writer to
consider his subject "in all its relations" and "will not suffer
him to be superficial."[4] Aware, then, that he wrote not as an
isolated thinker, such as the Spinoza he had depicted, but as
a critic who addressed an audience to which he was account-
able—an audience that was in part resistant if not openly hostile to his ideas but that he wished finally to persuade and
convert—Arnold utilized the opposition he encountered to
reexamine his positions, to qualify what had been inexactly
stated or modify what had been insecurely supported, even
to make the kind of return upon himself that he had praised
Burke for doing, and to expand and develop his original argument until his reply sometimes assumed greater importance
than the document that had initially provoked criticism.

Hence, although he was never more completely immersed
in his age than when he was involved in controversy, Arnold
in his most successful replies to criticism produced essays that
transcended the circumstances in which they were written.
It is true that most of his opponents were minor and now
largely forgotten figures—Rintoul, Frank Newman, Colenso,

Fitzjames Stephen, Harrison, Hutton, and Goldwin Smith, to name a few of the most obvious. But if it is true that he infrequently engaged in debate with opponents equal to himself, it is also true that he turned even the opposition of lesser persons to significant account, answering criticism that has not endured with works that have. To his controversies are owed such legacies as the 1853 preface, which has been described as "one of the classics" of English criticism;[5] the almost universally praised fourth lecture on Homer; "The Function of Criticism at the Present Time," probably the most widely reprinted essay of the Victorian era; *Culture and Anarchy*, a book that has influenced generations of readers; and portions of his theological writings, which are as pertinent to the religious difficulties of the twentieth century as to those of the nineteenth. The contemporary scene that Arnold rejected in much of his poetry he depicted in his controversial prose, with the very qualities he most admired: sanity, lucidity, wit, and seriousness. He thus survives his age as, to use his own favorite term, the most adequate of all the Victorians.

NOTES

Titles frequently referred to are cited in abbreviated form as follows:

Buckler William E. Buckler, *Matthew Arnold's Books: To-ward a Publishing Diary* (Geneva: Librairie E. Droz, 1958).

Lowry *The Letters of Matthew Arnold to Arthur Hugh Clough*, ed. Howard Foster Lowry (London: Oxford University Press, 1932).

Neiman *Essays, Letters, and Reviews by Matthew Arnold*, ed. Fraser Neiman (Cambridge: Harvard University Press, 1960).

Russell *Letters of Matthew Arnold, 1848–1888*, ed. George W. E. Russell. 2 vols. (New York: Macmillan, 1895).

Super *The Complete Prose Works of Matthew Arnold*, ed. R. H. Super. (Ann Arbor: University of Michigan Press, 1960–).

Whitridge *Unpublished Letters of Matthew Arnold*, ed. Arnold Whitridge (New Haven: Yale University Press, 1923).

Manuscript materials from two collections are cited as follows:

Whitridge Family letters, quoted by permission of the late Arnold
Papers Whitridge.

Yale Papers Manuscripts in the Beinecke Rare Book and Manuscript Library, quoted by permission of the Yale University Library.

I express here my gratitude for permission to quote these materials, as well as my gratitude for similar permissions granted, and individually acknowledged in the notes, by Mr. Evelyn de Rothschild, the British Museum, and Wellesley College.

Several unpublished dissertations have been of considerable use, and where they have directed me to specific items, I have so indicated with abbreviations as follows:

Gudas   Fabian Gudas, "The Debate on Matthew Arnold's Religious Writings" (University of Chicago, 1952).

Kirby   *Friendship's Garland*, ed. with an introduction by John P. Kirby, 2 vols. (Yale University, 1937).

SenGupta   Satyaprasad SenGupta, "The Reception of Matthew Arnold as Poet and Critic (1849–1871)" (University of London, 1961).

Wilkins   Charles T. Wilkins, "The English Reputation of Matthew Arnold, 1840–1877" (University of Illinois, 1959).

CHAPTER ONE: The Writer and His Mission

For the epigraphs see: "Balliol Scholars 1840–43: A Remembrance," *Macmillan's Magazine* 27 (Mar. 1873): 381; "Matthew Arnold," *English Illustrated Magazine* 1 (Jan. 1884): 246, quoted by John Henry Raleigh, *Matthew Arnold and American Culture* (Berkeley: University of California Press, 1957), p. 38; *Poetry and Prose of William Blake*, ed. Geoffrey Keynes (London: Nonesuch Press, 1948), p. 190; *Conversations of Goethe with Eckermann and Soret*, trans. John Oxenford, rev. ed. (London: G. Bell, 1883), p. 223; A. Norman Jeffares, *W. B. Yeats: Man and Poet* (New York: Barnes & Noble, 1966), p. 268.

1. Evelyn Abbott and Lewis Campbell, *The Life and Letters of Benjamin Jowett*, 2nd ed. (London: J. Murray, 1897), 1: 88–89; 2: 338.

2. *Forty Years of Friendship as Recorded in the Correspondence of John Duke, Lord Coleridge and Ellis Yarnall During the Years 1856 to 1895*, ed. Charlton Yarnall (London: Macmillan, 1911), p. 279.

3. Frederic W. Maitland, *The Life and Letters of Leslie Stephen* (London: Duckworth, 1906), p. 442.

4. William S. Peterson, "G. W. E. Russell and the Editing of Matthew Arnold's Letters," *Victorian Newsletter*, no. 37 (Spring 1970), p. 28.

5. *Letters of Charles Eliot Norton*, ed. Sara Norton and M. A. DeWolfe Howe (Boston: Houghton Mifflin, 1913), 1: 237.

6. *Leslie Stephen: His Thought and Character in Relation to His Time* (Cambridge: Harvard University Press, 1952), p. 277.

7. Samuel Butler, *The Way of All Flesh*, chap. 86.

8. E. H. Coleridge, *Life and Correspondence of John Duke Lord Coleridge* (London: Heinemann, 1904), 1: 145.

9. *My Autobiography: A Fragment* (New York: Scribner's, 1901), p. 283.

10. *Reminiscences*, ed. Arnold Haultain (New York: Macmillan, 1910), p. 71.

11. "Matthew Arnold. By One Who Knew Him Well," Manchester *Guardian*, May 18, 1888, p. 8.
12. Blanche Athena Clough, *A Memoir of Anne Jemima Clough*, new ed. (London: E. Arnold, 1903), p. 55.
13. *The Correspondence of Arthur Hugh Clough*, ed. Frederick L. Mulhauser (Oxford: Clarendon Press, 1957), 1: 178–79.
14. *Auld Lang Syne* (New York: Scribner's, 1898), p. 143.
15. Letter of Feb. 15, 1865 (Whitridge Papers).
16. Russell, 1: 390.
17. Letter of Feb. 13, 1869 (Whitridge Papers).
18. Letter dated [Dec. ? 1864] in Arthur Kyle Davis, Jr., *Matthew Arnold's Letters: A Descriptive Checklist* (Charlottesville: University Press of Virginia, 1968), p. 58 (Whitridge Papers).
19. Russell, 1: 450.
20. Letter of Dec. 5, 1867 (Whitridge Papers); largely quoted by Super, 5: 414.
21. [Hallam Tennyson], *Alfred Lord Tennyson: A Memoir* (New York: Macmillan, 1898), 2: 225. But, according to M. E. Sadler, " 'Mat's sublime wagging' amused Tennyson" ("Matthew Arnold," *Nineteenth Century* 93 [1923]: 204); quoted by Kirby, 1: 209–10.
22. *Unforgotten Years* (Boston: Little, Brown, 1939), p. 124.
23. "Arnold's Marguerite," *Booker Memorial Studies*, ed. Hill Shine (Chapel Hill: University of North Carolina Press, 1950), p. 98.
24. "The Death of Matthew Arnold," *Times Literary Supplement*, Oct. 10, 1968, p. 1159.
25. Russell, 1: 165.
26. George W. Smalley, *London Letters and Some Others* (London: Macmillan, 1890), 1: 348.
27. Russell, 1: 17.
28. *Matthew Arnold's "England and the Italian Question"* (Durham: Duke University Press, 1953), p. viii.
29. Russell, 1: 113, 150, 125.
30. Letter of Oct. 21, 1863 (Whitridge Papers).
31. Russell, 1: 263, 442, 48, 420.
32. Letter of Christmas day 1869 (Whitridge Papers).
33. "The Buried Life," 1: 97.
34. Super, 8: 12, 56, 59, 80, 146, 152.
35. *Modern Philology* 48 (1951): 281.
36. *Studies of a Biographer* (New York: Putnam's, 1898), 2: 104.
37. *Recollections* (New York: Macmillan, 1917), 1: 130.
38. "Matthew Arnold," *New Review* 1 (Aug. 1889): 218, from which it is quoted by E. H. Coleridge, *John Duke Lord Coleridge*, 2: 387.
39. *A Writer's Recollections* (New York: Harper, 1918), 2: 81.
40. *Henry Crabb Robinson on Books and Their Writers*, ed. Edith J. Morley (London: J. M. Dent, 1938), 2: 806.
41. Letter to Arthur Galton, Dec. 27, 1888 (Yale Papers).
42. *Some Authors: A Collection of Literary Essays, 1896–1916* (Oxford: Clarendon Press, 1923), p. 308.
43. Buckler, p. 72.
44. *Studies of a Biographer*, 2: 78.
45. Russell, 1: 282, 234.

46. Letter to Frances Arnold, Athenaeum, Tuesday [1864?] (Whitridge Papers).
47. *Auld Lang Syne*, p. 135.
48. *Matthew Arnold*, English Men of Letters Series (New York: Macmillan, 1902), pp. 125–26.
49. Russell, 1: 447; 2: 6.
50. "Matthew Arnold's Prose: Theory and Practice," *The Art of Victorian Prose*, ed. George Levine and William Madden (New York: Oxford University Press, 1968), p. 98.
51. Letter of July 16, 1867 (Whitridge Papers).
52. Letter of Nov. 23, 1867 (Whitridge Papers).
53. Russell, 1: 452, 183, 211, 282–83, 377.
54. Letter of Mar. 10, 1869, to Grant Duff.
55. Super, 7: 436.
56. I cite the latter example not because I consider it especially appropriate but because it is so often mentioned. My own opinion is that R. H. Super is right in believing that the passage was intended as a joke that was later deleted when almost no one got it or thought it amusing (see Fred G. Walcott, *The Origins of "Culture and Anarchy"* [Toronto: University of Toronto Press, 1970], p. 130, n. 70).
57. *Matthew Arnold: A Study in Conflict* (Chicago: University of Chicago Press, 1948), pp. 18, 103.
58. Russell, 1: 289.
59. Brown, *Arnold: Study in Conflict*, p. 183.
60. Super, 7: 203.
61. Russell, 1: 225, 250, 255.
62. After his retirement Arnold remarked, "Abroad probably a Minister might have known more about my performances; but then abroad I doubt whether I should ever have survived to perform them. Under the strict bureaucratic system abroad, I feel pretty sure that I should have been dismissed ten times over for the freedom with which on various occasions I have exposed myself on matters of Religion and Politics. Our Government here in England takes a large and liberal view about what it considers a man's private affairs, and so I have been able to survive as an Inspector for thirty-five years ; and to the Government I at least owe this—to have been allowed to survive" (G. W. E. Russell, *Matthew Arnold* [New York: Scribner's, 1904], pp. 54–55). The risk Arnold incurred in publishing "The Twice Revised Code" may be judged from a passage in a letter to his wife: "I don't think . . . they can eject me, though they can, and perhaps will, make my place uncomfortable. If thrown on the world I daresay we should be on our legs again before very long. Any way, I think I owed as much as this to a cause in which I have now a deep interest, and always shall have, even if I cease to serve it officially" (Russell, 1: 194–95).
63. *Sartor Resartus*, ed. C. F. Harrold (New York: Odyssey, 1937), p. 129.
64. Russell, 1: 255.
65. "Matthew Arnold. By One Who Knew Him Well," p. 8.
66. Letter of Aug. 1, 1863 (Whitridge Papers).
67. Russell, 1: 233–34, 400.
68. Ibid., 1: 420.
69. Letter of Nov. 23, 1867.
70. Russell, 2: 41, 45, 135, 146.

71. Ibid., 1: 6, 10.
72. Ibid., 1:129, 285–86, 360.
73. Ibid., 1: 444.

CHAPTER TWO: The Poet and His Readers

For the epigraphs see: T. Percy Jones [pseudonym of W. E. Aytoun], *Firmilian: A "Spasmodic" Tragedy* (New York: Redfield, 1854), pp. 26–27; Oxenford, *Conversations of Goethe*, p. 32; *Laocoön*, trans. Ellen Frothingham (Boston: Little, Brown, 1898), p. 127; *The Sacred Wood* (New York: Knopf, 1921), pp. 52–53; *Miscellaneous Works* (New York: D. Appleton, 1845), p. 337.

1. The phrase is that of one of the ablest and most sympathetic of Clough's critics, Walter E. Houghton, in *The Poetry of Clough: An Essay in Revaluation* (New Haven: Yale University Press, 1963), p. 56.

2. Lowry, p. 56.

3. *Sun*, Sept. 10, 1855, p. 3 (SenGupta). Arnold described the *Sun*'s review as "a flaming account" (Russell, 1: 54).

4. Alan D. McKillop, "A Victorian Faust," *PMLA* 40 (1925): 744, 746, 765. The quotation from Emerson is from the *Journals*, ed. Edward Waldo Emerson and Waldo Emerson Forbes (Cambridge: Riverside Press, 1909–14), 7: 285.

5. The phrases, by James Montgomery, R. H. Horne, and Ebenezer Elliott, respectively, are quoted at the end of the first American edition of *Festus: A Poem* (Boston: Mussey, 1845), p. 415. A reviewer of Arnold's *Poems* (1854) was to say, "Poems like those before us, and the 'Festus' of Mr. Bailey, stand at opposite extremes. The admirers of the former will be tempted to account Bailey's work a gorgeous incoherence—a mass of materials for poetry rather than a poem; while those who are enthusiastic for 'Festus' will complain of tameness in Mr. Arnold" (*British Quarterly Review* 19 [Apr. 1854] 581–82).

6. Quoted by Mark A. Weinstein, *William Edmondstoune Aytoun and the Spasmodic Controversy* (New Haven: Yale University Press, 1968), p. 83.

7. Robert A. and Elizabeth S. Watson, *George Gilfillan: Letters and Journals, with Memoir* (London: Hodder & Stoughton, 1892), pp. 155, 194–95, 200; T[homas] Brisbane, *The Early Years of Alexander Smith, Poet and Essayist* (London: Hodder & Stoughton, 1869), pp. 130–32, 145. More than thirty years later, in the essay on Sainte-Beuve that he wrote for the *Encyclopaedia Britannica*, Arnold described praise of Hugo's poetry as "in the vein of Mr. George Gilfillan" (*Five Uncollected Essays of Matthew Arnold*, ed. Kenneth Allott [Liverpool: Liverpool University Press, 1953], p. 74). As Allott points out (p. 105), Gilfillan was on Arnold's reading list for May 1855.

8. Jerome Hamilton Buckley, *The Victorian Temper: A Study in Literary Culture* (Cambridge: Harvard University Press, 1951), p. 52.

9. Alexander Smith, *Poems* (Boston: Ticknor, Reed, and Fields, 1854), pp. 5, 6, 83, 85–86, 24. Nearly thirty years later, in his essay on Keats, Arnold observed, "Young poets almost inevitably over-rate what they call 'the might of poesy,' and its power over the world which now is" (Super, 9: 210).

10. *The Life and Letters of Sydney Dobell*, ed. E[mily] J[olly] (London: Smith, Elder, 1878), 1: 257. Gilfillan apparently took offense at this criticism of his protégé.

11.   *The Letters of Elizabeth Barrett Browning,* ed. Frederic G. Kenyon (New York: Macmillan, 1898), 2: 134, 138.

12.   *Letters of James Russell Lowell,* ed. C. E. Norton (New York: Harper, 1893), 1: 210–11 (SenGupta).

13.   *Letters of Dante Gabriel Rossetti,* ed. Oswald Doughty and John Robert Wahl (Oxford: Clarendon Press, 1965), 1: 136.

14.   Rossetti's letter is dated April 17. Three days earlier, Arnold had written to "K" of his intention to publish "Sohrab and Rustum," together with several other narrative poems, "in February next, with my name and a preface" (Russell, 1: 34).

15.   *The Poems of Matthew Arnold,* ed. Kenneth Allott (New York: Barnes & Noble, 1965), p. 589; the passage appears in somewhat different form in Ward, *Writer's Recollections,* 1: 71. Arnold later translated *bedeutendes Individuum* as "the noble or powerful nature" (Super, 1: 189). The *Nonconformist* reviewer of Arnold's *Poems* was later to say of his "polemical preface," "In very truth we took it, at first glance, for a manifesto against Alexander Smith and his admirers" (14 [Apr. 27, 1854]: 340).

16.   Lowry, p. 144.

17.   Whitridge, p. 22.

18.   Super, 1: 3, 256.

19.   J. W. Robertson Scott, *The Story of the "Pall Mall Gazette"* (London: Oxford University Press, 1950), p. 51.

20.   *Spectator* 22 (Mar. 10, 1849): 231; 25 (Oct. 30, 1852): 1046 (for the first of these references I am indebted to Wilkins).

21.   J. D. Jump, "Matthew Arnold and the *Spectator,*" *Review of English Studies* 25 (1949): 61.

22.   Whitridge, p. 22.

23.   "Theories of Poetry and a New Poet," *North British Review* 19 (Aug. 1853): 338, 317–18. For Masson's authorship see Walter E. Houghton, ed., *The Wellesley Index to Victorian Periodicals* (Toronto: University of Toronto Press, 1966–   ), 1: 677.

24.   Whitridge, p. 20.

25.   *The Note-Books of Matthew Arnold,* ed. H. F. Lowry, Karl Young, and W. H. Dunn (London: Oxford University Press, 1952), pp. 553–54.

26.   Lowry, pp. 96–97, 124, 136.

27.   Ibid., pp. 63, 145.

28.   See, for example, Arnold's statement that the blank verse used in translating Homer "must not be Mr. Tennyson's blank verse," his description of Tennyson as "a most distinguished and charming poet," and his distinction between the natural simplicity of Wordsworth and the artificial simplicity of Tennyson (Super, 1: 147, 204–07).

29.   R. H. Super, "Matthew Arnold and Tennyson," *Times Literary Supplement,* Oct. 28, 1960, p. 693.

30.   Lowry, pp. 147, 154.

31.   Russell, 1: 147, 278.

32.   E. H. Coleridge, *John Duke Lord Coleridge,* 1: 211.

33.   *Times,* Nov. 4, 1853, p. 5. For Smith's supposed authorship see E. H. Coleridge, *John Duke Lord Coleridge,* 1: 211.

34.   *Germ,* no. 2 (1850), p. 96.

35.   *Blackwood's Edinburgh Magazine* 66 (Sept. 1849): 344–45. For Aytoun's authorship see Houghton, *Wellesley Index,* 1: 87.

36.   "Glimpses of Poetry," *North British Review* 19 (May 1853): 212.

For Patmore's authorship see J. C. Reid, *The Mind and Art of Coventry Patmore* (London: Routledge & Paul, 1957), p. 334, and Houghton, *Wellesley Index*, 1: 676, where it is given as questionable.

37. *English Review* 13 (Mar. 1850): 212.

38. "Recent Poetry, and Recent Verse," *Fraser's Magazine* 39 (May 1849): 575. For Kingsley's authorship see Margaret F. Thorp, *Charles Kingsley, 1819–1875* (Princeton: Princeton University Press, 1937), p. 192, and Houghton, *Wellesley Index*, 2: 405.

39. Kathleen Tillotson has observed that although the preface does not mention Tennyson, "it implies him, in more than one passage" ("Rugby 1850: Arnold, Clough, Walrond, and *In Memoriam*," *Review of English Studies* 4 [1953]: 137), and Paull F. Baum went so far as to assert that the preface "might have been a deliberate refutation of Tennyson's aims" (*Tennyson Sixty Years After* [Chapel Hill: University of North Carolina Press, 1948], p. 249).

40. Russell, 1: 33.

41. Lowry, p. 136.

42. *Matthew Arnold*, 2nd ed. (New York: Columbia University Press, 1949), p. 146. Of the numerous discussions of the complex relationship between Arnold and Clough the following, in addition to Trilling, are especially helpful: Michael Timko, "Corydon Had a Rival," *Victorian Newsletter*, no. 19 (1961), pp. 5–11; Katharine Chorley, *Arthur Hugh Clough, the Uncommitted Mind: A Study of His Life and Poetry* (Oxford: Clarendon Press, 1962), pp. 118–20; Paul Veyriras, *Arthur Hugh Clough (1819–1861)* (Paris: Didier, 1964), pp. 427–30; David J. DeLaura, "Arnold, Clough, Dr. Arnold, and 'Thyrsis,'" *Victorian Poetry* 7 (1969): 191–202; and Robindra K. Biswas, *Arthur Hugh Clough: Towards a Reconsideration* (Oxford: Clarendon Press, 1972), pp. 213–21.

43. Mulhauser, *Correspondence of Clough*, 2: 424, 434, 414.

44. Lowry, p. 136.

45. "Recent English Poetry," *North American Review* 77 (July 1853): 16, 17, 24, 1–4. Clough's review has recently been made more accessible in its entirety in *Selected Prose Works of Arthur Hugh Clough*, ed. Buckner B. Trawick (University, Ala.: University of Alabama Press, 1964), pp. 143–71. For Arnold's attempt to meet Clough's objections to the "obscurity" of *Tristram and Iseult*, see Roger L. Brooks, "Matthew Arnold's Revision of *Tristram and Iseult*: Some Instances of Clough's Influence," *Victorian Poetry* 2 (1964): 57–60.

46. Clough, "Recent English Poetry," pp. 18, 20, 22.

47. Lowry, p. 140.

48. Clough, "Recent English Poetry," pp. 12, 24–25.

49. *Aurora Leigh*, Fifth Book, lines 189–90, 200–22. The passage helps explain the comment of apparently unprovoked severity that Arnold made about Mrs. Browning in 1858: "I regard her as hopelessly confirmed in her aberration from health, nature, beauty, and truth." He had just requested Madame du Quaire to show a copy of *Merope* to Browning, for "one of the very best antique fragments I know is a fragment of a Hippolytus by him" (Russell, 1: 70). The impulses producing *Aurora Leigh* and *Merope* were, of course, antipodal.

50. Lines 391–93. William Clyde DeVane showed how the poem refers by implication to Arnold's 1853 preface and answers it (*Browning's Parley-*

ings: The Autobiography of a Mind [New Haven: Yale University Press, 1927], pp. 234–40.

51. "The Epic," lines 35–38. For Tennyson's comment see Hallam Tennyson, *Memoir*, 2: 364. At Cambridge Ernest Pontifex wrote an essay on Greek drama in which he said "that a faithful rendering of contemporary life is the very quality which gives its most permanent interest to any work of fiction, whether in literature or painting" (*The Way of All Flesh*, chap. 46). For the Victorian preoccupation with the contemporary, the relevant, the immediate present, see Jerome Hamilton Buckley, *The Triumph of Time: A Study of the Victorian Concepts of Time, History, Progress, and Decadence* (Cambridge: Belknap Press of Harvard University Press, 1966), pp. 116–36.

52. *Festus: A Poem*, p. 7.

53. "The Poet," lines 1, 7, 56, 26.

54. *Sordello*, V: 506. The line was brought to my attention by Daniel Stempel ("Browning's *Sordello*: The Art of the Makers-See," *PMLA* 80 [1965]: 560), who points out that the poem itself repudiates the widespread notion here expressed by Sordello.

55. Quoted by Edgar F. Shannon, Jr., *Tennyson and the Reviewers* (Cambridge: Harvard University Press, 1952), p. 87.

56. Robert B. Martin, *The Dust of Combat: A Life of Charles Kingsley* (London: Faber and Faber, 1959), p. 160.

57. Kingsley, "Recent Poetry, and Recent Verse," pp. 578, 575.

58. *Germ*, no. 2, pp. 88–89.

59. *Gentleman's Magazine* 32 (Sept. 1849): 284 (Wilkins).

60. Whitridge, p. 15.

61. Mulhauser, *Correspondence of Clough*, 1: 270.

62. Lowry, p. 114.

63. Russell, 1: 36. In the general condemnation of Arnold's subject matter, a dissenting voice was raised by the *Globe and Traveller* (May 28, 1849, p. 1), which said, "We have rarely seen so striking a proof that a writer has been 'nourished on the milk of a better time,' and has prepared himself for illustrating the present by long and laborious seclusion in the past" (Wilkins).

64. *New Zealand Letters of Thomas Arnold the Younger*, ed. James Bertram (London: Oxford University Press, 1966), p. 164.

65. Kingsley, "Recent Poetry, and Recent Verse," p. 579.

66. Patmore, "Glimpses of Poetry," pp. 210, 213–14.

67. *Blackwood's Edinburgh Magazine* 66: 345.

68. *English Review* 13: 211–12.

69. *Guardian* 7 (Dec. 8, 1852): 823.

70. Mulhauser, *Correspondence of Clough*, 1: 251.

71. Ibid., 2: 401, 437. Shairp continued to insist that Arnold should assume the role of prophet, concluding his review of Arnold's poetry in the *North British* in August 1854 by saying that "Arnold must learn . . . that whatever are the faults or needs of our own time, the heart has not yet died out of it; that if he thinks it bad, it is the duty of poets, and all thoughtful men, to do their part to mend it, not by weak-hearted lamentations, but by appealing to men's energies, their hopes, their moral aspirations" (21: 504). For Shairp's authorship see Houghton, *Wellesley Index*, 1: 678.

72. Super, 1: 1.

73. Whitridge, pp. 15–17.

74. Russell, 1: 71–73.

75. *Poems of Arnold*, p. 399. Allott later elaborated on the point in "A Background for 'Empedocles on Etna,' " *Essays and Studies by Members of the English Association* 21 (1968): 80–100, reprinted in *Matthew Arnold: A Collection of Critical Essays*, ed. David J. DeLaura, Twentieth Century Views (Englewood Cliffs: Prentice-Hall, 1973), pp. 55–70.

76. Lowry, p. 65. Although the letter breaks off, "my sinews cracking under the effort to unite matter . . .," it would seem almost certain that "with form" followed. See R. H. Super, *The Time-Spirit of Matthew Arnold* (Ann Arbor: University of Michigan Press, 1970), p. 95, n. 21.

77. Waldo H. Dunn, *James Anthony Froude: A Biography* (Oxford: Clarendon Press, 1961–63), 1: 134. Froude's comment is understandable in view of the fact that he was writing to Kingsley on the very day that William Sewell ostentatiously burned a copy of *The Nemesis of Faith*.

78. *The Autobiography of William Butler Yeats* (New York: Macmillan, 1938), p. 267; similarly quoted by Barbara Charlesworth, *Dark Passages: The Decadent Consciousness in Victorian Literature* (Madison: University of Wisconsin Press, 1965), p. 6. For an essential difference between Yeats and Arnold, however, see Frank Kermode, *Romantic Image* (New York: Macmillan, 1957), p. 19.

79. Super, 1: 8.

80. Oxenford, *Conversations of Goethe*, pp. 17, 52, 32, 165, 19–20, 236.

81. Super, 1: 4, 9, 12.

82. Ibid., 1: 13, 223.

83. Russell, 1: 18.

84. Lowry, p. 99.

85. Russell, 1: 5.

86. Super, 1: 14–15.

87. *Examiner*, Apr. 29, 1854, p. 260.

88. *Daily News*, Dec. 26, 1853, p. 2. The review was so unfavorable that Arnold said it "must have been written" by Clough, who thought it was "probably" by Harriet Martineau (Mulhauser, *Correspondence of Clough*, 2: 471).

89. *Christian Remembrancer* 27 (Apr. 1854): 316–17.

90. *Athenaeum*, Mar. 11, 1854, pp. 304–05. The notice is attributed to Heraud by Leslie A. Marchand, *"The Athenaeum": A Mirror of Victorian Culture* (Chapel Hill: University of North Carolina Press, 1941), p. 215.

91. "The Poems of Matthew Arnold, and of Alexander Smith," *Prospective Review* 10 (Feb. 1854): 111–12. For the attribution of the review to Roscoe see T. B. Smart, *The Bibliography of Matthew Arnold* (London: J. Davy, 1892), p. 56.

92. *Personal and Literary Letters of Robert, First Earl of Lytton*, ed. Lady Betty Balfour (London: Longmans, Green, 1906), 1: 50, quoted by SenGupta, p. 138.

93. "Arnold's Poems," *Westminster Review* 61 (Jan. 1854): 158–59.

94. "Arnold's Poems," *Spectator* 26 (Dec . 3, 1853): supplement, 5–6.

95. See Alice R. Kaminsky, *George Henry Lewes as Literary Critic* (Syracuse: Syracuse University Press, 1968), p. 203, and *Literary Criticism of George Henry Lewes*, ed. Alice R. Kaminsky, Regents Critics Series (Lincoln: University of Nebraska Press, 1964), pp. 82–84, where portions of Lewes's two review articles are reprinted.

96. Quoted by Ann Theresa Kitchel, *George Lewes and George Eliot: A Review of Records* (New York: John Day, 1933), p. 107. The praise of

Alexander Smith helps explain Arnold's comment that the *Leader* was "certain to disparage" the 1853 volume (Russell, 1: 37). Arnold later came to "have a very high opinion of [Lewes's] literary judgment" (ibid., 1: 67), but one suspects that in 1853, when he described Keats's "Isabella" as a failure despite its being "a perfect treasure house of graceful and felicitous words and images" (Super, 1: 10), he was ironically echoing Lewes's praise of Smith's "luxuriant imagery and exquisite felicity of expression."

97. "Schools of Poetry," *Leader* 4 (Nov. 26, 1853): 1147; (Dec. 3, 1853): 1170.

98. *Daily News*, Dec. 26, 1853, p. 2.

99. "A Raid Among the Poets," *New Quarterly Review* 3 (Jan. 1854): 40.

100. "The Two Arnolds," *Blackwood's Edinburgh Magazine* 75 (Mar. 1854): 308–12. For Aytoun's authorship see Houghton, *Wellesley Index*, 1: 97.

101. *Christian Remembrancer*, 27: 318–20. Important material pertaining to the review is found in E. H. Coleridge, *John Duke Lord Coleridge*, 1: 207–13, and an account of the relationship between the two men is given by W. P. Fishback, *Recollections of Lord Coleridge* (Indianapolis and Kansas City: Bowen-Merrill, 1895), pp. 25–27, 46–47. Coleridge afterwards "bitterly repented" of the review (see his article on Arnold in the *New Review*, 1: 122, where he is almost certainly referring to himself).

102. *Christian Remembrancer*, 27: 329–33.

103. Ibid., p. 322.

104. E. H. Coleridge, *John Duke Lord Coleridge*, 1: 210–12.

105. Super, 1: 16–17.

106. Oxenford, *Conversations of Goethe*, p. 380.

107. Allott, *Poems of Arnold*, pp. 612–15. The note was published only in 1854; for a possible explanation for Arnold's never reprinting it, see C. B. Tinker and H. F. Lowry, *The Poetry of Matthew Arnold: A Commentary* (London: Oxford University Press, 1950), pp. 82–85.

108. Russell, 1: 40.

109. *Matthew Arnold, Poète: essai de biographie psychologique* (Paris: Libraire Marcel Didier, 1947), p. 363.

110. See R. H. Super, "Documents in the Matthew Arnold–Sainte-Beuve Relationship," *Modern Philology* 60 (1963): 206.

111. Bonnerot, *Matthew Arnold, Poète*, p. 522.

112. Super, "Documents," pp. 206–07, corrects the erroneous dating of the letter in Whitridge, p. 68.

113. Whitridge, p. 69. The bracketed additions are Bonnerot's, p. 351.

114. The passage is quoted by Bonnerot (*Matthew Arnold, Poète*, pp. 351–52, n. 1) from the third edition of *L'Etude sur Virgile* (Paris: Calmann-Lévy, 1878), pp. 72–73.

115. Russell, 1: 48, 66. Arnold's relationship with Temple is described in some detail by Eugene L. Williamson, Jr., in "Matthew Arnold and the Archbishops," *Modern Language Quarterly* 24 (1963): 250-52.

116. "Matthew Arnold. By One Who Knew Him Well," p. 8. Arnold gave to "Rugby Chapel" the subtitle, "November 1857." For the possibility of a later date and the linking of the poem with Fitzjames Stephen's attack not on Thomas but on Matthew Arnold, see Harvey Kerpneck, "The Road to Rugby Chapel," *University of Toronto Quarterly* 34 (1965): 178–96. In recent years "Rugby Chapel" has attracted considerable scholarly and critical attention, at least partly because it reflects Arnold's growing veneration for his

father. See especially Wendell Stacy Johnson, " 'Rugby Chapel': Arnold as a Filial Poet," *University Review* 34 (1967): 107–13; John O. Waller, "Doctor Arnold's Sermons and Matthew Arnold's 'Rugby Chapel,' " *Studies in English Literature* 9 (1969): 633–46; and, for the argument that veneration for his fa'her was expressed at the sacrifice of "his own poetic imagination," Jonathan Middlebrook, " 'Resignation,' 'Rugby Chapel,' and Thomas Arnold," *Victorian Poetry* 8 (1970): 291–97.

117. Letter of Feb. 13, 1869.
118. Super, 1: 19–30.
119. Ibid., 1: 32–36.
120. Lowry, p. 146.
121. Super, 1: 33. René Wellek, in *The Later Nineteenth Century*, vol. 4 of *A History of Modern Criticism: 1750–1950* (New Haven: Yale University Press, 1965), p. 159, points out the shifting meanings in Arnold's use of the word *adequate*. At the beginning of the lecture it describes a literature commensurate with the age in which it is created, but later, beginning with the treatment of Menander, it comes to imply intrinsic moral qualities. The shift underscores the general change in Arnold's critical stance between 1853 and 1857.
122. The fact that Arnold did not publish the lecture for more than a decade reflects his lack of regard for it; and when he finally published it, he spoke scornfully of its "rather high-horse academic style" (Buckler, p. 154) and its "broad clear generalisations" (letter of Feb. 13, 1869). His disparagement of the lecture, however, does not conceal its importance in showing the development of his thought.
123. Super, 1: 14.
124. First published by William T. Arnold, "Thomas Arnold the Younger," *Century Magazine* 66 (1903): 124, n., and later by Robert L. Lowe, "Two Arnold Letters," *Modern Philology* 52 (1955): 263.
125. Russell, 1: 68, 69.
126. Super, 1: 39, 64.
127. "Stanzas in Memory of the Author of 'Obermann,' " lines, 95–96.
128. *The Swinburne Letters*, ed. Cecil Y. Lang (New Haven: Yale University Press, 1959–62), 1: 115; 3: 55.
129. "Matthew Arnold's Tragedy of Merope," *Spectator* 31 (Jan. 2, 1858): 25.
130. *Mythology and the Romantic Tradition in English Poetry* (Cambridge: Harvard University Press, 1937), p. 262.
131. Russell, 1: 69–70.
132. Super, 3: 259.

CHAPTER THREE: Homer and His Translators

For the epigraphs see: Lang, *Swinburne Letters*, 4: 280; *Poetics*, 4; *Modern Painters*, vol. 3, pt. 4, chap. 1, section 18; Arnold Whitridge, "Matthew Arnold and Sainte-Beuve," *PMLA* 53 (1938): 312; *Introductory Lecture Delivered before the Faculties of Arts and Laws and of Science in University College, London, October 3, 1892* (New York: Macmillan, 1937), pp. 24–25.

1. Russell, 1: 146, 150.
2. "On Translating Homer," *Spectator* 34 (Feb. 16, 1861): 170.

3. On Nov. 6, 1861, Arnold wrote to his mother, "The notice in the *Times* was by Dallas, a Scotchman, their ordinary reviewer of poetry and poetical criticism. I have once met him at dinner" (Whitridge Papers).

4. "On Translating Homer," *Times*, Oct. 28, 1861, p. 8.

5. *Daily News*, Mar. 25, 1861, p. 2.

6. Letter of Feb. 13, 1861 (Whitridge Papers).

7. For Arnold's comment on the motto see Russell, 1: 191.

8. Ibid., 1: 161.

9. Ibid., 1: 177, 183–84.

10. T[homas] Mozley, *Reminiscences Chiefly of Oriel College and the Oxford Movement* (Boston: Houghton Mifflin, 1884), 1: 17.

11. Basil Willey, *More Nineteenth Century Studies: A Group of Honest Doubters* (New York: Columbia University Press, 1956), pp. 11–52; William Robbins, *The Newman Brothers: An Essay in Comparative Intellectual Biography* (Cambridge: Harvard University Press, 1966); J. M. Cameron, in his review of Robbins, *Victorian Studies* 10 (1967): 442.

12. *The Letters of Mrs. Gaskell*, ed. J. A. V. Chapple and Arthur Pollard (Cambridge: Harvard University Press, 1967), p. 89; *The George Eliot Letters*, ed. Gordon S. Haight (New Haven: Yale University Press, 1954-55), 2: 85.

13. Watson, *George Gilfillan*, p. 144.

14. *The Works of Thomas Carlyle*, Edinburgh ed. (New York: Scribner's, 1903–04), 11: 184; Moncure D. Conway, *Autobiography, Memories and Experiences* (London: Cassell, 1904), 2: 188; E. Jane Whately, *Life and Correspondence of Richard Whately* (London: Longmans, Green, 1866), 2: 153.

15. Mulhauser, *Correspondence of Clough*, 1: 63. Dr. Arnold presumably had the same sense of Frank's spiritual superiority that in 1875 led A. P. Stanley to write to Frances Power Cobbe, "When the sum of the theological teaching of the two brothers is weighed, will not 'the *Soul*' of Francis be found to counterbalance, as a contribution to true, solid, catholic (even in any sense of the word) Christianity, all the writings of John Henry?" (*Life of Frances Power Cobbe as Told by Herself* [London: Swan Sonnenschein, 1904], p. 531).

16. Lowry, p. 86.

17. Ibid., p. 115.

18. A. W. Benn, *The History of English Rationalism in the Nineteenth Century* (London: Longmans, Green, 1906), 2: 26.

19. *Phases of Faith; or, Passages from the History of My Creed*, new ed. (London: Trübner, 1881), p. 1.

20. Willey, *More Nineteenth Century Studies*, p. 18.

21. For Arnold's attitude toward perplexity over pedobaptism see his essay, "Equality," in Super, 8: 296–97.

22. Newman, *Phases of Faith*, p. 68.

23. I. Giberne Sieveking, *Memoir and Letters of Francis W. Newman* (London: K. Paul, Trench, Trübner, 1909), p. 59.

24. *Essays, Reviews and Addresses* (London: Longmans, Green, 1890–91), 3: 2–3.

25. Letter, "Brighton 1861," partially quoted by Super, 1: 249 (Whitridge Papers).

26. Letter to Arthur Galton, Dec. 21, 1897 (Yale Papers). Mrs. Arnold must have been thinking of a separate publication of *On Translating Homer*,

since it was republished in an American edition of *Essays in Criticism* in 1865 and with *On the Study of Celtic Literature* in 1883.

27. Lowry, p. 153.
28. Super, 1: 140–41.
29. *The Iliad of Homer Faithfully Translated into Unrhymed English Metre* (London: Walton and Maberly, 1856), p. xvi; Newman's italics.
30. *Homeric Translation in Theory and Practice: A Reply to Matthew Arnold*, in Matthew Arnold, *Essays, Literary and Critical* (Everyman's Library; London: J. M. Dent, 1950), p. 309.
31. Newman, *The Iliad of Homer*, p. xvi; Newman's italics.
32. Arnold, *Essays, Literary and Critical*, pp. 310-11.
33. Newman, *The Iliad of Homer*, p. iv.
34. Ibid., pp. iv, vi, x.
35. Ibid., pp. v–viii.
36. Super, 1: 118.
37. Ibid., 1: 97.
38. "To a Friend," lines 1–2.
39. Super, 1: 168, 119.
40. Ibid., 1: 119–20, 124.
41. Ibid., 1: 121–22.
42. Ibid., 1: 123, 125.
43. Ibid., 1: 111, 128, 134, 152.
44. Ibid., 1: 103, 139–40.
45. Arnold, *Essays, Literary and Critical*, pp. 303, 313, 295.
46. A more sympathetic and discerning critic, "K," also complained that Arnold was dogmatic. He facetiously dismissed the criticism in speaking of it to his mother—"Jane thinks me too dogmatic—but you see nobody else complains of this, as when one is on the side of *commonsense* much positiveness is forgiven" (letter of Feb. 13, 1861); but he took it more seriously in writing to "K" herself: "No one else has yet made this complaint, and you must remember that the tone of a lecturing professor to an audience supposed to be there to learn of him, cannot be quite that of a man submitting his views to the great world. . . . But enough of all this—certainly I must and will take care not to fall into an offensive tone of dogmatising, on any subject, for that is always in bad taste, and therefore always excruciating" (Whitridge, pp. 51–53). More than two years later, when "K" said that he "was becoming as dogmatic as Ruskin," Arnold "told her the difference was that Ruskin was 'dogmatic and *wrong*'" (Russell, 1: 233). Later, however, he wrote to her, "I thought there was some truth in your objection to the dogmatic tone of the Homer lectures, and I have ever since tried to be on my guard against that (letter of [Dec. ? 1864]).
47. Arnold, *Essays, Literary and Critical*, pp. 296–98, 325, 336. Newman expresses surprise that Arnold should have found some of his diction unintelligible. The word *bragly* ("proudly fine"), he says, should be recognized because it approximates in sound the word *brag*; *plump* ("mass"), because it is a modification of *lump*; *bulkin* ("calf"), because it is related to *lambkin*. Newman not only fails to see the absurdity of this argument, he also misunderstands Arnold's objection to archaic diction as such when he says that "Arnold appears to regard what is *antiquated* as *ignoble*" (p. 324). Arnold's sole objection to intelligible archaisms is that they may surprise the reader by their incongruity.
48. Ibid., p. 302.

49. Ibid., pp. 303, 325.
50. Ibid., pp. 306, 304, 307–08; Newman's italics.
51. Ibid., pp. 320, 313–14, 319.
52. Ibid., pp. 315–18.
53. Ibid., pp. 308–09, 329, 331. Newman's defense of his diction includes a defense of his translating the names of horses (such as "Spotted" for Balius), a practice Arnold said was as if a Frenchman called Mr. Bright "M. Clair." Newman believes that if he had translated the names of persons (such as "Highmind" for Agamemnon) Arnold's criticism would have been just; but he maintains that since the Greeks called a spotted horse *balios* they read the name of Achilles' horse with a sense of its meaning.
54. Ibid., pp. 286, 288–89; Super, 1: 118; Newman, *The Iliad of Homer,* p. xvii; Newman's italics.
55. Arnold, *Essays, Literary and Critical,* pp. 279–80, 300; Newman's italics.
56. Ibid., pp. 281–83.
57. Russell, 1: 161–62.
58. Letter of Jan. 1, 1862 (Whitridge Papers).
59. Letter of Mar. 28, 1861 (Whitridge Papers).
60. Letter of Jan. 1, 1862.
61. W. C. Brownell, *Victorian Prose Masters* (New York: Scribner's, 1901), p. 156.
62. Super, 1: 168–71.
63. Ibid., 1: 170–72, 185.
64. Ibid., 1: 174–75.
65. Ibid., 1: 180–83.
66. Ibid., 1: 185.
67. Ibid., 1: 175–76.
68. T. S. Omond has observed, "Descriptions of pig-killing or boat-launching can hardly have sounded so 'heroic' to a Greek hearer as they do to us. On the other hand, we have the testimony of Greek writers as to the place which Homer held in their estimation. He is . . . the master-artist, to whom a critic like Dionysius of Halicarnassus pays almost idolizing homage, not merely for his thoughts, but for the magical perfection of his style. We can hardly be wrong, therefore, in believing that the unassuming majesty, the unforced 'nobleness,' of Homer's language, recognized by readers in all ages, is not wholly the creation of our fancy, or of that removal to a distance which an alien tongue causes. . . . Besides, it is of *general effect* that Arnold speaks, and as to that there is hardly a dissentient voice" ("Arnold and Homer," *Essays and Studies by Members of the English Association* 3 [1912]: 74).
69. Super, 1: 186–87, 177–78.
70. A decade later Newman reviewed *Literature and Dogma* for *Fraser's Magazine* (8 [June1873]: 114–34), generally condemning it but not really exacting vengeance for Arnold's treatment of his translation of Homer; Arnold made no public recognition of the review.
71. Russell, 1: 109.
72. "Homer and His Translators," *Macmillan's Magazine* 4 (Aug. 1861): 269–70.
73. Ibid., pp. 272, 277.
74. Super, 1: 207–11. René Wellek, like Frank Newman and several other critics of Arnold, is too absolute in his judgments when he writes, "The whole discussion *On Translating Homer* into English shows Arnold's constant

assumption of inherent fixed characteristics in special metrical forms. He considers the ballad meter essentially inferior to the 'hexameter and argues that Homer *must* be translated in hexameters. . . . Arnold does not recognize that the English hexameter is quite different from Homer's and thus just as 'inadequate' as blank verse or Chapman's long line, and that insistence on a particular metrical pattern begs the question of *English* poetry. The whole theory of the grand style is vitiated by this belief in form apart from meaning" (*A History of Modern Criticism*, 4: 169; Wellek's italics). This passage contains so many misrepresentations that it is difficult to unravel them all, but three in particular should be singled out. Arnold never says that Homer *must* be translated into hexameters; he does not believe "in form apart from meaning" (speaking as a practicing poet, he argues, rather, that the ballad does not lend itself to a long narrative poem of sustained nobility); and far from begging the question of English poetry, he is, on the contrary, specifically concerned with that very question—to find the best possible English counterpart of the Greek original.

75. Super, 1: 210–12.
76. *Letters of Edward FitzGerald* (London: Macmillan, 1894), 2: 302.
77. Letter of May 29, 1861 (Whitridge Papers).
78. Lowry, p. 156.
79. "Arnold on Translating Homer," *Fraser's Magazine* 63 (June 1861): 703–04, 707.
80. Ibid., pp. 706–07.
81. Ibid., pp. 710, 705, 709.
82. Ibid., pp. 711–12, 714.
83. "On a Metrical Latin Inscription copied by Mr. Blakesley at Cirta and published in his 'Four Months in Algeria,' " *Transactions of the Cambridge Philosophical Society*, vol. 10, pt. 2 (1864), pp. 377, 379; Munro's italics. Spedding answered Munro the following year in "Note, By the Author of the Review on Mr. Arnold in 'Fraser's Magazine' for June, 1861," *Fraser's Magazine* 65 (June 1862): 780–84.
84. Munro, "On a Metrical Latin Inscription," pp. 404–06.
85. Ibid., p. 408.
86. Super, 1: 193–95.
87. Ibid., 1: 192, 194, 201.
88. Ibid., 1: 198, 196, 199.
89. Ibid., 1: 203–06. In this passage Arnold may have been writing with one eye on the *Spectator*, which had been unable to decide whether Tennyson was or was not Homeric. Although the reviewer of Arnold's lectures had declared that "Ulysses" was not Homeric (34: 169), the reviewer of Newman's reply asserted that "nothing so truly Homeric . . . has ever yet been written in English" (34: 703). (The latter review has been attributed to Hutton by Robert H. Tener, "R. H. Hutton: Some Attributions," *Victorian Periodicals Newsletter*, no. 20 [June 1973], col. 9.) Arnold was also motivated by the "ridiculous elevation" of Tennyson above Wordsworth, whose poetry had the real quality of *simplicité* (Russell, 1: 191).
90. Super, 1: 202, 197.
91. Letter of Feb. 18, 1861; quoted by permission of Wellesley College. Three days later Arnold wrote to Gladstone, "I attach very little importance to my own 'hexameters, and have no design in attempting to translate Homer in that or any other measure. Still, I confess I want to see the hexameter thor-

oughly tried" (W. H. G. Armytage, "Matthew Arnold and W. E. Gladstone: Some New Letters," *University of Toronto Quarterly* 18 [1949]: 219).
92. Super, 1: 212–13.
93. Ibid., 1: 199.
94. *The Odyssey of Homer Translated into English Verse in the Spenserian Stanza* (Edinburgh and London: William Blackwood, 1861–62), 1: x–xii.
95. Super, 1: 200.
96. Letter of Jan. 1, 1862.
97. *The Odyssey of Homer*, 2: vii–viii.
98. Letter of Oct. 30, 1861 (Whitridge Papers). One paper that at first praised Arnold's hexameters later reversed itself. In its review of the Homer lectures, the *Nonconformist* said, "No one . . . will read Mr. Arnold's own specimens of translation, without desiring that he would attempt the entire Iliad. The form of metre he prefers is the hexameter; and we fully agree with him that that metre keeps the translator more nearly to 'Homer's movement' than any other, and assists the reproduction of the general effect of the original" (21 [May 1, 1861]: 356). But four years later, in a review of Wright's *Iliad*, the paper asserted, "Mr. Matthew Arnold has given the prestige of his academic position to a metre, against which lies the one sweeping and decisive objection, that it is not English" (25 [March 22, 1865]: 237). I am indebted to SenGupta for both references.
99. Super, 3: 486. At least Arnold *supposed* the compliment directed to him.
100. "Attempts at Classic Metres in Quantity," *Cornhill Magazine* 8 (Dec. 1863): 707–08. A footnote to Tennyson's comment is provided by Alexander Macmillan, who wrote to Ichabod Charles Wright on Oct. 28, 1864: "I spent three days with [Tennyson] about a fortnight ago, and the question [of hexameters] was debated between him and two scholars of eminence—one a distinguished Senior Classic of Cambridge. Beyond a general conclusion that you could not make English hexameters like Greek ones, I could see no result. It was not denied that a powerful and effective metre analogous to the Hexameter, and suited to the genius of the English language, would be a great thing" (Charles L. Graves, *Life and Letters of Alexander Macmillan* [London: Macmillan, 1910], p. 231). In a letter to Macmillan (p. 116), Charles Kingsley had earlier described the English hexameter as "that king of metres," and later, in March 1890, George Meredith was to write to Sir Frederick Pollock: "In my opinion the whole *Iliad* is open to a rendering in fluent hexameter lines. And I am sure that all other measures are inefficient [insufficient?] to give a single tone of the Homeric" (*The Letters of George Meredith*, ed. C. L. Cline [London: Oxford University Press, 1970], 2: 993).
101. *Forty Years of Friendship of Coleridge and Yarnall*, p. 10. Walter Bagehot described the *Saturday Review* as "a nearly perfect embodiment of the corrective scepticism of a sleepy intellect" (F. W. Hirst, *Early Life and Letters of John Morley* [London: Macmillan, 1927], 1: 47).
102. Scott, *Pall Mall Gazette*, p. 28.
103. *The Letters of John Addington Symonds*, ed. Herbert M. Schueller and Robert L. Peters (Detroit: Wayne State University Press, 1967–69), 1: 259.
104. Russell, 1: 157.
105. Letter of Nov. 6, 1861.

106.   Letter of Oct. 30, 1861.
107.   E. K. Chambers was clearly mistaken in supposing the author to be James Spedding (*Matthew Arnold: A Study* [Oxford: Clarendon Press, 1947], p. 70). Merle M. Bevington, who provides a good account of Arnold's conflict with the journal in *The Saturday Review, 1855–1868* (New York: Columbia University Press, 1941), pp. 136–52, says that the author was not Fitzjames Stephen, who was off the paper at the time, but he seems mistaken in describing the reviewer as "one of the Oxford men of the staff, obviously a friend of Francis Newman" (p. 138). Some of the comments about Newman scarcely suggest friendship.
108.   Letter of Dec. 3, 1862 (Whitridge Papers).
109.   Russell, 1: 155.
110.   "Homeric Translators and Critics," *Saturday Review* 12 (July 27, 1861): 95.
111.   Ibid., p. 96.
112.   Russell, 1: 165.
113.   "Homeric Translators and Critics," p. 96.
114.   Russell, 1: 164.
115.   Super, 1: 169–71, 182, 188, 214.
116.   Ibid., 1: 103.
117.   *A Letter to the Dean of Canterbury, on the Homeric Lectures of Matthew Arnold, Esq.* (London and Cambridge: Macmillan, 1864), pp. 5–6, 8, 11–16, 20.
118.   Russell, 1: 283.
119.   Buckler, p. 153.
120.   Super, 3: 286–87, 536. Professor Super observes (p. 486) that "Arnold was somewhat disingenuous to protest his ignorance that the line was aimed at himself, since he had supposed the prose compliment was for him."
121.   Ibid., 3: 287, 538. The 1865 preface serves also as the occasion for Arnold's answer to Edward Earl of Derby, chancellor of the University of Oxford and translator of Homer. In the introduction to his translation of the *Iliad*, which Arnold thought "creditable" but without "the soul of poetry," Derby obviously alluded to Arnold when he spoke of "that 'pestilent heresy' of the so-called English Hexameter; a metre wholly repugnant to the genius of our language; which can only be pressed into service by a violation of every rule of prosody." In his reply Arnold said that this criticism by his "illustrious Chancellor" and "severe chief" did not prevent his admiring Derby's translation: "I admire its freshness, its manliness, its simplicity; although, perhaps, if one looks for the charm of Homer, for his play of a divine light. . . ." (pp. 489–90, 539).
122.   Ibid., 3: 536.
123.   Russell, 1: 196.
124.   Ibid., 1: 203–04.

CHAPTER FOUR: Bishop Colenso and the Pentateuch

For the epigraphs see: R. T. Davidson and William Benham, *Life of Archibald Campbell Tait, Archbishop of Canterbury* (London: Macmillan, 1891), 1: 334–35; *The Letters of William and Dorothy Wordsworth: The Later Years*, ed. Ernest de Selincourt (Oxford: Clarendon Press, 1939), 2: 911; *Essays and Reviews* (London: J. W. Parker, 1860), pp. 372–73; A. P. Stanley, *The Life and Correspondence of Thomas Arnold*, 4th ed. (London: B. Fellowes, 1845), 1:361; Florence Emily Hardy, *The Later Years of Thomas Hardy, 1892–1928* (New York: Macmillan, 1930), p. 58.

1. Russell, 1: 111.
2. *On Liberty and Considerations on Representative Government*, ed. R. B. McCallum (Oxford: B. Blackwell, 1946), pp. 33–34.
3. *Essays and Reviews*, n. p. and p. 47.
4. Abbott and Campbell, *Life of Jowett*, 1: 210.
5. *Essays and Reviews*, pp. 180, 433.
6. *The Winnington Letters*, ed. Van Akin Burd (Cambridge: Harvard University Press, 1969), p. 379.
7. George W. Cox, *The Life of John William Colenso, Bishop of Natal* (London: W. Ridgway, 1888), 1: 2–3.
8. Schueller and Peters, *Letters of Symonds*, 1: 92.
9. In a leading article on Nov. 4, 1853, just three weeks before Colenso's consecration, the *Church and State Gazette* said that "if Professor Maurice be dismissed for his teaching, what then is to become of Dr. Colenso, the newly-appointed Bishop of Natal, who declares in his recently published volume of sermons that, if he knows much of Christianity, almost all his knowledge is owing to the teaching to which he listened at the feet of the Professor" (quoted by Wyn Rees, *Colenso Letters from Natal* [Pietermaritzburg: Shuter and Shooter, 1958], p. 34).
10. A. O. J. Cockshut, *Anglican Attitudes: A Study of Victorian Religious Controversies* (London: Collins, 1959), p. 92.
11. Cox, *Life of Colenso*, 1: 483–85.
12. Peter Hinchliff, in *John William Colenso, Bishop of Natal* (London: Nelson, 1964), p. 113, writes: "The real issue at stake was whether a missionary bishop should be allowed to preach a universalist gospel as official Anglican doctrine. As soon as *Pentateuch and Joshua* appeared, all this was forgotten. 'Biblical criticism' was an easier heresy to pin on Colenso. People felt more strongly about it."
13. Davidson and Benham, *Life of Tait*, 1: 333.
14. *Guardian* 17 (April 9, 1862): 353.
15. Davidson and Benham, *Life of Tait*, 1: 334.
16. Hinchliff, *Colenso*, p. 109, n. 4.
17. Russell, 1: 204.
18. Super, 3: 40–41. For the possibility of John Henry Newman's influence on Arnold's position in the Colenso controversy, especially in regard to the distinctions between the few and the many and between instruction and edification, see David J. DeLaura, "Matthew Arnold and John Henry Newman: The 'Oxford Sentiment' and the Religion of the Future," *Texas Studies in Literature and Language* 6 (Supplement 1965) : 591–98, and *Hebrew and Hellene in Victorian England: Newman, Arnold, and Pater* (Austin: University of Texas Press, 1969), p. 28–39.
19. Super, 3: 43–47.
20. Ibid., 3: 48.
21. Cockshut, *Anglican Attitudes*, p. 94.
22. Super, 3: 49.
23. Lowry, p. 117. At the outset of his lucid account of Spinoza's influence on Arnold, R. H. Super, *Time-Spirit*, p. 65, says that 1850 "is almost certainly too late a date for first acquaintance."
24. Super, 3: 49–53, 170–71, 523.

25. From an unpublished letter to Lady de Rothschild, no date; quoted by permission of Mr. Evelyn de Rothschild.

26. Letter of Dec. 9, 1862; quoted by Super, 3: 415.

27. Russell, 1: 205–06.

28. Ethel H. Thomson, *The Life and Letters of William Thomson, Archbishop of York* (London: John Lane, 1919), p. 151.

29. J. M. Robertson, *Modern Humanists Reconsidered* (London: Watts, 1927), p. 123.

30. Samuel C. Chew, in *A Literary History of England*, ed. Albert C. Baugh (New York: Appleton-Century-Crofts, 1948), p. 1298.

31. See, for example, "Bishop Colenso on the Pentateuch," *Saturday Review* 14 (Nov. 29, 1862): 657–59; "Mr. Matthew Arnold on the Aristocratic Creed," *Spectator* 35 (Dec. 27, 1862): 1438; *The Life of Frederick Denison Maurice, Chiefly Told in His Own Letters*, ed. Frederick Maurice (London: Macmillan, 1884), 2: 423; Frederic Harrison, *Autobiographic Memoirs* (London: Macmillan, 1911), 1: 284; and Charles Morgan, *The House of Macmillan (1843–1943)* (New York: Macmillan, 1944), p. 65.

32. *The Pentateuch and Book of Joshua Critically Examined* (London: Longman, Green, Longman, Roberts & Green, 1862), p. 5.

33. Hallam Tennyson, *Memoir*, 2: 172.

34. Mark Pattison, *Memoirs* (London: Macmillan, 1885), pp. 315–16.

35. *An Essay on the Development of Christian Doctrine* (New York: Longmans, Green, 1900), pp. 327–28.

36. *Apologia Pro Vita Sua*, ed. A. Dwight Culler, Riverside ed. (Boston: Houghton Mifflin, 1956), p. 244.

37. Super, 3: 68.

38. The passage, quoted by Cockshut, *Anglican Attitudes*, pp. 99–100, appears in the *Guardian*'s review of Colenso's volume, 17 (Dec. 3, 1862): 1148–50.

39. Davidson and Benham, *Life of Tait*, 1: 343.

40. Quoted by Abbott and Campbell, *Life of Jowett*, 1: 295, n.

41. Davidson and Benham, *Life of Tait*, 1: 291. Temple later changed his mind. After seeing him in 1870, when he was bishop of Exeter, Arnold wrote to his mother: "I told him I approved of his withdrawal of his Essay, which the Liberals, who turn religion into mere politics, are so angry with him for; he seemed pleased. I told him also that I thought the *Essays and Reviews* could not be described throughout as 'a free handling, in *a becoming spirit*, of religious matters,' and he said he quite agreed with me" (Russell, 2: 32).

42. Quoted by Cockshut, *Anglican Attitudes*, pp. 98–99.

43. Quoted by Cox, *Life of Colenso*, 1: 492. Stanley's article was attacked by Goldwin Smith in a manner that "made much noise" (Russell, 1: 157), but to the end Stanley remained loyal to Colenso. He had regretted the book "extremely" but had refused to "join in the indiscriminate outcry against an evidently honest and single-minded religious man" (R. E. Prothero and G. G. Bradley, *The Life and Correspondence of Arthur Penrhyn Stanley* [New York: Scribner's, 1894], 2: 100). In 1865, before the Lower House of Convocation, he spoke against a motion in effect denouncing Colenso (Cockshut, *Anglican Attitudes*, p. 108), and the following year he defended him in a speech in Convocation, quoting an artisan's remark to a missionary clergyman: "I would go twenty miles to hear Bishop Colenso preach, he is so honest like" (Cox, *Life of Colenso*, 2: 104). One of Stanley's strongest statements was made at a meeting of the Society for the Propagation of the Gospel: "The

Bishop of Natal is the one colonial bishop who has translated the Bible into the language of the natives of his diocese. He is the one colonial bishop who, when he believed a native to be wronged, left his diocese, journeyed to London, and never rested till he had procured the reversal of that wrong. He is the one colonial bishop who, as soon as he had done this, returned immediately to his diocese and his work. For these acts he has never received any praise, any encouragement, from this the oldest of our Missionary Societies. For these deeds he will be remembered when you who censure him are dead, buried, and forgotten" (quoted by William Knight, *Retrospects* [New York: Scribner's, 1905], p. 165). According to Moncure Conway, Ruskin "honoured Stanley for the high position he took in standing by Colenso" (*Autobiography*, 2: 100). To all of this might be added the judgment that Francis Palgrave passed on Stanley: "He has *les défauts de sa qualité*: so chivalrous, that he, perhaps open-eyed-ly, perpetually backs men he only half or not at all agreed with from pure charity" (Gwenllian F. Palgrave, *Francis Turner Palgrave: His Journals and Memories of His Life* [London: Longmans, Green, 1899], p. 246). Arnold's friendship with Stanley has been treated by Eugene L. Williamson in "Words from Westminster Abbey: Matthew Arnold and Arthur Stanley," *Studies in English Literature* 11 (1971): 749–61.

44. Letter of Dec. 25, 1862; quoted by Super, 3: 420.
45. Russell, 1: 206–07.
46. Super, 3: 51.
47. Cox, *Life of Colenso*, 1: 235.
48. Russell, 1: 211.
49. Super, 3: 57, 64.
50. "Mr. Matthew Arnold on the Aristocratic Creed," *Spectator* 35 (Dec. 27, 1862): 1438–39; attributed to R. H. Hutton by Tener, col. 15.
51. "Spinoza and Professor Arnold," *Spectator* 36 (Jan. 3, 1863): 1472–74.
52. To George Eliot, Maurice was "dim and foggy" (Haight, *George Eliot Letters*, 2: 125); to Jowett, "misty and confused" (Abbott and Campbell, *Life of Jowett*, 2: 45); to John Moreley, "nebulous" (*Recollections*, 1: 276). Listening to Maurice was for Aubrey de Vere "like eating pea-soup with a fork" and for Grant Duff like drinking "spiritual champagne"; someone remarked of one of his books that it read "as if all the good words in the language had got drunk, and were wandering up and down in it" (Mountstuart E. Grant Duff, *Notes from a Diary 1851–1872* [London: J. Murray, 1897], 1: 78–79; 2: 143). Arnold said of him after his death, "I cannot read Maurice, but then I never could read him when he was alive" (letter to his sister Frances, April 29, 1884; Whitridge Papers).
53. Frederick Maurice, *Life of Maurice*, 2: 490. Colenso's widow later recalled with bitterness what she regarded as Maurice's injustice to her husband (Rees, *Colenso Letters*, pp. 390–91, 395–96, 411).
54. "Professor Arnold's Review of Stanley's *Jewish Church*," *Spectator* 36 (Feb. 7, 1863): 1608.
55. Letter of Jan. 21, 1863 (Whitridge Papers).
56. "The Bishop and the Professor," *Examiner*, Jan. 10, 1863, p. 20.
57. "The Bishop and the Professor," *Examiner*, Jan. 17, 1863, p. 36. "I hope these liberals, and I, and all of us," Arnold wrote with wry amusement to his mother, "shall improve as time goes on" (letter of Jan. 21, 1863).
58. J. G., "The Bishop and the Professor," *Examiner*, Jan. 17, 1863, p. 36.
59. "Bishop Colenso and His Critics," *Examiner*, Jan. 24, 1863, p. 52.

60. *Memorials of Albert Venn Dicey,* ed. Robert S. Rait (London: Macmillan, 1925), p. 138.
61. Graves, *Life of Macmillan,* p. 197.
62. Schueller and Peters, *Letters of Symonds,* 1: 377.
63. Letter of Jan. 21, 1863.
64. "The Educated Few," *Saturday Review* 15 (Jan. 17, 1863): 71–72.
65. "The Few and the Many," *London Review* 6 (Jan. 31, 1863): 111.
66. "Bishop Colenso's Criticisms; and Mr. Isaac Taylor's Considerations," *Nonconformist* 23 (Feb. 4, 1863): 96 (SenGupta).
67. *John Bull,* Jan. 3, 1863, p. 11 (SenGupta).
68. *English Churchman,* Jan. 8, 1863, p. 35; Jan. 15, p. 59.
69. Russell, 1: 205.
70. Graves, *Life of Macmillan,* pp. 197–98.
71. Russell, 1: 208–09, 212.
72. Ibid., 1: 212.
73. Conway, *Autobiography,* 2: 100.
74. Super, 3: 65.
75. Ibid., 3: 65–66, 80.
76. Ibid., 3: 68.
77. Brown, *Arnold: Study in Conflict,* p. 76.
78. Super, 3: 66, 75.
79. Ibid., 3: 68–69. Arnold's use of the concept of a spirit of the time has been fully treated by Fraser Neiman in "The Zeitgeist of Matthew Arnold," *PMLA* 72 (1957): 977–96.
80. *Englishman* 37 (Feb. 14, 1863): 1 (SenGupta).
81. "Literary Honesty," *Saturday Review* 15 (Feb. 7, 1863) : 169–70.
82. Letter of Feb. 18, 1863 (Whitridge Papers).
83. Frederick Maurice, *Life of Maurice,* 2: 442.
84. "Professor Arnold's Review of Stanley's *Jewish Church,*" p. 1608.
85. Letter of Feb. 11, 1863 (Whitridge Papers).
86. *Reader* 1 (Feb. 7, 1863): 152.
87. Russell, 1: 219.
88. "Truth *versus* Edification," *Westminster Review* 23 (April 1863): 512–13. Greg's article appeared anonymously in the *Westminster* but is reprinted in his *Literary and Social Judgments* (London: N. Trübner, 1868), pp. 380–403.
89. Russell, 1: 211.
90. Ibid., 1: 242. For Arnold's previous plans for the article see pp. 208, 212.
91. Ibid., 1: 208.
92. Maurice, "Spinoza and Professor Arnold," pp. 1472–74.
93. Super, 3: 159, 174–75, 178.
94. Ibid., 3: 445–46.
95. Buckler, pp. 66–67.
96. Super, 3: 276, 537–38.
97. Ibid., 5: 206.
98. *Morning Star,* Feb. 13, 1869, p. 3.
99. *The Creed of Christendom,* 4th ed. (London: Trübner, 1875), 1: xxiii. Greg's criticism was first made in the preface to the third edition, here reprinted.
100. Super, 7: 147.
101. Ibid., 3: 282.

102. Ibid., 3: 262, 264–66, 275.
103. Ibid., 3: 268, 270, 274.
104. Ibid., 3: 277–79, 533.
105. Ibid., 3: 278, 282; my italics.
106. Ibid., 3: 261, 268, 284, 281, 271; my italics.
107. Rees, *Colenso Letters*, pp. 181, 206.

CHAPTER FIVE: Philistinism and *Geist*

For the epigraphs see: *Collected Letters of Samuel Taylor Coleridge*, ed. E. L. Griggs (Oxford: Clarendon Press, 1956–71), 3: 253–54; *Nostromo*, chap. 13; *Journal*, trans. Mrs. Humphry Ward (London: Macmillan, 1891), p. 60; *The Idea of a University*, Discourse 7; Oxenford, *Conversations of Goethe*, p. 433.

1. Russell, 1: 240.
2. *Essays of George Eliot*, ed. Thomas Pinney (New York: Columbia University Press, 1963), p. 247. George Eliot's article on Heine originally appeared in the *Westminster Review* 65 (Jan. 1856): 1–33.
3. See, for example, Elsie M. Butler, "Heine in England and Matthew Arnold," *German Life and Letters* 9 (1956): 157–65; Sol Liptzin, "Heine, the Continuator of Goethe: A Mid-Victorian Legend," *Journal of English and Germanic Philology* 43 (1944): 317–25; and Charles D. Wright, "Matthew Arnold on Heine as 'Continuator of Goethe,' " *Studies in Philology* 65 (1968): 693–701.
4. The essay on Heine is in Super, 3: 107–32.
5. Ibid., 3: 183–211.
6. Ibid., 3: 232–57.
7. Ibid., 3: 258–85.
8. Letter to Lady de Rothschild, dated "Monday morning"; quoted by permission of Mr. Evelyn de Rothschild.
9. Letter of Oct. 29, 1864; quoted by permission of Mr. Evelyn de Rothschild.
10. Norton and Howe, *Letters of Norton*, 1: 476.
11. R. J. White, ed., *Liberty, Equality, Fraternity* (London: Cambridge University Press, 1967), pp. 3, 7, 10, 12, 14.
12. Norton and Howe, *Letters of Norton*, 1: 476.
13. *Letters to a Victorian Editor, Henry Allon, Editor of the "British Quarterly Review"*, ed. Albert Peel (London: Independent Press, 1929), p. 179.
14. Rait, *Memorials of Dicey*, p. 139.
15. Haight, *George Eliot Letters*, 3: 438.
16. White, *Liberty*, p. 16.
17. *A Selection from Goldwin Smith's Correspondence*, ed. Arnold Haultain (London: T. W. Laurie, n.d.), p. 183.
18. White, *Liberty*, p. 9.
19. *Edinburgh Review* 107 (Jan. 1858); 183.
20. Lowry, p. 164. But Kenneth Allott has pointed out that Arnold's memory of reading the review was so tied up with his memory of reading Hughes's novel that he later assigned it undue importance (*Poems of Arnold*, p. 444). See also the previously cited article by Harvey Kerpneck, "The Road to Rugby Chapel."
21. Russell, 1: 118. Stephen's review, "Mr. Matthew Arnold on the Italian Question," *Saturday Review* 8 (Aug. 13, 1859): 188–89, is reprinted by Merle

M. Bevington in *Matthew Arnold's "England and the Italian Question"*, pp. 59–74.

22.   *Matthew Arnold the Ethnologist* (Evanston: Northwestern University Press, 1951), p. 197.

23.   Super, 3: 250.

24.   Russell, 1: 282, where the clause concerning "the judicious" has been deleted.

25.   Letter of Dec. 30, 1864 (Whitridge Papers).

26.   *Saturday Review* 18 (Dec. 3, 1864): 683–85.

27.   Russell, 1: 282; letter of Dec. 20, 1864.

28.   Letter of Dec. 1, 1864; quoted by Super, 4: 345.

29.   Russell, 1: 282–83.

30.   Ibid., 1: 286, 288–89, 291.

31.   Augustine Birrell, *Frederick Locker-Lampson: A Character Sketch* (London: Constable, 1920), p. 127. The passage was called to my attention by Geoffrey Tillotson's use of it in "Matthew Arnold's Prose: Theory and Practice," p. 97.

32.   Super, 3: 482. Arnold's preface is found in the same volume, pp. 286–90, 535–39.

33.   Russell, 1: 225. The *Guardian* was a Church of England weekly founded in 1846 and owned by Gladstone.

34.   *Guardian* 18 (May 13, 1863): 454.

35.   *Guardian* 16 (May 29, 1861): 514.

36.   *Guardian* 20 (May 17, 1865): 502. In "My Countrymen" Arnold would answer, "So I take comfort when I find the *Guardian* reproaching me with having no influence; for I know what influence means,—a party, practical proposals, action . . ." (Super, 5: 28).

37.   *Guardian* 28 (June 11, 1873): 781.

38.   W. F. Monypenny and G. E. Buckle, *The Life of Benjamin Disraeli, Earl of Beaconsfield* (New York: Macmillan, 1910–20), 4: 370–73.

39.   "Mr. Disraeli at Oxford," *Examiner*, Dec. 3, 1864, p. 773.

40.   "Mr. Clay on the Classics," *Saturday Review* 18 (Nov. 12, 1864): 593.

41.   Super, 3: 530–34.

42.   Ibid., 3: 243, 247.

43.   "Provincial Style," *Saturday Review* 18 (Aug. 6, 1864): 175.

44.   Morley, *Recollections*, 2: 334. John Douglas Cook, the editor of the *Saturday Review*, once spoke of Smith as his "most effective pen" (W. R. Nicoll, *James Macdonell, Journalist* [London: Hodder and Stoughton, 1890], p. 188).

45.   Rait, *Memorials of Dicey*, p. 182.

46.   In chapter 24. The enmity between Smith and Disraeli went back to 1850, when Smith attacked him in a series of anonymous articles in the *Morning Chronicle*.

47.   Haultain, *Reminiscences*, p. 71.

48.   Elisabeth Wallace, *Goldwin Smith: Victorian Liberal* (Toronto: University of Toronto Press, 1957), p. 57, n. 4.

49.   Lowry, p. 142; Russell, 1: 157.

50.   "On a Citation from M. Renan in the 'Cornhill Magazine' for August," *Daily News*, Aug. 4, 1864, p. 2. For Arnold's attribution of the article to Smith see Russell, 1: 272.

51.   Russell, 1: 294.

52. Letter of Mar. 18, 1865; quoted by Super, 3: 483. One sign of the topical nature of the preface was the continuing debate in the *Examiner* concerning the Victorians' capacity for appreciating a joke. Presbyter Anglicanus solemnly protested that he had understood Disraeli's joke but thought it contemptible ("The Philistines of the Nineteenth Century," Mar. 11, 1865, p. 148); the paper itself pointed out that "earnest men" had censured Disraeli for trifling with "the good feeling of the country" (review of *Essays in Criticism*, Mar. 4, 1865, p. 134); and a correspondent sarcastically wrote that he now recognized Colenso's real crime to have been that he "was too serious; he should have written a Comic History of the Deluge, and Mr. Arnold's criticisms would have been disarmed" ("Comic Theology," Mar. 25, 1865, p. 180).

53. Letter of Feb. 15, 1865; quoted in part by Super, 3: 482.

54. Russell, 1: 288. In a passage imperfectly reproduced by Russell, Arnold adds: "then Mrs. Arnold is always thrown into a nervous terror by my writing anything which she thinks likely to draw down attacks on me."

55. Letter of Feb. 15, 1865.

56. *North American Review*, 101 (July 1865), 207. Arnold said that he liked this article "as well as anything" he had seen (Russell, 1: 359).

57. *Examiner*, Feb. 18, 1865, p. 104.

58. *Westminster Review* 27 (Apr. 1865) : 634–35.

59. "Arnold's Essays in Criticism," *Pall Mall Gazette*, Feb. 24, 1865, p. 7.

60. "Matthew Arnold's Essays," *Spectator* 38 (Feb. 25, 1865): 214–15. Arnold's comment on the review, quoted earlier, was that it had "Hutton's fault of seeing so very far into a millstone" (Russell, 1: 289).

61. *North British Review*, American ed., 42 (Mar. 1865): 88. Arnold liked the rest of the review, explaining the objection to his "vivacities" as being due to "a Scotchman who writes" (Russell, 1: 290). The reviewer was H. H. Lancaster, lawyer and essayist (Houghton, *Wellesley Index*, 1: 689).

62. "Essays and Essayists," *London Review* 10 (June 10, 1865): 616.

63. *British Quarterly Review* 41 (Apr. 1865): 544.

64. "Mr. Matthew Arnold Amongst the Philistines," *Saturday Review* 19 (Feb. 25, 1865): 235–36.

65. Russell, 1: 290.

66. It is found in Super, 2: 3–29.

67. Russell, 1: 153.

68. *Athenaeum*, July 6, 1861, pp. 15–16.

69. "Popular Education in England," *Edinburgh Review* 114 (July 1861): 11. The writer was Henry Reeve, the editor (Houghton, *Wellesley Index*, 1: 510).

70. "The New Minute on Education," *Eclectic Review*, 8th ser., 1 (Oct. 1861): 495–96.

71. *Inquirer* 20 (Nov. 2, 1861): 787.

72. "Popular Education," *Literary Gazette* 6 (May 18, 1861): 462.

73. Russell, 1: 157, 174, 183, 185, 187.

74. Super, 2: 244–51, 257–61.

75. Ibid., 4: 1–7. The *Pall Mall Gazette*'s criticism appeared in a leading article, Dec. 20, 1865, pp. 1–2.

76. Letter of Jan. 30, 1864, in W. H. G. Armytage, "Matthew Arnold and Richard Cobden in 1864: Some Recently Discovered Letters," *Review of English Studies* 25 (1949): 251.

77. Russell, 1: 241.
78. The first two numbers of *A French Eton* are reprinted in Super, 2: 262–301.
79. *Spectator* 37 (Feb. 6, 1864): 162.
80. "Middle Class Public Schools," *Museum and English Journal of Education*, n.s. 1 (Apr. 2, 1864): 14–15.
81. *Nonconformist* 24 (Feb. 10, 1864): 118.
82. Armytage, "Arnold and Cobden," p. 252.
83. *Athenaeum*, July 6, 1861, p. 16.
84. The last number of *A French Eton* is in Super, 2: 301–25.
85. *Athenaeum*, July 30, 1864, pp. 137–38. The review was by C. Cordy Jeaffreson (Marchand, *"Athenaeum": Mirror of Victorian Culture*, p. 86, n. 227).
86. *Educational Times* 17 (Sept. 1864): 134 (SenGupta).
87. *Westminster Review* 26 (Oct. 1864): 500.
88. "Middle-Class Education in England," *Cornhill Magazine* 10 (Oct. 1864): 418, 423. For the authorship see Houghton, *Wellesley Index*, 1: 338.
89. Russell, 1: 360.
90. It is reprinted in Super, 5: 3–31.
91. Russell, 1: 366–69.
92. *Letters from Owen Meredith (Robert, First Earl of Lytton) to Robert and Elizabeth Barrett Browning*, ed. A. B. Harlan and J. L. Harlan, Jr., Baylor University's Browning Interests, Series 10 (Waco: Baylor University, 1936), p. 224. He added that "ever since" reading "that excellent paper" he had "been propagating copies of it."
93. *London Review* 12 (Feb. 3, 1866): 155; (Feb. 10, 1866), 165.
94. *Sunday Times*, Feb. 11, 1866, p. 2 (SenGupta).
95. *Court Circular* 17 (Feb. 10, 1866): 135 (SenGupta).
96. *Press* 14 (Feb. 3, 1866) : 115.
97. *Westmorland Gazette and Kendal Advertiser*, Feb. 17, 1866, p. 3 (SenGupta).
98. Edinburgh *Evening Courant*, Jan. 31, 1866, p. 4. Two more leading articles based on "My Countrymen" appeared on Feb. 2 (p. 4) and 3 (p. 6), the latter being reprinted in the supplement of Feb. 6 (p. 11).
99. Russell, 1: 367.
100. *Illustrated Times* 8 (Feb. 10, 1866): 90 (SenGupta).
101. *Illustrated London News*, Feb. 10, 1866, p. 142.
102. "An Intellectual Angel," *Spectator* 39 (Feb. 3, 1866): 126. The offending passage was later withdrawn (Super, 5: 372, 488–89), presumably in response to the *Spectator*'s criticism and Kinglake's courtesy at a dinner party in 1867.
103. F., "Mr. Sampson," *Examiner*, Feb. 17, 1866, pp. 99–100 (SenGupta). Arnold thought the parody so amusing that he wanted his wife to see it, a wish he did not always express about criticism of his writings (Russell, 1: 372).
104. "Mr. Arnold on the Middle Classes," *Saturday Review* 21 (Feb. 10, 1866): 163.
105. "Your Countrymen," *Pall Mall Gazette*, Mar. 14, 1866, pp. 4–5; March 17, pp. 4–5.
106. Russell, 1: 374.
107. It is reprinted in Super, 5: 32–36. The original title was later changed to "A Courteous Explanation."
108. Russell, 1: 376–77. Five days later, on March 29, the *Pall Mall*

ɢᴀᴢᴇᴛᴛᴇ published a third letter from Horace (Kirby), which Arnold apparently saw no need to acknowledge.

109. "The Part of England in the European Crisis," *Daily News*, July 17, 1866, p. 5.

110. Super, 3: 298–99, 328, 341–42, 382.

111. Ibid., 5: 37–42.

112. Russell, 1: 390.

113. Buckler, p. 93.

114. "The Part of England in the European Crisis," *Daily News*, July 25, 1866, p. 5.

115. "The End of the War," *Illustrated Times* 9 (July 28, 1866): 49–50 (SenGupta).

116. " 'Get Geist,' " *Spectator* 39 (July 28, 1866): 828–29.

117. Super, 5: 43–47.

118. Ibid., 5: 48–56.

119. Ibid., 3: 390.

120. Ibid., 5: 29.

121. *Times*, Sept. 8, 1866, p. 8.

122. *Times*, Sept. 14, 1866, p. 9.

123. *Times*, Sept. 14, 1866, p. 6.

124. *Daily Telegraph*, Sept. 8, 1866, pp. 4–5.

125. Nicoll, *James Macdonell*, pp. 164, 199. Macdonell's authorship was first noted by Super, 5: 394.

126. Russell, 1: 393.

127. Super, 5: 57–58, 67.

128. See Buckler, p. 93, and Russell, 1: 339–40, 399.

129. "Stein in Ireland," *Pall Mall Gazette*, Nov. 13, 1866, p. 3, and reprinted by Neiman, pp. 114–15.

130. Super, 5: 62–64.

131. *Standard*, Nov. 12, 1866, p. 4 (SenGupta).

132. Russell, 1: 399, 419. The introduction is in Super, 3: 387–95.

133. An account of *On the Study of Celtic Literature* would be incomplete without some mention of Lord Strangford, "a *savant* of the very first force on these subjects" (Russell, 1: 376) who gave Arnold assistance, mostly philological, in the preparation of the lectures for publication in a single volume, and whose notes and comments Arnold "inserted, as a check upon some of the positions adopted in the text." In the introduction, moreover, he answered Lord Strangford's objection to classifying D. W. Nash as a "Celt-hater" ("Mr. Arnold on Celtic Literature," *Pall Mall Gazette*, Mar. 19, 1866, pp. 3–4); and he responded to his comment on "the impracticability of finding a suitable professor" to fill a Chair of Celtic ("Celtic at Oxford," *Pall Mall Gazette*, Sept. 22, 1866, pp. 11–12) by withdrawing the proposal.

134. *Westminster Review* 32 (Oct. 1867): 605.

135. *British Quarterly Review* 46 (July 1867): 244.

136. "Mr. Arnold on the Celtic Genius," *Spectator* 40 (June 22, 1867): 696; attributed to Hutton by Tener, "R. H. Hutton," col. 33, where the pagination is incorrectly given.

137. Russell, 1: 397.

CHAPTER SIX: The Apostle and the Enemies of Culture

For the epigraphs see: *Notebooks*, ed. Kathleen Coburn (New York: Pantheon Books, 1957–   ), vol. 1, entry 1072; *Nostromo*, chap. 6; *Works* (London: Henry G. Bohn, 1854–58), 2: 370, the use of the quotation being suggested by Ian Gregor's doctoral dissertation (1954) at the University of Durham; *Notes towards the Definition of Culture* (New York: Harcourt, Brace, 1949), p. 19; *Biographia Literaria*, chap. 11.

1. "Our Venetian Constitution," *Fortnightly Review*, n.s. 1 (Mar. 1867), 268, 270, 276–77.

2. Maurice Cowling, *1867: Disraeli, Gladstone, and Revolution* (London: Cambridge University Press, 1967), pp. 22, 31–32.

3. Russell, 1: 406.

4. Buckler, p. 85.

5. See Russell, 1: 406–20, *passim*, and William E. Buckler, "Studies in Three Arnold Problems," *PMLA* 73 (1958): 260.

6. Harrison's article fixed itself in Arnold's memory; nearly twenty years later, in "The Nadir of Liberalism," he quoted from it again (*Nineteenth Century* 19 [May 1886]: 653–54). For a detailed account of the relationship between Arnold and Harrison see Martha Salmon Vogeler, "Matthew Arnold and Frederic Harrison: the Prophet of Culture and the Prophet of Positivism," *Studies in English Literature* 2 (1962): 441–62.

7. Super, 5: 75–76.

8. Ibid., 5: 87, 109, 112.

9. Mrs. Arnold's personal diary, June 7, 1867 (Yale Papers).

10. Super, 5: 87–114.

11. Russell, 1: 251, 237.

12. Letter of July 4, 1867 (Whitridge Papers).

13. *Morning Star*, June 28, 1867. John Bright's association with the *Star*, amounting to editorial influence, is described by Justin McCarthy, *Reminiscences* (New York: Harper, 1899), 1: 161–63.

14. *Daily Telegraph*, July 2, 1867, pp. 6–7.

15. Russell, 1: 431.

16. "Mr. Matthew Arnold Again," *London Review* 15 (July 13, 1867): 39–40.

17. *Illustrated Times* 10 (July 6, 1867): 10 (SenGupta).

18. Russell, 1: 428.

19. "Mr. Matthew Arnold on the *Nonconformist*," *Nonconformist* 28 (July 10, 1867): 557–58.

20. Leeds *Mercury*, July 15, 1867, p. 2.

21. "Mr. Arnold on the Enemies of Culture," *Spectator* 40 (July 6, 1867): 746–48; attributed to Hutton by Tener, "R. H. Hutton," col. 33.

22. Letter of July 26, 1867 (Whitridge Papers).

23. Aberdeen *Free Press*, July 12, 1867, p. 2.

24. "Mr. Arnold's Theory of Perfection," Aberdeen *Free Press*, July 19, 1867, p. 5.

25. "The Enemies of Culture," *Globe and Traveller*, June 29, 1867, p. 2.

26. "Literary Notes from London," Liverpool *Daily Post*, July 17, 1867, p. 7.

27. "A Philistine," "A Plea for the Uncultivated," and [E. L. Godkin], "Sweetness and Light," *Nation* 5 (Sept. 12, 1867): 215, 212–13.

28. *Westminster Review* 32 (Oct. 1867): 602–03.

29. "The Poet of Culture," *Eclectic and Congregational Review* 13 (Sept. 1867): 184.

30. Haight, *George Eliot Letters*, 5: 445

31. Letter to his mother, dated "Thursday morning" (Whitridge Papers).

32. "The Prophet of Culture," *Macmillan's Magazine* 16 (Aug. 1867): 271–80; reprinted in *Miscellaneous Essays and Addresses* (London: Macmillan, 1904), pp. 40–58. Sidgwick further criticized Arnold's concept of culture in "The Pursuit of Culture," *Practical Ethics: A Collection of Addresses and Essays* (London: Swan Sonnenschein, 1898), pp. 205–34.

33. Russell, 1: 432–33. Years later, after the publication of Arnold's letters, Harrison rejoiced to learn that his "little piece gave him such innocent pleasure" (*Tennyson, Ruskin, Mill and Other Literary Estimates* [London: Macmillan, 1899], p. 129).

34. *Fortnightly Review*, n.s. 2 (Nov. 1867): 603–14; reprinted in *The Choice of Books and Other Literary Pieces* (London: Macmillan, 1899), pp. 97–118.

35. *Morning Star*, Nov. 4, 1867, p. 3.

36. "Mr. Matthew Arnold on Culture," *Saturday Review* 24 (July 20, 1867): 79.

37. "Culture and Action," *Saturday Review* 24 (Nov. 9, 1867): 593.

38. Buckler, p. 86.

39. A notable exception was George Eliot, who wrote to Harrison that she "regarded the word 'culture' as a verbal equivalent for the highest mental result of past and present influences" (Haight, *George Eliot Letters*, 4: 395).

40. Letter dated "Thursday morning."

41. *Matthew Arnold*, pp. 252–55.

42. Super, 5: 115–36.

43. *Illustrated London News*, Jan. 4, 1868, p. 10.

44. *Daily Telegraph*, Dec. 27, 1867, p. 4.

45. *Illustrated Times* 12 (Jan. 4, 1868): 7 (SenGupta).

46. *Daily News*, Dec. 30, 1867, p. 4.

47. William E. Buckler (in "Studies in Three Arnold Problems," p. 261) has pointed out that there is no evidence that Arnold originally intended to write more than one of the "Anarchy and Authority" papers, but by the middle of December he had decided that at least two or perhaps even three would be necessary. "I am getting on with the second paper," he wrote to George Smith, the publisher, on December 18, "but matter is so abundant that it will very likely run into a third—but the third will certainly end it. I suppose there is no objection to a third and I need not put a bridle on my fine frenzy?"

48. Super, 5: 505. How well Arnold knew Comte is difficult to ascertain, but his slight regard for him goes back to at least 1848, when he wrote to Clough: "By trivialities do you mean novels as opposed to Comte and them of that kidney—Figaro as opposed to the Contrat Social. For amongst a *people* of readers the litterature [*sic*] is a greater engine than the philosophy. Which last they change very fast—oh said a F[renc]hman to me the other day— Comte—Comte has been quite passé these 10 years" (Lowry, p. 74). But according to Harrison, on the subject of Comte Arnold did not know what he was talking about. Years later, after Arnold's death, Harrison recalled Arnold's "telling us with triumph that he had sought to exclude from a certain library a work of Herbert Spencer, by reading to the committee a passage therefrom which he pronounced to be clumsy in style. He knew as little about Spencer's *Synthetic Philosophy* as he did about Comte's, which he pretended to discuss with an air of laughable superiority, at which no doubt he was himself the first to laugh (*Tennyson, Ruskin, Mill*, p. 132).

49. Super, 5: 137, 139, 143.

50. Arnold never permitted Harrison to forget the phrase "coherent, interdependent, subordinate, and derivative principles," which had been employed against him in "Culture: A Dialogue," and continued to use it as late as *God and the Bible* (Super, 7: 520), published two years after he had expressed, in *Literature and Dogma*, a "hope to make our peace with the Comtists" (Super, 6: 174). The phrase became a familiar part of Arnold's strategy of upholding flexibility of mind (which he implied he had) as opposed to systematic thought (to which he modestly made no claim at the same time that he ridiculed it).

51. *Times*, Jan. 3, 1868, p. 7; Dec. 2, 1867, p. 9.

52. Super, 5, 157.

53. Ibid., 5: 159–60.

54. *Morning Star*, Jan. 30, 1868, p. 4.

55. See Frederic E. Faverty, *Matthew Arnold the Ethnologist*, pp. 162–85.

56. Sidgwick, "Prophet of Culture," p. 275.

57. Super, 5: 184, 186, 190.

58. Ibid., 5: 191.

59. *Globe*, July 2, 1868, p. 1 (Wilkins).

60. "The Politics of Young England, II," *Fraser's Magazine* 77 (Mar. 1868): 351.

61. *Illustrated London News*, July 4, 1868, p. 3.

62. "Matthew Arnold *versus* Thomas Carlyle," *Spectator* 41 (July 4, 1868): 789–90; attributed to Hutton by Tener, "R. H. Hutton," col. 37.

63. Super, 5: 205–21.

64. Russell, 1: 452.

65. *Spectator* 39 (Sept. 15, 1866): 1028.

66. Russell, 1: 394.

67. Ibid., 1: 452.

68. See *David Gray, and Other Essays, Chiefly on Poetry* (London: Sampson Low, Son, and Marston, 1868), p. 291, where Buchanan apparently alludes to a letter that Arnold wrote to him in October 1866 (see Russell, 1: 394).

69. Letter of Mar. 2, 1868 (Whitridge Papers). In the same letter Arnold says that he has been told that Buchanan "has a long article, in the strain of what he has already vented, to appear as soon as he can find an editor to take it." For an account of the crisis in Buchanan's life see Harriett Jay, *Robert Buchanan* (London: T. Fisher Unwin, 1903), pp. 125–31.

70. *Spectator* 41 (Feb. 8, 1868): 170.

71. Russell, 1: 452.

72. Buchanan, *David Gray*, pp. 177–200.

73. Ibid., pp. 290–91, 296.

74. "Mr. Buchanan's Essays," *Spectator* 41 (Feb. 8, 1868): 165; attributed to Hutton by Tener, "R. H. Hutton," col. 36. For Buchanan's phrase, "fate-stricken men," see Buchanan, *David Gray*, p. 299.

75. "Mr. Buchanan on Literary Morality," *Spectator* 41 (Feb. 15, 1868): 197–98.

76. "Mr. Buchanan and His Reviewer," *Spectator* 41 (Feb. 22, 1868): 227.

77. And from the *Pall Mall Gazette*, which attacked Buchanan on Feb. 21, 1868, pp. 11–12.

78. Super, 5: 214–18. Arnold's gentleness in dealing with Buchanan's unprovoked attacks was perhaps responsible for turning an acerbic critic into a warm admirer. Four years later, signing himself as Walter Hutcheson, Bu-

chanan wrote in *St. Paul's Magazine* (11 [Sept. 1872]: 344): "Just at this present moment we want a great poet, if we want anything; and we particularly want a great poet with the courage to 'loosen' the conventional poetic speech. . . . Among living men, one poet at least is to be applauded for having, inspired by Goethe, 'kicked' at the traces of rhyme, and written such poems as 'The Strayed Reveller,' 'Rugby Chapel,' and 'Heine's Grave' " (quoted by SenGupta, p. 18). And still later Arnold credited Buchanan with the authorship of a "rhapsodical" review of his poetry (Russell, 2: 172) in which he, "of all living poets," was said to have "most nearly attained the golden mean" (*Light*, Aug. 31, 1878, p. 649).

79. *Oxford Chronicle and Berks and Bucks Gazette*, Aug. 15, 1868, p. 6 (SenGupta).

80. *Illustrated London News* 53 (Aug. 8, 1868): 127.

81. " 'Anarchy and Authority,' " *London Review* 17 (Aug. 1, 1868): 136–37.

82. Buckler, p. 91.

83. A. C. Benson, *Memories and Friends* (New York: G. P. Putnam's, 1924), p. 143.

84. *Quarterly Review* 125 (Oct. 1868): 473–90.

85. Russell, 2: 4. The passage was deleted, accordingly, when *Culture and Anarchy* was published in a second edition (1875).

86. Super, 5: 236.

87. *Daily News*, Feb. 10, 1869, p. 4.

88. *Morning Star*, Feb. 13, 1869, p. 3.

89. *Fortnightly Review* 5 (Mar. 1869): 372.

90. "Mr. Matthew Arnold's Praise of Culture," *Spectator* 42 (Mar. 6, 1869): 296.

91. Letters of Jan. 23 and Mar. 6, 1869 (Whitridge Papers).

92. Letter of Mar. 10, 1869, to Grant Duff.

93. Eliot, *Definition of Culture*, p. 20.

94. Letter of Jan. 23, 1869.

95. Letter of Mar. 6, 1869; quoted by Super, 5: 457.

96. Letter of Mar. 10, 1869, to Grant Duff.

97. *Rome and Venice, with Other Wanderings in Italy, in 1866–7* (London: Tinsley, 1869), p. 23.

98. Super, 5: 313–16. I have treated this episode in greater detail in "Matthew Arnold and the *Daily Telegraph*," *Review of English Studies* 12 (May 1961): 173–79.

99. Super, 5: 319–24.

100. Ibid., 5: 327–33, 347, 474–75.

101. "The German Invasion.—I," *Pall Mall Gazette*, Dec. 6, 1870, p. 3 (SenGupta).

102. Super, 5: 353, 355.

103. Letter of Nov. 21, 1869 (Whitridge Papers).

104. *British Quarterly Review* 49 (Apr. 1869): 570–71.

105. Peel, *Letters to a Victorian Editor*, pp. 170–71, 187–88.

106. *North British Review* 47 (Sept. 1867): 42.

107. *Tablet* 2 (Aug. 7, 1869): 310; quoted by Wilkins, p. 255.

108. *Morning Star*, Feb. 13, 1869, p. 3.

109. "Arnold on Culture and Anarchy," *London Quarterly Review* 33 (Oct. 1869): 213–14.

CHAPTER SEVEN: The Bible and Its Interpreters

For the epigraphs see: *Miscellaneous Works*, p. 73; *Loss and Gain* (New York: Longmans, Green, 1900), p. 38; *Tess of the d'Urbervilles*, chap. 18; *Lay Sermons, Addresses, and Reviews* (New York: D. Appleton, 1876), p. 18; Oxenford, *Conversations of Goethe*, pp. 234–35.

1. Russell, 2: 20.
2. Super, 5: 181–82.
3. *Saint Paul* (Paris: Michel Lévy, 1869), esp. pp. 568–70.
4. Russell, 2: 101. For a more detailed comment on Arnold's divergence from Renan's view of Paul, see Flavia M. Alaya, "Arnold and Renan on the Popular Uses of History," *Journal of the History of Ideas* 28 (1967): 571.
5. Edward Reuss, *History of Christian Theology in the Apostolic Age*, trans. Annie Harwood from the 3rd ed., with preface and notes by R. W. Dale (London: Hodder and Stoughton, 1872–74), 1: xiii; 2: 6–9, 90, 147–49, 195.
6. Russell, 2: 11.
7. Super, 6: 5–33.
8. "Mr. Matthew Arnold's Poems," *Nonconformist* 30 (Sept. 8, 1869): 866.
9. Letter of Sept. 25, 1869 (Whitridge Papers); quoted in part by Super, 6: 419.
10. Letters of Oct. 2, 1869 (Whitridge Papers) and Oct. 16 (quoted by Super, 6: 419).
11. "St. Paul and Protestantism," *Nonconformist* 30 (Oct. 6, 1869): 962.
12. *Freeman* 16 (Oct. 15, 1869): 831.
13. "Mr. Matthew Arnold and St. Paul," *English Independent* 3 (Oct. 7, 1869): 979–80.
14. Super, 6: 33–71.
15. Russell, 2: 24.
16. "Matthew Arnold on Protestantism," *Nonconformist* 30 (Nov. 10, 1869): 1081; quoted also by Super, 6: 441.
17. "Mr. Matthew Arnold on St. Paul and Puritans," *English Independent* 3 (Nov. 4, 1869): 1088.
18. Letter of Dec. 5, 1869 (Whitridge Papers); referred to by Super, 6: 419.
19. Letter of Nov. 21, 1869.
20. Letter of Dec. 5, 1869.
21. Russell, 2: 24, and letter of Nov. 21, 1869.
22. Super, 6: 72–107.
23. In December 1869, two months before the publication of "Puritanism and the Church of England," Arnold heard Frederick Temple deliver his final sermon as headmaster of Rugby and called it "remarkable as showing his strong Church feeling and sense of the value and greatness of the historic development of Christianity, of which the Church is the expression" (Russell, 2: 29).
24. In sending his mother the first of the *English Independent*'s reviews, Arnold commented that "when they say the Nonconformists preach *righteousness* I should like them to go over my list from the Galatians and tell me *how much* of righteousness" (letter of Oct. 16, 1869; Whitridge Papers).
25. The revisions were largely mechanical or stylistic, affecting punctuation and diction, but the additions, for the most part, were made to refine or strengthen Arnold's thesis. The most important of these are as follows: a

paragraph developing the idea that biblical language is poetic rather than scientific (Super, 6: 20–21); four paragraphs comparing the conversions of Paul and a Methodist soldier named Staniforth to show the irrelevance of an alleged miracle to the truth of a doctrine taught (pp. 34–35); a paragraph explaining that Paul used the word *faith,* even though he meant something different by it, because he wished to gain scriptural sanction for his idea (pp. 44–45); a portion of a paragraph clarifying the account of the significance of Christ's crucifixion (p. 53); a paragraph expanding what had been said regarding the apparent support given the doctrine of atonement by the Epistle to the Hebrews (pp. 63–64); several altered or added paragraphs providing a naturalistic interpretation of expiation (pp. 65–68); and portions of two paragraphs concerning the relationship between the Church of England and the Roman Catholic Church (pp. 99–100).

26. Buckler, pp. 100–01.
27. Super, 6: 108–27.
28. "Arnold on Puritanism and National Churches," *Edinburgh Review* 133 (Apr. 1871): 399; for the authorship see Houghton, *Wellesley Index,* 1: 519.
29. Russell, 2: 65.
30. Ibid., 2: 40.
31. "Arnold on Puritanism and National Churches," pp. 399–400.
32. "The Church and Nonconformity," *Quarterly Review* 130 (Apr. 1871): 440–41; for the authorship see Houghton, *Wellesley Index,* 1: 753.
33. *Christian Observer,* May 1871, pp. 363, 354.
34. Russell, 2: 52.
35. *Guardian* 25 (Nov. 9, 1870): 1325.
36. "Mr. Matthew Arnold and Puritanism," *British Quarterly Review* 52 (July 1870): 174, 187.
37. *Nonconformist* 31 (June 8, 1870): 550.
38. *London Quarterly Review* 34 (July 1870): 478.
39. "A Puritan's Apology," *Macmillan's Magazine* 22 (Aug. 1870): 266.
40. "Mr. Matthew Arnold and the Nonconformists," *Contemporary Review* 14 (July 1870): 540–71.
41. A. W. W. Dale, *The Life of R. W. Dale of Birmingham* (London: Hodder and Stoughton, 1899), p. 379. Arnold, on the other hand, regarded Dale as "a brilliant pugilist" (Super, 8: 84).
42. *Guardian* 25 (Nov. 9, 1870): 1325.
43. "Mr. Matthew Arnold and the Church of England," *Fraser's Magazine,* n.s. 2 (Oct. 1870): 431.
44. "Mr. Arnold on St. Paul and His Creed," *Contemporary Review* 14 (June 1870): 339–41.
45. "Arnold on Puritanism and National Churches," p. 424.
46. Super, 6: 420.
47. Russell, 2: 48.
48. Ibid., 2: 55, 60.
49. Super, 7: 45.
50. Russell, 2: 41, 50–51. The effect on Arnold of Lord Salisbury's remarks is treated by William Blackburn in "The Background of Arnold's *Literature and Dogma,*" *Modern Philology* 43 (1945): 131–33.
51. Super, 6: 196, 200–02, 279.
52. Ibid., 6: 147–411.
53. Arnold uses this point for answering an objection to his parallel be-

tween Paul and Sampson Staniforth that had been made by the *Guardian*
(25 [Nov. 9, 1870]: 1326), quoted by Super, 6: 482, which argued that Paul
had witnesses to his conversion. Arnold observes that the testimony about the
event as recorded in Acts is contradictory (Super, 6: 250–51).

54.   On this vexed question see, in addition to Super, 6: 449–51, E. K.
Brown, *Studies in the Text of Matthew Arnold's Prose Works* (Paris: Librairie E. Droz, 1935), p. 131, and *Arnold: Study in Conflict*, p. 212, n. 30;
Blackburn, "Background of *Literature and Dogma*," p. 131, n. 11; and Francis G. Townsend, "The Third Instalment of Arnold's *Literature and Dogma*,"
Modern Philology 50 (1953): 195–200, and "*Literature and Dogma*: Matthew Arnold's Letters to George Smith," *Philological Quarterly* 35 (1956):
195–98. Brown maintained that either George Smith, the publisher of the
Cornhill, or Leslie Stephen, the editor—or both—objected to the third paper
and terminated the series. Blackburn challenged this conclusion, suggesting
instead that the controversy over the Athansian Creed led Arnold to expand
"his original argument into a book." Arnold's letters to Smith, published by
Townsend, show that the series was terminated, though for precisely what reason is not clear.

55.   *Dublin Review* 20 (Apr. 1873): 360–61, 378. The reviewer is un-
identified in Houghton, *Wellesley Index*, 2: 86.

56.   *Tablet* 9 (Mar. 29, 1873): 400.

57.   "Matthew Arnold's New Gospel," *Congregationalist* 2 (June 1873):
342, 345.

58.   "Doctrine and Dogma," *London Quarterly Review* 40 (July 1873):
412–13.

59.   *British Quarterly Review* 57 (Apr. 1873): 585.

60.   *Scotsman*, Mar. 21, 1873, p. 3.

61.   *Westminster Review*, 43 (Apr. 1873), 559.

62.   "Mr. Matthew Arnold's New Religion of the Bible," *Contemporary
Review* 21 (May 1873): 842.

63.   On Sept. 12, 1873, Arnold wrote to Charles Appleton, editor of the
Academy, to thank him "for putting me into such hands as Réville's, and producing so interesting a notice as that which I have just read. I think so highly
of Réville and of his opinion that I should have read with interest even the
most hostile judgment from him; how much more a judgment which is in
many respects so favourable! It is curious that the two most valuable and
serious notices have come from Holland; this of Réville's and Rauwenhoff's.
I hope to notice both of them in a new preface at the beginning of next year.
. . . The English notices have for the most part been wholly unprofitable, concerning themselves with the mere fringes and externals of the book only."
And he went on to ask Appleton to convey to Réville his "warm thanks"
(Diderik Roll-Hansen, "Matthew Arnold and the *Academy*: A Note on En-
glish Criticism in the Eighteen-seventies," *PMLA* 68 [1953]: 388–89).

64.   *Academy* 4 (Sept. 1, 1873): 328, 330.

65.   "Matthew Arnold," *Theologisch Tijdschrift* 7 (1873): 340.

66.   Super, 8: 150.

67.   Arnold at first misread Gubernatis' *oscenità* and translated it "obscuri-
ties" (ibid., 8: 500).

68.   Angelo de Gubernatis, "Rassegna delle Letterature Straniere," *Nuova
Antologia di Scienze, Lettere ed Arti*, 2nd ser., 3 (Dec. 1876): 880–81.

69.   Super, 6: 451.

70.   Norton and Howe, *Letters of Norton*, 1: 443.

71. Buckler, p. 96.
72. Russell, 2: 134.
73. Letter of Sept. 21, 1874 (Yale Papers).
74. Super, 7: 391–92, 150.
75. Manchester *Guardian*, May 16, 1873, p. 7 (Wilkins).
76. "Modern Culture," *Quarterly Review* 137 (Oct. 1874): 407. For the authorship see Houghton, *Wellesley Index*, 1: 757.
77. "Doctrine and Dogma," p. 420.
78. W. H. G. Armytage, "Matthew Arnold and T. H. Huxley: Some New Letters 1870–80," *Review of English Studies* 4 (1953): 349. Arnold told Huxley that he would "be sorry to have said anything which enables the enemy to divert attention from his damaged position by raising a cry of *scoffing* and *scandal.*"
79. F. Max Müller, *Auld Lang Syne*, p. 135.
80. Super, 7: 151.
81. Brown, *Studies in the Text of Arnold*, p. 75.
82. Arnold wrote to "K" on Oct. 5, 1883, "If you see the new edition of *Literature and Dogma*, you will like what I have said of Lord Shaftesbury, in leaving out the too famous illustration; he is a man to whom I have always felt myself drawn" (Russell, 2: 254–55).
83. *Guardian* 28 (June 11, 1873): 781.
84. Super, 7: 154.
85. Quoted by P. T. Marsh, *The Victorian Church in Decline: Archbishop Tait and the Church of England 1868–1882* (London: Routledge & K. Paul, 1969), p. 28.
86. Arnold's criticism of the two bishops is no doubt in questionable taste. But E. K. Brown indulged in hyperbole when he called the passage "a radical critic's equivalent for a service of excommunication" and "the last resort of an outraged controversialist" (*Studies in the Text of Arnold*, p. 154). The kingdom of God to which Arnold referred was earthly, not heavenly, and one can scarcely conceal the truth contained in his judgments of both bishops. Nor can he conceal the truth in his comments on Maurice, which had also caused offense (Super, 6: 383).
87. *The New Republic*, ed. J. Max Patrick (Gainesville: University of Florida Press, 1950), p. 181. Mallock's satirical novel appeared originally in 1877.
88. "Mr. Matthew Arnold's New Religion of the Bible," pp. 860–64.
89. "Amateur Theology: Arnold's *Literature and Dogma*," *Blackwood's Edinburgh Magazine* 113 (June 1873): 685, 689. Portions of Tulloch's anonymous review were reprinted in his *Modern Theories in Philosophy and Religion* (Edinburgh and London: W. Blackwood, 1884), pp. 277–315.
90. Letter dated "Thursday morning," [1867]. Arnold told his mother that he had "been reading in the Revue des 2 Mondes [Réville's] two excellent articles on Isaiah . . ., which have made me think of Papa." Later, in *Culture and Anarchy*, he described Réville's "religious writings" as "always interesting" (Super, 5: 251).
91. *Academy* 4 (Sept. 1, 1873): 329–30.
92. "Mr. Matthew Arnold on Dogma," *Saturday Review* 35 (Mar. 1, 1873): 284–86.
93. *Christian Observer*, Aug. 1873, p. 581.
94. "Dogmatic Extremes," *Contemporary Review* 23 (Jan. 1874): 184.
95. "Mr. Arnold on God," *Spectator* 44 (July 8, 1871): 827 (Gudas).

This, as well as the two *Spectator* reviews cited in notes 97 and 98 following, are attributed to Hutton by Tener, "R. H. Hutton," cols. 46, 50.

96.   Super, 6: 190 n.

97.   "Mr. Arnold's Gospel," *Spectator* 46 (Feb. 22, 1873): 243–44.

98.   "Mr. Arnold on Christianity," *Spectator* 46 (Mar. 1, 1873): 279. During the next few weeks the *Spectator* received several letters objecting to its articles on *Literature and Dogma.* J. Scot Henderson wrote that since the book brought out the very least that the Bible contains, it served a useful purpose ("What Mr. Arnold's Analysis Involves," *Spectator* 46 [Mar. 15, 1873]: 337–38). A month later a correspondent signing himself "A." declared that the Christian element in Arnold's writings was "not a diminishing but an increasing quantity" and that his books had "their whole raison d'être in their affirmations; . . . while the negations are of the most common-place sort, the affirmations are fresh, striking, and peculiar, and have every appearance of constituting the substance and stuff of the book. What I wish to point out is . . . this,—that so far as Mr. Arnold can be called a Christian, he is a convert to Christianity." For this reason the writer maintained "that the testimony now borne by Mr. Arnold is on the whole, as far as it goes, unique, a new fact in the history of Christianity. He has undertaken to estimate the value of the Bible considered purely as a book. . . . there could hardly be a greater triumph for the Bible than the empire it has established, gradually and in mature life, upon so sceptical and so cultivated a mind." Arnold's affirmation of the value of the Bible, the writer concluded, "so made, and by such a man, outweighs by itself half the anti-religious writing of the age" ("The Clergy and the Church. I," *Spectator* 46 [Apr. 12, 1873]: 472–73).

99.   *Facts, Not Fairy-Tales: Brief Notes on Mr. Matthew Arnold's "Literature and Dogma"* (London: Simpkin, Marshall, 1873), pp. 35–36, 32.

100.   "Personality and the Infinite," *Contemporary Review* 28 (Oct. 1876): 786–87.

101.   "Neo-Christianity and Mr. Matthew Arnold," *Contemporary Review* 45 (Apr. 1884): 572.

102.   Roll-Hansen, "Arnold and the *Academy*," p. 388.

103.   Super, 7: 156.

104.   "Dr. Strauss's Confession," *Edinburgh Review* 138 (Oct. 1873): 552–53, quoted by Gudas, p. 220, n. 59. The *Edinburgh* reviewer was G. H. Curteis (Houghton, *Wellesley Index*, 1: 522).

105.   Super, 7: 160–61.

106.   *Guardian*, 28: 780.

107.   Super, 7: 164, 170.

108.   Letter of Oct. 26, 187[4] (Yale Papers); largely quoted by Super, 7: 436, 439.

109.   Arnold was answered by Shadworth H. Hodgson in *Mind* 1 (Oct. 1876): 568–70.

110.   Super, 7: 191–92.

111.   Abbott and Campbell, *Life of Jowett*, 2: 80.

112.   Super, 7: 193–99.

113.   "The Bible as Interpreted by Mr. Arnold," *Westminster Review* 45 (Apr. 1874): 309–23.

114.   Super, 7: 528, 537. Professor Walter E. Houghton informs me that "the card for the review of *Literature and Dogma* in the *Westminster* [is] absolutely blank."

115.   Super, 7: 203–16.

116. Ibid., 7: 220–21.
117. "Modern Culture," p. 397.
118. Super, 7: 222–27.
119. *Bibliothèque Universelle et Revue Suisse* 49 (1874) : 342–59. In "A Speech at Westminster" Arnold described the journal as "one of the most seriously conducted and trustworthy reviews in Europe" (Super, 7: 80).
120. Super, 7: 230–31.
121. Ibid., 7: 233–34.
122. "Mr. Arnold's Sublimated Bible," *Spectator* 47 (Oct. 10, 1874): 1257 (Gudas). Hutton's review is reprinted in *Criticisms on Contemporary Thought and Thinkers* (London: Macmillan, 1894), 1: 214–20, and is cited by Robert H. Tener, "The Writings of Richard Holt Hutton: A Checklist of Identifications," *Victorian Periodicals Newsletter*, no. 17 (Sept. 1972), col. 8.
123. Super, 7: 232–33.
124. "Modern Culture," p. 397.
125. Super, 7: 234–35.
126. Rauwenhoff, "Matthew Arnold," p. 338.
127. *Academy* 4 (Sept. 1, 1873): 330.
128. *Westminster Review*, 43 (Apr. 1873), 559.
129. *Fraser's Magazine* 8 (July 1873): 122.
130. Newman, *Phases of Faith*, p. 81.
131. *Life of Jesus*, trans. from the 23rd and final ed. by Joseph Henry Allen (Boston: Roberts Brothers, 1896), pp. 17–18.
132. *Supernatural Religion*, 6th ed. (Toronto, 1879), 2: 692. It is in this same edition that Cassels answers Arnold's criticism of his work (1: 52–53) (Gudas).
133. Super, 7: 241–42.
134. As Gudas observes, Arnold's reiterated phrase seems to have been suggested by Réville, who had said that *Literature and Dogma* presents a theory "which does not err either by excess of vigor or excess of rigor" (*Academy* 4 [Sept. 1, 1873]: 329).
135. Super, 7: 243–44, 263, 267, 269–71.
136. Ibid., 7: 286–88. For the possibilities other than those allowed by Arnold, see Raymond E. Brown, ed., *The Gospel According to John (i–xii)*, The Anchor Bible (Garden City: Doubleday, 1966), pp. lxxi–lxxii, lxvii, 440, 44.
137. Brown, *Gospel According to John*, p. lxxx, xcvii, c.
138. Super, 7: 289–90, 296.
139. Ibid., 7: 305–25.
140. See Brown, *Gospel According to John*, pp. 388–400, 169, 429–31.
141. Super, 7: 325–27, 358.
142. Ibid., 7: 370–73.
143. Davidson and Benham, *Life of Tait*, 2: 303–04.
144. "Scepticism of the Day.—Matthew Arnold," *Church Quarterly Review* 2 (July 1876): 328, 332.
145. *Westminster Review* 49 (Jan. 1876): 223.
146. *Academy* 8 (Dec. 18, 1875): 618.
147. Super, 8: 63–86.
148. After publication of Arnold's address in *Macmillan's*, James Martineau wrote to Henry Allon that the "paper should be met by a reply conceived in the spirit of Nonconformist English History," and continued, "I

earnestly wish that you would take the matter up. No one would bring to it greater resources or a higher spirit. And no one is more entitled to rebuke the supercilious levity with which, too often, great principles and good men are treated by our most popular literateur [*sic*]" (Peel, *Letters to a Victorian Editor*, pp. 329–30). Martineau's differences with Arnold were of long standing. In 1871 he had delivered an address in answer to *St. Paul and Protestantism* and later explained to Arnold that although he favored a national Church, he did not believe that an approach to unity could be made until the Church allowed in its worship only what was "true to the conscience of all" (James Drummond and C. B. Upton, *The Life and Letters of James Martineau* [London: J. Nisbet, 1902], 2: 6–7). When Arnold rightly surmised that their ideas were more akin than dissimilar, Martineau implied that he was annoyed instead by "the merely literary spirit" in which Arnold dealt with important issues. "Let him fall in love with something!" he impatiently exclaimed (Conway, *Autobiography*, 2: 292).

149.   Russell, 2: 147.

150.   Super, 8: 111–47.

151.   Letter of Mar. 10, [1876], to James T. Knowles (Yale Papers); quoted in part by Super, 6: 450.

152.   Super, 8: 148.

153.   R. H. Super has discovered the review in *La République française*, of which Challemel-Lacour was a founding editor (ibid., 8: 415).

154.   Ibid., 8: 149–53.

155.   Ibid., 8: 153–57.

156.   "La Philosophie Religieuse en Angleterre: Une nouvelle forme du Christianisme (1): M. Matt. Arnold," *Revue Scientifique*, 2nd ser., 11 (Oct. 21, 1876): 385–92.

157.   Super, 8: 161–62.

158.   Peel, *Letters to a Victorian Editor*, p. 304.

159.   Neiman, pp. 255–60.

160.   "Mr. Arnold's Lay Sermon," *Spectator* 57 (Dec. 6, 1884): 1610–11. The essay is reprinted in *Aspects of Religious and Scientific Thought*, ed. Elizabeth M. Roscoe (London: Macmillan, 1899), pp. 322–29, and is cited by Tener, "Writings of Hutton," col. 13.

161.   "Mr. Matthew Arnold's Gospel for the Poor," *Guardian* 39 (Dec. 10, 1884): 1867.

162.   *Guardian* 39 (Dec. 17, 1884): 1919. Arnold later wrote to "K," "Were you not interested in the Sheffield clergyman's letter to the *Guardian*, rebuking them for speaking evil of me? He has written me a very sensible letter since. Do you know anything of him?" (letter of Dec. 25, 1884; Whitridge Papers).

163.   They were written by T. N. Staley, 39 (Dec. 24, 1884): 1961; C. A. Goodhart, 40 (Jan. 21, 1885): 113; and E. S. Talbot, 40 (Feb. 4, 1885): 191 (Gudas).

164.   *Contemporary Review* 47 (Apr. 1885): 457–72.

165.   The essay was answered in turn by the bishop of Carlisle ("A Comment on 'A Comment on Christmas,' *Contemporary Review* 49 [Feb. 1886]: 178–93) and by R. A. Watson ("The Counterfeit Gospel of Nature," *British and Foreign Evangelical Review* 35 [Oct. 1886]: 627–50).

166.   Super, 6: 3–4.

167.   Russell, 2: 187.

168.   *Notes from a Diary, 1889–1891* (London: J. Murray, 1901), p. 48.

Chapter Eight: The Humanist and His Adversaries

For the epigraphs see: *Middlemarch*, chap. 9; "Two Theories of Poetry," *Macmillan's Magazine* 44 (Aug. 1881): 271; A. P. Stanley, *The Life and Correspondence of Thomas Arnold*, 7th ed. (London: B. Fellowes, 1852), pp. 376–77; "America's Impressions of Matthew Arnold," *Andover Review* 1 (Jan. 1884): 86, quoted by Raleigh, *Arnold and American Culture*, p. 72; "Letter on the Affairs of Ireland, Written in the Year 1797," *The Works of Edmund Burke* (Boston: Wells and Lilly, 1826–27), 5: 301.

1. Brown, *Arnold: Study in Conflict*, p. 156.
2. Russell, 2: 156–57.
3. Ibid., 2: 219.
4. Coleridge's remark is variously quoted; I have followed the wording that prompted the article, "Genius and Versatility," *Macmillan's Magazine* 49 (Dec. 1883): 87–94, by H. D. Traill (Houghton, *Wellesley Index*, 1: 619).
5. Florence Emily Hardy, *The Early Life of Thomas Hardy, 1840–1891* (New York: Macmillan, 1928), p. 175. Meeting him a year and a half later, Meredith likened him to "a parson washed half white" and said that one saw in him "the great brain grafted on the cleric" (Cline, *Letters of Meredith*, 2: 643).
6. Russell, 2: 181, 267, 163, 220–21.
7. Super, 8: 188–207. The significance of Arnold's view of Falkland has been treated most fully by John P. Farrell, "Matthew Arnold's Tragic Vision," *PMLA* 85 (1970): 107–17, reprinted in DeLaura, *Arnold: Critical Essays*, pp. 99–118.
8. Super, 8: 169.
9. "Falkland and the Puritans. In Reply to Mr. Matthew Arnold," *Contemporary Review* 29 (Apr. 1877): 925–43.
10. Brown, *Studies in the Text of Arnold*, pp. 96–97.
11. Super, 8: 189, 502.
12. Ibid., 8: 277–305.
13. Lucy Hutchinson, *Memoirs of the Life of Colonel Hutchinson*, 7th ed., Bohn's Standard Library (London: H. G. Bohn, 1848), pp. 299–300.
14. "Mr. Arnold's New Poems," *Fortnightly Review*, n.s. 2 (Oct. 1867): 414–45. I have traced the Swinburne-Arnold relationship at greater length in *Philological Quarterly* 49 (1970): 211–33, on which the following section is largely based. My essay has been supplemented by Terry L. Meyers, "Swinburne's Later Opinion of Arnold," *English Language Notes* 10 (1972): 118–22.
15. Super, 7: 49.
16. Ibid., 8: 230, 253.
17. Russell, 2: 184.
18. Ibid., 2: 434–35, 438–39, 444. In the essay on Maurice de Guérin, Arnold had expressed the same objection to the alexandrine (Super, 3: 14), as he had also done, Professor DeLaura reminds me, as early as the preface to *Merope* (1858) (ibid., 1: 50).
19. *The Complete Works of Algernon Charles Swinburne*, ed. Edmund Gosse and T. J. Wise, Bonchurch ed. (New York: Wells, 1925–27), 19: 156.
20. Ibid., 11: 114.
21. Lang, *Swinburne Letters*, 4: 117.
22. Ibid., 4: 142, and Gosse and Wise, *Complete Works of Swinburne*, 4: 20.

23. Russell, 2: 195.
24. Gosse and Wise, *Complete Works of Swinburne*, 4: 21.
25. Lang, *Swinburne Letters*, 4: 142, 145, and Gosse and Wise, *Complete Works of Swinburne*, 13: 194.
26. *Civilization in the United States* (Boston: Cupples and Hurd, 1888), p. 92, and *Discourses in America* (London: Macmillan, 1896), p. 97.
27. Super, 9: 181, 204.
28. Ibid., 3: 14, 516; Gosse and Wise, *Complete Works of Swinburne*, 15: 108.
29. Lang, *Swinburne Letters*, 4: 109, and Gosse and Wise, *Complete Works of Swinburne*, 14: 152.
30. *Gray*, English Men of Letters Series (New York: Harper, n. d.), pp. vi, 98, 65.
31. British Museum MS. Ashley 23; quoted by permission.
32. *Discourses in America*, p. 157.
33. Lang, *Swinburne Letters*, 4: 76.
34. Super, 9: 45.
35. Gosse and Wise, *Complete Works of Swinburne*, 13: 417–18; 16: 132–40; 13: 242–44.
36. Ibid., 14: 157–61.
37. Super, 3: 132.
38. Gosse and Wise, *Complete Works of Swinburne*, 15: 120–21.
39. Super, 9: 232.
40. "Lord Byron: Arnold and Swinburne," *Proceedings of the British Academy* 9 (1919–20): 458.
41. Russell, 1: 227–28, and Gosse and Wise, *Complete Works of Swinburne*, 14: 85.
42. *Apes, Angels, and Victorians: The Story of Darwin, Huxley, and Evolution* (New York: McGraw Hill, 1955), p. 283. For an excellent account of Arnold's attitude toward science see Fred A. Dudley, "Matthew Arnold and Science," *PMLA* 57 (1942): 275–94.
43. Super, 5: 231; Leonard Huxley, *The Life and Letters of Thomas Henry Huxley* (New York: Appleton, 1897), 1: 335; Armytage, "Arnold and Huxley," pp. 349–50.
44. Walcott, *Origins of "Culture and Anarchy"*, p. 106.
45. Quoted by Walcott, *Origins of "Culture and Anarchy,"* p. 109.
46. Super, 4: 292.
47. Russell, 2: 41, 50–51.
48. Super, 6: 165.
49. Ibid., 9: 21–22.
50. *Science and Education* (New York: Appleton, 1896), pp. 139–52.
51. Armytage, "Arnold and Huxley," p. 352.
52. Super, 5: 244–45.
53. "Literature and Science," *Nineteenth Century* 12 (Aug. 1882): 216–30.
54. Russell, 2: 233. For additional details about the lecture, see David J. DeLaura, "Four Arnold Letters," *Texas Studies in Literature and Language* 4 (1962): 280–82.
55. *Civilization in the United States*, pp. 69–108.
56. Russell, 2: 232–33.
57. Ibid., 2: 253, 270, 258.

58. M. E. Grant Duff, *Notes from a Diary, 1892–1895* (London: J. Murray, 1904), 1: 71, quoted by Chilson H. Leonard, "Arnold in America: A Study of Matthew Arnold's Literary Relations with America and of His Visits to This Country in 1883 and 1886" (Ph.D. diss., Yale University, 1932), pp. 144–45.

59. Russell, 2: 254. Arnold's attitude toward Carlyle has been treated at length by Kathleen Tillotson, "Matthew Arnold and Carlyle," *Proceedings of the British Academy* 42 (1956): 133–53 (reprinted in Geoffrey and Kathleen Tillotson, *Mid-Victorian Studies* [London: University of London, The Athlone Press, 1965], pp. 216–38), and by David J. DeLaura, "Arnold and Carlyle," *PMLA* 79 (1964): 104–29. To these should be added C. J. Rawson, "Matthew Arnold to Henry Reeve: An Unpublished Letter," *Notes and Queries* 18 (1971): 251, who prints a letter of Mar. 29, 1887, in which Arnold writes: "Carlyle is so distasteful to me that I do not promise myself much pleasure from the reading [presumably of *Conversations Between Goethe and Carlyle*], but I am glad Goethe comes out well." Arnold's regard for Emerson has been treated by R. H. Super in "Emerson and Arnold's Poetry," *Philological Quarterly* 33 (1954): 396–403 and *The Time-Spirit of Matthew Arnold*, pp. 7–8.

60. *Discourses in America*, pp. 138–207.

61. Russell, 2: 277, 279.

62. *Nation* 37 (Dec. 6, 1883): 460.

63. "Matthew Arnold's Visit," *Literary World* 14 (Dec. 15, 1883): 446, quoted by E. P. Lawrence, "An Apostle's Progress: Matthew Arnold in America," *Philological Quarterly* 10 (1931): 69. In reviewing *Discourses in America*, the *Literary World* altered its opinion of the Emerson lecture: "Since Mr. Arnold left us we have had time to ponder his remarks concerning the unsoundness of the majority and the literary claims of Emerson, and the truth of his utterances on these topics is now more generally acknowledged than was the case when we heard them for the first time" (Oct. 3, 1885, p. 346, quoted by Leonard, p. 256).

64. *Nation* 37 (Dec. 20, 1883): 500.

65. "The Lounger," *Critic* 4 (Feb. 2, 1884): 57, quoted by Lawrence, "Apostle's Progress," p. 69.

66. "Literary Notes," New York *Daily Tribune*, Dec. 15, 1883, p. 6, quoted by Lawrence, "Apostle's Progress," p. 70. According to Leonard, "Arnold in America," p. 143, the passage on Hawthorne read in the original: ". . . Hawthorne's observation in *Our Old Home* is the work of a man chagrined. The author's attitude in each of these cases can easily be understood . . . ." In the margin Arnold wrote in pencil, to be inserted after the sentence ending "chagrined," the following: "Hawthorne's literary talent is of the first order. His subjects are not generally to me, subjects of the highest interest, but his literary talent is of the finest kind, finer a great deal than Emerson's."

67. Russell, 2: 270, 277.

68. Brown, *Studies in the Text of Arnold*, pp. 114–16.

69. Russell, 2: 279.

70. Leonard, "Arnold in America," p. 230, says that they were usually from two to four hundred.

71. Russell, 2: 296.

72. Neiman, pp. 253–54.

73. Melville E. Stone, *Fifty Years a Journalist* (London: Heinemann, 1922), pp. 122–23.

74. Lawrence, "Apostle's Progress," p. 77. The Chicago visit has also been treated by John P. Long, "Matthew Arnold Visits Chicago," *University of Toronto Quarterly* 24 (1954): 34–45.

75. "The Matthew Arnold Myth," *Literary World* 15 (Apr. 19, 1884): 132–33, quoted by Lawrence, "Apostle's Progress," pp. 73–74.

76. "Matthew Arnold," *North American Review* 138 (May 1884) : 432.

77. "Matthew Arnold," *Nation* 46 (Apr. 19, 1888): 316. A discriminating explanation of Arnold's failure in America, caused largely by mutual ignorance and misunderstanding, is to be found in David J. DeLaura, "Matthew Arnold and the American 'Literary Class': Unpublished Correspondence and Some Further Reasons," *Bulletin of the New York Public Library* 70 (1966): 229–50.

78. Russell, 2: 364.

79. Armytage, "Arnold and Huxley," p. 353.

80. Neiman, p. 338.

81. Letter of Aug. 1, 1863.

82. Neiman, p. 312.

83. Russell, 2: 429.

84. Ibid., 2: 309, and *Civilization in the United States*, pp. 127, 133, 141.

85. *Gladstone and the Irish Nation* (Hamden, Conn.: Archon Books, 1964), esp. pp. 650–51, 730. On this matter as well as Arnold's view of the entire Irish question, see the admirable article by William Robbins, "Matthew Arnold and Ireland," *University of Toronto Quarterly* 18 (1947): 52–67.

86. Neiman, pp. 269, 284–85, 289.

87. Ibid., pp. 314, 338–39, 352.

88. "American Opinion on the Irish Question," *Nineteenth Century* 22 (Aug. 1887): 291.

89. Neiman, pp. 362, 364–65.

90. *Civilization in the United States*, p. 149.

91. Haultain, *Goldwin Smith's Correspondence*, pp. 176, 184.

92. Neiman, p. 377.

93. Russell, 2: 433.

94. Ibid., 2: 396.

95. *Civilization in the United States*, pp. 161, 192. Despite this moving rhetoric, however, the essay was bitterly resented by George W. Smalley, London correspondent for the New York *Tribune*, who thought it "deplorable" to spread in England a misleading impression of American life and accordingly sought to correct it, sending Arnold a copy of his answer. Arnold politely replied that he had been determined to comment on the deficiencies of American newspapers and concluded with the prediction that Smalley would "end by judging this article of [his] less unfavourably" (Smalley, *London Letters*, 1: 337–38). The words were presumably the last of Arnold's responses to his critics. Two days later, in Liverpool, he dropped dead of a heart attack.

CONCLUSION

1. Super, 1: 8.

2. Ibid., 7: 280–81.

3. *Matthew Arnold: A Survey of His Poetry and Prose*, Masters of World Literature Series (New York: Macmillan, 1971), p. xv.

4. Super, 3: 2.
5. H. W. Garrod, "Matthew Arnold's 1853 Preface," *Review of English Studies* 17 (1941): 310.